Militant Citizenship

NUMBER TWENTY-ONE
PRESIDENTIAL RHETORIC SERIES

Vanessa B. Beasley, General Editor

Belinda A. Stillion Southard

MILITANT CITIZENSHIP

RHETORICAL STRATEGIES OF THE NATIONAL WOMAN'S PARTY, 1913–1920

TEXAS A&M UNIVERSITY PRESS | College Station

First edition
This paper meets the requirements of ANSI/NISO Z39.48-1992
(Permanence of Paper).
Binding materials have been chosen for durability.

Library of Congress Cataloging-in-Publication Data

Stillion Southard, Belinda A., 1978–
Militant citizenship : rhetorical strategies of the National Woman's Party, 1913–1920 / Belinda A. Stillion Southard.—1st ed.
p. cm.—(Presidential rhetoric series ; no. 21)
Includes bibliographical references and index.
ISBN 978-1-60344-281-7 (paper with deluxe flaps : alk. paper)—
ISBN 978-1-60344-282-4 (trade pbk. : alk. paper) 1. Women—Suffrage—United States—History—20th century. 2. National Woman's Party—United States—History. 3. Political leadership—United States—History—20th century. 4. United States—Politics and government—1913–1921. 5. Rhetoric—Political aspects—United States—Case studies. I. Title. II. Series: Presidential rhetoric series ; no. 21.
JK1896.S82 2011
324.2732—dc22
2011005218

DEDICATION

To my daughters, Ella Rose and Finna Helene

Contents

Acknowledgments

The publication of this book can be attributed to the academic and personal support shown to me over the last six years. This project began as a seminar paper and a dissertation at the University of Maryland, was revised when I was an assistant professor in the Department of Communication at Indiana University–Purdue University Fort Wayne (IPFW), and went through the final publication steps when I taught as an adjunct professor at Lewis & Clark College.

Most significantly, I owe a debt of gratitude to Shawn J. Parry-Giles for reading a seminar paper that eventually became an inexcusably long dissertation. She read and offered feedback to chapters without complaint; likewise, she was willing to entertain my multiple academic queries and crises throughout the dissertation-writing process. I'm fortunate to have her as a good friend and a generous mentor. Also, I must thank James F. Klumpp, Shirley Wilson Logan, Trevor Parry-Giles, and Mari Boor Tonn for their contributions to the earlier stages of this project. Many thanks are also owed to Martin J. Medhurst, editor of *Rhetoric & Public Affairs,* Susan Zaeske, and Angela G. Ray for their feedback on an earlier version of chapter 4. Last, I wish to thank Vanessa B. Beasley for her invaluable advice on transitioning my dissertation into a book manuscript.

I feel very fortunate that I landed in the IPFW Department of Communication (if only for a year), where my chair, Marcia Dixon, took great measure to protect my time as a junior faculty member. Moreover, I was lucky to be surrounded by youthful and encouraging faculty, including Irwin Mallin, Adam Dircksen, Jane Banks, and Jules Rosskam.

This book is also a product of the rhetoric and public address scholarly culture—one that is shaped and reflected by its participants. To me, those participants and my peers who discussed the content of the book and the process of writing a book, or who offered a model research activity, include Lisa Corrigan, Kristy Maddux, Jason Black, Kelly Carr, Ben Krueger, Dave Tell, Kim Thomas, Carinna Tarvin, and Bjørn F. Stillion Southard.

This book would not exist if I didn't have a wonderful partner, teammate, cheerleader, and would-be stay-at-home dad, Bjørn F. Stillion Southard. In addition to the scholarly input he has offered over the years, he vehemently insisted that I use our family time to edit, revise, and polish this manuscript in its every stage. In addition to relieving my parental guilt, Bjørn has managed to hang with me throughout this process and still claim to like me.

I am also quite fortunate to have the ongoing support of a humorous and loving family. My siblings, Jennifer, Alyson, and Jeffrey, provide hilarity and deserving ridicule from a distance. Moreover, my parents, Karen Turner and David Stillion, remain vigilantly supportive of my academic endeavors, even if these endeavors have kept me at the farthest reaches of the country. My in-laws, Fred and Barb Southard, have also shown unfailing support in our family's academic journey, and selflessly provide babysitting services.

Last, I am fortunate to have had two amazing daughters throughout the process of writing this book. I recall taking notes on the *Suffragist* while holding a three-week-old Ella Rose in my arms. Six years later, I am writing acknowledgments while a four-month-old Finna Helene waits for me at home. It is because of and for them that I write of militant women.

Militant Citizenship

Introduction
The Making of Militants

On the day of Pres. Woodrow Wilson's second inauguration, marchers sloshed through the soggy streets of Washington, D.C. The daunting weather did not stop the ceremonial parade or discourage the growing crowds. One report noted that "[i]n spite of steady and drenching rain, thousands of people congregated about the White House" in anticipation of the formal procession.[1] Months of orchestration culminated in "bands playing stirring airs [as] the line of lifted banners swung out down Madison Place, cheered by the spectators, between smiling rows of policemen."[2] The unrelenting weather enhanced the spectacle of the pageant, as the wet pavement "project[ed] the long oscillating reflections of the many banners which the gray day and the steady rain threw into extraordinary brilliancy."[3] Onlookers were so excited by "the gay sight" that many spontaneously joined in. Marchers from every state in the union carried banners bearing President Wilson's name over four miles of unforgiving concrete as they participated in the great American tradition of political pomp.[4]

Yet these banners, these signposts of democracy, did not regale the reelected president. Instead they insisted, "Mr. President, how long must women wait for liberty?"[5] The force behind this demonstration was the National Woman's Party (NWP)—an organization determined to direct a stern message to President Wilson: "We demand an amendment to the Constitution of the United States enfranchising women."[6] The suffragists' provocative protest exacerbated the "solemn mood" of Wilson's inauguration, particularly as the US entrance into World War I seemed inevitable. As the *New York Times* reported of Wilson's inauguration parade: "It was not a festive occasion, it was not a holiday, it was not a merrymaking."[7]

Not surprisingly, when President Wilson and the first lady returned from the inauguration, neither of them acknowledged any of the four hundred women surrounding the White House.[8] Perhaps this was so because the woman suffrage demonstration marked another high point in the NWP's militant campaign for fully enfranchised citizenship rights. Consider, for example, that in the months preceding Wilson's second inauguration, the NWP's "Silent Sentinels" stood quietly at the White House gates eight hours a day, six days a week; NWP members heckled Wilson during a Senate speech;[9] and on the day before Wilson's 1913 inauguration, the group led a national suffrage parade through the streets of Washington. Certainly by his second inauguration, President Wilson had grown weary of the NWP.

Between the organization's inception in early 1913 and the conclusion of the suffrage movement in August 1920, the NWP pursued a relentless, militant campaign for woman suffrage. More specifically, this book shows that through a rhetoric of political mimesis, the NWP enacted key political rituals and rhetorics in order to empower themselves as US citizens. In early 1913, for example, the NWP mimicked the inauguration ritual through its national suffrage parade, in which more than five thousand women marched.[10] Throughout the 1914 and 1916 election cycles, the NWP sensationalized and mimicked third-party strategies and then actually formed a third party, the Woman's Party, to organize women voters in the western states to vote against non-suffrage-supporting Democrats—including President Wilson.[11] In 1917, NWP members employed the mimetic forms of parody and quotation as they adopted Wilson's rhetorical authority while silently protesting him in front of the White House. Last, throughout 1918 and 1919, NWP members mimicked Wilson's rhetorical leadership by incorporating his international rhetoric of democracy into their statue protests and "Watch Fires of Freedom."[12]

To best locate the rhetorical thrust of the NWP's campaign, this book asks three questions. First, how did the NWP's rhetoric of political mimesis target President Wilson and members of Congress as change agents for women's full enfranchisement? Next, how did the process of mimicking key political rhetorics and militantly entering reserved political spaces empower NWP members to constitute their citizenship identities and help reenvision women's roles in the nation-state? Last, to what extent did a rhetoric of political mimesis both enhance and restrict the empowering potential of social change, particularly as it simultaneously helped liberate and oppress US women? To help answer these questions, NWP suffrage discourse, including all issues of the NWP's weekly organ, the *Suffragist,* and all correspondence, pamphlets, campaign booklets, and ephemera produced between early 1913 and August of 1920, are examined to demonstrate the ways in which the group's rhetoric political mimesis both reified and challenged progressive notions of US nationalism and citizenship throughout its militant campaign for woman suffrage.[13]

PROGRESSIVE ERA POLITICS

The NWP members who circled the White House in the rain clearly viewed the presidency as a site of potential change. This possibility for political empowerment was enhanced by the power dynamics of the Progressive Era, a time of great social and political transformation. Thus, it is necessary to view the NWP's seven-year campaign as one steeped in the ideological and institutional forces of the late nineteenth and early twentieth centuries, when the rise of the rhetorical presidency, progressivism, and a host of social movements took hold. A brief discussion of these forces shows how this climate of social and institutional change created the optimal conditions for the women of the NWP to assert their political agency and demand women's national citizenship rights.

Wilson's Rhetorical Presidency

In part, the NWP's protests on President Wilson may be considered a response to Wilson's enactment of what has come to be known as the "rhetorical presidency"—a phenomenon that emerged as presidents began to appeal to the American people more so than to Congress. Although the lineage of the rhetorical presidency can be traced back to the earliest presidents, the rise of the rhetorical presidency is typically associated with early-twentieth-century presidents who claimed to appeal to the American people as activists on their behalf.[14] As presidents promoted and shaped their policy agendas based on the needs of the American people, the people were empowered with a political voice to engage in a dialogue with their leader as a means to effect policy change. President Wilson, in particular, viewed himself as an advocate for the American people and through the rhetorical presidency attempted to create a more unified American polity.[15] Paradoxically, the NWP's protests suggested that Wilson's more direct appeals to the American people invited the response of the NWP—one that attempted to expose Wilson's efforts to unite the nation as hypocritical. Viewing the response of the NWP to Wilson's rhetorical presidency as an enactment of the democratic principles he valued also suggests that perhaps the rhetorical presidency did not solely belong to the president.

Understanding the genesis of the modern rhetorical presidency reveals how the institution is situated to invite the participation of the American people. The scope and character of the rhetorical presidency have been contested;[16] nonetheless, Mary E. Stuckey and Frederick J. Antczak argue that the presidency represents "a symbol of national identity, a voice for our national values," and a defining force of "the American polity."[17] In the early 1900s, Theodore Roosevelt's presidency emerged as such a symbol and a voice as he targeted the American people through the bully pulpit.[18] Roosevelt explained: "I acted for the public welfare, I acted for the common well-being of all people, whenever and in whatever manner was necessary, unless prevented by direct constitutional or legislative prohibition."[19] According to Jeffrey K. Tulis, Roosevelt's successful use of popular leadership allowed Wilson to adopt the "second constitution, which puts a premium on active and continuous presidential leadership of popular opinion" more so than conceived in the "first" constitution, the US Constitution.[20]

Like Roosevelt before him, President Wilson was enamored with the rhetorical power of the presidency to shape a national identity. James Andrews argues that Wilson believed such rhetorical leadership "was clearly the president's responsibility, indeed a measure of his fitness to hold office, to grasp the 'meaning' of America and to use the rhetorical power of the presidency to fix that meaning in the minds of an American community."[21] To such ends, Wilson sought to hear the voices of the American people in a more democratic fashion. Tulis details Wilson's idea of political representation: "He favored an interplay between representative and constituent that would, in fact, educate the constituent. This process differed, at least in theory, from the older attempts to 'form' public opinion: it did not begin in the minds of the elite but in the hearts of the mass. Wilson called the process of fathoming the people's desires (often only vaguely known to the people until instructed) 'interpretation.' Interpretation was the core of leadership for him."[22]

As the nation's chief "interpreter," Wilson served as a "lobbyist for the people," since "he alone could hear the 'true' voice of the people; he alone had the ear."[23] Wilson considered himself as a leader *of* the people—and less so *above* the people.[24] Wilson's rhetorical presidency, thus, can be considered a shared construct—one that relied, to an extent, on the input of "the people" it sought to serve. However, as Wilfred E. Binkley observed, "The reign of public opinion through presidential leadership was unquestionably the dream of Woodrow Wilson."[25] As such, Wilson's "interpretation" of the people's voices served political ends, potentially mitigating the rhetorical presidency's democratic promise. The women of the NWP worked to ensure that Wilson made good on this promise.

Wilson's Progressivism

Also key to situating Wilson's rhetorical presidency and the NWP's campaign is understanding the empowering and disempowering contours of progressivism—or, the ideological beliefs of the Progressive Era. Undergirded by progressivism, Wilson's rhetorical presidency sought to restore and empower those who endured the physical and spiritual costs of industrialization. Wilson's sense of progressivism, however, also promoted a racialized and gendered notion of the ideal US citizen, precluding him from advocating for the citizenship rights of those who did not fit into his vision of America—including women. However, the promise of progressivism to place power back in the hands of the marginalized provided the impetus for African Americans, wage laborers, immigrants, American Indians, and women to vie for enhanced citizenship rights.[26] Thus, the paradox of Wilson's rhetorical presidency and visions of progressivism is exposed, as he sought to interpret the will of a select group of people while quelling the voices of the very groups seeking progressive reform. The NWP's exploitation of this paradox, however, helped mark Wilson's second presidential term with the successful conclusion of the woman suffrage movement.

That the NWP and President Wilson pursued seemingly divergent social and political goals as part of progressive reform is not surprising considering that politicians, social activists, and intellectuals adopted different understandings of progressivism and different means of implementing progressive measures.[27] The forces that gave rise to the Progressive Era help explain these often-competing goals. Between 1870 and 1900, the nation's population exploded, the number of farms doubled, urban population tripled, immigration peaked, and railroads networked across the nation.[28] Such "progress" left many powerless; farmers and workers were often exploited by mammoth national corporations and corrupt city bosses. Political power became concentrated in the hands of the very wealthy, which compelled those languishing in urban slums and rural wastelands to assert political voice.[29] Agrarian revolt came to a climax in 1896 when William Jennings Bryan ran on a Populist platform as the Democratic presidential candidate; his defeat left a residual "rebelliousness and suspiciousness" of governmental abuses of power.[30]

Political efforts to ameliorate this oppressive climate took hold in the White House as an organized political platform upon President Wilson's 1912 election.[31] Wilson belonged in what Rogers M. Smith identifies as the centrist camp of progressives, which "believed that the US should be a modern democratically and scientifically guided nation that was also culturally ordered, unified, and civilized due to the predominance of northern European elements in its populace and customs."[32] Wilson's centrist progressivism thus valued cultural homogeneity and the preservation of racial and gendered hierarchies to help cultivate a national community in which all could participate as citizens and learn what it meant to be "American."[33] The glorification of Anglo-Saxon culture and ideals, however, reinforced the notion that the ideal American was white and male.

Wilson's progressive ideals functioned in tandem with the rhetorical presidency to establish an empowering dialogue with a select group of the American people. In his first inaugural address, Wilson focused on the "task" of securing the needs of the American people: "We know our task to be no mere task of politics but a task which shall search us through and through, whether we be able to understand our time and the need of our people, whether we be indeed their spokesmen and interpreters, whether we have the pure heart to comprehend and the rectified will to choose our high course of action."[34] Wilson pursued progressive policies, such as urban sanitation, labor laws, and tariff and commerce reform, to empower the citizenry of "all honest men, all patriotic, [and] all forward-looking men."[35] This progressive vision, then, relied on a renewed understanding of citizenship, one that simultaneously helped empower the American people to effect positive social change, and yet reinforced a masculine, Anglo-Saxon citizenship ideal.

The onset of World War I compounded Wilson's efforts to shape a united American polity and to silence those who resisted such efforts. In part, Wilson won his presidential reelection in 1916 by promising to keep the United States out of war; therefore, it became necessary for Wilson to justify the subsequent entrance of the United States in "American" terms. Recall Wilson's famously uttered words in his war address: "The world must be made safe for democracy."[36] In support of America's war efforts, as Geoffrey R. Stone puts it, "the nation was whipped into a fever pitch of patriotism"—so much so, voices of dissent were considered disloyal to the Wilson administration and to America's plight to liberate oppressed nations.[37] In fact, Wilson created the Committee on Public Information, a wartime propaganda program designed to help create "a uniform national opinion" in support of the war.[38] Shortly after Congress declared war on April 6, 1917, the Espionage Act was introduced, which, according to Stone, was distorted by the Wilson administration and the federal courts "to suppress a broad range of political dissent."[39] The following May, President Wilson signed the Sedition Act of 1918, which prohibited the willful utterance of disloyal language about the United States, the use of language to bring the United States into disrepute, and the interference of the things necessary to the production of war.[40] Along with a heightened sense of war hysteria, these acts were used to arrest socialists, anarchists, and German immigrants (or those perceived to be so), to say nothing of the abuses inflicted upon these groups by mobs and other "patriotic" citizens.[41] As such, US involvement in World War I worked to construct a unified American identity and severely limit the expression of marginalized voices, creating the impetus for these voices to rise up in protest.[42]

The presidency was not the only site of inclusion and exclusion at the time, as legislative and judicial discourses often worked to restrict women's citizenship rights. For example, in 1904, the Supreme Court ruled that husbands had "certain personal and exclusive" property rights to sexual intercourse with their wives.[43] Further, women did not have the right to sue their husbands for battery or physical abuse, let alone acquire separate state citizenship from their husbands.[44] Women's citizenship rights were further abridged by the passage of the 1907 Expatriation Act, which dictated that if a woman married a foreigner, she forfeited her US citizenship.[45] In 1908, the Supreme Court ruling on *Muller v. Oregon* showed that, with women's expanding roles in the workplace, the courts would extend their impulse to "protect" women by abridging their rights.[46] Justice David Brewer contended that women needed special protections in the workplace because of their motherly duties and physical needs. The ruling may have been considered a victory for wage-earning women, but it also reinforced the notion that women did not share equal rights with men.[47]

As progressive trends worked to marginalize women from fully participating in the national community, the empowering potential of progressivism motivated the women of the NWP to demand social change through civic participation. At the core of progressive movements was the belief in activism, that "social progress was not to be realized by sitting and praying, but by using the active powers [and] . . . by a revivification of democracy."[48] Like the women of the NWP, activists were inspired to implement referendum and recall measures, create city reform, and institute presidential primaries to help shift political power from party bosses to the people.[49] Further, "muckrakers" worked to expose the corrupt practices of politics and industry through vigilant journalism.[50] This contentiousness fostered a climate of robust civic engagement. J. Michael Hogan describes the scene: "ordinary citizens of the Progressive Era gathered in schools, in churches, and even in tents to listen to speakers, to debate among themselves, and to render their judgments on the issues of the day."[51] Although not empowered with the same voting rights as such "ordinary citizens," NWP members asserted their voices as they demanded the power of the vote.

The National Woman's Party

Although many scholars note the significance of Alice Paul and the militant contributions of the NWP to the US woman suffrage movement, studying the rhetorical strategies of the NWP in the context of the genesis of the rhetorical presidency offers an area of untapped scholarly pursuit.[52] If, as Stuckey and Antczak argue, the rhetorical presidency offers the possibility of "studying how the nation chooses among visions of itself," we must also consider that the rhetorical presidency offers the possibility of examining the contestations to visions of national identity.[53] The NWP's rhetoric of political mimesis, thus, allows us to question the extent to which the rhetorical presidency is shared not only by the president and the American people, but shared by the president and the people who contest who "the people" are.

As such, the NWP provides an example of the ways in which disenfranchised members of the American public responded to the president's power to shape a national identity and a vision of citizenship—one in which women could not participate as fully as their white male counterparts. In fact, Linda G. Ford characterizes the NWP's militancy as "the readiness to resist governmental authorities and break the law for the cause of women's rights, developed gradually from men's (non)reaction to women's political claims to equal citizenship."[54] In order to get the government's attention, the NWP embraced a theory of agitation wherein the president and members of Congress were held responsible for social change. Hence, the NWP's campaign emerged as a symbolic response to institutional and ideological resistance to woman suffrage.

Coming off of the heels of "the doldrums" of the US woman suffrage movement, the NWP's militancy helped reenergize a movement that had begun almost seventy years earlier when historic women's rights leader Elizabeth Cady Stanton had advocated for woman suffrage at the Seneca Falls Convention.[55] Over the course of the decades that followed, the early women's rights movement endured legal and cultural resistance, internal strife, and yet made incremental progress at acquiring state-level policy changes. Alice Paul's entrance into the US woman suffrage scene in 1912 aimed to challenge the moderate and state-level strategies favored by the dominant National American Woman Suffrage Association (NAWSA). Paul's resistance to those strategies, such as petitioning, lobbying, and relying on personal relationships with legislators, can be attributed to her previous participation in England's militant suffrage movement wherein Paul repeatedly protested and heckled members of parliament, for which she was arrested five times. Even so, Paul and fellow activist Lucy Burns initially worked with the NAWSA as leaders of its Congressional Committee to pursue a federal amendment for woman suffrage.[56] Soon after, Paul and Burns moved on to establish an independent organization committed to agitating political leaders, thus beginning the NWP's seven-year journey toward women's fully enfranchised citizenship rights.[57]

THE RHETORIC OF PROTEST

The drenched NWP protesters marched around the White House ten times in hopes that President Wilson might answer their simple question: "How long must women wait for liberty?" NWP members clearly wished to be fully endowed with the rights and privileges of US citizens, and sought to do so in one of the most provocative manners of protest in US history. To these extents, the NWP's rhetoric of protest invites theoretical discussions on nationalism, gendered citizenship, and militant social change. Moreover, because these women voiced their concerns as though they *were* fully enfranchised US citizens, this book embraces the concept of political mimesis to help explain this rhetorical phenomenon.[58]

Forming a National Identity

Put briefly, NWP members protested to be part of the nation. Thus, when placed within the broader context of President Wilson's efforts to form a national identity, the US woman suffrage movement can be seen as a movement to access the symbolic strength of what it meant to fully participate in the nation. To explore the relationship between nationalism and woman suffrage, this section asks three questions: What does it mean to belong to a nation? What roles do the president and the disenfranchised play in creating that meaning? How is this meaning sustained and revised?

Nationalism—or a sense of national identity—takes hold through a discursive process that undergoes constant revision. Belonging to a nation allows one to identify with a large community, which provides "a sense of security, a feeling of belonging, and prestige."[59] A shared sense of belonging fosters feelings of nationalism, which, according to Anthony D. Smith, is more than just pride in one's country, but "an ideological movement for the attainment and maintenance of autonomy, unity and identity."[60] Likewise, as Benedict Anderson puts it, a nation is "an imagined political community" composed of people who remain connected by the shared "image of their communion."[61] Similarly, Otto Bauer argues that nations are defined less by geography or natural inheritance, and more by what he terms "national character."[62] Such character is formed through shared struggle, shared language and habits, and shared political institutions, all of which create a shared will or the drive to achieve a common destiny.[63]

The formation of a US national identity intensified in the few decades preceding the inception of the NWP. In fact, the concept of nationalism emerged in the United States during the late nineteenth and early twentieth centuries as part of larger social phenomena, including the onset of modernity, the stratification of classes and subsequent urbanization, the influx of immigration, increasing industrialization, and Reconstruction.[64] Rogan Kersh argues that in response to the massive wave of immigration during the 1880s and 1890s, "virulent antiforeign sentiment"—"xenophobia, imperialism, and intolerance"—surfaced throughout the nation.[65] The perceived threat that immigrants posed to national unity, coupled with the rise of the United States as an international power, compelled Americans to embrace a "hyperpatriotic" sense of national identity.[66] A treatise by Pres. Theodore Roosevelt, *The New Nationalism,* reflected the growing desire to establish a shared, national identity that eschewed the threat of a diverse national polity and bolstered America's presence in the international arena.[67] Further, as Geoff Eley and Ronald Grigor Suny argue, the "triumph of Wilsonian principles" between 1917 and 1919 transformed the meaning of nationalism into "full political sovereignty," the very thing demanded by "even the smallest national minority."[68]

The rhetorical study of US nationalism attends to the rhetorical negotiations of power between such political leaders and social groups. After all, the meanings of "nation" are symbolic and emerge from "a continuously changing discursive formation."[69] Specific to the US political context, Kersh argues that "[t]he United States, like all nations, was constructed over time, a process requiring rhetorical affirmation and reproduction"[70]—a discursive exchange that involved members of the political elite and everyday Americans. M. Lane Bruner emphasizes this exchange as he posits the formation of a national identity as "a never-ending and politically consequential rhetorical struggle," in which groups compete for differing "accounts of national character."[71]

Significant to this study is the power that presidents hold in shaping a national identity. According to Erwin C. Hargrove, the president's "first task is to 'teach reality' to publics and their fellow citizens through rhetoric."[72] Likewise, Vanessa B. Beasley argues that presidents "promote the *idea* of an American people *to* the American people."[73] While historically presidents have always articulated a vision of an American identity, the rise of the rhetorical presidency in the early twentieth century elevated the president's role in the "national conversation" as "a surrogate of 'the people,' simultaneously enacting and enunciating our national values and national identity."[74] Consequently, a critical examination of Wilson's discourse provides an institutional perspective on how the nation's identity has been constructed, maintained, and challenged by the NWP.

Articulations of a unified American identity, however, often represent a deceptively homogenous version of the American people. Given the diversity of the American public along lines of race, class, gender, religion, sexuality, and even nationality, uniting the nation often begets simplification. In Stuckey's words, "Nation building thus inevitably requires reduction."[75] At times, presidential efforts made in the name of US nationalism have encouraged acts of "exclusion, intolerance, and even inhumanity."[76] Further, Katherine Verdery argues that "[n]ationalism is a quintessentially homogenizing, differentiating, or classifying discourse," thus creating multiple group identities—one composed of those privileged enough to be considered "American," and many composed of "others."[77] Similarly, Prasenjit Dura points out that exclusion, or the identification of "the Other," is essential to the nation-defining process, in that a nation must define itself in terms of what or who it is not.[78]

Given this book's focus on how the NWP challenged the perception that women were not to participate in the nation as fully enfranchised citizens, it is necessary to see the nation not as "a rigid thing" but rather as "a process of becoming."[79] The ways in which diverse groups attempt to participate in the national imaginary help ensure that a US national identity is continually reflective. Verdery, for example, argues that when studying nationalism, "the point is to see how a single symbol, nation, takes on multiple meanings. Groups orientating to it all take the nation to be the paramount symbol, but they have different intentions for it. Various things enter into their conflicts—contrasting ideas about authenticity, about the nation's true mission, about cultural patrimony or heritage, about national character, and so forth."[80] As such, this study recognizes and examines the historical contestation over the meanings of an American identity as historically excluded groups vied for full citizenship rights in the nation-state.

Gendered Citizenship

The women marchers did not simply wish to belong to a national community—they wished to have a voice in it. Possessing the right to vote as fully enfranchised US citizens would ideally provide them with this voice. Thus, the marchers also attempted to challenge shared meanings of citizenship. Reviewing theories of citizenship helps answer the following questions: What is citizenship? How does it function to include and exclude members of the national imaginary? Last, how is it markedly gendered?

To begin, we can turn to theories that link citizenship to political agency. As Karlyn Kohrs Campbell argues, "rhetorical agency refers to the capacity to act, that is, to have the competence to speak or write in a way that will be recognized or heeded by others in one's community. Such competency permits entry into ongoing cultural conversations and is the *sine qua non* of public participation."[81] Those considered citizens are granted political agency or participation in these "cultural conversations."[82] In the context of US nationalism, citizens with a "voice"—or the right to vote—can fully participate in the nation.

According to Rogers M. Smith, theories of citizenship can be placed into at least three different categories: republican, liberal, and ascriptive inegalitarian.[83] Scholars generally agree that all three of these categories have shaped notions of US citizenship since the nation's founding, and that the first two privileged a distinctly public and "male" form of citizenship because of their emphases on civic participation and the pursuit of individual rights—activities which were typically reserved for men.[84] The third of these categories, however, recognizes the roles of race, sex, class, ethnicity, nationality, religion, and sexuality in the enforcement and enactment of citizenship.[85] Smith elaborates: "Rather than stressing protection of individual rights for all in liberal fashion, or participation in common civic institutions in republican fashion, American law had long been shot through with forms of second-class citizenship, denying personal liberties and opportunities for political participation to most of the adult population on the basis of race, ethnicity, gender, and even religion."[86] Further, Smith argues that a combination of republican, liberal, and ascriptive forms of citizenship have been used to aid political leaders to create a shared identity of the "people" who can participate in the national imaginary, and further, to convince the "people" that their leadership and vision was necessary and beneficial.[87] Thus, just as notions of ascriptive citizenship were inscribed with power, they nevertheless also contained the impetus for social protest. In part, such citizenship rhetoric helped constitute identities of dominant and subordinate members of a national community, suggesting the hegemonic potential of such identity formations as well as the exigency for political challenge when such identities oppressed the rights of marginalized and socially aware groups.[88]

Ascriptive inegalitarianism also explains how citizenship acquired gendered meanings. Resonating with Smith's notion of ascriptive citizenship, Pnina Werbner and Nira Yuval-Davis adopt a differentiated notion of citizenship—a notion that views citizenship as "inflected by identity, social positioning, cultural assumptions, institutional practices and a sense of belonging."[89] The authors contend that, given such historical, social, and legal inequities, it is necessary to consider how a group's "gender, nationality, religion, ethnicity, 'race,' ability, age or life cycle stage mediates the construction of their [members'] citizenship as 'different' and thus determines their access to entitlements and their capacity to exercise independent agency."[90] As Robert Asen argues, one can perform citizenship without full citizenship rights; however, to an extent, state-recognized citizenship grants political agency.[91] Furthermore, women not privileged enough to participate in the public sphere as members of a civic community encountered a restrictive form of citizenship pertaining to their identities as women, not as independent beings deserving of natural rights.

Gendered citizenship highlights the tension between republican, liberal, and ascriptive forms of citizenship. Though in different ways, republicanism and liberalism both promised a vision of equality and participation in a larger, national community, which required that one subordinate ties to other communities centered on gender, race, class, or sexuality.[92] Ironically, citizenship was often ascribed to a group based on perceptions of race, class, and gender; in the context of US history, for example, voting rights were typically ascribed to privileged, white, Christian males. Specifically, as women attempted to access the privileges bound up in citizenship, they challenged a distinctly masculine realm of power, and, further, were often positioned as "the Other."[93] Women's identities were thus subjugated within the masculine spaces of citizenship as they pursued such rights and privileges.[94]

Furthermore, when US women pursued citizenship, they negotiated their identities among the public and private, the universal and the particular, and the community and the individual. Feminist scholars have long noted that the masculine, abstract conceptualization of citizenship as public and universal egalitarianism runs contrary to the feminist project of revaluing the public sphere to include "the personal," concrete, lived experiences of women and women's bodies.[95] As such, the pursuit of citizenship forced women to balance their identities *as women* and *as citizens,* forming the "dual nature" of women's citizenship.[96] Yuval-Davis elaborates: "[O]n the one hand [women] are included in the general body of citizens; on the other hand there are always rules, regulations, and policies which are specific to them."[97] Because women often encountered citizenship in conflicting and dichotomous ways, it was necessary to challenge traditional meanings of citizenship. Contesting and transforming meanings of citizenship allowed women to assert their political agency, and, further, to move closer to participating in the national community.

Citizenship, thus, shapes the ways in which people engage in the national community. Although shared notions of citizenship are ascribed to a narrower portion of "the people," alternative perspectives on citizenship allow marginalized groups to challenge liberal, republican, and ascriptive forms of citizenship and to assert political agency. More specifically, recognition of ascriptive inegalitarianism helps us see how difference plays a role in the enforcement and enactment of citizenship. Gendered citizenship in particular speaks to the ways in which citizenship has been mediated by sex, and further, how women have transformed meanings of citizenship to expand understandings of civic engagement.

Militant Social Change

As self-proclaimed "militants," the marchers outside Wilson's door demanded social change in a confrontational and controversial way. The NWP's methods appeared particularly troubling and sensational compared to those of the reigning moderates. But what exactly is militancy? Rhetorically, how does it function as a form of social protest? Last, how could the NWP protesters secure citizenship rights through such nontraditional means?

To begin, theories of social change help explain how marginalized groups gain access to and transform institutionalized power. A rhetorical movement perspective in particular examines the ways in which social change occurs through discourse, which necessitates the interrogation of the "themes, strategies, arguments, ethos, values, [and] rhetorical forms" of social movements.[98] Additionally, this study views the process of social change as an ongoing rhetorical exchange of power among those groups conceived of as more powerful or powerless, rather than perceiving social change as a top-down, bottom-up, or outside-in process.[99] To point, Hogan argues that a social movement perspective is characterized as a "collective, evolutionary, and dialectical process."[100]

Reflecting this dialectic of power, militant and moderate groups seek to negotiate institutional opposition in different ways, while often working in tension with one another. The NWP, for example, employed more militant and confrontational methods for change while the NAWSA used more reformist methods for change.[101] Moreover, Paul's impatience with the NAWSA's moderation provoked the NWP's militancy, just as the NWP's militancy influenced the NAWSA's moderation. Martin Duberman elaborates on the moderate-militant relationship: "Militants are tough-minded realists. Their refusal to place entire faith in an appeal to conscience, or in the benevolent workings of time, separates them from the genteel mainstream of American reform tradition. That tradition has always been grounded in a double optimism—that the world can be made better, and that this can be done through an appeal to 'right reason' rather than force and fear. The militants share the belief that the world can be made a better place, but they put their faith for change in power, not goodwill."[102] In short, militants engage in a rhetorical process that aims to confront institutional power more so than it aims to appeal to institutional power.

Constituting a group identity and asserting political agency are particularly significant processes for militant groups who typically lack validation and recognition from the institutions they seek to alter. Thus, as militants resort to nontraditional forms of communication after exhausting traditional means of political persuasion, they engage in the process of validating who they are and making themselves matter. As Jean L. Cohen asserts, "the process of identity formation, however, involves *nonnegotiable* demands," demands made by militant groups, particularly once more moderate modes of negotiation seem futile.[103] In part, militants are their own audience of their protests as such acts perform the necessary behavior to satisfy a need when no other behavior suffices.[104] However, as militants constitute their identities, they in turn invite other "audience[s] to experience the world in certain ways."[105] For example, as the NWP constituted its militant identity, it invited US women to participate in its vision of fully enfranchised US citizenship, women who in turn constituted their own citizenship identities. As militants engage in this constitutive process, they are called into valuable being and can then assert their political agency.[106] Put quite simply by Robert S. Cathcart, "[T]he enactment of confrontation gives a movement its identity, its substance, its form."[107]

Revealing further intricacies in identity formation, militants must forge identities with the majority they seek to join. Mari Boor Tonn argues that effective agitation emerges from negotiating militant appeals with dominant ideologies.[108] The NWP, although a self-proclaimed "militant" organization, aimed to make a policy change and to be represented in the US democratic system. To this extent, the NWP needed to negotiate its militant identity with that of the political mainstream. Political agency, thus, is not an unmitigated force; "agency is constrained by externals, by the community that confers identities related to gender, race, class, and the like on its members and by so doing determines not only what is considered to be 'true,' but also who can speak and with what force."[109] In terms of women's political agency, feminist theorist Arlene Elowe MacLeod argues, "women, even as subordinate players, always play an active part that goes beyond the dichotomy of victimization/acceptance, a dichotomy that flattens out a complex and ambiguous agency in which women accept, accommodate, ignore, resist, or protest—sometimes all at the same time."[110] Power and identity, thus, are constantly negotiated between those perceived to be the powerful and the oppressed. Given the NWP's militant demands to access institutionalized power through the vote, and, given the resistance of President Wilson and Congress to the woman suffrage movement, a social movement perspective allows for the interrogation of the NWP's negotiation of political power and constitution of a militant identity from a more disempowered position.

Political Mimesis

As mentioned before, the women marching around the White House demanded rights as though they already possessed them. Such gusto can be attributed to their militant identities, but it can also be explained through the rhetorical process of mimesis. The marchers viewed themselves as political actors and as citizens on equal footing with the political elite of the time. Thus, this section seeks to understand: What is mimesis? How does it function socially and politically? Last, what liberatory potential does a rhetoric of political mimesis offer?

To summarize, this study embraces the concept of political mimesis to explain how the NWP exacted its militancy by adopting the accepted rhetorics and rituals of political behavior in a manner that simultaneously challenged and reified shared meanings of nation and gender. In light of the NWP's policy-oriented campaign, rhetorical acts of political mimesis allowed the group to access symbols of political power and thus to enact more traditional strategies of effecting policy change. As Rhys Williams argues, social movement rhetors will often tap into an "established repertoire" of "clearly recognizable elements [to] give movements easier entrée into 'legitimate' politics" and into "the political arena."[111] In this sense, however, the potential for political mimesis to effect radical change is mitigated as political mimesis can reproduce the same political and social processes that worked to oppress US women. Then again, political mimesis can serve militant ends in that it allowed US white women to boldly enter reserved political spaces, assert political agency, and contest the meanings of otherwise restricted symbols and rhetorics.

The rhetorical complexities of political mimesis can be derived from the way in which the concept of mimesis has evolved throughout ancient, medieval, and contemporary rhetorical contexts.[112] Initially, Plato valued mimesis for its instructional qualities, but also dismissed it as the imitation of mere appearance.[113] Aristotle's *Poetics* elevated *mimēsis* to the art (or *technē*) of imitating or representing nature in paintings, literature, and music. Moreover, Aristotle considered mimesis as a natural instinct and a pleasurable process as it not only offered a means for learning, but for understanding and acquiring knowledge.[114] Classical notions of mimesis persisted in the notion of *imitatio* throughout the medieval era and the Renaissance, particularly as it pertained to the arts of writing fiction and theater.[115] In the eighteenth century, aesthetic theorists sought to expand mimesis beyond the arts to explain the formulation of social life.[116]

Building upon these conceptualizations, recent theoretical developments reappraise mimesis for the part it plays in "the *constitution* of reality."[117] For example, Samuel Ijsseling highlights mimesis as a fundamental mechanism for meaning-making, in which "doubling" and "repetition" create "the identity and recognizability of beings."[118] The power of mimesis to construct meaning and identities is attributed to the dialectical relationship created between the original and the representation of the original. Arne Melberg's articulation of this relationship stresses mimesis as a "meeting-place of two opposing but connected ways of thinking, acting, and making: similarity and difference."[119] Michael Taussig's *Mimesis and Alterity* argues that "the construction and subsequent naturalization of identities" rests upon such "similarity and difference," insofar as the exploration of such difference creates the potential to "yield into and become Other."[120] Inhabiting the identity of the Other—or that which is mimicked—can function as a strategy of empowerment. Taussig continues: "The wonder of mimesis lies in the copy drawing on the character and power of the original, to the point whereby the representation may even assume that character and that power."[121]

Significantly, Gunter Gebauer and Christoph Wulf offer *social mimesis* as a way to explain the processes through which mimetic acts shape and are shaped by our interpersonal and material realities.[122] They argue that "mimesis itself is inseparable from practical action, from interplay among perception, evaluation, and interpretation between fictional elements and active interventions in worldly events."[123] Extending this theory, Deborah Jensen argues that acts of social mimesis "could include everything from speech systems to the performance of gender norms to religious or philosophical proselytizing to currency exchange; . . . any domain of culture is mimetic where likeness is the basis on which we are able to perceive or act within overarching collectivities or systems."[124] In fact, many cultural critics link mimesis and hybridity to the processes of constituting cultural identities, particularly in postcolonial and intercultural contexts wherein power and ideologies are constantly in flux.[125]

Emerging from such previous scholarship, *political mimesis* is considered a strategy of political empowerment in which disempowered rhetors mimic political rhetorics, rituals, and practices to assert political agency, constitute political identities, and earn political legitimacy. Political mimesis is particularly amenable to the rhetorical processes through which marginalized groups negotiate power and constitute identities. Gebauer and Wulf argue: "In many usages mimesis entails an *identification* of one person with another. People identify themselves by means of their mimetic abilities when they see themselves in the Other and perceive a state of mutual equality. . . . There is a complementarity of perspectives in mimesis: a person regards the Other as equal and assumes the Other to be doing the same in reverse. Such an act of complementary seeing produces a correspondence between people. Complementarity is manifest in physical form when one person clings to another; it is a sensuous, bodily act, but it is penetrated by order; the Other is assimilated to the world of the person who is clinging."[126]

Mimetic rhetorics hold the potential to empower a marginalized group to identify and create "a correspondence" with those voicing institutional opposition. While the NWP did not attempt to literally cling to President Wilson or members of Congress, its members did insert themselves into reserved political spaces and physically confront the public-private boundaries placed on women. Moreover, the NWP's mimetic adoption of political discourses and rituals helped its members assert their political authority and force a discursive exchange with those in positions of political power, working to renegotiate the power relationships embedded in a world "penetrated by order."

Political mimesis also accentuates the NWP's use of militant methods to effect social change. Gebauer and Wulf explore the "extent to which the author [of a mimetic act] resists social pressure and produces a counterpressure, [and] whether the author's strategy in relation to the medium generates a codification system through which he or she gains symbolic power."[127] Here political mimesis can be considered a strategy of resistance to the "social pressure" of accepting and participating in the hegemonic processes of preserving male dominance. Similarly, in her discussion of cultural mimesis or "the political consequences of pointed imitation," Barbara Fuchs argues that "ideology pirated or ventriloquized becomes surprisingly vulnerable" and that this allows marginalized subjects to "undermine imperial claims to originary authority."[128] In the case of the NWP, political mimesis motivated members to militantly interrogate and make "vulnerable" the ideological forces that restricted women's roles in the nation-state.

To an extent, however, political mimesis reinforces institutional and ideological forces of tradition. In attempting to create a likeness in political power between their members and political leaders, protest groups necessarily accept some of the institutional rituals, reifying their exclusion and the exclusion of others, limiting the liberating potential of their social protest. Consequently, mimesis has been criticized, for example, as a "cultural site for the (re)production of the patriarchal political economy of signification as the 'real' and for perpetuating its hegemony."[129] As such, the NWP's rhetoric of political mimesis allowed the organization to engage in more traditional forms of social agitation while it also mimicked the oppressive ideological forces that the group often attempted to disrupt.

Taken together, nationalism, citizenship, militant social change, and political mimesis provide critical perspectives that account for the ways in which power is negotiated among dominant and subordinate members of society. More specifically, these lenses illuminate the ways in which marginalized groups contest and transform prevailing meanings of membership in a national community and assert political agency. Nationalism and gendered citizenship offer both restricting and empowering conceptions of community membership, particularly as oppressed groups engage institutional and ideological forces. Militant groups seek to confront these forces in traditional and nontraditional ways; through political mimesis in particular, militant groups can gain access to reserved political spaces and earn the necessary political legitimacy to ingratiate themselves into the institutional and ideological favor of the national polity while reconstituting citizenship identities and reenvisioning the boundaries of the nation-state.

OUTLINE FOR STUDY

Situated within a larger context of increased presidential power, national and international campaigns for democracy, progressive change, and the renewed scrutiny over notions of US citizenship, this book looks at the rhetorical strategies of the NWP's militant pursuit of the Nineteenth Amendment. While the seven-year campaign of the NWP helped enfranchise US white women in 1920, its rhetoric of political mimesis offered US women the opportunity to enact women's citizenship rights and thus offered a vision of women's expanded roles in the nation-state. Simultaneously, however, the NWP's rhetoric of political mimesis reified the strength of US political leaders and institutions as it vied for institutional legitimacy. Eventually, the viability of political mimesis as a strategy of social change is demonstrated by the ways in which the NWP's rhetoric circulated within the woman suffrage debate and solicited a response from political leaders, the US news media, and those individuals who became NWP members and opponents. Thus, this study argues that political mimesis offered the NWP the means to achieve both constitutive and political gains.

In addition, the NWP's rhetoric of political mimesis empowered its campaign for national suffrage rights in many ways. By mimicking the rituals of politics, such discourse helped the NWP negotiate the gendered boundaries of political participation and assuage the opposition to their actions as such rituals were accepted means of political engagement. Enacting the political legitimacy they sought, NWP members inserted themselves into national and state political spaces, which included the streets of Washington, D.C., the halls of capitol buildings, and presidential spaces of power. This strategy not only provided NWP members access to otherwise unavailable spaces, but it forced political leaders to engage them in a deliberative process over national woman suffrage, ultimately offering them a sense of political authority and legitimacy. However, as others, including the president, attempted to ignore or silence the NWP, the militancy of the NWP's assertion of citizenship rights was exposed.

Political mimesis also allowed the NWP to parody and quote the rhetorical strategies employed by the political elite to shape a nationalist and internationalist identity, and to link woman suffrage to the nation's vision of democracy. By parodying and quoting the democratic rhetoric espoused by President Wilson and members of Congress, the NWP demonstrated the variable ways in which mimesis can function as a strategy of empowerment. Through parody and quotation, the NWP rhetorically fused woman suffrage to America's democratic program during a time of war. In so doing, the NWP helped expand women's roles in the nation-state beyond more private, domestic concerns.

As a constitutive process, moreover, political mimesis helped empower NWP leaders with a sense of authority and agency to effect political change, and allowed women to envision themselves as fully participating US citizens; such constitutive efforts served as a motivating force throughout their campaign. In terms of the NWP's militancy, constituting themselves as citizens was integral toward helping women realize their citizenship identities and reenvision the gendered nation. However, as a more traditional strategy of social change, political mimesis provided NWP members the necessary political legitimacy and recognition to codify women's national citizenship rights into the US Constitution in ways less threatening to the political establishment. Such inclusion, however, often came with certain costs, considering that their political empowerment was dependent on the ultimate endorsements of male political leaders, which reified the latter's authority. The racism of the period was likewise reproduced as the NWP consistently subordinated African American women's rights throughout its campaign. As such, this study demonstrates the potential for political mimesis to expand *and* restrict citizenship rights.

Chapter 1 first situates the NWP within a larger context of US nationalism, citizenship, and woman suffrage from the seventeenth century through the genesis of the NWP in early 1913. This chapter traces gender ideologies embedded in US political culture to demonstrate the ways in which women interacted with constructions of nationalism and citizenship. Throughout US history, women appropriated nationalist and citizenship ideals to argue for their rights and challenge the public-private doctrine. This chapter also emphasizes the changing political climate of the early twentieth century, which marked a significant shift in the ways women could access political power in the context of the growing alliances between the labor and international women's rights movements.

Chapter 2 focuses on how the NWP's militant underpinnings shaped its first act as an organization—its national suffrage parade held the day before Wilson's first inauguration ceremony in 1913. By mimicking the inauguration ritual, the NWP's national suffrage parade helped shape woman suffrage as part of America's democratic tradition, as a matter of national rights, and as a force of coalition politics. As a strategy of social change, organized militancy had yet to enter the US woman suffrage scene on a national level, even after more than sixty years of agitation for enfranchisement.[130] Harriot Stanton Blatch's role in linking the growing international militant labor movement and woman suffrage helped create the opportunity for Alice Paul and Lucy Burns to make made their first statement as a militant force in the woman suffrage movement. Mimicking the inauguration ritual allowed the NWP to confront the public-private boundaries placed on women's participation in *national* spaces, elevate woman suffrage as a *national* issue, and offer a vision of a united, mass movement across race, class, and regional lines. Moreover, Mikhail Bakhtin's discussion of the medieval carnival helps show how the NWP's 1913 parade directly confronted President Wilson's nationalist authority.

Chapter 3 focuses on the ways in which the NWP's campaign exploded into the spaces of national politics through the mimetic adoption of third-party strategies and the ultimate formation of a new political party—the Woman's Party. Once severed from the NAWSA, the NWP mobilized members into every state and congressional district in the nation in order agitate the US Congress as its primary change agent for woman suffrage. In the process, the NWP worked to nationalize the suffrage movement while constituting enfranchised and disenfranchised US women as citizens. Accentuating a more traditional role of political mimesis, this chapter demonstrates how the NWP worked to nationalize the movement by adopting the strategies of a national political party throughout the 1914 and 1916 election cycles.

Chapter 4 turns to the NWP's mimetic strategies employed between 1917 and 1918. Situated within the rise of Wilson's rhetorical presidency, World War I, and gendered militarism, this chapter argues that the NWP mimicked Wilson's rhetorical campaign for democracy through parody and quotation. Specifically, the NWP's "Silent Sentinels" parodied the bully pulpit as the protesters went over Wilson's head and appealed to the American public to empower their fight for woman suffrage. Also, as the NWP directly quoted Wilson's war discourse, it constituted the Sentinels as soldiers fighting to liberate the oppressed and thus justified their abuses and motivated further action in the war for woman suffrage.

Chapter 5 analyzes the NWP's rhetorical acts of mimesis throughout 1918 and 1919, as the group adopted Wilson's international ethos to rhetorically link woman suffrage to Wilson's campaign for world democracy.

Now backed by Wilson's endorsement for woman suffrage, the NWP turned their protesting energies onto the Senate—and back again onto the president for failing to motivate the Senate to pass the suffrage measure. Contextualized amidst US internationalist ideology, gendered internationalism, and the internationalization of the woman suffrage movement, this chapter analyzes the NWP's protests at the Lafayette and Rochambeau statues, at the Senate buildings, and at their "Watch Fires of Freedom." These protest strategies helped promote the NWP in the international arena, but, more so, offered woman suffrage a rhetorical force that encouraged the nation and the US Senate to view suffrage as part of the democratic tradition and to pass the measure onto state ratification.

The afterword explores this study's historical and theoretical contributions as it deepens the appreciation of the NWP's role in national politics, citizenship discourses, and woman suffrage, as well as the understanding of political mimesis as a strategy of social change. The NWP's militant campaign certainly did more than help enfranchise US white women; significantly, the NWP impacted national politics, internationalist discourse, and multiple communities of women citizens. The force of political mimesis as a strategy for social and political change is also discussed, particularly as it helped the NWP to constitute citizenship identities while reaching its goal of enfranchising US white women in the process of reenvisioning the gendered nation.

Before turning to the NWP's rhetoric of political mimesis and its militant campaign for woman suffrage, this book offers a historical explanation of the strategies employed by the NWP to confront nationalist, citizenship-based, and gendered ideological forces.

1

Women, Citizenship, and US Nationalism

Months following the colonies' spirited declaration of independence from Great Britain, the people of New Jersey reached a breaking point. Patriotism wore thin as some considered taking up an amnesty proclamation offered by Lord Cornwallis after he and his British army set up camp in Elizabethtown. Late one December night, a group of New Jersey men gathered in Isaac and Hannah Arnett's home to deliberate the proposed amnesty and wearily concluded that they had no choice but to submit. Having overheard this conversation from an adjacent room, Hannah Arnett burst into the parlor, only to be shooed by her husband: "Hannah, Hannah, this is no place for you, we do not want you here just now. . . . Do you not see these are not questions for you? . . . Women do not understand these things." In response, she declared to the crowd, "And you call yourselves men; the sons who gave up homes and fortune and fatherland to make for themselves and for dear liberty a resting-place in the wilderness! Oh, shame upon you, cowards!" She warned, "Isaac, we have lived together for twenty years and for all of them I have been a true and loving wife to you. But I am the child of God and of my Country, and if you do this shameful thing, I will never again own you for my husband."[1]

Hannah Arnett's declared allegiance to her country over her husband suggested that her identity as a citizen of the young nation took precedence over her identity as a wife. Moreover, Arnett's ability to assert her political agency and address a room full of men reflected a deep commitment to the growing nationalist ideology of the young republic. Considering that between 1776 and 1807, property-owning New Jersey women possessed the right to vote and, further, that many of these women actively participated in the war and in New Jersey's post-revolutionary political culture, Arnett's passionate devotion to her country may not be surprising.[2] However, when seen within the larger, nationalist context of the revolutionary era, particularly in light of issues pertaining to citizenship, suffrage, and gender, Arnett's political consciousness was quite impressive. Most women of this time could not vote, were preoccupied with economic and familial survival, and were not educated enough to comprehend republican conceptualizations of virtue and nation.[3] Thus, while property-owning New Jersey women could assert their political agency and vote, most women of the time were not afforded such a privilege.

To help the reader fully appreciate the political and social value of the National Woman's Party (NWP), this chapter offers a historical look at how women such as Arnett have asserted political agency in US nationalist contexts. Often women have made arguments rooted in nationalist, citizenship-based, and gendered ideologies in opposition to those resisting advances for women's rights.[4] Thus, the women of the NWP were able to assert their citizenship rights by building upon the strategies of political and social empowerment employed by women since before the nation's founding. For example, the NWP's campaign echoed and expanded upon the ways in which women of the immediate post–American Revolution era embraced motherhood as a republican civic duty, abolitionist women petitioned their government to free slaves, and suffragists marched in state suffrage parades. Most women argued that these acts were performances of ideal citizenship behavior; however, what was considered "ideal" has differed throughout US history and often reflected gendered and racialized beliefs of the day.[5] Women activists themselves were not immune to such beliefs, and thus this historical look also shows that many strategies of empowerment also worked to exclude women of color and of the lower classes. NWP leaders were no exception as they often reified the notion that only white women deserved the right to vote.

This chapter also accentuates the forces of inclusion and exclusion that women faced over the course of US nationalist history—forces that likewise shaped the Progressive Era and the NWP's campaign. For example, although women in the early twentieth-century were more liberated than women in any US period before them, the women of the NWP challenged the legally and culturally enforced notion that women were dependents of men. Looking to the early national period, this discussion shows how women's dependent status was established through competing citizenship ideals and the struggle to become "American." Also key to understanding the NWP's struggle is that during eras of democratic proliferation and heightened nationalism—much like during the Progressive Era—women and most minorities typically did not benefit from expanding voting and citizenship privileges. Last, the NWP's efforts to elevate woman suffrage beyond a state-level issue to a national one can be explained by tracing state-level control over citizenship and voting laws back to the Constitution. Even with the passage of the Civil War amendments, which enhanced the federal government's ability to enforce voting rights, the early twentieth-century saw great resistance to the federal government's role in deciding who got to participate in the nation-state as citizens proper.

Amidst these historically grounded forces of oppression and activism, the women of the NWP sought to assert themselves as US citizens. This chapter highlights women's activism over four key periods of social change inflected by intense national activity and altered meanings of citizenship and gender.

WOMEN IN COLONIAL AMERICA AND THE EARLY REPUBLIC

The following elaboration upon women in America's colonial, revolutionary, and postrevolutionary eras informs the political and social barriers that the women of the NWP faced centuries later. The ways in which government shapes women's citizenship identities is introduced, as are the ways in which women have asserted their political agency in spite of such limits. Specifically, the formation of women's dependent status is explained as part of the political system of deference the colonies inherited from Great Britain. Also, this section shows how women's domestication became tied to national ideals as elite, white women were construed as carriers of the nation's prerevolutionary republican ideals. Last, this section helps explain the NWP's struggle to amend the Constitution as the founding document empowered states with the authority to define parameters of citizenship—parameters that often excluded women from participating in state or national communities.

Legal Dependents and Cultural Domestication

In colonial America, prior to revolutionary times, colonists were less united by a strong sense of nationalism and more so by their common European heritages and their commitments to family and community.[6] Also, most were considered dependent subjects of the British crown and to a great extent, parliamentary law.[7] As such, the tension between the reach of British law and colonial communities posed great potential for struggle as colonists worked to establish life in the New World. Nonetheless, inheriting British customs of law and government shaped the politics and identity of colonial life, an identity that was simultaneously mediated by race, class, religion, and, gender.[8]

In part, the struggle between Britain and colonial America explains how women's exclusion from politics was established in this period. Although Britain and colonial America held different ideals of citizenship and participation in public life, both held exclusive notions regarding who could possess the right to vote.[9] Colonists, for example, were eager to naturalize people of Anglo-Saxon descent because of their need to build communities that reflected a sense of themselves as chosen people.[10] The right to vote, thus, was greatly limited to Protestant, white, and propertied men—or to those who owned and paid taxes on property and held a literal "stake-in-society." Conversely, those without such property (in addition to the appropriate race, religion, and gender), were considered economically dependent and thus, subject to undue influence.[11] African Americans, American Indians, men under the age of twenty-one, those without established residency, Catholics, Jews, members of minority Protestant sects, servants, lower- and middle-class farmers, unnaturalized settlers, and women remained unrepresented at the polls.[12]

While it was legally and culturally accepted that women were the dependents of men, women possessed some rights as subjects of the British crown and thus engaged in colonial life in empowering yet complicated ways.[13] For example, as subjects, women were entitled to own and convey land; however, as dependents of their husbands and fathers, women had to defer to men when performing legal actions pertaining to the land.[14] Similarly, widows could inherit their husband's property, but the notion of *femme covert*—the idea that women were legally dead—often left widows at the mercy of their male children.[15] Eventually, colonial widows established critical mass and gained more legal power.[16] Still, in the absence of a will, all property went to the eldest male heir.[17]

Economically, women were similarly caught between the demands of colonial life and social customs. In some urban and commercial areas, women could work as *feme sole* traders; they were given the right to sue, conduct businesses, enter into contracts, sell property, and function as attorneys-in-fact.[18] Likewise, some married women were considered "help-meets" to their husbands or partners in managing the familial and physical demands of frontier and farm life.[19] As colonial markets prospered, some women began manufacturing goods at home and established trading networks. In seaport towns, spinning factories employed widows and poor white women, while other women became seamstresses and nurses. Still, most of these women were not entitled to their earnings, and, in remote frontier locations, impoverished conditions required that women work the land.[20]

Despite a few economic advances, the idea that women belonged in the home took hold in this period. The notion of women as "helpmeets" emphasized women's wifely and domestic duties under what was thought to be the more moral and intellectual guidance of their husbands.[21] Further, the geographic isolation of families in earlier colonial times emphasized the family structure around the home, as opposed to the more extensive webs of kinship found in England. As such, women were expected to be mistresses of the household. Eventually, Puritan and Quaker beliefs focused on the spiritual upbringing of children, and narrowed northeastern women's duties to the home and to child rearing. Additionally, the Great Awakening of the 1740s stressed private morality over public piety, thus contributing to the moral and domestic aspects of motherhood. Similarly, with the increased wealth of plantation life, southern women experienced a shift from managing all domestic work to focusing more on raising children. Of course, the gradual domestication of colonial women did not affect poor white women or slave women—rather, these religious and social forces worked to divide women along race and class lines.[22]

The experiences of colonial women, thus, were often shaped by the gap between the demands of establishing life in the New World and the legacy of English law and customs concerning women's dependence. Although mediated by race, class, and geography, the lives of colonial women gravitated toward the home. In varying degrees, religious and economic factors allowed some women to assert themselves as providers and spiritual leaders. Nonetheless, in the context of establishing a shared colonial identity, women's rights often fell to the wayside. Rogers M. Smith argues, "The new protonationalist political identity that British Americans were forming still largely presumed men's continuing legal right to govern women both in state institutions and in the home." Smith continues, "It is possible, moreover, that male desires to control women were enhanced by the increased emphasis on the racial and ethnic conceptions of their identity that British Americans formed to defend the subjugation of American Indians and African slaves."[23] Smith suggests that the growing nationalist ideology, which emphasized the superiority of white, Protestant, wealthy men, employed a protection myth, which constructed women as vulnerable and weak and depicted racial minorities as deviant sexual aggressors. This protection myth worked to simultaneously justify women's exclusion from legal or social rights, as women needed to be "spoken for" and protected as property.

Are Women Citizens?

Revolutionary thought provided the philosophical reasoning for women to embrace political participation in the nation-state, a rhetorical strategy employed by women throughout the following century and more, including NWP members. Turning to John Locke's Enlightenment ideals, colonists embraced liberal individualist views yet built upon republican principles of local community to justify a revolution.[24] Consequently, the ideal citizen of the young nation retained a republican sense of virtue and duty, but also possessed the right to individual freedom and voluntary citizenship.[25] In revolutionary terms, the liberal subject would choose to create a republican assembly that represented all people, offering more legitimate political participation.[26] This iteration of republicanism also promoted the belief that the people of the new nation were a chosen people, or "the *sole* bearers of the providentially favored Anglo-Saxon mission to build a realm of enlightenment and spiritual and political liberty."[27] As such, new state governments revised voting laws that allowed many minorities to vote, including New Jersey women.[28] Even so, William Blackstone's "stake-in-society" philosophy of voting had not faded, keeping most women, immigrants, paupers, and members of the lower classes from the polls.[29]

Nonetheless, revolutionary thought forced a discussion of women's roles in society and created small, but distinct openings for women to assert political agency.[30] The basic principles of Lockean liberalism begged the question of women's equality. However, John Adams's famed response to Abigail Adams's warning, "Remember the Ladies"—that he could only "but laugh" at—demonstrated the great resistance to extending equal rights to all individuals.[31] To an extent, however, notions of political liberty motivated some states to increase rights for widows and offer women the right to divorce.[32] Additionally, some revolutionary thinkers theoretically conceived of women as their equals.[33] But strands of American republicanism were used to argue against gender equality.[34] For example, republican thought stressed that independence meant economic independence, which not only limited women's ability to vote, but women's ability to be considered "individuals."[35] Thus, the potential contradictions of America's revolutionary sense of republicanism were exposed in the legal status of women following the revolution, forcing the question that would continue to provoke debate over women's rights for the next 150 years: Are women citizens?

The question over women's equal rights was also compelled by women's experiences in the war. Some women left their homes and trades to fight and camp alongside their husbands, fathers, and brothers. Class, however, mediated these women's experiences. Most women campers were poor and even considered prostitutes; however, the more privileged women campers, such as Martha Washington, were considered noble leaders.[36] Economic necessity compelled most of these women to return to their domestic lives following the war, although widows and poorer women confronted a harsher reality than others.[37] Ironically, men who had fought in the war were rewarded with voting rights, reflecting a link between war service and citizenship as well as a devaluation of women's roles in military combat.[38] Some women who did not participate in the war showed support by joining patriotic organizations, such as the Daughters of Liberty, or by boycotting English goods and by spinning and weaving their own clothes. For wealthier women, this meant participating in an activity often reserved for middle- and lower-class white women, servants, and slaves. Further, wartime inflation limited the extent to which lower-class working women and widows could participate in these patriotic activities; most of these women were preoccupied by providing a living for themselves and their children.[39]

In addition to these economic hardships, the rise of "republican motherhood" following the war constructed social barriers to women's independence. The gradual domestication of women before the war coupled with the limited extension of liberal rights to women after the war helped create a perception of motherhood as the ultimate performance of republican virtue and self-sacrifice. Linda Kerber argues that the emergence of republican motherhood was motivated by desires to limit the radical potential of individualist thought and retain the conservative strands of civic republicanism in the new nation.[40] As such, Kerber describes the scope of the republican mother: "[Her] life was dedicated to the service of civic virtue: she educated her sons for it, she condemned and corrected her husband's lapses from it."[41] Ideologically, republican motherhood created a "distinction between feminine virtue and masculine self-interest," enabling a growing distinction between the domain of white women's work and the world in which men could assert their independence and flourish as political actors.[42] These "separate spheres"—the public and the private—were complementary and, in political terms, greatly benefited men.[43] In Joan R. Gundersen's words, men exercised individual freedom "by virtue of women's dependence."[44]

Republican motherhood, however indirectly, carried some political import that, over time, women activists exploited in pursuit of enhanced rights.[45] By securing the virtuous citizenry of the new nation, mothering became linked to national duty. Further, women became empowered as the educational and spiritual authorities in households, compelling many to advocate on behalf of women's education.[46] Moreover, the greater emphasis on women's morality allowed white women to forge relationships and networks through the church, empowering women to participate in semipublic acts of benevolence without transgressing the parameters of their proper sphere.[47] Of course, white women were generally the only ones privileged enough to focus all energies on mothering. Even white women's political consciousness during this time cannot be overestimated, however. Most women were overwhelmed with the demands of survival in the post–Revolutionary War period and did not possess the privileges of education and wealth to consider the implications of republicanism on motherhood.[48] The few women that did contemplate such matters, such as Mercy Otis Warren, Judith Sargent Murray, and Abigail Adams, considered republican motherhood "a stage in the process of women's political socialization" and a concept that "legitimized a minimum of political sophistication and interest."[49] Thus, to an extent, republican motherhood ideologically justified women's political participation, although simultaneously restricted such participation to the private sphere. Eventually, the tension between women's domestic and civic roles would compel many women to address the inconsistent use of liberal and republican ideals in forming the new nation. To such ends, republican motherhood, more than anything else, provided the ideological foundation that eventually helped give rise to women's political activism.

Citizenship and the Constitution

Even with the potential to participate in nation building, women were excluded from the citizenship and voting parameters set forth in the Constitution. The Constitution's position on citizenship and suffrage was the result of differing views on the role of government.[50] Ultimately, the Federalist–Anti-Federalist debate shaped a provision that gave states the power to decide who had the right to vote and left the federal government without the means to override state suffrage laws except through a constitutional amendment.[51] Additionally, Congress acquired the power to establish naturalization policies, separating the issues of suffrage and citizenship along state and federal lines.[52] Thus, although the Constitution was designed to ensure representation of "the people," states retained the power to define who could vote—or to define who constituted "the people."[53] Such state power created a tension between federal and states' rights that would greatly limit the ability of the NWP to challenge voting laws or other measures that limited women's civic participation.

WOMEN AND DEMOCRATIC EXPANSION, 1790–1840

Following the establishment of women as dependents and republican mothers, the Jacksonian era saw increased political opportunity for women and yet continued restriction of women's rights. This section shows how this era—much like the Progressive Era—is considered one of the greatest periods of democratic expansion in US history and yet is also marked by the sharp exclusion of women and minorities. This era, characterized by the empowered citizenship rights of "the common [white] man," nonetheless inspired privileged US women to assert political agency, advocate for enhanced education, and form benevolent societies. Simultaneously, during this era the struggle between women's domestication and political activism intensified with the rise of the "true woman" ideology and women's increased participation in moral reform and abolition. The shared belief that the home was a (wealthier, white) woman's "proper place" as well as the severe resistance to women's participation in the public sphere persisted beyond this era and presented social and political obstacles to the women of the NWP.

Democratic Expansion (for White Men)

The early nineteenth century didn't see great advances for women's rights; however, during this time, the idea that the vote offered a sense of national belonging took hold—especially to those previously thought unfit to vote. Specifically, the rise of the two-party system in the 1820s became a way for white men to link their local interests with national politics.[54] Additionally, the commercial revolution and the rise of an industrial working class helped shift economic and political power away from property-owning men to white men of all classes.[55] According to Michael McGerr, increased participation in political parties "gave men a sense of their true collective agency."[56] The right to vote, then, no longer symbolized independent wealth, but it grew to symbolize the right to participate in the US democratic process as a free citizen.[57] Simultaneously, however, the vote became less attainable to marginalized groups, including African Americans, American Indians, Catholics, non–Anglo-Saxon immigrants, and women.[58] Arguments of natural superiority and competence were used to maintain a link between whiteness, US nationalism, and citizenship.[59] Needless to say, by the 1840s, the vote represented "a key symbol of [white] male political privilege."[60]

The general move toward recognizing individual rights, however, earned women a few more legal advances than most other minorities. For example, in 1823, Maine granted married women some property rights if their husbands deserted them; Massachusetts, Mississippi, New York, and Pennsylvania did the same in the following decades.[61] In 1838, Kentucky allowed propertied widows and unmarried white women to vote in school elections.[62] Also, many northeastern women worked in factories and earned wages of their own, though, as Sharon Harley writes, African American women were not privileged enough to have the opportunity to earn a working wage in these factories.[63] Norma Basch argues that these few gains—for white women—were the crucial "first steps toward integrating women into an egalitarian political ethos."[64] Nonetheless, Blackstonian notions of coverture prevailed in legal decisions regarding women and in early-nineteenth-century American culture in general.[65] Legally speaking, most women were still denied the right to their wages or to sell, sue, or contract without their husbands' approval.[66]

Most significantly, the idea that women were dependents prevailed, thus constructing women as incapable of making responsible voting decisions and appreciating the privilege of the vote.[67] Even New Jersey revised its constitution to prohibit women from voting in 1807.[68] As the public sphere increasingly became a political and male space, the private sphere increasingly became the reign of the republican mother.[69] Women were still largely recognized first and foremost *as women;* but in a few legal cases, often shaped by the democratic thrust of the post-revolutionary era, women were considered *citizens.*[70] In Kerber's words, the American woman "was a citizen but not really a constituent."[71]

Moral Reform and Abolition

Women's ability to assert political agency throughout the early nineteenth century, however, was not completely determined by state-sanctioned limits on citizenship or societal views regarding a woman's proper sphere, limits that the NWP would later push as well. Indeed, women engaged the US political process in ways that both reinforced and defied these limitations, and ultimately in ways that stretched the legal and social parameters of women's citizenship.[72] Women pushed for and attained increased access to education, formed religious organizations, performed acts of benevolence, and participated in reform movements and abolition, all activities with political implications that eventually continued to force the question of women's citizenship rights.

Access to equal education, then, was the first movement toward women's rights in the United States.[73] One of the first advocates for women's education was an English woman, Mary Wollstonecraft, who, in *A Vindication of the Rights of Women,* argued that women and men were naturally equals and that boundaries between the public and private spheres should be eliminated.[74] Women's education became more plausible as the demands of republican motherhood led to a female seminary movement. Founders of female seminaries, however, faced many obstacles, including fund-raising, developing curriculum, finding trained female teachers, and persuading opponents to support women's education.[75] Even so, Emma Willard opened the first endowed educational institution for young women. After she was denied a formal education, Willard believed her self-taught mathematical and physiological training should be put to use. For two years she privately lobbied New York Governor DeWitt Clinton and many legislators. In 1821, she opened the Troy Female Seminary.[76]

The increased focus on women's morality, enhanced by women's participation in the growing evangelical Protestant movement, provided the rhetorical means for women to gather and organize on behalf of moral causes of the time.[77] Also, the onset of "true woman" values—piety, purity, domesticity, and submissiveness—motivated these activities as extensions of women's moral and domestic duties.[78] Women developed organizations to train other women to become housekeepers and seamstresses; to aid poor women, elderly women, orphans, and victims of domestic abuse; to advocate for fair treatment of women in prisons, dress reform, and health and sex education; and to marshal support against prostitution, brothels, and alcoholism.[79] These organizations provided women the opportunity to enact the political rights of their male counterparts. Ann Boylan details the political characteristics of these organizations: "Every group—no matter how small or how modest—had a constitution and bylaws, held regular elections, and followed set agendas, members were able to vote, run for office, hammer out platforms, and make decisions that affected others directly."[80] She adds that these women were endowed with more rights as a group than as individuals. For example, incorporated groups could own substantial amounts of property, invest money, sue and be sued, and pressure politicians for city funds and favors.[81] One organization mobilized over fourteen hundred women to sign a petition against controversial American Indian removal policies, which, according to Alisse Portnoy, was "the first announced instance of women's federal activism in a space declared national and political."[82] Furthermore, these organizations fostered a sense of solidarity and civic identity among members; the petitioners against Indian removal, for example, acted out of "national faith and honor."[83] This sense of a shared identity, however, was mostly limited to wealthy white women, whose senses of religious and moral superiority often translated into self-righteous and classist attitudes toward the underprivileged.[84]

Although works of benevolence crossed over into the political sphere, many benevolent organizations insisted that their work was a function of their religious and domestic duties. In fact, some benevolent organizations resisted identifying themselves as "political." Lori D. Ginzberg writes: "Benevolent women—and men—were quite prepared to use the ideology of femininity against female organizing that served interests they thought too radical. The language of gender spheres, with its charge of 'straying,' was often used less to describe the boundaries of women's benevolent activity than to assert the unpopularity of a cause."[85] The rhetorical power of women's inherent religiosity and morality, thus, could also work to restrict women's political agency. Moreover, many of these benevolent organizations relied on the political and economic resources offered by men, thus restricting the extent to which women asserted their political independence through these organizations.

In the 1830s, however, moral reform and abolitionist societies emerged, providing women the opportunity to engage the political sphere in a more ardent and therefore controversial way, laying the groundwork for the NWP's militancy. Boylan describes the shift in organizational participation: "Unlike benevolent women who presented to local politicians deferential petitions from prominent individuals for specific favors, antislavery women circulated their petitions to mass audiences. . . . Moral reformers in the 1830s shouted their cause from the housetops and invited controversy as a means of publicizing their work."[86] Female reformers and abolitionists modeled popular political strategies of the Jacksonian era, including the use of the popular press and mass petitioning.[87] More so than their benevolent counterparts, these organizations pushed the boundaries of women's political and civic participation by assuming the political authority of their male counterparts.

The abolition movement, in particular, challenged codes of womanly behavior by encouraging women to speak publicly. For example, Frances

Wright, a Scottish freethinker, was greatly influenced by the Jacksonian workingmen's movement for economic equality.[88] Between 1828 and 1829, she delivered antislavery speeches and advocated for gender and racial equality.[89] Many women abolitionists invoked the rhetoric of morality to speak publicly against slavery and, further, to construct the bonds of "sisterhood" between themselves and enslaved women.[90] Sarah and Angelina Grimké were compelled by their upbringing on a slave-owning plantation and their Quaker faith to wage a public abolitionist campaign between 1835 and 1838; accordingly, they worked for the American Anti-Slavery Society in Boston, writing editorials and delivering lectures. Ultimately the Grimkés advocated a woman's right to speak publicly in order to further the abolitionist cause.[91]

Not surprisingly, moral reformers and women abolitionists were met with great resistance, even from within abolitionist circles. Addressing "promiscuous audiences"—groups comprised of both men and women—and publicly deliberating political issues were considered outrageous violations of gendered codes, both socially and politically.[92] Although some women worked to empower the citizenship rights of others, some women insisted on perpetuating conservative ideas of gender roles, thus limiting their own citizenship rights.

Although many white women were chastised for publicly decrying slavery, most African American women abolitionists were silenced altogether. Four founders of the Female Anti-Slavery Society of Philadelphia were African American women.[93] These women attended the first two national antislavery conventions, where the question of African American women's involvement was debated. Ultimately, between the 1830s and 1860s, the majority of white women and African American male abolitionists marginalized the participation of African American women abolitionists. Rosalyn Terborg-Penn argues that, although scholars more often note the participation of African American men, "black women were equally involved in the movement."[94] Some of these women included Mary Ann Shadd Cary, Josephine St. Pierre Ruffin, and Sojourner Truth. Resisting marginalization in a predominantly white women's movement, Truth delivered her historic "Ar'n't I a Woman" speech at the 1851 Woman's Rights Convention in Akron, Ohio, where, as Carla Peterson argues, Truth "claim[ed] privilege on the basis of neither whiteness nor maleness."[95]

The need for a women's rights movement was growing among both white and African American women. American women still lived with severe economic, legal, and social restrictions, all woven into a seemingly impenetrable web of laws and social customs. A woman had no right to her own wages; upon being widowed, the state took most of her family's possessions, and if she did seek divorce, she forfeited custody of her children.[96] Most women could not challenge these forces, let alone forge their own identities—especially nonwhite, working-class women. But some women wished to expand the boundaries of women's political and civic participation. Thus, while advocates for women's education and benevolence reified traditional gender ideologies, moral reformers and abolitionists dared to challenge them.[97] It was not lost on early women's rights leaders that the vote had become "a key symbol of male political privilege."[98]

THE WOMEN'S RIGHTS MOVEMENT, 1840–1890

Following the more democratizing forces of the early- to mid-nineteenth century came an era of more restrictive citizenship rights. Nonetheless, this time period marked the inception of the women's rights movement that would conclude seven decades later with the help of the NWP. The struggles of the early women's rights movement shaped the struggles later encountered by the NWP, including the complex relationship between the African American and women's rights communities, the exclusion of women from the Civil War constitutional amendments, the expansion and resentment of the federal government's role in citizenship rights, and the internal struggle between equal rightist and conservative approaches to women's rights. Even so, the women of the NWP inherited the opportunities that the early movement provided—to engage political life and even vote at the local, state, and national levels. Additionally, the NWP greatly benefited from the alliance that leaders established with the labor movement. The following discussion shows how these struggles and opportunities gave rise to the NWP's own battle for women's rights.

The Question of the Vote

Despite the relative expansion of citizenship rights in the first half of the nineteenth century, the 1840s marked a shift in this pattern. The issue of the franchise remained in the forefront of American politics, but primarily because of the threat posed to the traditional white male electorate by African Americans, women, Catholics, American Indians, paupers, and immigrants not considered "white" enough. Fears of these groups gaining too much political ground led to a gradual restriction of citizenship and voting rights that, despite the enfranchisement of African American males in 1870, held fast through the early decades of the twentieth century.[99] For example, throughout the 1840s and 1850s, Indiana, Illinois, Iowa, and Oregon voted to prohibit African Americans from entering their territories.[100] Additionally, fears that immigrant votes could easily be bought by promising naturalization were fueled by the increasing perception that Catholic immigrants were dirty, alcoholics, morally impure, and lawless. These fears contributed to the meteoric success of the anti-immigrant Know-Nothing Party, which pushed for a twenty-one-year naturalization period for immigrants (in contrast to a five-year period).[101] Although the party dissolved shortly after its rise, the Know-Nothings demonstrated the preeminence of the white, male, Protestant, and native-born citizen.

Within this context of restrictive political power, a women's rights movement was underway, providing a small group of women avenues to assert political agency. Historic leader Elizabeth Cady Stanton helped initiate a movement after her marginalizing experiences with abolition. In 1840, Stanton and her activist husband attended the first World Anti-Slavery Convention in London. Many notable abolitionists were in attendance, including Angelina Grimké Weld, Wendell Phillips, and William Lloyd Garrison. Most exciting to Stanton, though, was the presence of Lucretia and James Mott. Lucretia Coffin Mott was an ordained Quaker minister, who at forty-seven years of age became an immediate mentor and confidante to Stanton. The two women bonded through adversity—on the first day of the convention, when a vote was held as to whether the American women would be welcome to sit with the men. Out of protest, Garrison joined the women who had been relegated to the periphery of the convention floor. Stanton and Mott boycotted the rest of convention and decided that someday they needed to hold a convention of their own.[102]

Before Stanton and Mott could make such plans, eight farm women presented a petition to the New York State Constitutional Convention in 1846, arguing for a woman's right to vote. Although they were all but laughed out of the convention, they had introduced the idea of woman suffrage into the political arena, a discussion that would not abate for another seventy years.[103] It was perhaps not entirely coincidental that, two years later, Stanton helped persuade the New York state legislature to adopt the Married Woman's Property Law, which granted land-owning rights to women.[104] A few months later, the historic Seneca Falls Convention took place.

The success of the Seneca Falls Convention showed that both women and men were eager to fight for women's rights, constituted an alliance with the abolition movement, and demonstrated that among the rights sought after, the right to vote was the most controversial. On July 13, 1848, Stanton, Mott, Martha Coffin Wright, Jane Hunt, and Mary Ann McClintock gathered in Stanton's parlor and drafted an announcement of a two-day "Woman's Rights Convention," a notice that appeared in the *Seneca County Courier* the next day.[105] On July 19, 1848, over one hundred men and women filled a small Wesleyan chapel "to discuss the social, civil, and religious rights of woman" as the announcement had promised.[106] While the first day of the convention was reserved for women only, more than forty men were admitted. McClintock addressed the promiscuous audience on the purpose of the convention, which was followed by a lively debate over the resolutions drafted in the foundational "Declaration of Sentiments." On the second day, even more men attended, including abolitionist Frederick Douglass. For the first order of business, Stanton presented the revised "Declaration of Sentiments," which was surprisingly embraced by the audience.[107] After debate and discussion, all resolutions of the "Sentiments" passed unanimously with one exception—the resolution for enfranchisement. Sixty-eight women as well as thirty-two men signed the document.[108]

Stanton and the other convention leaders intentionally modeled the "Sentiments" after the Declaration of Independence, showing how women's rights leaders often made arguments grounded in equal rights.[109] Ellen Carol DuBois argues that the strategy "involved the extension of natural rights egalitarianism from men to women—especially the principles of individualism, the universal capacity for reason, and political democracy."[110] The "Sentiments" declaration was so directly modeled after the Declaration of Independence that it too began, "When in the course of human events."[111] The most obvious revision lay in the opening of the second paragraph, "We hold these truths to be self-evident: that all men *and women* are created equal."[112] The "Sentiments" declaration was structured "in the tradition of declarations as a genre" by listing a host of grievances and then resolutions.[113] Thus, as both an extension and a revision of the Declaration of Independence, the "Sentiments" offered what Stanton believed to be a statement of natural rights—that women were also human, and that they too were born with the innate right and responsibility to revolt when abused by the government.

The Seneca Falls Convention and the signing of the "Declaration of Sentiments" constituted the beginning of a women's rights movement and the debate over woman suffrage. Before the Civil War, the movement was carried on through a series of conventions held in 1850, 1851, 1852, and

1860. These conventions provided stages for women to argue publicly for women's equal rights.[114] Many of these women, including Stanton, Lucy Stone, and Ernestine Potowski Rose, argued for independence from men, spoke out against laws of coverture, and even broached the contentious issue of divorce.[115] The arguments made during the "divorce debates" of the 1860 convention demonstrated that many were uncomfortable with the full realization of "women's equal rights" and more so, that conservative beliefs regarding a woman's proper place posed the greatest obstacle to women's rights.[116] Nonetheless, in a little over a decade, the women's rights movement provided women a place to assert political agency and make arguments for women's rights, including the right to vote.

The Civil War and Woman Suffrage

Much of this momentum, however, slowed down considerably as the Civil War and the enfranchisement of African American males took hold of the nation's attention and established ongoing rifts within the women's rights movement and between the women's rights and African American communities. Additionally, the successes of the Civil War amendments and the Radical Republicans' theory of impartial and universal rights offered some promise to the women's rights movement, yet exacerbated the struggle between federal and states' rights. The internal and external struggles experienced by the women's rights movement during this time persisted throughout the late nineteenth century and shaped the NWP's campaign in poignant ways, particularly in terms of race relations and the South's resentment of the federal government.[117]

The language of the Civil War amendments both elided the women's rights movement and provided the rhetorical means for women leaders to argue for a constitutional amendment. The Thirteenth Amendment and the Civil Rights Act of 1866, for example, provided the first constitutional definition of citizenship and introduced equal citizenship rights before the law.[118] Furthermore, these measures helped empower the federal government to intervene in state affairs if individual rights or citizenship rights were thought to be violated. Additionally, the Fourteenth Amendment declared, "All persons born or naturalized in the United States, and subject to the jurisdiction thereof, are citizens of the United States and of the State wherein they reside." Moreover, this amendment prohibited states from abridging citizens' "privileges and immunities" or denying them "equal protection of the laws."[119] The amendment was also considered a repudiation of the 1857 *Dred Scott v. Sandford* Supreme Court ruling that declared African Americans were not citizens.[120] Congress extended the reach of the federal government in March 1867 with the passage of the Reconstruction Act, which required southern state constitutions to ratify the Fourteenth Amendment and allow African Americans to vote on the same terms as whites.[121] In light of these measures, African American political participation in the South flourished. African Americans served as congressmen, legislators, sheriffs, justices of the peace, and school board officials; one African American even served as governor of Louisiana. Many African Americans attended political events and up to 90 percent of the population voted in elections.[122]

The passage of the Fifteenth Amendment, however, incensed women's rights leaders and drove a wedge between them and African American leaders. The final version of the amendment, which protected the rights of African American males to vote, reflected a much more narrow interpretation of who was deserving of suffrage. The amendment prohibited discrimination on the basis of race and color, but left out the language that prohibited discrimination based on "nativity, property, education or creed," and, quite noticeably, sex.[123] The absence of this language showed the women's rights movement that a similar amendment would be necessary to ensure woman suffrage.

The idea of women acquiring the right to vote did not seem to concern legislators, but the promise of equal treatment before the law provided the means for women to levy arguments for woman suffrage. Additionally, the Civil War offered women the empowering experiences of organizing the Sanitary Commission and adopting a style of leadership that emphasized "cooperation, prevention, and expertise."[124] After the war, women's rights leaders focused on earning constitutional recognition of women's citizenship and suffrage rights, and expected support from their abolitionist allies. In 1865, however, abolitionist leaders including William Lloyd Garrison wanted to pursue enfranchisement for black men exclusively. Remaining firm in acquiring suffrage for men and women, Susan B. Anthony and Elizabeth Cady Stanton formed the American Equal Rights Association (AERA) in May 1866. Prominent African American women abolitionists held leadership and support roles in the organization, including Frances Ellen Watkins Harper and Harriet and Hattie Purvis.[125] By 1869, however, differences over the proposed language of the Fifteenth Amendment fractured the organization. Some leaders of the abolitionist community, including Frederick Douglass and Frances Harper, left the organization and contended it was the "Negroe's Hour" for constitutional enfranchisement.[126] Others, including Mary Ann Shadd Cary, agreed that the word "male" should not have been included in the amendment.[127]

Correspondingly, Anthony and Stanton established the National Woman Suffrage Association (NWSA) in May 1869 to extend their national campaign for women's equal rights.[128] The ideological foundation of the NWSA greatly influenced the founders of the NWP, as Alice Paul thought of Anthony as her personal hero. The NWP later inherited the NWSA's expansive and restrictive trends; for example, both organizations addressed a host of equal rights issues, including divorce, oppression in the church, and equal wages, yet both organizations excluded participation of nonwhite women. In contrast to the NWSA, former abolitionist leaders and other women's rights leaders established the American Woman Suffrage Association (AWSA) in November 1869.[129] The AWSA focused mostly on securing suffrage for white women on the state level and articulated a more conservative gender ideology toward women's rights.[130] The establishment of these two women's rights organizations—the more radical NWSA and the more conservative and moderate AWSA—would develop over time into a similar pair at the conclusion of the woman suffrage movement: the militant NWP and the more moderate National American Woman Suffrage Association (NAWSA).

Meanwhile, new relationships between the women's rights and labor movements were forged, establishing a link that later shaped the NWP's membership of both woman suffragists and labor activists. In 1866, Anthony and Stanton attempted to ally with the National Labor Union (NLU), which focused primarily on empowering the working class. However, the alliance was fragile due to the disparity between Anthony and Stanton's middle-class position and the working-class roots of NLU leaders.[131] Shortly after, in September 1868, Anthony formed the Working Women's Association (WWA) made up of wage-earning women. The WWA sent a delegation of women to the 1868 National Labor Congress, promising to forge a link between middle-class suffragists and wage-earning women. However, the association between the two movements lasted no longer than a year. In part, male trade unionists remained hostile toward women, and believed the labor movement should primarily benefit men. DuBois argues that while workingwomen were doubly exploited—on the bases of gender and class—relieving class oppression was paramount to relieving gender oppression. Furthermore, she argues that women's rights leaders took a somewhat patronizing attitude toward wage-earning women, considering them powerless victims.[132] Nonetheless, Anthony and Stanton had established the beginning of a relationship between the woman suffrage and labor movements that would strengthen over time.

Meanwhile, women's rights leaders embraced a constitutionally based argument for enacting voting rights. Introduced by Francis and Virginia Minor as the New Departure Theory, the argument drew upon the first section of the Fourteenth Amendment, which extends citizenship protection and rights to all persons born in the United States, and the Fifteenth Amendment's reaffirmation of suffrage as a citizenship right. Virginia Minor thus argued that women were citizens entitled to the right to vote, and said that "the immunities and privileges of American citizenship, however defined, are National in character and paramount to all State authority."[133]

The New Departure strategy provoked a series of revolutionary events in the suffrage movement, providing women the opportunity to assert political agency, intrude upon political spaces, and expand their roles in the nation-state. First, after the NWSA embraced the strategy, Stanton presented its principles to the Congressional Committee on the District of Columbia in January 1870. She aimed to enfranchise the women of the District, but was blocked by the outcome of a Supreme Court case, *Minor v. Happersett* (1875), which was the first case to reach the Court that addressed woman suffrage. Reese Happersett refused to register Virginia Minor to vote in an 1870 election.[134] When the Court's decision was finally issued in 1874, it argued that, first, citizenship did not ensure suffrage, and, second, states could elect to withhold voting rights from women.[135] Also influenced by the New Departure strategy was free-love feminist, Virginia Claflin Woodhull, who delivered a memorial to the House Judiciary Committee in January 1871, arguing for women's constitutional equality. Although the committee rejected Woodhull's memorial, two members of Congress issued a minority report in support of woman suffrage.[136] Additionally, her address coincided with the NWSA's national convention in Washington, D.C., allowing Anthony and Stanton to witness Woodhull's public action and suffrage arguments.[137]

As the New Departure strategy provoked debate in Congress and the Supreme Court, it pressed the issue of woman suffrage into the privileged spaces of national politics and created the opportunity for women to enter these spaces and enact the citizenship rights they sought. Most significantly, the New Departure prompted women to leave their homes, walk to voting polls, and cast ballots. Beginning on November 19, 1868, 174 women, four of whom were African American, voted in Vineland, New Jersey. In

1870, forty women, including Angelina Grimké Weld and Sarah Grimké, similarly cast ballots in Hyde Park, Massachusetts. Between 1871 and 1872, seventy more women successfully voted across the country, including African American women in South Carolina.[138] Voting peaked during the presidential election of 1872. On November 5, 1872, Anthony led over fifty women in Rochester, New York, to register and vote, leading to her much-famed arrest and subsequent trial.[139] Similarly, the New Departure Theory was used to urge female property owners not to pay taxes on their property.[140]

Key to this strategy was the understanding that *action* made social change. Not only did these women make an equal rights argument for the right to vote, but also they enacted their equal rights convictions by mimicking the actions of their fully-enfranchised male counterparts.[141] Further, the Enforcement Acts of 1870 and 1871, which were passed to protect the voting rights of African American males, strengthened the notion that voting was the ultimate act of citizenship to be protected by federal law.[142] While the ruling of *Minor v. Happersett* argued that suffrage was not a citizenship right, and, further, that states could enforce their own definitions of citizenship (ones that excluded women), these women constituted themselves as political actors by actively and militantly upholding their interpretation of constitutional law.

Increased Activism

Although the New Departure Theory was met with strong opposition, the woman suffrage movement experienced incremental and state-level success throughout the 1870s and 1880s that paved the way for larger successes at the turn of the century. These successes may be owed to the reinstated state-level control over voting rights, considering that, by 1878, Democrats had secured control of Congress, signaling the end of the federal government's attempts to protect black male suffrage.[143] In turn, suffrage efforts were more successful at local and state levels, while efforts for a national amendment were largely ignored.

Even so, multiple organizations such as the AWSA, the NWSA, and the Woman's Christian Temperance Union (WCTU) waged national-level campaigns for women's rights by adopting the traditions of national political organizations. Women's rights leaders conducted regularly held conventions, published pamphlets, petitioned state legislatures and Congress, and lobbied congressmen.[144] By pressing themselves into the spaces of national politics, these women helped elevate women's rights issues to matters of national significance. The question of a federal woman suffrage amendment, however, was still met with resistance. In 1882, for example, the NWSA pushed both houses of Congress to appoint committees on woman suffrage, both of which recommended passage of a federal amendment. In 1886, an amendment came to a vote in the Senate; this was ultimately defeated in 1887. Congress debated the issue for another six years, although to no avail.[145] Another suffrage amendment would not be introduced until the NWP's time; like the NWSA, the NWP would help spark debate in the national arena.

The focus of the AWSA on promoting state suffrage amendments, in concert with state suffrage organizations, lent greater success for woman suffrage. Between 1870 and 1910, referenda were held in eleven states; the territory of Wyoming enfranchised women in 1869, followed by the territory of Utah in 1870, the territory of Washington in 1883, Colorado in 1893, and Idaho in 1896. Holly J. McCammon attributes these successes to many factors. First, she points to the willingness on behalf of state legislatures to grant partial suffrage; Montana's legislature, for example, allowed women to vote for school officials in 1887 and 1889. She also argues that the growing presence of third parties—such as the Populist Party, the Progressive Party, the Prohibition Party, and the Socialist Party—increased the opportunity for social change. Last, McCammon links these successes to the overall increased participation of women in organizations, such as the WCTU and the General Federation of Women's Clubs (GFWC). Western states seemed to be more willing to grant women the right to vote, which some scholars attribute to the belief that an agrarian lifestyle promoted more egalitarian roles between men and women. Many suffrage scholars argue that these political successes were due to women's ability to assert themselves amidst larger cultural and structural forces that favored the blurring of gendered spheres.[146]

The NWP also expanded upon the internationalization of the women's rights and suffrage movements, which can be attributed in large part to the WCTU, founded in 1874 and led by the charismatic Frances E. Willard. The WCTU was the largest women's organization in the late nineteenth century, consisting of over forty departments charged with addressing issues such as labor, peace, social purity, health, and education. Willard used arguments championing women's morality and purity to advocate for woman suffrage, in contrast to the equal rights arguments espoused by the NWSA. Willard was a socialist and formed alliances with labor organizations, such as the Knights of Labor and the Populist Party, and eventually transformed the WCTU's mission to help redress the excesses of capitalism and male political power.[147] Additionally, in 1884, Willard helped form the World's Woman's Christian Temperance Union (WWCTU), taking the WCTU's mission to an international level. WWCTU leaders targeted the issues of wage-earning women in Australia, New Zealand, and England. In England, WWCTU leaders formed an alliance with Sylvia Pankhurst and other leaders of women's trade union and labor organizations. Thus, while the WCTU's position on morality and family were quite conservative, its class and economic positions were left-leaning. The WWCTU's class consciousness, however, was not unchecked by its racist undercurrents; the organization excluded indigenous Maori women in New Zealand and was criticized for excluding African American women in the United States.[148]

Similarly, the NWP's militancy was influenced by the solid link forged between the women's rights and international labor movements with the help of Elizabeth Cady Stanton. After spending a considerable amount of time in England in the late 1880s, Stanton helped found the Women's Franchise League (WFL), a radical suffragist organization with close ties to the labor and socialist movements in England. The organization took a radical approach to women's rights, arguing that all women's work—whether paid or unpaid—was "labor" and deserved certain legal protections. The WFL also argued on behalf of wage-earning women and pushed for the eight-hour workday. Further, the organization took a militant approach toward woman suffrage. For example, in 1892, when WFL members were unsatisfied with a suffrage bill, they stormed the stage in Parliament.[149] This militant activism would eventually capture Alice Paul's attention.

By the 1890s, however, it seemed that the more women asserted their political agency and expanded gendered boundaries through political participation, the more resistance these women faced from social and institutional forces. Brewers and liquor retailers took a strong anti-suffrage position for fear that women might help enact prohibition. As political power shifted to party bosses in urban areas populated by immigrant workers, party machines opposed woman suffrage for fear of an uncontrollable and uneducated electorate. Southern women were particularly fearful of woman suffrage because of more traditional gendered ideals and for fear of black women attaining the vote. Western states appeared more eager to grant women the right to vote, but anti-Chinese prejudices kept many from wanting to extend voting rights.[150] Considering the sharp restrictions of African Americans' voting rights in the post-Reconstruction era, it seemed almost impossible for women to earn a constitutional amendment granting equal voting rights. Nonetheless, women worked and organized tirelessly, united with other movements inspired by class and economic oppression, raised awareness, and altered movement strategies.

WOMEN AND THE PROGRESSIVE ERA, 1890–1913

The following section traces the growing momentum of the woman suffrage movement as it interacted with shifting nationalist and civic ideals just prior to the NWP's inception in 1913. As in the post–Civil War era, heightened activism and severe resistance characterized the last thirty years of the first women's rights movement. The Progressive Era promise of enhanced citizenship rights and the rise of the rhetorical presidency encouraged minority groups to assert their political agency more than ever before, despite a revival of racist and nativist nationalism. Women actively sought political, economic, and social liberation as they joined reform societies, women's clubs, and local, state, and national woman suffrage organizations. Moreover, the growing alliances between the woman suffrage, labor, and settlement house movements empowered women to act in the political sphere.

Suffrage Regeneration

Between 1890 and the 1910s, citizenship and voting rights became more narrowly defined, while simultaneously a wave of social and political movements worked to expand these rights. As the excesses of capitalism, industrialization, political corruption, and racial supremacy took its toll on the American people, many groups rose up in protest. Some groups took the form of third parties—such as Progressives, Populists, and Socialists—and some took the form of organized agitators, such as the Knights of Labor, the American Federation of Labor, and the Women's Trade Union League (WTUL). These somewhat contradictory patterns of restricting and expanding citizenship rights created an optimal environment for woman suffrage activists to regenerate momentum.

Although voter turnout in the late nineteenth century was exceptional, corruption, southern "Redeemers," and the aftermath of Reconstruction shaped the political environment.[151] The institution of Jim Crow laws prevented African Americans from voting; literacy and education tests disenfranchised a new wave of immigrants from Asian and European countries; property and tax requirements limited many working-class and poor white Americans from voting; and strict assimilation laws applied to the voting rights of American Indians.[152] Although many whites opposed these restrictions, nationalist feelings of superiority prevailed. One way late-nineteenth-century presidents tried to allay fears of expanding citizenship laws was by rhetorically constructing the "good citizen," whose hard work was the ultimate performance of an American identity. Immigrants, for example, could be "Americanized" by participating in the hard, strenuous labor of building a nation.[153] Nonetheless, many resisted an expanded electorate.

Meanwhile, a general shift in the relationship between American politics and people took place. Michael McGerr argues that in the final decades of the nineteenth century, education and advertising replaced the extreme partisanship and party loyalty of the early nineteenth century. For example, candidates took train and automobile tours and advertised themselves and their platforms for voters to compare and ultimately "buy into."[154] Thus, the voting experience became less an act of party loyalty and community belonging and more an act of choice and independence. This shift can be attributed, in part, to Theodore Roosevelt's innovative use of the presidency to appeal directly to the American people through rhetoric.[155] Roosevelt's predecessor, William McKinley, encouraged this development, as he was one of the first presidents to speak across the country. Likewise, during the 1896 presidential election, William Jennings Bryan spoke to voters during a whistle-stop tour.[156] As presidential candidates shifted toward a more direct relationship with the electorate, the potential for voters to voice their concerns directly to the president increased.

In the last decade of the nineteenth century, the women's rights movement also experienced a shift in leadership and strategy. In 1890, the NWSA and the AWSA united into one organization, the NAWSA. Originally led by Anthony and Stanton, the organization was taken up by a younger generation of suffragists with new strategies in mind. Carrie Chapman Catt transformed the NAWSA into an efficient organization with headquarters in each state and with hands in local suffrage campaigns.[157] Focusing on state suffrage, the NAWSA voted to hold annual conventions outside of Washington, D.C., every other year to mobilize different parts of the country.[158] The western states, in particular, enjoyed local and state success during the 1890s.[159] Prevailing racist and classist attitudes, however, tempered these developments. NAWSA leaders appealed to wealthy white women by assuring them that the vote would help prevent the uneducated and ignorant from voting. Even Stanton, in her waning years, advocated for literacy tests.[160] Western suffragists, too, are also noted for making arguments grounded in scientific racism by promising to "civilize" American Indians through the vote.[161]

Despite the prevalent racism and classism in the woman suffrage movement, African American women continued to assert their political voices.[162] For example, in 1880, Mary Ann Shadd Cary organized the Colored Women's Progressive Franchise Association, and in 1887 Frances Watkins

Harper became the Superintendent of Work Among Colored People for the WCTU.[163] In the early 1890s, Ida B. Wells-Barnett waged multiple campaigns to fight mob violence and lynching.[164] African American women also thrived in women's clubs throughout the 1890s. In 1895, for example, fifty-two women founded the National Federation of Afro-American Women, which, in 1895, merged with the National League of Colored Women to form the National Association of Colored Women. Well-known African American woman suffragist Mary Church Terrell was elected its first president.[165] Other women, such as Fannie Barrier Williams and Anna Julia Cooper, sought to establish identification with white women, while also forcing white women to recognize black women's relative oppression.[166] Such arguments were necessary considering that African American women remained marginalized within the woman suffrage movement. Even by 1913, with the inception of the more equal-rightist National Woman's Party, African American women were subject to the movement's expedient racism.

Overall, women's participation in club activities flourished throughout the 1890s. Even the NAWSA, the dominant national suffrage organization, was outnumbered during this time with only thirteen thousand members in 1890, compared to the GFWC's twenty thousand members in 1892, and the WCTU's one hundred fifty thousand members.[167] These clubs promoted the idea that women were a purifying force in American society and extended the growing progressive faith in activism, bureaucracy, and efficiency.[168] Most significantly, club participation helped close the gap between the public and the private.

Suffrage Acceleration

In the early years of the twentieth century, support for woman suffrage grew immensely and yet stalled in many ways, creating the ideal context for the NWP's campaign. For example, in 1910, Pres. Howard Taft addressed the annual convention of the NAWSA. Moreover, in 1912, the Progressive Party endorsed woman suffrage, while the movement grew popular among Republicans. In 1914, a draft of a suffrage bill was brought to the Senate floor for the first time since 1893.[169] Woman suffrage thrived in the West with Washington State's enfranchisement of women in 1910, California in 1911, Arizona, Alaska, and Oregon in 1912, and Montana and Nevada in 1914.[170] Support for woman suffrage grew among southern women as a growing class of young, educated women—termed "New Women"—enacted the political independence they sought in the vote.[171] This younger, more charismatic generation of suffrage leaders used innovative strategies to bring visibility to the movement, including suffrage parades, open-air meetings, and soapbox speeches.[172] With increased visibility, however, came increased opposition. Democrats were particularly fearful of expanding the franchise, along with liquor interests who feared prohibition, and southerners who still feared racial equality.[173]

Much of the suffrage success during this time can be attributed to the movement's alliance with labor movement organizations.[174] Participation in the labor movement provided women the opportunity to assert political agency to alter their material realities.[175] Although shaped by ideological and demographic differences, the American Federation of Labor, the Knights of Labor, the Grange, the Farmers' Alliance, and the Populists encouraged women's membership.[176] Nonetheless, women tended to be marginalized in the leadership of these organizations, as the focus tended to stay on liberating the male worker.[177]

The NWP in particular benefited from the efforts of Harriot Stanton Blatch, daughter of Elizabeth Cady Stanton, to organize an enduring relationship between all classes of women. Blatch later played an integral role in the NWP's leadership and helped recruit many working-class and immigrant women. Her efforts began in the mid-1890s, when she and Anthony attempted to unite upper-class and working-class women in a political reform movement in New York. Upon her failure, Blatch realized that upper-class suffragists overlooked the needs of working-class women; thus, she began dedicating her work toward liberating working-class women with the vote.[178] She felt so strongly about the rights of these women that she engaged in a public debate with her mother, sharply opposing the implementation of literacy tests at the polls.[179]

Following her mother's death in 1902, Blatch joined the WTUL, aiming to work with—not for—working-class women.[180] Blatch believed that all women's work was valuable, whether in the home or in the factory. She appealed to upper- and middle-class women by arguing that they should use their educations, careers, and the vote for the greater good. To working-class women, the vote represented the promise of changing the material conditions of their everyday lives. To be sure, Blatch's own middle- to upper-class positioning did not go unchecked, as she argued that women worked for psychological reasons—an argument that did not seem to resonate well with working-class women, who worked primarily out of necessity.[181]

Meanwhile, the strengthening ties between woman suffrage and settlement house movement leaders also shaped the NWP's membership. Progressive emphases on expertise and detached observation sharpened the movement's focus on enacting social reform and demanding a voice in urban policy making.[182] After her experiences as a social worker, for example, Jane Addams aimed to provide sanitary living environments for lower-class women, children, and immigrants.[183] Similarly, Florence Kelley's work with Chicago's Hull House inspired her to help found the Children's Bureau later in 1912. Addams and Kelley saw the vote as a way to improve the living conditions of working-class women and thus they became vociferous suffrage supporters.[184] Like Blatch, Addams and Kelley later became members of the NWP's executive board.

In 1907, Blatch founded the Equality League of Self-Supporting Women, which adopted a militant philosophy toward enfranchising working white women. She united educated and professional women, who valued the work of wage-earning and industrial-working women. Working-class members became articulate in the arguments for enfranchising trade union women, and even testified before the New York state legislature in early 1907. Additionally, Blatch's ongoing alliance with the Pankhurst family in England, leaders of the militant Women's Social and Political Union (WSPU), encouraged the Equality League's participation in militant acts. For example, Blatch organized a large crowd—two-thirds of which were trade unionist men—to gather at Cooper Union to hear a WSPU member testify about her protests and imprisonment in England. Blatch also encouraged Equality League members to participate in the first open-air meeting held on behalf of woman suffrage and many subsequent open-air meetings and trolley campaigns throughout 1907 and 1908. Although WTUL members had been speaking on street corners for years, the Equality League's militancy exhibited an intensified faith in asserting political agency in public spaces reserved primarily for men. Furthermore, these militant acts provided the Equality League with increased publicity—an invaluable asset considering that working-class women could not afford to bring awareness to their issues.[185]

The growing internationalism of the labor and suffrage movements also brought militancy to the forefront of social activism. Between 1907 and 1915, the predominant socialist organization, the Second International, coordinated a socialist movement between many western, central, and eastern European nations, Australia, and the United States.[186] Soon, as DuBois argues, "militant suffragism around the world" took hold.[187] The influence of the WSPU's militancy spread throughout the network of international women's organizations.[188] The International Woman Suffrage Association's 1906 meeting in Copenhagen reported on the WSPU's success, helping spread news to Hungary and Russia. In 1909, Sylvia Pankhurst toured central Europe, raising awareness of working-class militant techniques, such as marches, open-air meetings, and civil disobedience. Moreover, militancy inspired women's rights movements in Ireland, China, and Argentina.[189]

By 1910, the strength of international networks and this heightened sense of militancy cultivated a mass US woman suffrage movement and ultimately offered Alice Paul and Lucy Burns the opportunity to establish their own organization. The coalition between the woman suffrage and labor movements was so strong that it was difficult to distinguish among trade unionist, socialist, and militant suffragists. Even the NAWSA reversed its position on literacy tests and began emphasizing the needs of working-class women.[190] Soon after, in 1912, Paul's work with the WSPU caught the eye of NAWSA's leaders, who employed Paul and Burns to establish the Washington, D.C., headquarters. Greatly influenced by their international experiences with militant activism, Paul and Burns were determined to ignite the national wing of the woman suffrage movement and inspire women to assert political agency by introducing contentious protest strategies aimed at earning fully enfranchised citizenship rights.

Throughout US nationalist history, women have asserted political agency despite restrictive ideological and institutional forces. Just as nationalist, citizenship, and gender ideologies worked to limit women's political participation in the national community, such ideologies provided them the resources to challenge and expand upon women's rights. Whether women adopted the equal-rightist arguments informed by Lockean liberalism or extolled women's natural virtue through republican motherhood, women forced themselves into the public and political spheres to advocate for education, moral reform, abolition, and, eventually, a woman's right to vote. Moreover, women asserted their political agency and constituted their citizenship identities by adopting the political practices of men as they formed organizations, held conventions, petitioned, lobbied, and even voted. By 1913, the growing strength of the woman suffrage movement and the empowering forces of the Progressive Era fueled a group of young suffragists to rise up and demand US women's fully enfranchised citizenship rights and to reenergize the US woman suffrage movement for the following seven years.

2

Mimesis and Political Ritual

The National Woman Suffrage Parade

By 1913, the woman suffrage movement had gained some political strength and social appeal. Many western states had enacted woman suffrage, working-class women joined the movement in droves, and the National American Woman Suffrage Association (NAWSA) had developed strong political ties. However, the movement's leaders were primarily focused on securing woman suffrage at the state level. Even the NAWSA had adopted a more decentralized policy as it loosened its control over state suffrage efforts. This focus on state suffrage was enhanced by the persistent notion that states controlled citizenship and voting laws. Thus, attempting to acquire women's full citizenship rights through a federal amendment meant transcending state lines and uniting the movement across regional, ideological, and racial differences.

The restricting and expanding forces of the Progressive Era shaped these differences. Progressivism helped inspire changes that were intended to place political power back in the hands of US citizens—changes such as primary elections, state referenda, and secret ballots.[1] However, progressive efforts to empower and rehabilitate the US citizenry typically privileged Anglo-Saxon identity and culture. Discourse from the presidential, judicial, and legislative branches constructed the ideal US citizen as white, "civilized," and male. Such discourse reflected exclusionary and protectionist attitudes toward African Americans, immigrants, American Indians, and women, ensuring that these groups remained subordinated and marginalized as US citizens. As Mary E. Stuckey claims, "The American polity was no more unified at the end of the Progressive Era than it had been in the movement's infancy."[2]

Accordingly, by 1913, the discourse of the US woman suffrage movement both reflected and challenged these differentiating progressive ideals. Because US women comprised a significant portion of the population, woman suffragists could potentially shape and benefit from empowering progressive measures. However, the movement still faced political and social opposition, and thus woman suffrage leaders often adopted more expedient and socially appealing strategies. These strategies were typically aimed at enhancing the citizenship rights of middle- and upper-class white women and tended to ignore the rights of African American, working-class, and immigrant women. Thus, the power dynamics of the woman suffrage movement reflected the power dynamics of progressivism.

The discourse of the woman suffrage movement in the early 1910s was also shaped by regional and ideological differences pertaining to states' rights. Voting rights and the power to define citizenship remained within the purview of states' rights. These rights were staunchly defended in southern states, which typically resented the federal reach of the Civil War amendments. Such regional complications explain, in part, why woman suffrage leaders remained preoccupied with winning suffrage at the state level as an incremental, moderate approach toward national suffrage. This state-based approach, however, facilitated the racist and nativist suffrage agenda in some southern and western states. Moreover, the success of this state-by-state approach depended on the efforts of state suffrage organizations to raise support among voters, a more diffuse strategy than raising support among legislators. These state-level constraints made it very difficult for the woman suffrage movement to gain broad, national appeal. Thus, by the end of 1912, the US woman suffrage movement lacked an organized national or militant force directed toward acquiring women's full citizenship rights through a federal amendment. Amidst a time of heightened social and national change, the NWP emerged as such a force.

The Congressional Committee (the NWP's first iteration) instituted a militant campaign for a federal amendment, working to force the issue of woman suffrage into the arena of national politics, while attempting to transcend state and ideological differences in the woman suffrage movement. In support of such ends, the Committee orchestrated its first order of business—a national woman suffrage parade. Held the day before President Woodrow Wilson's first inauguration ceremony, the Committee's parade functioned as an act of political mimesis in which Committee members mimicked the ritual of the president's inauguration parade to help promote a vision of woman suffrage as a united, national movement and to constitute the identities of women as *national* citizens. While inserting women into the reserved spaces of national politics, the parade cast woman suffrage as part of the democratic ideals of the United States, promoted federal suffrage over state suffrage, and exhibited progressive coalition building.

A host of contextual elements shaped the Committee's strident efforts for social change, including the prevalence of progressivism, the growing collaboration between the labor and woman suffrage movements, and Alice Paul's personal tenacity and militant vision. In what follows, a discussion of these forces will inform a rhetorical analysis of the Committee's mimetic parade and its overall contribution toward the Committee's militant efforts to nationalize the woman suffrage movement and constitute US women's national citizenship identities. An analysis of photographs, the parade's "Official Program," the "Pageant Outline," and newspaper accounts reveals that the Committee's national parade established woman suffrage as part of the nation's pursuit to fulfill US democratic ideals, portrayed state suffrage as instrumental but subordinate to federal suffrage, and promoted coalition building across marginalized groups.

THE RISE OF THE CONGRESSIONAL COMMITTEE

In 1913, Pres. Woodrow Wilson's "rhetorical presidency" sought to empower Americans with the ability to approve his policy agenda by championing shared democratic principles and promoting "a fundamental unity of all Americans."[3] Stuckey cautions, however, that Wilson's civic notions of nationalism were often compatible with racialized notions of nationalism, which constructed Anglo-Saxon people and culture as the embodiment of US democratic ideals. Consequently, Wilson's rhetorical efforts to unite and empower the American people also worked to exclude and disempower many groups attempting to participate in a US nationalist identity. American Indians and African Americans in particular were excluded from Wilson's vision of US nationalism, and immigrants confronted the reality of losing their ethnic identity in favor of inclusion and US citizenship.[4]

The presidency was not the only site of inclusion and exclusion during this time, considering that the courts and Congress also championed progressive ideals that tended to marginalize certain groups. The denial of citizenship and voting rights for African Americans, for example, became more institutionalized. Despite the "separate but equal" treatment promised through *Plessy v. Ferguson* (1898), unequal racial segregation flourished in southern and western states that codified segregation through Jim Crow laws.[5]

In effect, the Civil War amendments were rendered all but obsolete during the Progressive Era. Ian F. Haney López observes that during this time, a white-black dichotomy dominated discourse pertaining to naturalization and citizenship laws, which helped construct "whiteness" as the preferred racial make-up of the American citizenry.[6]

The desire to preserve whiteness shaped institutional discourse pertaining to immigration as well. Between 1900 and 1910, the United States experienced a highest rate of immigration in its history. Anti-immigrant sentiment flourished following "a marked increase of nativism" in the late nineteenth century and was enhanced by the Progressive Era's renewed senses of racial and national superiority.[7] This sentiment culminated in more stringent naturalization policies, resulting in what Rogers M. Smith considers second-, third- and fourth-class forms of US citizenship for women, African Americans, American Indians, and immigrants from Puerto Rico, Guam, China, and the Philippines.[8] Reinforced by America's growing sense of international superiority, progressive beliefs in inclusion stressed the "civilization" and the ultimate Americanization of these immigrants and other non-Anglo-Saxon groups.[9]

By 1913, the US government portended that it would expand citizenship rights in light of progressive efforts to empower and protect the powerless; however, these efforts placed severe limits on the extent to which certain groups could participate in the much-heralded nationalistic vision of democratic citizenship. Women were no exception.

Progressive Exclusions

In the early 1910s, the woman suffrage movement both confronted and internalized these institutional and cultural forms of oppression. Demonstrating the movement's headway, for example, Pres. Howard Taft addressed the national convention of the NAWSA in 1910. Although he was very careful not to endorse the movement, his presence offered it some political legitimacy. In 1910, Congress also received a petition of four hundred thousand women's signatures, and in 1912, the Progressive Party, which some contend was the strongest third party in history, endorsed the movement.[10] Nonetheless, the movement resisted embracing a fully fledged campaign for a federal amendment. The NAWSA's primary focus was on securing women's citizenship rights through an incremental, state-by-state campaign strategy. It was thought that once women had the right to vote at the state level, they could also vote at the national level. Even so, it had been over forty years since states began granting suffrage rights and by 1913, only one-third of American women possessed these citizenship rights.

The state-by-state strategy embraced by most suffragists in the early twentieth century was inflected by ideological, regional, and racial tensions. More specifically, ideological differences pertaining to federal rights and states' rights reflected regional differences between the North and the South during this time. The framers of the Constitution granted states the power to write voting and citizenship laws, which established a system that, according to Kirt H. Wilson, "effectively protected state officials from federal intervention."[11] Despite differing interpretations of this system, it was generally agreed that civil matters and the rights of citizens fell within the purview of state power.[12] This precedent was challenged and redefined in the 1870s and 1880s when the Civil War amendments empowered the federal government to define the parameters of US citizenship and voting rights.

The Fourteenth Amendment, in particular, introduced the notion of equality before the law and rights of *national* citizenship, particularly in the first section: "All persons born or naturalized in the United States, and subject to the jurisdiction thereof, are citizens of the United States and of the State wherein they reside."[13] However, following Reconstruction, the federal government slowly lost its ability to enforce the Civil War amendments in southern states, which fought to redeem their states' rights. The weakening of the Civil War amendments and the rise of Jim Crow laws heightened regional tensions between the North and South and ideological contestations between federal and states' rights. Moreover, the South's fear of empowering African Americans' citizenship rights exacerbated its resistance to constitutional actions pertaining to voting rights.[14]

These regional, ideological, and racial differences shaped the way southern women viewed women's citizenship rights. Compared to most northern women, for example, southern women typically were more resistant to a federal amendment. Jacqueline Glass Campbell argues that following the Civil War, southern women helped preserve their southern identity by constructing southern men as heroes. Southern women, correspondingly, were depicted as pillars of "sentimentality, patience, and endurance" and as "cultural guardians rather than the makers of nations and nationalisms."[15] Throughout Reconstruction and into the early twentieth century, southern women transformed their identities as victims of Union soldiers into potential rape victims of African American males, entrenching fears of African Americans and encouraging acts of discrimination and violence.[16] Amidst such racial tensions, many southern women feared that a federal mandate to enhance women's rights would simultaneously enhance African Americans' rights. Additionally, southern women often retained more conservative views of gendered behavior, resisting the image of themselves as political actors.[17] Acquiring woman suffrage through a constitutional amendment, such logic suggested, represented a direct threat to state power and white privilege.

Reflecting such sentiments, racism in the woman suffrage movement was particularly strong in the South. Even as support for woman suffrage in the South grew (by 1913, every southern state had an NAWSA organization), southern leaders more ardently pursued suffrage as a right for white women only.[18] Further, white suffrage leaders staunchly defended states' rights, fearing that a federal suffrage amendment could override the power of segregationist laws and lead to the enfranchisement of African Americans. In 1906, for example, Laura Clay of Kentucky and Kate Gordon of Louisiana led statewide suffrage campaigns promoting a "whites-only" version of the law.[19] Further, in 1913, Gordon organized the Southern States Woman Suffrage Conference in response to the NAWSA's establishment of a committee designed to pursue a federal amendment exclusively. Gordon, formerly an NAWSA leader, worked to preserve states' rights in order to maintain white supremacy in the woman suffrage movement.[20]

Regional tensions over federal and states' rights were not unique to the North and South. Although more eager to grant women the right to vote at the state level, the West had its own racially driven concerns about a federal woman suffrage amendment. More specifically, western states feared that such an amendment could potentially expand citizenship rights to Chinese, Japanese, and Mexican immigrants, and to American Indians.[21] Some western suffragists made racist and nativist arguments by promoting the idea that the vote would empower white women to "civilize" American Indians.[22] Nonetheless, the woman suffrage movement in western states thrived and had more success winning partial and state suffrage than the movement in the northeastern and the southern states. Scholars argue that western states and municipalities were more willing to grant women citizenship rights due to the egalitarian nature of the region's agricultural society and to the newer states' desire to attract inhabitants and establish a voting population.[23]

Racism and nativism in the woman suffrage movement, however, was not always a regional characteristic. Many woman suffrage leaders embraced philosophies reflective of the racist and exclusionary tendencies of most progressive efforts. For example, in 1895, long after the split between the abolition and suffrage movements in the 1860s, Susan B. Anthony asked Frederick Douglass not to attend an NAWSA convention in Atlanta.[24] In

1899, the NAWSA refused to advocate on behalf of Lottie Wilson Jackson against segregated seating on trains. Anthony insisted that woman suffrage for white women and for African American women were separate causes.[25] In 1900, Josephine St. Pierre Ruffin and Mary Church Terrell were ostracized at a General Federation of Women's Clubs meeting in Wisconsin. Furthermore, in 1903, at a convention of the NAWSA held in New Orleans, the national board adopted a policy allowing states to develop their own suffrage positions, which gave southern states the freedom to pursue racist suffrage efforts. Prominent suffrage leaders, including Anthony, Carrie Chapman Catt, Anna Howard Shaw, Kate Gordon, and Alice Stone Blackwell signed the statement. In fact, in 1911, Shaw was accused of barring an African American woman from the NAWSA's Louisville convention and was noted for placating white southern suffragists during her tenure as the NAWSA president between 1910 and 1915.[26]

Racist and nativist arguments regarding citizenship and voting rights also persisted in the anti-suffragist movement. The National Association Opposed to Woman Suffrage (NAOWS), founded in 1911, was particularly strong in the southern states because it relied on conservative arguments regarding a woman's proper place and fears of African American women. It was thought that black women were more aggressive than black men and would be more difficult to keep from voting polls. The efforts of the NAOWS, in addition to the strength of such gendered and racist beliefs, resulted in many failed attempts at state and local suffrage in the South.[27] Deep-seated beliefs in preserving social, cultural, and political modes of power relied on the persistent subordination not only of women, but also of nonwhite women. As such, opposition to woman suffrage on behalf of political machines, liquor interests, and even immigrants (who feared that woman suffrage would result in the loss of their jobs), resulted in multiple failed state suffrage referenda between 1912 and 1914. Throughout these years, more referenda failed than succeeded.[28]

Reform and "social control" efforts of the Progressive Era also reflected classist attitudes toward working-class and immigrant women. For example, the Children's Bureau, founded in 1912, was the first all-woman branch of the federal government, which offered professional women a place to push policies on improving infant health care and regulating child labor. However, enforcing these progressive efforts required extending the reach of the federal government into the lives and homes of working-class and immigrant women. According to Molly Ladd-Taylor, this perceived elitist push for "social control" was met with resistance from "an unreceptive working class."[29] Thus, as Eileen Boris argues, "social control can therefore be more accurately interpreted as intervention into families on the part of the state and professional experts, mediated by the gender, class, race, and ethnicity of both family members and interveners."[30]

Despite the racist, classist, and sexist tendencies of progressivism and the woman suffrage movement, minority and working-class women managed to assert their political agency and push forward for full citizenship rights. Nancy A. Hewitt documents the activist efforts on behalf of Tampa's black, Latina, and Anglo women in the first decade of the twentieth century. She argues that elite Anglos and Latinas participated in clubs, social welfare associations, revolutionary organizations, and mutual-aid societies, while working-class Latinas and black women "employed domestic resources and skills as instruments of class and racial struggle." These women managed to form their own mutual-aid societies and welfare institutions to resist class-based discrimination.[31]

Wage-earning black women were typically excluded from efforts of trade unions, and were often shamed within the black community for transgressing their domestic duties and for perpetuating the belief that black males couldn't independently provide for their families. Nonetheless, these women managed to establish workingwomen's associations, clubs, occupational training programs, and cooperative daycares. Eventually, the Associations for the Protection of Negro Women was formed in 1905, which became the National League for the Protection of Colored Women in 1909.[32] Black women in Atlanta—the most segregated city in Georgia at that time—organized the Neighborhood Union in 1908, for example. The union's relentless research and petitioning resulted in improved facilities, teachers' salaries, and classroom spaces for black schools.[33]

Thus, the woman suffrage movement incorporated the empowering and differentiating ideals of the Progressive Era, particularly as they pertained to geographical region, federal and states' rights, race, and class. In light of these differences, and despite the NAWSA's success as a reputable national organization, the woman suffrage movement remained committed to a state-by-state strategy. Additionally, the woman suffrage movement had yet to be considered a legitimate force in politics at the national level. In other words, the majority of leaders in the presidential, legislative, and judicial branches of the US government refused to address the grievances expressed by the national woman suffrage movement. The Senate Woman Suffrage Committee, for example, which had been in existence since 1877, had not formally met since 1878.[34] By 1913, no sitting president had publicly endorsed woman suffrage, despite President Taft's relationship with the NAWSA and former President Roosevelt's endorsement during his campaign as the Progressive Party candidate. As such, although woman suffrage had been part of the political vernacular for some fifty years, the woman suffrage movement lacked national cohesion.

Militancy in America

The inception of the NWP's militancy was greatly influenced by the suffrage movement's growing alliance with the labor and settlement house movements. Specifically, Harriot Stanton Blatch's formation of the Equality League of Self-Supporting Women in 1907 promoted unity between wage-earning and professional women, and enacted a militant approach toward social change. In the 1880s and 1890s, Blatch earned her militant training in England as an apprentice of Ursula Bright, a radical reformer with close ties to Harriot's activist mother. Having also served in an apprenticeship position under Bright, Emmeline Pankhurst founded a militant woman suffrage organization in England, the Women's Social and Political Union (WSPU). Working alongside her daughter, Christabel Pankhurst, Emmeline deployed militant tactics that "electrified the country and galvanized the whole of the suffrage movement" between 1903 and 1911.[35]

In its beginnings, the WSPU employed nonviolent protest strategies by harassing members of Parliament, leading marches, and infiltrating and disrupting private parliamentary meetings.[36] However, the proactively violent stages of the WSPU's militant campaign began after Christabel's arrest on October 13, 1905, prompting the WSPU to declare that Parliament had declared war on them.[37] Between 1909 and 1910, WSPU members engaged in a series of violent and terrorist acts, including launching rocks into crowds of government officials and innocent citizens, pouring acid on public property, cutting telegraph wires, slashing pictures in galleries, and setting fire to empty buildings. Often, while imprisoned, a number of "suffragettes" went on hunger strikes and demanded to be treated as political prisoners instead of common criminals. Their demands were met with force-feedings—an extremely painful process, which WSPU members often likened to the act of rape.[38] Ultimately, England's entrance into World War I brought an end to the WSPU's militant campaign efforts, shifting Emmeline and Christabel's efforts toward mobilizing support for the war.[39]

Having maintained close ties with the Pankhursts and the WSPU, Blatch infused her campaign for workingwomen's rights and US woman suffrage with similar militant tactics. Blatch organized women to attend open-air meetings (large public gatherings featuring multiple speakers), deliver soapbox speeches, and wear sandwich boards on street corners.[40] Most significantly, Blatch introduced the mass suffrage parade as a new tactic in the woman suffrage movement. In early 1908, Bettina Borman Wells, a visiting member of the WSPU, attempted an all-woman suffrage parade in New York. Only twenty-three women marched, however, and the parade received very little public attention.[41] Additionally, many state woman suffrage organizations held suffrage parades, beginning in California and Iowa in 1908.[42] However, on May 21, 1910, Blatch's Equality League took to the streets of New York in the largest organized woman suffrage parade yet, in which several hundred suffragists marched.[43] Blatch organized annual suffrage parades in New York between 1910 and 1913, aiming to push the public-private boundaries imposed upon women. Blatch's most successful parade took place on May 4, 1912, with over ten thousand men and women marching in New York, wearing costumes, holding banners, singing songs, giving speeches, and representing delegations of woman suffragists all over the country. Women of diverse races, ages, and classes marched together, with prominent suffragist Inez Milholland leading the parade on horseback.[44]

Blatch's innovative tactics held many implications for the woman suffrage movement in the early years of the century's second decade. To begin, the publicity of the parades helped force the suffrage question into the minds of many Americans. On one hand, the parade functioned as an exhibition of femininity and celebrated women's traditional gender roles as they provided a spectacle for others to admire or gaze upon. On the other hand, the parade represented the intrusion of women into the public sphere and women's demand for equal rights. Such insistent demands for equal rights were a reflection of Blatch's militant vision. According to Holly J. McCammon, parades "not only allowed [suffragists] to claim the streets as women's terrain, but the parades also permitted women to lay symbolic claim to the polity as they demanded the right to vote. Their use of the tactic helped the suffragists redefine themselves as men's equals in the public sphere."[45]

Blatch's militant strategies also helped foster solidarity with working-class women and the labor movement. Forging a shared identity between elite and working-class women was not without its problems, however; Blatch was aware that an elite woman delivering a soapbox speech garnered more press than a working-class woman doing the same.[46] Nonetheless, these militant efforts helped establish a sense of collectivity for suffragists as working- and upper-class women marched side-by-side in Blatch's parades. As Ellen Carol

DuBois argues, participating in these public protests "intensified women's commitment to the movement."[47] Blatch's efforts were also the result of pursuing a single-issue approach toward woman suffrage. In fact, she had been criticized for ignoring other women-related issues in order to focus solely on attaining women's voting rights.[48] Alice Paul would face similar criticism.

Enter Alice Paul

Alice Paul's entrance into the US woman suffrage scene was motivated by her participation in the WSPU's militant campaign throughout 1909 and 1910. In fact, the NWP attributed its militant campaign to Emmeline Pankhurst's militancy in England.[49] Throughout Paul's time with the WSPU, she was arrested five times, and while in prison she went on hunger strikes, refused clothing, and endured force-feedings.[50] Soon after, Paul returned to the United States ready to thrust the suffrage movement forward. At this point, Paul was twenty-seven years of age and had earned multiple advanced degrees, including a BA, MA, and PhD, in addition to attending the London School of Economics.[51] Prior to her work with the WSPU, Paul had participated in the settlement house movement in England, which instilled in her the notion that social reform and woman suffrage were inextricably linked movements. Thus, upon her return to the United States, Paul found good company among the settlement house and trade unionist leaders with inroads to the NAWSA's executive board.[52] In fact, Paul delivered a speech at the 1910 NAWSA convention discussing and defending the WSPU's militant campaign.[53]

Instigating a militant woman suffrage campaign in a US political context required Paul to adjust her sense of militancy. Cheryl R. Jorgensen-Earp argues that, despite the violent outcome of the WSPU's campaign in England, militancy is the result of an ongoing negotiation between the marginalized and the politically powerful, and thus "new protest strategies must be justified in terms that are socially intelligible."[54] In the context of England's suffrage movement, suffragettes felt they had exhausted traditional means of negotiation with Parliament, and thus justified their move to property destruction as a last resort. In the United States, suffragists had yet to reach this point of exhaustion.[55] In part, the movement's incremental successes at the state level may have precluded state activists from realizing a collective sense of national defeat. Moreover, in England, where political power is bound up in the parliamentary process, suffragettes had agitated members of Parliament, cabinet ministers, and the prime minister prior to escalating to acts of violence.[56] At this point, US suffragists had yet to agitate those with political power in a collective, organized fashion, let alone militantly protest against figures of national political authority.

Thus, Paul's militant vision did not take a violent form. Nevertheless, it did adopt many key principles from the WSPU's campaign. First, militancy was viewed as a form of action. As the WSPU's slogan commands, "Deeds Not Words"—Paul did not mince words seeking approval from NAWSA leaders or political figures. Rather, Paul made her suffrage demands through a series of highly publicized acts.[57] Next, Paul knew that militant strategies pushed the boundaries of socially acceptable behavior, and thus generated publicity. As Andrew Rosen simply declared, "Militancy *was* news."[58] At best, publicity attracted sympathizers, and, at worst, such publicity generated opposition yet potentially forced political leaders to address the movement. Finally, Paul embraced the WSPU's theory of agitation, which entailed holding those with political power responsible for social change. Thus, in an effort to secure a federal suffrage amendment, Paul directed her militant efforts toward the president and members of Congress. Such efforts were focused on nationalizing the woman suffrage movement and forcing the issue into the fray of national-level politics.

Guided by these militant principles, Paul spent the summer of 1911 organizing open-air meetings for the Pennsylvania Suffrage Association in Philadelphia.[59] Then, in 1912, Paul met several times with fellow WSPU activist Lucy Burns to discuss ways to more forcefully implement their militant philosophy of agitation. Inspired by the state-level enfranchisement of two million American women, Paul and Burns thought that mobilizing these women to vote against non-suffrage-supporting legislators could potentially force these political leaders to take woman suffrage seriously. Such agitation could help bring woman suffrage to the forefront of electoral politics and constitute these women as citizens with political power.

Paul and Burns decided that the NAWSA would allow them the organizational legitimacy to put this plan into practice. Fortuitously, the 1912 NAWSA national convention was to be held in Philadelphia, which prompted Paul to pressure Anna Howard Shaw and Harriot Stanton Blatch—a couple of her reform-minded acquaintances—to move forward her proposal. Resistant to its militant approach, NAWSA leaders rejected the plan. Paul and Burns then turned to the NAWSA vice president, Jane Addams, who managed to persuade the NAWSA to accept their proposal. The final proposal, however, was accepted, on the condition that Paul and Burns curtail their anti-Congress strategy and instead orchestrate a parade to be held in Washington, D.C., on the day before President Wilson's first inaugural ceremony. Given Blatch's recent success with suffrage parades, this strategy seemed more palatable to the NAWSA leaders. As such, the NAWSA's Congressional Committee was established, with Paul as president, Burns as vice chair, and socialist-feminist radical Crystal Eastman as a committee member at large.[60]

Paul began her work immediately. Without financial support from the NAWSA, Paul raised some funds in Philadelphia before whisking off to Washington, D.C., the ideal location for pressing woman suffrage into the national political agenda and for planning a suffrage parade. Upon her arrival in December 1912, she found no office space, no active NAWSA members interested in a federal amendment, and an outdated list of potential volunteers. In fact, the NAWSA member previously in charge of pursuing a federal amendment had been unable to spend all of her ten-dollar annual budget.[61] After securing space for the Congressional Committee's official headquarters, Paul and other members called upon friends, former classmates, and a larger network of activists for support.[62] On January 2, 1913, the Committee held its first formal meeting, where Paul laid out plans for the parade to be held in just two months time.[63]

The Committee's militant approach to pursuing a federal amendment went hand in hand with Paul's "swift, decisive leadership."[64] Paul once conceded to Blatch, "I am not a speaker at all," suggesting that Paul knew her strengths lay in organizing and delegating.[65] Her talent for inspiring others attracted many recruits, including elite and working-class white women of the settlement house and labor movements. Among these women were Dora Kelley Lewis, a coworker of Paul's from Philadelphia, Mary Ritter Beard, a New York writer and reformer, and Lavinia Dock of the Henry Street Settlement house.[66] Notable wage-earning women who joined the Committee included Margaret Hinchey of the Women's Trade Union League, Rose Winslow of the National Consumers' League, and Josephine Casey, a Chicago trade unionist.[67] Despite lacking racial diversity, the organization's membership was considered youthful, temperamental, and uncompromising. Even though some members were not technically young (such as Harriot Stanton Blatch, who at the time was older than the NAWSA's Carrie Chapman Catt), the Committee's membership promised a fresh and defiant approach to woman suffrage.[68] However, like Blatch's leadership, Paul's single-issue approach was at times considered autocratic and top-down. Furthermore, Paul's militancy faced criticism for facilitating acts of expedient racism, which discouraged the participation of African American suffragists.[69]

In all, these swift developments in early 1913 brought invigorating change to the woman suffrage movement. Strategically, Paul and her fellow suffragists intended to subordinate the state-by-state campaign strategy and focus directly on acquiring a federal amendment to the Constitution. Additionally, their faith in militant tactics stood in sharp relief against the moderate methods of the NAWSA and other woman suffrage organizations. Ideologically, their belief in equal rights posed a threat to many southern suffragists who stuck to a states' rights position and invoked racist fears of expanding citizenship rights to minority groups. Nonetheless, the newly formed Congressional Committee thrust itself into the contested arena of national politics, where it had to negotiate the regional, racial, and ideological differences characteristic of US nationalism and Progressive Era beliefs.

THE INAUGURAL PARADE RITUAL

The Committee's national suffrage parade mimicked the ritual of the inaugural parade in a militant effort to agitate President Wilson, insert women into the nationalized spaces of Washington, D.C., and nationalize the suffrage movement. More specifically, the Committee's intrusion into the streets of Washington, D.C., challenged the politicized and gendered spaces of the nation's capital, targeted Wilson as the key change agent for woman suffrage, and illustrated woman suffrage as the pursuit of freedom, justice, liberty, and equality. By aligning the pursuit of woman suffrage with nationalistic ideals that transcended state differences and helped unite disenfranchised groups across race and class lines, the Committee further justified its demands for a suffrage amendment at the federal level and allowed US women to participate in a vision of US democratic citizenship.

The Committee's national parade functioned as a mimetic enactment of part of the president's ritual transition into the presidency—the inauguration. Karlyn Kohrs Campbell and Kathleen Hall Jamieson's discussion of the generic elements of inaugural addresses speaks to the overall symbolic meanings of the ritual: "[Inaugurals] are an essential element in a ritual of transition in which the covenant between the citizenry and their leaders is renewed," in which "a newly elected president is invested with the office of the presidency."[70] With the rise of the rhetorical presidency and the democratizing wave of Progressive Era politics, Wilson's presidential inauguration ritual acquired particular significance in reinforcing this covenant. Since the election of George Washington, the inauguration ritual called upon newly elected presidents to take oath of office and deliver an inaugural address after traveling through the streets in a formal procession, now considered the inauguration parade.[71] The parade typically represents the longest part of the inauguration ritual, providing crowds the greatest opportunity to come face to face with their newly elected leader on a street level before the president-elect rises above the crowds to deliver an address. Thus, inauguration parades shape the inauguration ritual as an occasion in which the US citizenry and the president share an intimate and symbolic space in which the president's covenant with "the people" is renewed.

Targeting the inauguration parade as an object of political mimesis was particularly strategic toward negotiating the political terrain the early twentieth century. That the Committee mimicked only part of the inauguration ritual—the parade—can be explained by Gunter Gebauer and Christoph Wulf's theory of mimesis: that "mimesis tends toward condensed symbols, for example, toward rituals and images."[72] This rhetorical act of political mimesis can also be explained by the generic aspects of parades that allowed the Committee to simultaneously confront and appeal to Wilson's political authority. Dominic Bryan observes that parades "are public events, frequently involving large numbers of people, frequently involving people from a wide range of social backgrounds," thus they provided a unique vehicle for the Committee to demonstrate the mass, national collectivity of the suffrage movement.[73] Moreover, parades force the negotiation of physical spaces; as such the Committee's parade announced that US women were entitled to a stake in the national spaces of the US capital and were empowered with the authority to engage the US public as political leaders. In the sense that the Committee's parade worked to both appeal to and contest President Wilson's authority, the dual functions of political mimesis are exposed: the parade drew upon the democratizing ritual of leaders and citizens sharing nationalistic spaces as it also served as a "confrontation between the powerful and the powerless."[74] In this sense, the Committee's parade invoked the rhetoric of inauguration parades in order to target President Wilson as an opponent to woman suffrage.

Understanding the ways in which the Committee mimicked the inauguration parade in order to fashion a militant act of protest is greatly enhanced by looking at Mikhail Bakhtin's discussion of the medieval carnival. In Bakhtin's analysis of the carnival ritual, he argues that it created a life "sharply distinct" and "completely different" from the social castes and hierarchies that ordered everyday life.[75] Simply put, Bakhtin said, "While carnival lasts, there is no other life outside it."[76] To the extent that US women did not fully participate in the political world led by their white, male counterparts, the national parade worked to offer a revisualization of women's participation in the nation-state—an alternate, "distinct," or "different" world in which women asserted their political subjectivity. Bakhtin argues that the carnival's marked distinction from "serious official, ecclesiastical, feudal, and political cult forms and ceremonials"[77] held great liberatory potential:

> One might say that carnival celebrated temporary liberation from the prevailing truth and from the established order; it marked the suspension of all hierarchical rank, privileges, norms, and prohibitions. Carnival was the true feast of time, the feast of becoming, change, and renewal. It was hostile to all that was immortalized and completed.
>
> The suspension of all hierarchical precedence during carnival time was of particular significance. Rank was especially evident during official feasts; everyone was expected to appear in the full regalia of his calling, rank, and merits and to take the place correspondingly to his position. It was a consecration of inequality. On the contrary, all were considered equal during carnival.[78]

That the Committee's national parade attempted to contest President Wilson's political power points to the Committee's rhetorical act of political mimesis as an attempt to cast off the "prevailing truth[s]" and the "hierarchical precedence" buttressed by gender and political norms of the early twentieth century. Moreover, the spatial challenge posed by masses of women marching down the political spaces of Washington, D.C., resonated well with Bakhtin's theory of carnival as an event that offered an experience of "change," "renewal," and "equal[ity]."

Yet, the Committee's goal of earning women full participation in national-level politics required that the parade offer a vision of women's political subjectivity that reflected some of the "prevailing truths" of the day. Bakhtin notes that the parodic performances of the medieval carnival took form because they acknowledged an established order of sorts;[79] in light of the Committee's efforts to effect social change, it would have to acknowledge and appeal to a similarly established political order. As such, the politically mimetic contours of the national parade exposed a tension between old and new, death and life, and the complete and incomplete. The following analysis points to the Committee's rhetorical efforts to shape woman suffrage as a part of the nation's existing democratic truths. And yet, the rebirth, renewal, and, to an extent, the novelty of women's political subjectivity is exhibited as the participants forced a vision of collectivity and change to the one of the nation's founding documents. Moreover, the Committee's challenge to the existing hierarchy and social order is further exposed in the brutal, physical backlash endured by the marchers.

NATIONAL SPACES AND DEMOCRATIC IDEALS

Through the parade held the day before Wilson's first inauguration, the Committee laid claim to nationalized spaces and democratic values. To begin, the location of the Committee's national parade symbolized the intrusion of women into national politics. Catherine Allgor argues that, following the War of 1812, Washington, D.C., became "the definitive center of power for the United States, an important player in international politics, and a focus for American nationalism."[80] As the center of national politics, Washington's public spaces were highly politicized, holding significant implications for the roles that women played in these spaces. Allgor documents how, in the early republic, Dolley Madison helped fashion Washington into "a third sphere between public and private," where it was common to see white, upper-class women intermingle freely with politicians in public and political spaces.[81] Eventually, with the rise of the Jacksonian era's emphasis on expanding democratic rights to "the common man," public spaces in Washington became more clearly reserved for men to conduct political affairs. As such, women's political activities were confined to the upbringing of virtuous citizens within the domestic sphere. Thus, in Washington, when a woman transgressed these political boundaries, she often was considered immoral and impure.[82] By the early twentieth century, however, the boundaries between the public and the private spheres were becoming "slightly less discrete."[83] Nonetheless, a mass woman suffrage parade aimed at agitating the president challenged the masculine preserve of the nation's most preeminent political spaces.

The Committee's mimetic parade, thus, literally and symbolically forced woman suffrage into the sacred spaces of national politics. Prior to the national suffrage parade, women had testified before Congress, presented petitions in Congress, and even held national conventions in Washington, D.C. However, the Committee's national parade was the first time that masses of women descended upon the streets of Washington, D.C., creating a visualization of a collective, national movement. For days prior to the parade, newspapers reported on the arrival of five thousand women by train, car, and even on foot as an "invasion" of suffragists ready to "take the city."[84]

Moreover, the parade was comprised of more than twenty floats proceeding in at least six sections, in addition to wagons, horseback riders, and a tableau performance.[85] The perception that large groups of women had intruded upon the politicized spaces of Washington, D.C., suggested that the Committee's mimetic parade held a *national* audience, which helped legitimize the Committee's efforts to nationalize the suffrage movement.

The Committee further mimicked the ritual of the inaugural parade by casting its militant quest for equal suffrage as a fulfillment of US democratic ideals. Mimicking one of the key epideictic functions of the presidential inaugural, the Committee "rehearse[d] communal values drawn from the past."[86] Drawing upon shared values held by the *national* community, particularly as they take root in the nation's narrative of democracy, helped the Committee to further nationalize the question of woman suffrage. The Committee invoked key democratic values through its parade. For example, one section of the Committee's national parade illustrated the history of the woman suffrage movement through four floats, each representing a stage of the movement between 1840 and 1913. The floats' narration of the woman suffrage movement was framed as a larger story of triumph by its leading two banners: "The 75 Years Struggle for Freedom" and "Justice Conquering Prejudice."[87] Both banners directed their audience to an endpoint—"freedom" or "justice"—to a "struggle" against "prejudice." The parade's "Official Program" reinforced this sense of triumph through the captions that narrated for the audience the struggle for women's rights. First, the women of the 1840 float were depicted as facing "a black wall of prejudice," which, in the 1870 float, had become "less defiant." The caption accompanying the 1890 float said that "prejudice [was] standing aside for progress," which, according to the caption for the 1913 float, had culminated in an abundance of "advocates of the cause."[88] In casting the woman suffrage movement as an ultimately triumphant battle against prejudice, the Committee elevated the movement as part of the nation's overall commitment to freedom and justice. The Committee linked its cause to the nation's revolutionary ideals of breaking free from tyranny and pursuing individual liberties. Ultimately, rehearsing these democratic values further strengthened the Committee's move to mimic the inauguration ceremony as a national celebration of democracy and to nationalize the suffrage movement as part of the larger pursuit of freedom and justice.

The Committee's mimetic enactment of political ritual took another form through a tableau staged on the steps of the Treasury Building. The tableau featured the character Columbia, who summoned the characters of Justice,

FIGURE 2.1. Congressional Committee members performing a tableau on the steps of the US Treasury during the national suffrage parade held March 3, 1913. Reproduced courtesy National Photo Company Collection, Library Congress, LC-DIG-npcc-19098.

Charity, Liberty, Hope, and Peace to fight the crusade of women's rights (see fig. 2.1).[89] The narrative structure of the tableau invoked the myths central to the nation's genesis. In the late eighteenth century, as the new nation struggled to establish a shared sense of nationalism, Christopher Columbus became a celebrated figure of the nation's history. A derivative of Columbus's name, "Columbia," soon came to symbolize British America as a reflection of the colonies' growing separation from Great Britain.[90] Phillis Wheatley personified Columbia through her 1775 poem, "To His Excellency General Washington."[91] Thomas Steele argues that Wheatley's Columbia represented the combination of two mythical characters: the more feminine Phoebus Apollo, "the god of poetry and poets" and the more masculine Pallas Athene, "the goddess of strategy and generals."[92] The tableau reinforced these gendered contours as women actors, representing the feminization of nationalistic values, performed as Columbia, Justice, Charity, Liberty, Hope, and Peace. However, the tableau characters united to fight the "crusade" for women's rights, the narrative suggested, with Columbia holding a spear and Justice carrying a sword, reflecting the nation's warlike tendencies to defend nationalistic principles. These gendered depictions resonated well with the Committee's militant quest for woman suffrage, as the Committee took a more masculine and fearless approach toward the fulfillment of feminized virtues, such as liberty and justice. In the tableau's conclusion, all of the women actors stood together in a triumphant pose, representing the collectivity and strength of the woman suffrage movement, while aligning the movement with the nation's mythic plight to fulfill US democratic ideals.

The Committee's mimetic parade also cast its pursuit of woman suffrage as the enactment of equality as based in conceptions of natural rights. The notion of natural rights is rooted in eighteenth-century political thought with the rise of Lockean liberalism, embodied in the iconic line of the Declaration of Independence: "We hold these truths to be self-evident: that all men are created equal."[93] Although most men resisted extending these principles of natural rights to women, women's rights activists historically drew upon these ideals to demand equal rights.[94] A more natural-rights-focused philosophy toward woman suffrage, of course, was considered more radical—and therefore, less popular—than a more conservative philosophy, which embraced the socially acceptable notion that men and women were inherently different. Thus, by casting its pursuit of woman suffrage as part of the nation's commitment to equality, the Committee militantly called upon a radical strand of political thought and risked losing broad social appeal.

The Committee exhibited its equal-rightist ideology by illustrating gender equality as part of the everyday experiences known to Americans. In particular, the parade's third and fourth sections demonstrated how men and women equally contributed to the nation's economic, religious, social, and militaristic stability. Consider, for example, the third section's leading banner: "Man and Woman Make the State, Man Alone Rules the State."[95] While the banner ultimately pointed to gender inequities, the Committee's logic also was premised on the notion that women already made an equal contribution to the well-being of the state. Further, the banner suggested the potential correction of this inequality by earning women an active position in "the State."

In the many floats following this banner, the Committee further visualized the ways in which women already contributed to the nation. For example, the float entitled "In the Field" featured men and women farmers who demonstrated women's equal participation in the agrarian and economic livelihood of the nation. Scholars have argued that western territories and states were more eager to grant women equal suffrage based on the perception that agrarian communities fostered more egalitarian gender roles.[96] Given the recent successes of the woman suffrage movement in western states, the Committee seemingly used the region's more egalitarian

FIGURE 2.2. Delegation of "American nurses" marching in the national suffrage parade, March 3, 1913. Reproduced courtesy Bain Collection, Library of Congress, LC-USZ62–35138.

politics as a representative example of the positive benefits of woman suffrage. Moreover, as the Progressive Era came off the heels of the Populist movement, this float invoked the glorification of the farmer as the backbone of America's economic livelihood and invoked the principles of community, hard labor, and virtue.

The Committee extended this vision of economic equality by stressing women's successful pursuits in multiple professions, through floats and delegations of women representing college students, lawyers, doctors, pharmacists, factory workers, civil servants, businesswomen, teachers, social workers, librarians, writers, artists, actresses, nurses, and musicians (see, for example, fig. 2.2).[97] Access to equal education was the first movement toward women's rights in the United States, and by the second decade of the twentieth century more women regularly attended college and aspired to achieve financial independence as wage earners.[98] Such progress was reflected through the Committee's float "In Education," which featured a man and a woman each wearing a "College cap and gown."[99] Over one thousand women marched as college students, helping to normalize women in college and in careers traditionally reserved for men. In the process, these women embodied the actuality of equality and demonstrated a collective demand for equal citizenship rights.[100]

The Committee also stressed women's equal contributions to the nation's social and religious stability through "The Homemakers," a float that depicted a family of three. According to the "Pageant Outline," the man was to be dressed in "Quaker gray"—a reference to a religion commonly known at the time to practice gender equality in the church, home, and politics.[101] Many leading abolitionists and woman's right activists were Quakers, including Alice Paul. Such religious commitments may well have influenced the inclusion of a float featuring "Women of the Bible Lands."[102] The float promoted women's religious equality by representing women from the Old Testament, including Deborah, Miriam, and Huldah, as well as women from the New Testament.[103] Moreover, the program noted that these women were also examples of political equality: "Women in Bible lands who hold property in real estate vote in local affairs."[104] This float provided a visualization of women's religious and political authority, and offered further support for women's political equality in the United States.

The "Homemakers" float also made an argument for social and familial equality through a banner: "Women Have Free Fathers. Let Men Have Free Mothers."[105] Here the banner reversed the premise that women were deprived of full citizenship rights and asserted conversely, that men lacked full citizenship rights because of their mothers' disenfranchisement. Although the banner ultimately made an argument for equal citizenship rights, such logic relied on the construction of women primarily as mothers and of men primarily as citizens. Simultaneously, the premise of the argument—that women were free because they had free fathers—reified the longstanding policies of coverture, wherein a woman's legal identity was absorbed into her father's or her husband's legal identity. Thus, the banner accentuated the inequities embedded in a traditional family structure to make a more socially palatable argument for equal rights.

The Committee also argued for women's political equality by demonstrating women's national allegiance through war service. Citizenship rights were often granted to marginalized groups based on their service in war. Ratification of the Fifteenth Amendment, for example, was motivated, in part, by the participation of African American males in the Union army. Thus, the float featured both soldiers and nurses, which was then followed by a mass of marching nurses carrying a sign bearing Florence Nightingale's name.[106]

Nightingale, who had died just three years earlier, transformed nursing into a noble career and a higher calling. Further, Nightingale's leadership in the Crimean War forged a link between nursing, war, and national health.[107] By making visible the equal contribution women made in war service, the Committee intimated that women deserved equal citizenship rights.

The Committee's militant parade worked to nationalize the woman suffrage movement by mimicking the political ritual of the presidential inauguration and by violating Washington's gendered spaces and casting woman suffrage as part of the fulfillment of US democratic principles, including freedom, justice, liberty, and equality. As a reflection of the Committee's militancy, the Committee resisted making more socially appealing arguments and challenged the commonly held assumption that women belonged outside the realm of politics, both literally and symbolically. Moreover, the Committee and protesters asserted their political agency by descending upon the streets of Washington, D.C., and claiming the spaces of national politics. As a rhetorical act of political mimesis, the parade pointed to President Wilson as the necessary change agent for woman suffrage, which simultaneously reified his position of power in more traditional ways yet also reflected the Committee's militant efforts to agitate those in political power. In this sense, the Committee encroached upon the symbolic territory of the rhetorical presidency, laying claim to the covenant instantiated through the inauguration ritual. These militant efforts, nevertheless, were couched in socially appealing terms, considering, for example, the feminine appearance of the tableau's actors and the Committee's normalization of equality as a part of everyday American life. Ultimately, by mimicking a ritual of national politics, Committee members and US women enacted their participation in the fulfillment of democratic ideals and worked to constitute their identities as US national citizens.

NATIONAL SUFFRAGE OVER STATE SUFFRAGE

Mimicking a political ritual that extolled the fulfillment of democratic principles helped elevate suffrage as an integral part of the nation's identity. One of the key functions of a presidential inauguration is to "unif[y] the audience by reconstituting its members as 'the people.'"[108] The Committee's national parade similarly functioned to reconstitute its audience and participants as members of a national community—the American "people."[109] Specifically, the Committee worked to shape women's enfranchisement as the means to participate in national political culture, beyond the realm of state-level citizenship. Historically, states retained the power to define citizenship rights. However, with the ratification of the Fourteenth Amendment in 1866, the federal government assumed the right to guarantee and protect national citizenship rights.[110] By 1913, the egalitarian thrust of the Fourteenth Amendment had waned significantly, explaining the suffrage movement's preoccupation with state-level enfranchisement. The Committee's national suffrage parade symbolized the organization's focus on citizenship politics at the federal level. More significantly, the national parade allowed women to embrace the national-level citizenship rights held by their male counterparts, and thus constitute themselves as members of a national community.

The Committee's national parade allowed over five thousand women to collectively demand women's citizenship rights at the federal level. One of the parade's most enduring images was of the famous "Demand" sign, which was carried by a wagon at the front of the parade. It read, "We Demand an Amendment to the Constitution of the United States Enfranchising the Women of this Country" (see fig. 2.3).[111] The Committee's demand for a constitutional change reified the federal government's power to protect national citizenship rights. More significantly, however, the "Demand" board constituted the marchers' collective identity as suffragists in pursuit of national citizenship rights.

Although suffragists came from forty-eight states and even marched in sections organized by state, they did so as part of the Committee's militant demand for a national right. For example, the order of the parade's sections privileged efforts for nationwide suffrage. The first section was dedicated to marching delegations of women from sixteen nations where women possessed full national suffrage, partial suffrage, or were close to acquiring national suffrage.[112] This first section, then, introduced the notion of woman suffrage as a national right. The second section of the parade shifted the focus to woman suffrage in the United States by offering a narrative of the US women's rights movement. The parade did not feature state suffragists until the sixth section of the parade, reflecting the Committee's militant commitment to national suffrage. Privileging national citizenship rights, particularly at a time when states staunchly defended their powers to define citizenship and voting rights, boldly pronounced the Committee's militant insistence on forcing woman suffrage into the arena of national politics.

Even within the sixth section dedicated to state suffrage, state-level suffrage efforts were symbolically subsumed as an integral part of the Committee's federal-level strategies. For example, a float that depicted the first women's rights convention held in Seneca Falls, New York, in 1848, led this

FIGURE 2.3. Mrs. Richard Burleson and Inez Milholland ride horseback as "grand marshall" and herald of the March 1913 national suffrage parade. They ride alongside the famous "Demand" float. Reproduced courtesy Library of Congress, LC-USZ62–22459.

section.[113] Scholars point to this event as the genesis of the women's rights movement and the introduction of some of the movement's greatest leaders, including Elizabeth Cady Stanton and Lucretia Mott. Representing the convention also invoked its Declaration of Sentiments, which intentionally modeled the Declaration of Independence.[114] By reaffirming the tradition of individual and equal rights in American political thought that helped provoke a revolutionary war, the Committee framed this section's focus on state suffrage as part of the larger, national project to achieve equal political rights.

The Committee further subsumed state-level suffrage as a part of national suffrage in the next float, which featured a map of the United States labeled "9 States of Light among 39 of Darkness."[115] Non-suffrage-granting states were blackened, while states considering woman suffrage were shaded gray, and states granting full suffrage rights were left as white space.[116] Using the binary metaphors of light-dark and white-black (despite the use of gray, which appears almost as dark as the blackened states in parade photographs), the Committee presented the United States as a nation divided and fractured over woman suffrage. Despite this fractured image, the states were depicted as parts of a *whole* nation. Thus, this float helped frame the representation of state delegations as a larger project to unite the nation in pursuit of women's national citizenship rights. As such, the nine delegations of women representing "The Equal Suffrage States," which followed this float, can be read less as representations of individual state campaigns, and more so as groups of women dedicated to earning equal suffrage rights for all states.

Importantly, however, these state delegations were followed by a banner which read: "'No Country Can Exist Half Slave and Half Free,' Abraham Lincoln."[117] This quotation, although inaccurate, invoked the president's ethos for uniting the nation following the debilitating Civil War, and more significantly, aligned a federal suffrage amendment with a vision of national unity.[118] Following the previous float, which portrayed a nation split over suffrage, this quotation suggested that, like slavery, women's disenfranchisement had divided the nation. This analogy likened women to slaves and women's oppression to slavery. In this metaphorical context, the map's use of white-black imagery not only indicated the demarcation of suffrage-granting and non-suffrage-granting states, but of free states and slave states as well. The Committee extended this light-dark and free-slave analogy, as the car following the banner carried women who represented suffrage-granting states and who wore *light* green, while the women who marched around the car represented suffrage-denying states and wore *dark* green. Implicit to this dramatization is a hierarchy of political power, wherein those with voting rights are given a seat of privilege "above" those without voting rights. As a reflection of their marginalized position in society, those representing disenfranchised women marched below and beyond the privileged spaces reserved for voting citizens. Here political power separated these two groups of women, not state differences, which reinforced the Committee's militant attempt to transcend state lines and constitute a larger collectivity of suffragists at the national level.

Moreover, the float's reference to Lincoln mimicked the ritual of the presidential inauguration and solidified the Committee's visualization of a national suffrage movement. Most presidential inauguration speeches invoke the words and authority of previous presidents "to affirm that as we overcame difficulties in the past, so will we now; the venerated past assures us that the nation has a future."[119] Thus, by invoking the words of a president who was remembered for uniting a divided nation, the Committee positioned itself as the leaders who would similarly unite a country at odds over woman suffrage.[120] Acquiring a federal amendment to the US Constitution for woman suffrage would, in part, extend Lincoln's vision of a liberated and united nation. Furthermore, a constitutional amendment for women's rights would mirror the Fifteenth Amendment to the Constitution, which empowered the federal government to ensure voting rights for African American males. With this focus on national unity, the subsequent division of marchers, featuring delegations of women from the eighteen "States Working for Equal Suffrage," symbolized the promise to fulfill this national vision.[121]

The Committee's focus on national suffrage thus reappraised the significance of state-level suffrage campaigns as instrumental to the larger project of acquiring women's national citizenship rights. As such, the Committee remained committed to state campaigns. For example, the Committee later agreed to help Harriot Stanton Blatch organize the "National Division" of the New York Woman Suffrage Parade. Blatch suggested they could aptly assemble a national section by advertising the New York parade to the suffragists gathered "from all over the country" for the Washington parade.[122] Additionally, Blatch's request suggested that in a very short period of time, the Committee had established itself as a force in the national suffrage movement. In fact, in early April, Blatch asked Paul if she would "use [her] kindly offices in persuading" Sen. Robert LaFollette (R-WI) to attend a meeting after the New York parade, further reifying the Committee's almost immediate prominence in political circles.[123] Moreover, the incorporation of a "National Division" into the New York Woman Suffrage Parade suggested that the planning of the Washington parade intensified the formation of a national identity for woman suffragists.

Thus, the Committee's mimetic parade shaped the pursuit of state-level suffrage as integral but subordinate to its militant pursuit of a federal amendment for woman suffrage. As a mimetic enactment of the inauguration of a national leader, the parade further shaped woman suffrage as an issue of national significance, but with state-level implications. In so doing, the Committee integrated its efforts with those of the greater suffrage movement and avoided isolating itself as radical organization. This approach also allowed the Committee to gather masses of women to march as representatives of their states in its national parade. This collectivity supported the Committee's militant goals of forming a national movement for woman suffrage, forcing woman suffrage into the fray of national politics, and, more importantly, constituting US women as national citizens beyond the parameters of their home states.

PROGRESSIVE COALITION BUILDING

The Committee's parade further established woman suffrage as a force in US national politics through its coalition-building efforts. State and federal measures often treated marginalized groups separately when it came to matters of citizenship rights, codifying laws specific to each group. Thus, as different laws pertained to each group, marginalized groups were often precluded from forming critical mass for a particular policy change. However, the promotion of certain progressive ideals to empower disenfranchised groups rhetorically united them in their common state of political oppression. Even while these marginalized groups—including women, American Indians, African Americans, and wage laborers—occupied different levels of citizenship, they could potentially find commonality in the absence of fully enfranchised citizenship rights. As Erika A. Kuhlman argues, progressive reformers "broadened their base of support by creating alliances among various political-interest groups . . . Progressivism, then, was an ideology, a way of looking at the world, with a corresponding mode of conduct: coalition building."[124] The uniting potential of these progressive ideals nevertheless was constrained by the shared notion that the ideal citizen was an Anglo-Saxon male.

To an extent, President Wilson's progressive politics shaped these uniting and dividing trends. As was discussed before, President Wilson was confronted with the task of constituting a unified, nationalist identity, particularly following the economic and social discontent of the late nineteenth century. Wilson's task was particularly difficult as he faced a diverse country whose people differed along gender, race, class, and national lines. His empowering progressive ideals were thus amenable to the Progressive Era trend of coalition building. Wilson, however, has been noted for excluding minorities of the US polity in order to form a homogenous, nationalistic vision of the citizenry. The process of forming a nationalist identity often privileged beliefs shared by the whole of the nation, and in turn overshadowed the particularities of the nation's polity and the differentiated experiences of marginalized groups. Vanessa B. Beasley further explains this process: "In a nation whose citizens may have little else in common, focusing on shared beliefs is an efficient way of accommodating other types of differences."[125] In light of such differences, many coalitions were formed to challenge presidential, legislative, and judicial power to enhance citizenship rights. Thus, Wilson's first inauguration ceremony represented a site in which the empowering and disempowering forces of Wilson's progressive nationalism were both realized and contested.

The Committee's national parade reflected these uniting and differentiating trends as it included the participation of women across race, class, and ideological lines, but did so in a way that subordinated these differences to the pursuit of national citizenship rights for white women. In his study of the Orange parades in Northern Ireland, Dominic Bryan argues that "providing [ritual events] with a dominant meaning rarely goes unopposed and . . . even within the parades there is resistance to these processes."[126] Thus, it is not surprising that while the Committee's parade demonstrated a preference for national unity over the particular demands of state, regional, or racial groups, marginalized participants found the means to contest the expedient racism reproduced by the Committee's rhetoric of political mimesis. As was noted before, acts of mimesis can facilitate the perpetuation of hegemonic processes, thus diminishing the potential for such acts to confront modes of power as they reproduce it.[127]

Nonetheless, the Committee's inclusion of socially diverse groups is somewhat remarkable considering the isolating and differentiating ways in which the federal and state governments treated the citizenship rights of minority groups. The Constitution left most citizenship and voting matters to the states, which ultimately facilitated the exclusionary tendencies particular to certain states and regions. Thus, throughout US history, voting rights for African Americans, immigrants, American Indians, and women varied from state to state, and laws varied from group to group within each state.[128] By 1913, marginalized groups possessed various forms of abridged citizenship rights, which not only limited the full participation of these groups in the national community, but also prevented them from collecting and uniting in pursuit of any one particular demand for citizenship rights.[129]

Even so, non-first-class citizens were gaining ground in national politics by forging coalitions. As was discussed before, the collaboration of the settlement house and trade unionist movements with the woman suffrage movement in the early 1900s helped fashion woman suffrage into a mass movement, which promised to enhance the rights of immigrant and wage-earning women. Since the latter decades of the nineteenth century, labor organizations had endorsed woman suffrage, which helped align the plight of wage-earning men and women. In fact, the parade's program featured the following quotation by Samuel Gompers, historic president of the American

Federation of Labor: "I am for unqualified woman suffrage as a matter of human justice."[130] And although the woman suffrage movement was not immune to expedient racism, some African American woman suffrage organizations worked alongside white woman suffrage organizations—a considerable development following the acerbic split between the abolition and woman suffrage movements following the Civil War. The strengthening ties among the immigrant, working-class, African American, and woman suffrage communities offered the promise of greater participation in US national politics and culture.

Insofar as acts of mimesis reproduce ideologies, the Committee's national parade reproduced the president's progressive attempts to unite a diverse nation as the Committee invited labor and trade union organizations, African American women, and state woman suffrage organizations to participate. The participation of labor and trade union organizations was less surprising considering Paul's personal experiences and alliances with the settlement house and labor movements. In fact, Paul originally asked Harriot Stanton Blatch to serve as chair of the National Parade Committee. In light of Blatch's recent successes in New York and her ties to the militant branch of the labor movement, this move seemed particularly strategic. After initially refusing, Blatch agreed to act as a member of the procession committee.[131]

The Committee's incorporation of labor-related organizations in particular promoted a vision of a mass suffrage movement. For example, one group of marchers was led by women upholding a banner, which read: "100,000 Socialists Work and Vote for Woman Suffrage."[132] According to the available photographs of the parade, this contingent of marchers appeared to be one of the parade's largest, and while they certainly did not amass to one hundred thousand women, the number on the banner gave the impression of an overwhelming collectivity of women in favor of woman suffrage. Moreover, these socialists both "work[ed]" and "vote[d]" for suffrage, reflecting the growing coalition between working-class and middle-class women and between the socialist and woman suffrage movements.

The parade further illustrated the coalition among classes of women by the participation of wage-earning women who marched alongside the educated and career-oriented women in the parade's third section.[133] Two large contingents of "Wage Earners" surrounded a float entitled "A Labor Story" and upheld banners that read "Woman's Place is in the Home" and "The Sweat-Shop is the Home of Thousands of Women."[134] Much like the floats promoting women's economic, social, and religious equality, these banners reified traditional notions about women to make a more liberal argument for political equality. While the first banner echoed the ideology of gendered spaces at the time, suggesting that women belonged in the domestic sphere, the second banner read as an interrogation of that ideology, suggesting that the experiences of working-class women contradicted the gendered expectations of middle- and upper-class women. Thus, the banners forced an expansion of the class-based definition of "woman" and implicitly pointed to the obsolescence of the doctrine of the public-private spheres.

The Women's Trade Union League of Chicago made a more overt appeal to women's equality. Their leading banner demanded "Self Government in the Work Shop."[135] As part of a national suffrage parade, the trade union's demand can be understood as part and parcel to the vote; once unionized, working-class women could vote, allowing them to "self-govern" in the workplace. Both representations of wage-earning women, however, invoked the image of working-class women in a "Sweat-Shop" or "Work Shop"—a stark contrast to the mythic imagery of the Columbia tableau or the image of the typical white, upper- or middle-class woman suffragist. As such, the representation of wage earners and trade unionists challenged the idea that suffrage was primarily a white, middle-class women's movement, and promoted a vision of unity and strength among all classes of women.

The Committee's militant push to nationalize the movement also encouraged the more radical participation of women across race and regional lines. The parade took place less than fifty years after the Civil War; thus, tensions persisted between the North and South and between black women and white women in particular. The ratification of the Fifteenth Amendment entrenched the separation of groups pursuing citizenship rights for African American men and white women, and moreover, entrenched the occlusion of African American women from these pursuits altogether. Regional differences exacerbated these tensions as many white southern suffragists pursued a "whites-only" campaign, which was tacitly condoned by national suffrage leaders. Because African American woman suffragists faced resistance from the suffrage movement in all regions of the country, many were compelled to form their own suffrage organizations. Thus, the participation of African American women in the national parade, which also featured white suffragists from all regions of the nation, promoted the notion that fully enfranchised national citizenship included women across ideological and racial lines.

Reflective of the Committee's efforts to transcend regional and ideological differences, the parade included delegations from forty-eight states in the union, organized into three groups. The first group included the nine suffrage-granting states; the second featured the states where a suffrage amendment had passed both houses; and the third was comprised of "other states" where suffrage movements struggled.[136] This third group was the most regionally and ideologically diverse, as it included northern and southern states, such as the more ardently racist state delegations from Louisiana and Kentucky.[137] Whether these state delegations liked it or not, they marched alongside the Illinois delegation, which, contrary to the Committee's wishes, included Ida B. Wells-Barnett, notable African American women's rights activist. Moreover, in a previous subsection, a contingent of African American women from Howard University marched alongside representatives of the National Men's League for Women Suffrage.[138]

The Committee's incorporation of African American women in the national parade reproduced both the empowering and exclusionary tendencies of progressivism. In fact, the contingent of African American college women was the result of a compromise. Prior to the suffrage parade, an African American sorority from Howard University approached Paul and requested to march in the section of college women. Prominent African American suffrage leader Mary Church Terrell was to lead the group.[139] After bringing the question before the Committee and some NAWSA leaders, Paul was strongly discouraged from allowing the participation of African American women. Alice Stone Blackwell, for example, advised Paul against the formation of a black contingent in the parade. Additionally, white southern suffragists threatened to withdraw from the parade if black women marched.[140] Paul was aware that the Committee could not afford to lose the support of white southern suffragists, particularly since the South was the most resistant region to woman suffrage. On the other hand, Paul realized that advocating for federal voting rights would benefit African American women's voting rights and, more so, would force the Committee to formulate a position on African American women's rights.[141] In the end, Paul arranged for black women to march in the men's section of the parade, so that the men could act as a "protective wedge" between the women and spectators who might be resistant to African American women marchers.[142]

Ida B. Wells-Barnett's frustrating experiences with white suffragists compelled her to protest Paul's decision and perform a more inclusive vision of national woman citizenship. Wells-Barnett had often faced racism within the suffrage movement. In 1894, for example, Wells-Barnett witnessed her good friend, Terrell, wait fourteen months for the Chicago Woman's Club to decide if an African American woman could be admitted. In 1900, the Illinois State Federation of Women's Clubs rejected Wells-Barnett because she was

African American. But in 1913, Wells-Barnett organized the Alpha Suffrage Club of African American women, the first African American women's club in Illinois—whose campaign efforts helped elect Oscar DePriest, a black man, to Congress.[143] One of the club's first activities was to send Wells-Barnett to the national parade as a leader of the Illinois suffrage movement. After learning of the separate African American women's section, Wells-Barnett and other Illinois suffragists confronted Committee members, who remained intransigent. A reporter from the *Chicago Tribune* described Wells-Barnett's reaction: "[Her voice] trembled with emotion and two large tears coursed their way down her cheeks before she could raise her veil and wipe them away."[144]

Despite her tears, Wells-Barnett transformed the parade into a site of her own protest. She waited until the parade was underway, and, from the crowded sidewalks full of spectators, she stepped in line with the Illinois delegation, linking arms with white suffragists Belle Squire and Virginia Brooks.[145] Facing a rowdy, anti-suffragist crowd, Wells-Barnett and her compatriots managed to finish the parade untouched. The *Chicago Defender* championed Wells-Barnett's radical protest, calling her "The Modern Joan [of] Arc." Moreover, the article echoed Wells-Barnett's universalist approach toward women's citizenship rights, highlighting unity along gender lines rather than difference on racial grounds: "Mrs. Barnett represents the highest type of womanhood in Illinois."[146]

More so than the Committee envisioned, Wells-Barnett's act of protest provided a visualization of unity across racial lines, as she marched alongside white women, not behind or separate from them. Further, her protest may have helped promote a greater coalition between white and African American women activists of the time. Wells-Barnett's actions demonstrated that marginalized women possessed the political agency to transform the parade into a site of contestation within which they could protest their oppression within the suffrage movement and US national culture in general. Reflective of the dialectical relationship between the politically powerful and those with more limited power, Wells-Barnett's protest forced the Committee to incorporate the demands of marginalized voices within the suffrage community.

Despite such glimpses of progressiveness on issues of racial inclusion, the Committee's inclusion of African American women mimicked the protectionist posture the federal government had taken toward women throughout US history. Paul argued, for example, that she wished to "protect" and even conceal the participation of African American women in the parade by placing them alongside the National Men's League delegation. Neither the "Pageant Outline" nor the parade's "Official Program" identified a contingent of African American women—only the inclusion of the men. Furthermore, newspaper accounts from the *Washington Post,* the *New York Times,* and the *Daily Picayune* omitted any mention of African American marchers.[147] The marginalization of African American women in the "national" parade not only reflected their denigrated social and political position in American culture, but also the tendency for the particularities of American culture to be overlooked in favor of sustaining a whole and homogeneous national identity.

Much like the president's goal to forge a unified, nationalist identity out of a diverse country, the Committee worked to forge coalitions across gender, racial, class, and ideological lines. Because the Committee's militancy was grounded in the coalition between the labor and woman suffrage movement, the parade facilitated the intersecting demand for citizenship rights among wage-earning and upper-class suffragists. These coalitions provided a visualization of a mass suffrage movement and helped form a collectivity of women marching in favor a federal amendment for national citizenship rights despite significant differences. However, the Committee also mimicked exclusionary and racist practices as it promoted the marginalization of African American women. Thus, the Committee diminished the extent to which African American women could demand full citizenship rights, as it favored full citizenship rights for the majority over the minority. Nonetheless, the participation of African Americans in the parade as well as Wells-Barnett's act of protest directly challenged the construction of the ideal US citizen as white and male.

CONCLUSION: NATIONALIZATION AND VIOLENT BACKLASH

The Committee's national woman suffrage parade mimicked the political ritual of the presidential inauguration, and thus inserted woman suffrage into the privileged spaces of US national politics, promoted a sense of national unity within the suffrage movement, and helped constitute the identities of women as US citizens. The national parade earned the Committee respect from within suffrage circles. Harriot Stanton Blatch, leader of the New York suffrage movement, wrote Lucy Burns: "The Washington Parade is getting a great deal of notice in the papers here, and we all feel that the work you and Miss Paul are doing is going to be a tremendous boon for suffrage all over the country."[148] The Committee's efforts also attracted a larger, national audience. Almost five hundred thousand people had turned out to watch the parade, creating "a solid mass of spectators," according to one report.[149]

Further, the *New York Times* said, "the capital saw the greatest parade of women in its history," representing "an astonishing demonstration."[150]

The Committee's mimetic efforts to effect social change at the national level, however, resulted in social control efforts exacted against the suffragists as the parade came to a violent close. Paul had anticipated the large crowds and requested extra police protection from the superintendent of police, Maj. Richard Sylvester. After he refused, Paul managed to persuade the outgoing secretary of war, Henry L. Stimson, to arrange the Fifteenth Cavalry from Fort Myer, Maryland, to wait on standby. Not long after the parade began, onlookers began insulting the marchers and shoving bystanders into the procession, inciting a riotous atmosphere. Quickly, the cavalry rode in and restored order. Nonetheless, the incident resulted in 175 ambulance calls and 200 reported injuries.[151] Marchers, including Sen. Miles Poindexter (P-WA), reported that the police did little, if anything, to control the crowds. One marcher reported that Nora Blatch de Forest, Harriot Stanton Blatch's daughter, "was struck in the face while a policeman was standing near. Some of the women were pinched black and blue."[152] De Forest herself testified: "My mother, Mrs. Stanton-Blatch, told an officer he must look out for the crowd there as the women were being crushed, and he replied: 'Oh, you go home!'"[153] One police officer reportedly said to marcher, Genevieve Stone, "If my wife were where you are I'd break her head."[154]

Resistance to the suffragists' parade demonstrated that the national spaces they invaded were staunchly protected. Everett Pepperrell Wheeler, an anti-suffragist lawyer in New York, suggested, in a letter to the *New York Times* editor, that the women had initiated the violent response: "[Women] exposed themselves to the gaze of the crowd which filled the streets of Washington. . . . Men with self-restraint in such circumstances would, of course, abstain from violence and keep away. The spectacle to them was disgusting in the main. But all the more the crowd, who had no self restraint, would go and express their disapproval the way that they did. . . . [Suffragists'] attempt to bring violence in political warfare with men would break down the protecting barriers which courtesy and chivalry have thrown around women. If women fight men, men will certainly come to fight back and whether they like it or not the suffragists will find that men despise them if, under the pressure of the fight, they whimper and complain."[155]

Wheeler accused the women of "bring[ing] violence in political warfare," thus, provoking men to "break down the protecting barriers" and "fight back." The militancy of the Committee's insinuation into political territory was most visible as the marchers' demands were perceived as violent threats.

Others denied that any violence was done upon the women at all, attempting to discredit the women. John A. Johnston, D.C. commissioner, reported, "I myself was at the head of the parade. . . . I noticed the faces of the marchers and saw no signs of distress. . . . It was a big, typical, good-natured American crowd and I witnessed no rowdyism."[156] That the commissioner described the crowd as "good-natured" as evidence of its presumed innocence suggested that any violence that may have ensued was surely not the crowd's fault. Further, aligning the crowd's good character with Americanism suggested that many in positions of political power still posited women—or women's efforts for social change—outside the boundaries of a US nationalist identity. As history has shown, and as was demonstrated during the parade, when those who are excluded from a shared US nationalist identity attempt to challenge those in power, they are often punished in either social or violent terms.

The parade's violent turnout, however, fostered greater solidarity in the suffrage movement and attracted national political attention to the issue. Anna Howard Shaw, president of the NAWSA, said: "Of one thing I am certain, and that is that this made us many friends. . . . I never saw an audience so stirred as the one at the mass meeting we held after the parade."[157] Suffering together created a sense of unity among the suffragists and generated support from within the halls of Congress. Within three days, a special investigation committee was formed in the Senate, soliciting four days of testimony.[158] Senator Poindexter reported the names of twenty-two officers who failed to aid the marchers. The subsequent firing of Police Superintendent Sylvester in part legitimized the suffragists' testimonies.[159] This small success demonstrated that although local police condoned violent reactions to the parade, woman suffrage was gaining ground as a national movement and earning national media attention. Wilson's inauguration and the suffrage parade even shared front-page coverage in the *Washington Post*, the *New York Times*, and the *Daily Picayune*.[160]

The Committee's efforts to nationalize woman suffrage also faced some resistance from within the suffrage movement. Soon after the parade, for example, Paul wrote to Blatch, asking that she "institute a vigorous campaign to secure the vote of [New York] Senator James A. O'Gorman for the Federal Amendment." Further, Paul added: "Now is the moment to help the Federal bill and it seems to me that everything else should be subordinated to it at this crisis."[161] Blatch's response matched Paul's militant immediacy, but rejected the premise of Paul's request:

"You know I fully appreciate all that you and Miss Burns are doing in Washington and I appreciate its wide propaganda value, but at the same time, I do not waver for one moment in my conviction that the winning of New York is the great and immediate thing to be accomplished. . . . I regret that we have not an ounce of energy nor a postage stamp to devote to Senator O'Gorman. You see in all the suffrage work there is a political side and even if we had time and energy and money to give to the National work I would not want to approach Senator O'Gorman in the way in which you suggest."[162]

Blatch's commitment to state-level suffrage revealed that, even among the most established and innovative suffrage leaders, the Committee's sense of national citizenship and campaign for a federal amendment were considered too militant an approach toward woman suffrage. Clearly, state suffrage was the favored approach among NAWSA leaders and highly esteemed state suffrage leaders such as Blatch. Further, Blatch's more moderate position was revealed as she explained the "political side" to maintaining the support of key political figures. Blatch's unwillingness to agitate Senator O'Gorman stood in contrast to Paul's fearlessness—after all, Paul did ask Blatch to "subordinate" all of her well-known efforts for New York woman suffrage to the task of securing a federal amendment.

Nonetheless, the Committee's rhetoric of political mimesis demonstrated the organization's militancy, as it generated publicity, agitated President Wilson, and most significantly, offered Committee members and US women the means to enact and participate in a vision of US national citizenship. Mimicking the inauguration ritual, thus, helped constitute the citizenship identities of Committee members. As Gebauer and Wulf declare, mimesis is "an actualization, a presentation of what has been mimetically indicated."[163] In the case of the Committee's national parade, the Committee actualized women's presence in national, political spaces, positioned themselves as political leaders, and helped shape woman suffrage as a national issue. Specifically, the parade cast the Committee's pursuit of woman suffrage as part of the nation's pursuit to fulfill democratic ideals, constructed state-level suffrage as subordinate to federal-level suffrage, and promoted coalition politics across race, class, and ideological lines. Although the Committee's militant efforts faced resistance from inside and outside the suffrage community and, to an extent, mimicked the differentiating tendencies of the Progressive Era, Committee members were further motivated to press onward in order fulfill their militant vision of citizenship rights for US women.

3

Mimesis and Third-Party Politics

The Woman's Party

The Congressional Committee's woman suffrage parade of 1913 launched the militant branch of the National American Woman Suffrage Association (NAWSA) into the arena of national politics. As a mimetic enactment of the inauguration ritual, the parade created a vision of a mass movement and worked to empower US women to demand citizenship rights as it cast woman suffrage as a national issue.

Following the parade, Alice Paul and Lucy Burns wasted little time expanding the national campaign beyond the streets of Washington, D.C., into every congressional district of the United States. As the Congressional Committee sharpened its focus on agitating Democratic members of Congress, it turned its rhetoric of political mimesis toward mimicking third parties as a strategy of both agitation and political participation. Exhibiting such motives, one Committee member wrote to another: "If we can but continue a constant agitation which will rivet the eyes of Congressmen upon our measure, there is great hope it may go through this Congress."[1] Thus, Paul and Burns's militant vision was fixed on positioning suffragists within the spaces of electoral politics in order to threaten the election or reelection of Democratic congressmen.

Committee leaders expedited their militant campaign against members of Congress by breaking from the NAWSA and forming the Congressional Union for Woman Suffrage (CUWS). The CUWS was an organization open to all women sympathetic to the Committee's militant approach toward acquiring a federal woman suffrage amendment.[2] As veterans of the militant movement in England, Paul and Burns attempted to uphold the three basic tenets that the Women's Social and Political Union (WSPU) espoused in its constitution: to hold the political party in power accountable, to generate publicity, and to engage in "vigorous agitation upon lines justified by the position of outlawry to which women are presently condemned."[3] The adoption of third-party strategies by the CUWS represented an extension of the WSPU's first method of agitating the party in power. Such an approach seems fitting, particularly since third parties are considered "an explicit and deliberate rejection of the two dominant parties."[4] In this sense, third-party strategies positioned the CUWS in opposition to the Democratic and Republican parties, exhibiting its militancy as these women inserted themselves and their own political organization into the masculine world of party politics.

Representing a departure from the WSPU belief in taking "action *entirely independent of* political parties," however, the mimetic adoption of third-party strategies by the CUWS also functioned as a more traditional strategy of political change.[5] The CUWS aimed to enter the arena of party politics and compete with the Democratic Party while forging alliances with other major parties. Although the differences between the militant campaigns of the WSPU and the CUWS have been attributed to their unique historical and political contexts, they can also be attributed to the WSPU's contingent definition of militancy.[6] Specifically, the third militant tenet of the WSPU argued that, so long as women were disenfranchised, "vigorous agitation" was justified.[7] Compared to the WSPU, the CUWS took a more moderate approach when targeting congressional leaders, at least in part by working with and in opposition to the party apparatus in the United States, thus agitating from within the system as a means to effect political change.

The militancy of the CUWS was most visible as it directly confronted the gendered boundaries that helped shape the nation's identity. Despite women's increased political participation in the early twentieth century, nineteenth-century notions of femininity and a woman's "proper sphere" lingered, allocating domestic concerns to women and demarcating the public as a space reserved for men.[8] Even as more and more women engaged in political activity, they often did so as advocates of health, education, and child-labor policies—issues thought to be more "domestic." Thus, women's political identities were often cultivated as extensions of their familial identities. Tamar Mayer explains how such gendered identities function to establish hegemony within the nation: "In determining who belongs to the nation and who does not, elites construct a code of 'proper behavior' for members of the nation which becomes a sort of national boundary. In each case, the code which the elites promote as essential to the continuation of the nation also furthers the elite's own interests; thus in the life of the nation one gender, one sexuality and one national narrative tends to rule."[9] Without question, white, wealthier men were still the ideal citizens of the US nation-state. This hierarchy of gender positioned women's political and citizenship roles on the periphery of the political sphere and discounted the political relevance of women's citizenship rights.

In light of such constraints, the militant campaign of the CUWS challenged the gendered and nationalistic codes of the early twentieth century. By mobilizing US women into the public and political spheres to demand the defeat of US congressmen, CUWS members asserted their political agency and worked to constitute US women's citizenship identities beyond their domestic and familial identities. As Floya Anthias and Nira Yuval-Davis argue, "Women are constituted through the state but are also actively engaged in countering state processes."[10] The CUWS likewise countered such processes by mimicking third-party politics and aggressively entering the masculine spaces of politics. As Andrew Rosen argues, militant tactics were those "that conventional society would regard . . . as acts of social and political bellicosity when employed by women."[11] Simultaneously, however, such militancy helped to feminize the political sphere and legitimize women's citizenship rights.

Third-party politics provided an ideal context in which CUWS members and US women could militantly challenge codes of gendered nationalism. First, third parties occupied a position that simultaneously participated in and critiqued mainstream electoral politics. Next, Progressive Era shifts toward democratic participation facilitated the rise of multiple third parties during this time. Moreover, third parties provided women with more opportunities to participate in political activism than the two major parties. For example, some women participated in and helped form the Socialist Party of America.[12] Finally, the passage of California's woman suffrage bill in 1911 is attributed in large part to the organizing efforts of the Women's Socialist Union and the socialist leaders within the California Equal Suffrage Association.[13] Given these dynamics, the CUWS was well positioned to mimic third-party strategies and ultimately form a new political party to gain political legitimacy and deploy its militant, anti-Democratic campaign.

As the CUWS turned to mimicking party politics, it employed the more traditional function of mimesis as a form of representation. Specifically, the CUWS explicitly modeled the political rhetorics and practices characteristic of third-party and electoral politics of the day. Teresa L. Ebert's theory of mimesis as representation speaks to the ways in which the CUWS rhetoric of political mimesis could potentially work to enhance its political legitimacy. She says, "Representation is always inscribed in the political, economic, and ideological practices within any given social formation and functions to legitimate the validity, unavoidability, and historical necessity of those practices."[14] The CUWS offered representations of political practices that included the election of delegates by an electorate, the constitution of these delegates as leaders of a party, the construction of these leaders as political allies and rivals to US congressmen, and the official formation of a third party, complete with a national convention and a party platform. Ebert warns, however, that such mimetic representations, particularly when produced by women, hold the potential to reify the hegemonic processes endemic to such political practices. She maintains, "The task of feminism is to demystify the politics of all kinds of representation and not to naturalize some of these."[15] Although to an extent, the campaign of the CUWS helped to "naturalize" relationships of power central to party politics, it simultaneously worked to "demystify" these practices as it confronted the codes of gendered nationalism that worked to stabilize gendered power in the national imaginary. In short, the mimetic representation of third-party rhetorics and practices allowed the CUWS to both legitimize and destabilize the political processes bound up in earning women's full citizenship rights in the early twentieth century.

Although empowered by the destabilizing potential of political mimesis, the militant national campaign of the CUWS faced many challenges. First, many women in western states already possessed state suffrage and were either ignorant or apathetic to the CUWS's drive to enfranchise all US women. Next, although the Committee's national parade promoted federal suffrage over state suffrage, many women remained committed to local and state efforts directed at passing state referenda. Additionally, as more and more women participated in politics—albeit in a limited fashion—the CUWS needed to motivate US women to escalate their demands beyond traditional avenues of political participation, such as petitioning and lobbying.

To overcome these obstacles, the CUWS drove a militant campaign to agitate members of Congress and to constitute US women's citizenship identities. The rhetorical processes through which the militant principles of the CUWS guided its mimetic adoption of third-party strategies and formation of a new political party also helped US women assert their political agency and expand their roles within the nation-state. Thus, the CUWS worked to mobilize women in each of the 435 US congressional districts by seeking to unite the voices of white women to demand a federal amendment, inspiring mostly white women to commit sensational acts of citizenship, constituting party leaders and an electorate, and, last, forming a political party—the Woman's Party. An analysis of discourse pertaining to multiple activist events between 1913 and 1916, including CUWS correspondence and articles of the *Suffragist,* exposes the rhetorical dimensions of the militant campaign of the CUWS against members of Congress. First this analysis is situated in the political and ideological context of these years.

THE RISE OF THE CUWS

The militant campaign of the CUWS against Democratic members of Congress was part of an ongoing struggle between the suffragists and resistant political institutions. The CUWS negotiated the political terrain of the early twentieth century in ways that reflected key shifts in presidential, congressional, and party politics. More specifically, the adoption of the primary system, Congress's increased promise to pass progressive legislation, the rising power of the Democratic Party, and the activist and political strategies of third parties inform the militant campaign of the CUWS. Finally, the formation of the CUWS and its split from the NAWSA can be understood in terms of the CUWS's turn toward more militant means of persuasion.

Presidential and Congressional Politics

The formation of the Congressional Union for Woman Suffrage, an organization whose title implies a focus on congressional politics, reflected many progressive shifts in the early twentieth century. One of the most significant developments in presidential politics was the institution of the presidential primary. Kathleen A. Kendall argues that presidential primaries "were seen by early reformers as a way to take away the power to nominate the president from the party bosses and give it back to the 'the people.'"[16] By the 1912 presidential election, as many as twenty-one states had adopted a presidential primary system, and by 1915, only a handful had yet to do so.[17] Kendall argues that because these primaries helped free candidates from party control, more candidates could openly compete against one another, thus encouraging them to communicate more directly with potential voters.[18] Presidential candidates began targeting the American people in the late nineteenth century as contenders like William Jennings Bryan and Theodore Roosevelt spoke directly to voters across the country.[19] Ideally, these shifts toward a more democratic relationship between US citizens and presidential candidates worked to empower the political voices of the American people.

Along with the presidency and presidential campaigns, the US Congress underwent significant progressive reforms during this time. Specifically, the increased power of majority rule in the House of Representatives expedited the passage of progressive legislation.[20] The leadership of Congressman Thomas Brackett Reed (R-ME) throughout the 1880s and the 1890s centered on streamlining the passage of laws and minimizing the power of the minority party.[21] Although Reed believed that increased majority rule would more effectively represent the American majority, such power worked to nearly silence minority voices. In fact, it became the means through which Speaker of the House Joe Cannon (R-IL) "gain[ed] near absolute control over his party" in the early 1900s.[22] Cannon's autocratic leadership and his resistance to President Roosevelt's progressive agenda led to a Democratic revolt in the Sixty-First Congress (1909–1911).[23] This revolt was considered "one of the most dramatic events in the early 20th-century Congress," because it reflected how the introduction of the primary system allowed representatives to act independently of their parties and act as "Progressive Insurgents."[24] Moreover, this revolt helped ensure a Democratic majority in the House.

After the first decade of the twentieth century, the Democratic Party secured control of the executive and legislative branches. The growing faction of Republican Party progressives, along with the failure of the Republican Party to lower tariffs as promised in the 1908 mid-term elections, positioned House Democrats for a takeover in 1910. House Democrats became known as the "King Caucus," which was characterized less by autocratic rule and more by the progressive-friendly trend of consensus building.[25] Even with the simultaneous rise of the Progressive Party, voters were attracted to the more centrist progressives of the Democratic Party, including presidential candidate Woodrow Wilson.[26] His election in 1912 solidified the strength of the Democratic Party in the US government.

The ratification of the Seventeenth Amendment in April 1913, which ensured the direct election of senators, also increased the potential of Congress to represent the political demands of US citizens. Prior to the amendment, US senators were selected by their state legislatures. Throughout the latter decades of the nineteenth century, the labor and agrarian movements pushed for the direct election of US senators as a way to curb the corrupt promotion of particular senators. By 1909, the Democratic, Populist, and Socialist Parties endorsed the amendment's passage. After much resistance from the Senate, both houses of Congress passed a version of the amendment, which was ratified by the required number of states in early 1913.[27] The direct election of senators, along with the solidification of a Democratic majority in Congress, increased the legislative branch's potential to directly represent the voices of the American people and to be more open to the will of those constituents who supported a federal amendment securing women's full citizenship rights.

The CUWS was clearly mindful of these shifting political dynamics. Early in its militant campaign against members of Congress, the CUWS noted: "[G]overnment is tending more and more towards centralization, and the really important questions of law are being dealt with not in State legislatures but in Congress."[28] As part of its philosophy of agitating the party in power, the CUWS focused on the Democratic Party's strength. The CUWS explained: "This policy is entirely non-partisan in that it handles all parties with perfect impartiality. If the Republicans were in power we would regard them, in their capacity as head of the Government, as responsible for the enfranchisement of women. . . . Today, the Democrats are in power. They control the Executive offices, the Senate, and the House. They can, if they will, enfranchise women in the present session; their refusal to do so establishes a record which must necessarily be taken into consideration by women when the party seeks the re-endorsement of the people at the polls."[29]

The CUWS considered its campaign against the Democratic Party as a way to keep Congress accountable for upholding the promise of representing the American people. Consequently, the CUWS cast women as part of "the people at the polls," recognizing the voting power of many US women in western states and further constituting all US women as potential members of the electorate to whom Congress was responsible.

Third-Party Politics

In addition to the potentially empowering changes in presidential and legislative politics, progressive ideals motivated the formation of prominent third parties. In fact, the years between 1904 and 1924 have been identified as one of the most intense periods of third-party activity in US history.[30] Regarding its anti-Democratic strategy, the CUWS once said: "This policy is based upon a recognition of the fact that our government is a government by party and that the will of the individual counts for little as against the will of his party."[31] In light of the considerable power of third parties in the early twentieth century, mimicking third-party strategies bolstered the legitimacy of the CUWS in national politics and helped position the CUWS as a threat to Democrats.

Third parties have been a part of US politics since the rise of the two-party system in the late 1820s.[32] In their comprehensive study on third parties, Steven Rosenstone, Roy L. Behr, and Edward H. Lazarus argue, "Periods of third party strength indicate that the major parties are not representing citizens' political demands."[33] Third parties provide alternative political outlets that hold the potential to simultaneously agitate mainstream US politics and to effect policy change.[34] With the rise of Progressive Era demands to empower the rights of marginalized groups, third parties played a significant role in the political landscape of the late nineteenth and early twentieth centuries.

Third parties can be characterized by the ways in which they emerge and by their lifespan. According to V. O. Key, short-lived parties typically take form when "splinter" candidates leave a major party to establish their own.[35] Theodore Roosevelt, for example, split from the Republican Party in 1912 after the party nominated William Howard Taft for president. Roosevelt became the presidential candidate of the Progressive "Bull Moose" Party; although he was more popular than Taft, he and Taft split the Republican vote, which allowed Wilson to secure the presidency with only 41.8 percent of the vote.[36] While some splinter candidates have made strong showings in national and local elections, typically, they re-assimilate with a major party, thus rendering their third parties somewhat defunct.

Some short-lived third parties form out of economic protest to the two dominant political parties. The formation of the People's Party in 1892, for example, was driven by populism, a radical agrarian movement that swept the South, Midwest, and West, and aimed to redress the economic and social exploitation of the rural working classes.[37] Women were particularly vocal in the populist movement, and in 1891, founded the National Woman's Alliance, an autonomous organization committed to many populist causes.[38] In 1892, the People's Party made a strong showing at the polls as the populist presidential nominee, James K. Weaver, earned over one million votes; additionally, supporters of the party elected five senators, ten congressmen, three governors, and over fifteen hundred local and state officials.[39] Part of the party's strength is owed to the Democratic Party's appropriation of its agenda, which helped populists secure complete control of the Kansas state legislature in 1892.[40] One way in which the People's Party gained broad appeal in other areas was by joining the Democratic Party to promote a common candidate or to agree not to challenge each other in certain races. This trend, entitled "fusion politics," helped third parties gain institutional legitimacy, but often forced them to compromise their political agendas.[41]

Additionally, short-lived third parties, such as the People's Party, gained popularity by adopting single-issue platforms. For example, mining communities in Colorado, Nebraska, and Illinois championed the issue of free silver as a populist cause.[42] In these cases, the People's Party better resembled a single-issue party, which focuses its energies on the passage of one particular policy.[43] During the nineteenth century, the Liberty Party and the Free Soil Party, for example, were formed to eradicate slavery. Similarly, the Greenback Party was formed by farmers to fight a weakening currency, just as the Prohibition Party was formed to combat rampant alcohol use.[44] However, once single-issue parties achieve some political success, they have little need to continue. Additionally, single-issue parties typically succeed at the cost of ignoring other demands for policy change. For example, while the issue of free silver grew out of populism's focus on economic justice, its prominence eclipsed other populist efforts to rehabilitate oppressed workers.[45]

The eventual fall of the People's Party illustrates the tenuous position that short-lived third parties hold in electoral politics. In 1896, the Democratic Party's nomination of William Jennings Bryan as its presidential candidate reflected the trends of fusion and single-issue politics. Bryan was a prominent champion of the silver issue, but the populists who originated in the Farmers' Alliance believed that he "was not a Populist and did not share the movement's commitment to grassroots empowerment and democracy."[46] Because these populists refused to support Bryan's candidacy, the party split and eventually disassembled. Bryan's potential to represent the ideological foundation of the populist movement, thus, was tempered by the need for a short-lived third party to gain broad appeal and institutional legitimacy. However, as some third parties are absorbed into major parties, their agendas hold the potential to reshape major-party platforms.[47] The People's Party, which had dissolved by 1900, is often credited for fueling many progressive efforts in the twentieth century.[48]

Key also discusses how continuing doctrinal parties have shaped US party politics. These parties are deeply committed to a reenvisioned social and economic order and are often able to sustain themselves over the course of many decades.[49] For example, in the wake of the People's Party, the Socialist Party of America was founded. As an amalgam of many socialist and labor organizations, the party united farmers and factory workers against the capitalist elite that kept many living in poverty.[50] Women were integral to the rise of the Socialist Party, which spoke to the turmoil of immigrant working-women. In New York, for example, Jewish factory women who were organized by the Socialist Party and by trade unions led multiple militant strikes between 1909 and 1913.[51] These garment workers were thrust into political action following the deaths of 146 women in the tragic Triangle Shirtwaist Factory fire of 1911.[52] The uprising of the working class helped Eugene V. Debs, the Socialist Party's 1912 presidential candidate, earn 6 percent of the popular vote.[53] The Socialist Party's platform continued to shape US politics throughout the twentieth century, although it maintained its position as a third party.

The formation of the Woman's Party (WP) by the CUWS in 1916 expanded upon women's experiences in third-party politics and exploited the unique political position of third parties to effect policy change. The WP resembled a short-lived party because of its single-issue platform to defeat Democratic candidates. However, like a continuing doctrinal party, the WP articulated a deep commitment to the party's longer-term mission to reconfigure women's citizenship identities within the nation-state. Most likely, the WP would dissolve once a federal amendment was secured, but the rhetorical processes through which WP members came to identify themselves as citizens and political actors suggests that the adoption of third-party strategies performed a constitutive function as well.

The WP held great potential to curb the election or reelection of Democratic candidates, considering that party loyalty was not very strong in the twelve suffrage-granting states. For example, in all presidential elections between 1896 and 1912, winning presidential candidates secured the electoral votes of suffrage states by an average of 9 percent of the popular vote. Additionally, since 1896, in 223 of the 301 congressional elections, an average sway of 10 percent of the vote would have resulted in the election of a different candidate. Thus, in 1916, when women possessed the power to elect a total of twenty-two US senators and forty US representatives, the WP was well positioned to affect the election or reelection of Democratic candidates.[54]

The CUWS

In light of these empowering developments in presidential, legislative, and party politics, the CUWS intensified its focus on agitating Democratic members of Congress through its mimetic adoption of third-party strategies. However, the ability of the CUWS to forcefully execute its militant campaign was tempered by its affiliation with the more moderate NAWSA. Following the conclusion of the high-profile parade in March 1913, the CUWS initiated its anti-Congress campaign by sending suffrage delegates to every member of Congress at the opening of a special session on April 7, 1913.[55] Throughout the ensuing summer months, the CUWS orchestrated numerous delegations to Congress. Not surprisingly, the NAWSA considered the efforts of the CUWS beyond the scope of its moderate, state-by-state approach to woman suffrage. Consequently, the NAWSA and the CUWS severed ties after a bitter dispute over ideological and financial differences.[56]

Losing its affiliation with the more moderately minded NAWSA allowed the CUWS to more rigorously pursue its militant campaign. One way the CUWS cultivated its militant identity was through its weekly organ, the *Suffragist.* Launched in late 1913, the *Suffragist* promoted the militant campaign of the CUWS to agitate members of Congress through third-party strategies. For example, the CUWS said it was determined "to make this paper a force to be reckoned with in the political life of the United States."[57] Moreover, as a reflection of the group's militant goal to generate publicity on a national level, it hoped the *Suffragist* would reach across state lines and appeal to a "national" audience, thereby forcing suffrage into the minds of the "general public."[58] Thus, with the *Suffragist,* the CUWS aimed to elevate the issue of woman suffrage beyond state-level politics and potentially constitute women's national citizenship identities. As Paul explained, "[the *Suffragist*] is not issued to appeal to women's clubs or to small suffrage organizations at all. . . . Our subscription list is national and our newsstand sales should be national."[59] Thus, the creation and circulation of the *Suffragist* enacted the militant push of the CUWS to enter the arena of national politics and to appeal to a national audience.

The *Suffragist* also played a key role in constituting CUWS members as national citizens and militant activists. While the *Suffragist* was intended for mass circulation, its subscription peaked at just over twenty thousand issues in 1917.[60] Most copies went to party members, advertisers, branch headquarters, and CUWS organizers, which strongly suggests that the suffragists themselves were a key audience of the publication. In 1914, for example, while working for the CUWS in Colorado, Mabel Vernon wrote, "I devour the news of you all in the Suffragist."[61] In this sense, the *Suffragist* functioned as a movement "handbook" that promoted CUWS strategies for mobilization and helped standardize strategies of agitation throughout its national campaign. Thus, in addition to targeting a national audience through the *Suffragist,* the publication also functioned as a means for the CUWS to construct its members as political change agents.

Along with the inception of the *Suffragist,* the growing number of woman voters in the western states strengthened the militant campaign of the CUWS which considered these voters as key assets in its campaign against members of Congress. In late 1913, Lucy Burns said:

"We have in our hands today not only the weapon of a just cause; we have the support of ten enfranchised States. More than 3,600,000 women have a vote in Presidential elections. It is unthinkable that a national Government which represents women and which appeals periodically to the suffrage of women, should ignore the issue of their right to political freedom."[62]

Given the upcoming midterm elections in 1914, and the congressional and presidential elections of 1916, the CUWS had its work cut out for them. The CUWS considered the empowered citizenship rights possessed by women in western states the necessary leverage to hold Congress accountable to the demands of its electorate.

African American women represented part of the voting electorate in these western states. One study shows that in 1906, more African American women voted than white women in a Denver, Colorado, election. In fact, African American women founded the Colored Women's Republican Club in Denver in 1901.[63] Prominent activists, such as Mary Church Terrell and Ida B. Wells-Barnett, participated in the founding of the National Association for the Advancement of Colored People (NAACP) in 1909.[64] Wells-Barnett went on to establish the Alpha Suffrage Club in 1913, the first African American women's club in Illinois, which she represented in the Congressional Committee's national woman suffrage parade in March of that year. Adella Hunt Logan, the only African American woman listed in the Alabama roster of the NAWSA in 1900, publicly argued that if white women needed political equality, African American women needed it even more.[65] Further asserting their political agency, women leaders within the NAACP established the National Association of Colored Women (NACW) in 1912. Margaret Murray Washington, who was married to Booker T. Washington, served as NACW president between 1912 and 1916; by the end of her term, more than fifty thousand women had joined the organization. The suffrage department of the NAWSA represented more than forty thousand African American women, who gathered petitions, educated voters, and voted where they could. By 1920, when a federal amendment was ratified, more than seventy-five thousand African American women were registered to vote in New York alone.[66]

Working-class and immigrant women also asserted their political agency in pursuit of women's political and economic rights. Throughout the first decades of the twentieth century, Mary Harris Jones, known as Mother Jones, militantly and vociferously spoke out on behalf of coal miners and other working-class communities.[67] The Women's Trade Union League (WTUL), formed in 1903, was integral toward organizing the New York shirtwaist factory strikes between 1909 and 1913. Four-fifths of the thirty thousand picketers were Jewish women, many of whom were also suffragists.[68] Also, the epic Lawrence, Massachusetts, textile factory strike of 1912 was led mostly by Italian, Polish, Lithuanian, Russian, and Syrian immigrant women.[69]

This climate of heightened activism helped forge an alliance between the CUWS and the labor movement. Wealthy CUWS member Alva Belmont participated in the New York shirtwaist strikes, which fueled her commitment to a federal woman suffrage amendment. Although Belmont was not a factory worker, the WTUL rhetoric of sisterhood helped to forge unity across class lines. During these strikes, the NAWSA refused to endorse the WTUL, demonstrating its resistance to more militant tactics.[70] The likewise militant CUWS, however, recruited many WTUL leaders and working-class protesters. Moreover, Harriot Stanton Blatch fused the militant tactics of the labor and woman suffrage movements and helped build cross-class alliances through her campaigns for New York state suffrage.[71] Notably, CUWS alliances with African American activists were either nonexistent or not documented. The demonstrated resistance of the CUWS to such an alliance would prove to be a missed opportunity to fully enact its equal-rightist philosophy.

Extending this trajectory of women's increased organizational and political activities, the CUWS aimed to enter party politics in order to agitate Democratic members of Congress and recruit US women as party members. The CUWS planned to establish headquarters in each state, promote the CUWS in local newspapers, enlist new members, arrange open-air street meetings, and persuade women voters to vote against Democratic congressmen. This national campaign required that the CUWS rhetorically unite the voices of American women in pursuit of a federal woman suffrage amendment.

MOBILIZING US WHITE WOMEN AND AGITATING US CONGRESSMEN

Prior to officially forming the Woman's Party in 1916, the CUWS mimicked the strategies of a third political party by establishing headquarters in every state, stationing organizers in every congressional district, and launching a number of nationwide campaign strategies.[72] To motivate these campaign efforts, the CUWS rhetorically united US white women's voices in pursuit of a federal amendment. The CUWS also worked to mobilize such women to commit sensational acts of citizenship, in which they invaded political spaces and created a militant sense of presence and ubiquity. Simultaneously, the CUWS mimicked acts of congressional deliberation by sending locally appointed and state-appointed representatives to the nation's Capitol to voice the demands of women as key constituents of the US electorate. Together these strategies bolstered the militant commitments of the CUWS to fashion a woman's political party, agitate members of Congress, and constitute US white women as US citizens.

Uniting US White Women

The CUWS worked to establish a national electorate by constituting the citizenship voices of white women all over the country as part of a united demand for woman suffrage. Asserting political voice was central to the militant philosophy of the CUWS. Just before waging its 1914 midterm election campaign, the CUWS said: "A movement is not really alive which does not ask for immediate action. . . . One thing we may be sure of—until *we ask* for instant action, no one else will ask for it."[73] Uniting US women's voices constituted a national community of white women citizens whose demands militantly expanded women's political identities in the political sphere.

First, the CUWS employed a rhetoric of national sisterhood to appeal to enfranchised western women, which called forth a sense of loyalty and reciprocity. Mari Jo Buhle argues that the rhetoric of sisterhood took root in the clubwomen's movement of the late nineteenth century, as wealthier women attempted to forge links with working-class women.[74] As recently as 1913, working- and upper-class women argued that the New York shirtwaist strikes promoted a "magnificent demonstration of sisterhood."[75] The CUWS similarly aimed to forge unity between enfranchised and disenfranchised women. For example, following the 1914 midterm elections, when California, Oregon, and Kansas granted women state suffrage, the CUWS framed these successes as the result of a united, national effort: "The Eastern States, the Middle States—States from all parts of the Union sent help and workers."[76] In light of this national support, the CUWS called upon the new western voters to "join hands and to use their power for their unenfranchised sisters. It is making the women all over the United States one united body, with a unity of purpose that shall override all State and sectional selfishness, and which in its large vision shall embrace the whole field of suffrage work and shall make possible the subordination of local work whenever such subordination shall be helpful to the greater work of the whole."[77]

Here the CUWS rehearsed its militant vision for the subordination of local and state work to national work as it rhetorically constructed "a unity of purpose" for the "one united body" of US women. By uniting US white women as "sisters," this rhetoric allowed women to identify with each other across state lines and transcend differences in political power, thus fostering a collective identity for white women as members of a national community. Moreover, this appeal encouraged western women to assert their political agency and reenvision their ability to participate in and transform the American political process. Thus, the CUWS rhetoric of national unity and sisterhood promoted its militant agenda of challenging those with political power and motivating western women to vote against Democratic members of Congress.

The CUWS furthered a rhetoric of unity between enfranchised and disenfranchised US women by pointing to their common state of *national* disenfranchisement. Although almost four million women were enfranchised by 1914, they were limited to voting on state- and local-level policies, reifying the state limits of women's citizenship rights. Because the US Constitution did not protect their voting rights, CUWS members argued that state-level citizenship actually limited women's political freedom.[78] One *Suffragist* article said, "A woman fit to vote in the West, loses her right to full citizenship if she crosses a state line. But American men and women do not fall steadily on one spot of ground; they move freely from place to place in pursuit of business and family interests."[79] The CUWS thus positioned state-level citizenship as a violation of key American rights, including the pursuits of freedom and happiness. One CUWS member termed this violation "interstate discrimination."[80] Making western women voters aware of the limits of their state-level enfranchisement would ideally motivate them to participate in the anti-Democratic campaign of the CUWS. In attempt to do just that, a prominent CUWS organizer, Gail Laughlin, argued: "Citizenship is not an attribute of the states, but of the United States, and there is no sense or logic in recognizing the right and ability of women to vote on matters of national policy and then denying that suffrage is a national issue."[81] Laughlin concluded: "The women of the western states have power. They need only recognize that power."[82] Thus, the CUWS attempted to unite US women in a common state of national disenfranchisement by constructing state-level citizenship as a delimitation of national citizenship rights. As such, the CUWS encouraged western women to participate in its anti–Democratic Party campaign to protect their own rights as well as the rights of their disenfranchised counterparts.

The rhetorical efforts of the CUWS to unite the voices of US women helped prepare the organization to enter electoral politics as it worked to constitute a national base of constituents. This rhetorical act of political mimesis was made most visible through its May 2, 1914, nationwide demonstrations. On this day, national, state, and local CUWS organizers orchestrated and participated in suffrage demonstrations in more than a thousand US cities. Many demonstrations included between five and ten thousand activists.[83] The synchronicity of these demonstrations allowed the CUWS to literally and symbolically claim the united voices of US women. For example, the *Suffragist* described the event as "a whole great country making a simultaneous demand for the complete reform of the electorate."[84] By implying that this demand was made on behalf of "a whole great country," the CUWS positioned its followers as representatives of the US electorate, helping to position the CUWS as a force in US politics.

Expanding upon the constitutive forces of these national demonstrations and reflecting the emergence of a national base of supporters, the CUWS said: "All over the country, on hundreds of platforms the women's cause is being argued, and . . . hundreds of people are listening. Tomorrow every newspaper in the United States will rehearse the story of the women's demonstration, thus swelling the audience to millions. Never, in the history of the world, have women been as vocal as they are on this day in May."[85]

Believing that women's political voices were heard locally through street meetings and parades, and heard nationally through newspaper coverage, the CUWS constituted these women as part of the American polity with the political agency to participate in party politics. Constructing itself as a ubiquitous force, the CUWS enhanced its rationale for entering party politics, particularly with "millions" of potential supporters. Further legitimizing its demands, the CUWS declared: "We claim that the will of the people has been expressed in favor of nation-wide woman suffrage."[86] Moreover, the CUWS argued that this demand "comes from [each Congressman's] constituents, the people to whom he is responsible, and to whom he must look for re-election."[87] By constituting these demands as "the will of the people" and positioning US women as "constituents" with the power to elect or defeat particular congressmen, the CUWS empowered US women to participate in electoral politics as citizens and as agitators.

Sensationalizing Citizenship

The militant campaign of the CUWS further prepared US women to compete in party politics as they committed sensational acts of citizenship. These acts were performed as large numbers of white women mimicked citizenship rituals within local, state, and national spaces. In so doing, the CUWS functioned as a third party demanding the attention of the political mainstream while it achieved more political ends (for example, acquiring national and local support). The sensational acts of citizenship by the CUWS thus furthered its anti-Democratic campaign, as it exhibited both militant and traditional strategies.

As a key tenet of militancy, creating a sensation helped position the CUWS as a militant threat. Andrew Rosen argues, "Militant acts were those tactics sufficiently combative as to be widely regarded as shocking, and therefore worthy of comment."[88] Thus, as masses of women invaded male, deliberative spaces, they challenged the gendered limitations of political participation and in many cases provoked responses from congressmen. Paul considered these acts as part of the national anti-Democratic campaign of the CUWS. She said, "[I]f the party which has it in its power to pass our measure fails to act, then we will send organizers to every State and district where we can do effective work, and do all we can to defeat the representatives of that party."[89] These sensational acts helped establish the CUWS as a militant threat to "every State and district" and to the public-private limits on political participation.

Throughout the 1914 and 1916 anti-Democratic campaigns, these sensational acts allowed US white women to adopt the authority of fully enfranchised citizens while also attracting publicity. To greet Maryland state congressmen at the opening of the state's legislative session in 1914, for example, at least thirty Maryland suffragists marched twenty-eight miles from Baltimore to Annapolis, where they presented the legislators with a petition of over two hundred thousand signatures of Maryland voters. The suffragists created a sensation as they physically marched across the state over the course of a day and were escorted by a marching band to the state capitol. The *New York Times* reported on the "army" who persuaded anti-suffragist delegate Cyrus Cummings to present their petition to the state legislature.[90] But by positioning themselves as representatives of Maryland state citizens, the suffragists also mimicked the political authority of elected officials, and thus constituted themselves as political actors independent of men.[91]

To an extent, this militant commitment to agitate the US government represented the ways in which a third party presses its agenda into mainstream party politics from an outside position. Likewise, the CUWS sensationalized these acts of citizenship as invasions of male political spaces.[92] For example, on April 30, 1915, two hundred New York women visited Sen. James A. O'Gorman. The meeting was preceded by an open-air meeting, and a marching band "playing national and popular airs [as it] made its own appeal to the rapidly gathering crowd which assembled on the Sub-Treasury steps and packed the sidewalk and all available space within hearing distance of the two automobiles."[93] Moreover, the *Suffragist* noted that when they arrived at the meeting, the women "filled the spacious outer room" of O'Gorman's private office.[94] By focusing on the ways in which the suffragists occupied spaces on the street and in spaces reserved for the senator, the CUWS constructed itself as a force breaking down the public-private boundaries placed on women's political participation in the early twentieth century. Also, the CUWS created an overwhelming sense of presence, mirroring the growing national suffragist movement and promoting the collectivity of US women's political voices. Such activities occupied the pages of the *Suffragist* throughout the anti-Democratic campaign of the CUWS between 1913 and 1916; the *Suffragist* reported on at least twenty-four such delegations to state congressmen.[95]

The sensational acts of the CUWS allowed US women to assert their citizenship rights in everyday public spaces, and thus naturalized their demands for woman suffrage. For example, the CUWS demonstrations on May 2, 1914, inspired US women to participate in suffrage parades, demonstrations, and open-air meetings all over the country on this same day.[96] Regarding the reach of these demonstrations, the *Suffragist* described women who lived outside of urban areas as "timid about demonstrating their faith" and "afraid to speak, especially on the streets, where all causes must be argued before they can win."[97] Here, the militancy of the CUWS shone through as it politicized "the streets" as the ideal place to engage in deliberative acts. This reference to "the streets" created the perception that CUWS members were omnipresent, while it also challenged the idea that women in the streets, particularly women who voiced political demands, openly violated gendered beliefs about a woman's "proper place." By encouraging women to infiltrate these public spaces, the CUWS inspired women to assert their political agency and redefine the gendered limits of public and political activity.

Last, these sensational acts positioned the CUWS as a threat to a major political party. The *Suffragist* said, "[The demonstrations] will certainly prove to the Democratic party that there is no section of the country where women are not actively campaigning."[98] Thus, the CUWS's sensational acts of citizenship allowed the organization to exert its militancy in political spaces while gaining national and local appeal. As women participated in acts of campaigning, they enacted the citizenship rights they demanded through the framework of a political party. By doing so on local levels, CUWS members created a sense of ubiquity that helped naturalize woman suffrage; as the article concluded, they created an "overwhelming public opinion in favor of real democracy."[99] As these sensational acts elevated the CUWS's local and state efforts into national efforts for woman suffrage, the organization inched closer to mimetically forming its own political party.

Mimicking Deliberative Acts

Prior to the official formation of its women's political party, the CUWS mimicked rhetorical acts of deliberation in order to liken its members to popularly elected officials and party leaders. These mimetic acts of deliberation reflected a militant assumption of political leadership within legislative arenas while it also helped constitute the CUWS as a player in national party politics. Such acts included the presentation of petitions to every member of Congress by 531 suffrage "delegates" representing every congressional district in the nation.[100] Likewise, two elected CUWS "envoys" took a cross-country road trip to Washington, D.C., during which they accumulated more than five hundred thousand signatures on a single petition more than eighteen thousand feet in length.[101] The following discusses how these two mimetic acts of deliberation helped position the CUWS as a legitimate political force.

On May 9, 1914, as participants gathered in Washington, D.C., from all areas of the country to present US congressional members with their suffrage petitions, CUWS leaders voiced these demands as though they were the appointed representatives of the US electorate. In a parade much like the one held the year before, thousands of women marched through the streets of Washington, D.C., to the Capitol. There, the chosen 531 delegates marched up the Capitol steps into the rotunda, where eleven senators and eleven representatives enthusiastically received them. From there, the suffragists delivered their petitions to their respective legislators.[102] Of the demonstration, the *Suffragist* reported: "It has to inform the Congress of the United States that in every Congressional District in every State in the Union, men and women, their constituents, have met and have bade them pass the suffrage amendment now before Congress, and to do it without unnecessary delay. The really important part of the May 9th procession will be the delegates from the Congressional districts. All the rest of the procession will be merely an escort of those women who go to the Capitol to present the resolutions adopted all over the country on May 2nd."[103]

As "delegates," CUWS members constructed themselves as party officials chosen to carry the demands of US "men and women" and voice them in the deliberative spaces of the Capitol. This rhetorical act of political mimesis endowed these CUWS representatives with political legitimacy, while it also constituted women as members of a new political party complete with delegates and representatives to Congress.

CUWS leaders further mimicked acts of deliberation and more explicitly modeled party politics through the cross-country journey of two envoys. The two women, Sara Bard Field and Frances Joliffe, were the elected delegates from the first convention held for women voters. Electing Field and Joliffe as the CUWS delegates reinforced the construction of the CUWS as a political party, particularly in light of the concurrent rise of the primary system that nominated and elected candidates at party conventions. Because enfranchised women chose these representatives, the CUWS further positioned the envoys as elected officials. A writer for the *Suffragist* said, "Surely Congress cannot fail to heed the voice of the new power, the woman's vote, which is now sounding its message and sending its messengers 35,000 miles, to bear its demands to Washington."[104] The envoys were thus empowered by "the woman's vote" as "messengers" chosen to represent the voices of enfranchised women in Washington, D.C. This "new power" also constituted the women's solidarity and shared identities as party members. Demonstrating the strength of the CUWS constituency at a reception in New York, Alva Belmont noted: "Suffrage petitions have been submitted to Congress from time immemorial, but none that was backed by the strength of four million voters."[105]

The CUWS further constructed the envoys as party leaders by charging them with the duty of representing those previously unrepresented by major parties. For example, at the conclusion of the Convention of Women Voters, ten thousand attendees gathered to bid the envoys farewell. As CUWS organizer Margaret Anglin presented the envoys with the petition, she said, "This is not paper only upon which is written our demands . . . [but] women give their most eager aspiration, their hopes and their hearts to your keeping[,] realizing you are to be the voice crying to Congress to make straight the path of justice for women."[106] Like other party representatives, the envoys were charged with representing the "hopes" and "hearts" of those in need. However, the envoys were constructed as outsiders to Congress charged with "making straight the path of justice for women." Thus, like third-party leaders, the envoys were motivated by the American promise of democratic representation, wherein the voices of the unrepresented could elect their own officials for political empowerment.

The CUWS further engaged the deliberative process as party leaders by constructing the envoys' trip as a series of public meetings with political allies. Considering a recent shift in campaign strategies, which encouraged direct contact between party candidates and their constituents, conceiving of the envoys' trip as a publicity tour was particularly strategic. In Salt Lake City, for instance, Utah's governor William Spry, Mayor Samuel C. Park, and US Rep. Joseph Howell greeted the envoys on the state capitol steps.[107] In Lincoln, Nebraska, Gov. John H. Morehead met the envoys as a procession of ten cars carried them to the capitol building.[108] Similarly, in Chicago, one thousand people and fifty cars gathered as Mayor William Hale Thompson and his wife met with the women and signed the petition.[109] The envoys enjoyed receptions such as these in at least twenty-three states and forty-two cities.[110] These public greetings and endorsements of local and state politicians offered the envoys and their message political legitimacy and suggested that the envoys also possessed the political authority to engage other elected officials. Moreover, the public setting of these meetings reinforced the CUWS's expansion of women's roles in the public-political sphere.

The CUWS further bolstered the envoys' political legitimacy as these receptions were often construed as stages of public deliberation between political counterparts. Toward such ends, the envoys often met with reluctant senators and representatives who favored a state-by-state approach to woman suffrage or who opposed the initiative altogether. Nonetheless, the willingness on behalf of these officials to engage the envoys in such public and political settings reinforced the strength of the envoys' political leadership. For example, in Evanston, Wyoming, the envoys met with Republican senator Clarence D. Clark in the city's courthouse, where the senator stated that he believed strongly in the state method. According to the *Suffragist,* Sara Field "told the Senator and the people present of the untold waste of women's life force which the state campaigns entailed."[111] To this, Senator Clark "listened attentively" and reported that he "was amazed and interested to learn of the difficulties of that form of work."[112] When Field pressed the senator to approve a printed statement of his endorsement, he relented: "Say anything you like and I will stand for it."[113] By noting that the senator listened and then capitulated to the envoys' case, the CUWS portrayed this event as a deliberative process in which the envoys stood on equal political ground with other elected officials. By emphasizing that Field spoke to the senator as well as to "the people," the CUWS further constituted the envoys as public officials with the authority to represent the demands of "the people." While such rhetorical acts of political mimesis reflected the CUWS's militant assumption of political authority, they also bolstered the political legitimacy of the CUWS as a third party through the endorsements of male political leaders.

The CUWS extended its construction of the envoys as party leaders by sensationalizing these public meetings as political rallies, where the envoys were received as political celebrities speaking to their constituents. For example, in her report on their visit to Des Moines, Sara Field said, "we had more people to talk to than our voices could reach."[114] She added: "As our auto procession passed down the street, crowds gathered to see it; and the windows of every business[,] house[,] and office building were lined with kindly faces. Often there was applause and cheers; when these were lacking, there was a peculiar sort of earnest curiosity. . . . [At] earnest street meetings afterwards, gravely interested crowds attended and the newspapers gave large space. The whole city talked national suffrage for at least two days."[115]

Here, Field constructed herself and the envoys as an irresistible sight and as political celebrities, who came to Des Moines to inspire and mobilize their constituents to support a federal woman suffrage amendment. Field strengthened the envoys' celebrity attraction by depicting the audience as willing sympathizers with "kindly faces"; by extension, Field interpreted the audience's silence as "earnest curiosity" rather than as resistance. Field's report ultimately reflected the CUWS's militancy as she emphasized the envoys' ability to generate publicity and conversation in public spaces and in the press, spaces still often reserved for the political activities of men.

The envoys' rhetoric of political mimesis helped achieve the goal to nationalize local and state efforts as CUWS members physically canvassed the United States and amassed the collective voices of US citizens and supportive politicians. By the end of the envoys' journey, for example, the petition bore the signatures of every governor of every state the envoys visited except Nebraska, as well as hundreds of thousands of citizens.[116] Like the CUWS did with other rhetorical strategies to constitute a national base of party members, the envoys also promoted the notion that woman suffrage was a collective, nationwide movement. As part of their overall campaign to agitate members of Congress and to build a women's political party, the envoys allowed a space for US women to unite as politically empowered constituents.

In all, the CUWS worked to rhetorically unite all US women by constituting white women as part of the American people, inspiring them to participate in sensational acts of citizenship, and by mimicking acts of party leadership. These rhetorical strategies reflected the militant approach of the CUWS toward social change as it encouraged women to assume citizenship identities and assert their political agency with or without enfranchised citizenship rights. The CUWS further formed these citizenship identities as it constituted US women as political party members whose chosen representatives would voice their demands in local, state, and national deliberative spaces. Moreover, the militancy of the CUWS shone through as it encouraged CUWS members to occupy public and political spaces often reserved for men, mimicking the actions of male political leaders while also acting independently of men. Ultimately, the CUWS's construction of the envoys as elected officials helped launch the CUWS as an organized, political force in national politics.

FORMING A THIRD PARTY

Building upon the CUWS's mimetic enactment of political party strategies between 1913 and 1916, the organization officially created its own political party—the Woman's Party (WP)—in July 1916. Forming the WP helped codify its activist and political party strategies, positioning the CUWS as an even greater threat as the WP boasted the strength of its local organizational networks and state headquarters. The party was open to all women voters, and did not require that members pay dues.[117] Even the official formation of the WP mimicked typical political party behavior; the WP was launched at a CUWS convention in Chicago, at the same time that the Republican and Progressive national party conventions were taking place. Over one thousand women attended and contributed to the party's platform.[118] Yet, unlike a typical party that works to secure the election of party candidates, the primary goal of the WP was to defeat Democratic candidates in all twelve suffrage states. Moreover, the WP was careful not to endorse any particular candidate. Paul wrote to one organizer: "It seems to us that [we] gain more publicity by our campaign of opposition than we could by one of support."[119] Thus, the WP best resembled a third party as it was positioned in opposition to one of the mainstream political parties. Positioning the WP as a third party reinforced the CUWS's militant philosophy of sustained agitation while it also helped the CUWS achieve its ultimate goal of effecting policy change.

Reflecting the militant and traditional goals of the CUWS, Paul hoped the WP would enter national politics with the same political authority and forcefulness of a third party. Of the WP, Paul wrote: "We want it to be a new political party which will have the same significance as a factor in the coming election as had the Progressive Party when it was launched four years ago.

We hope that if the political leaders see the women voters are forming an independent party they will regard the suffrage question as a more serious one than they have considered it in the past."[120]

Clearly influenced by the meteoric success of the Progressive Party, the CUWS, with its mimetic formation of a third party, aimed to transform the question of woman suffrage into a legitimate political issue worthy of legislative attention.

Just as third parties threaten the political viability of major political parties, the WP was considered a weapon against political oppression. One WP leader said that the party was determined to inspire western women voters "to organize their political power and use it for the freedom of all women."[121] The militant underpinnings of the WP were further revealed as it constituted itself as a militaristic threat to the Democratic Party while campaigning at the Republican, Progressive, and Democratic national conventions. Here, the CUWS more forcefully employed warlike metaphors. For example, while at the Progressive and Republican Party conventions, Blatch advocated lobbying "every man on a committee or in a convention" in order to "fight the Democratic Party [from the] ground down."[122] Shortly after, at the Democratic National Convention, WP member Rheta Childe Dorr described the WP as a "brigade." She continued: "The siege of St. Louis began on the morning of June tenth. . . . We seized, without resistance on the manager's part, a conspicuous corner of the lobby."[123] Constructing themselves as a part of a "siege" on the Democrats, and as soldiers who "seized" part of the Democrats' convention space, WP members constituted the WP as a militant threat to the Democratic Party. In so doing, the WP's political legitimacy as a third party became a vehicle for constituting the CUWS's militant identity and motivating its members to agitate the Democratic Party as though engaged in an all-out war.

The WP further mimicked third-party politics by forging alliances with other national political parties to help defeat Democrats.[124] Like a single-issue third party, the WP was centered on earning women's national citizenship rights by defeating Democratic candidates. As such, the WP could potentially benefit other parties by driving Democratic voters to endorse other candidates. For example, Paul advised one organizer in Phoenix, Arizona, to use "Socialist, Progressive, Republican and Prohibition newspapers" in order to get the WP's "press bulletins into nearly every part of the state."[125] Eventually former Progressive leader Theodore Roosevelt and Republican presidential candidate Charles Evans Hughes publicly endorsed the WP. Allying with other national political parties strengthened the political legitimacy of the WP and exerted pressure on the Democratic Party to endorse national woman suffrage.

Much in the same way a splinter candidate is enlisted to head a third party, the CUWS drafted Blatch to lead the WP's campaign in all twelve suffrage states.[126] Blatch had been a supporter of the CUWS since its inception, but had also expressed disapproval of Paul and Burns's nationwide campaign, particularly since the New York campaign of the CUWS had often competed with Blatch's own New York campaign.[127] Yet, Blatch's prominence as a state suffrage leader was an invaluable asset to the CUWS. Her willingness to work with the organization suggested that the strength of the US suffrage movement was transitioning toward a national movement—strength that was harnessed in the WP.

Blatch's rhetorical leadership positioned the WP as a politically legitimate force in electoral politics. Again, while the WP was poised to disrupt mainstream party politics, it also functioned to effect constitutional change. In an appeal to a leader of the Colorado Democratic Party, for example, Blatch grounded her argument for a national suffrage amendment in constitutional terms: "The National Constitution must be made to protect women as it protects men. As our fundamental law reads today, the political rights of even enfranchised women are not protected for in the Fourteenth Amendment[;] protection is extended to *male* inhabitants only and in the Fifteenth Amendment the word 'sex' is excluded. The demand which the women are making for an amendment to the United States Constitution, concerns enfranchised women quite as deeply as it concerns the disenfranchised."[128]

Blatch's appeal exuded the equal-rightist philosophy of the CUWS toward woman suffrage, stemming from the liberal tradition in US politics that assumed all are born with the rights to individual freedom and voluntary citizenship. These ideals were thought to motivate the Radical Republicans in their push for the ratification of the Civil War amendments, which empowered African Americans' citizenship rights. By recalling these amendments, Blatch relied on the more radical notion of equal rights and compared the oppression of black men to that of white women in order to make a compelling argument for a federal woman suffrage amendment. Considering that Blatch's audience was a white male politician, such a legal argument buttressed the WP's political goal of altering the US Constitution, targeting those with the political agency to achieve such constitutional change.

Blatch further revealed her ability to ingratiate the WP into mainstream US electoral politics as she also made arguments for women's rights that reinforced traditional gender roles. For example, after Paul attempted to arrange some CUWS speakers to tour through the western states, Blatch replied, "A tear rolling down a cheek of a Democratic woman with a few words from her, however stumbling, expressing her profound regret at not being able to support her party, would do more to move the political committees and conventions than the most unanswerable logic of the most eloquent woman coming from outside the state."[129] Blatch revealed her nuanced understanding of state-level politics, as she preferred that Democratic women speak within their native states. Blatch also argued that a pathetic appeal would be more forceful than a logical appeal, and, in doing so, she tacitly perpetuated the construction of women as more emotional and irrational. By invoking the image of a "tear rolling down a cheek of a Democratic woman," Blatch positioned women in a subordinate and vulnerable position, nearly pleading for support from other political organizations. Thus, Blatch's rhetorical leadership reflected a combination of more radical and traditional gendered appeals, the latter of which potentially undermined the political agency asserted by these Democratic women as they demanded national citizenship rights. Blatch's gendered suggestion, however, also revealed a deeper understanding of the CUWS's male audience, who may have been less threatened by stereotypical womanly behavior than by the CUWS's militancy. Such beliefs persisted; for example, one Ohio CUWS organizer reported hearing from "[m]en who don't want to see women in 'Machine politics.'"[130]

The WP's use of more traditional arguments helped legitimize the CUWS campaign and curbed the perception that it was a militant threat. For example, an article in the *Washington Times* said, "The Woman's Party . . . is not a fantastic dream of sex solidarity, but a practical political influence, a balance of power movement, which is a factor in national politics and must be reckoned with."[131] Thus, the creation of the WP eschewed the potential militant threat posed by the rhetorical efforts of the CUWS to constitute female "solidarity" and instead established the CUWS as an authoritative presence in national politics. Even prior to the WP's inception, the party-centered strategies of the CUWS were regarded as a reflection of the political situation. Spencer Miller Jr. of the *San Francisco Bulletin* wrote of the CUWS: "Political party pressure, far from being indictable, is highly commendable. It is not an attempt to embarrass a party, but rather to vitalize the contact between the people and the party. . . . [The CUWS] is an adaptation of twentieth century political machinery to twentieth century political conditions."[132] Again, the CUWS was regarded as a legitimate force in national politics. Moreover, Miller constituted CUWS members as part of the "people" as they attempted to "vitalize" political parties.

Simultaneously, however, the WP helped establish the CUWS as a militant presence. Part of the CUWS's militant campaign was to empower women to assert their political agency and function as independent political actors. Moreover, the CUWS's militancy worked to politicize everyday spaces of women's lives by encouraging women to demand citizenship rights in public. For example, on the day of the 1916 congressional and presidential elections, the WP organized women to take posts at twenty-one hundred polling booths in Chicago alone. Many of these women reported converting fifty to a hundred women voters before they cast their ballots.[133] Creating this sense of ubiquity, particularly on such a large scale and in such public spaces, reflected the militant commitment to challenge the private-public divide.

The CUWS further boasted of its militancy as it considered the WP's campaign a success less so because of the number of defeated Democratic candidates, and more so because it posed a threat to the major political parties and forced discussion of the issue. Of the WP's campaign, the *Suffragist* said, "It put the Democrats on the defensive. It forced them to declare greater and greater enthusiasm for national woman suffrage. The election ended with Democrats and Republicans vying with each other as to which was more devoted to the enfranchisement of women."[134] Here, the CUWS credited itself for spurring political debate about woman suffrage and contributing to its prominence as a political issue. While Democrats lost sixteen House seats and Wilson secured the presidency with 158 fewer electoral votes than he did in his 1912 election, the CUWS declared: "We did not care who won . . . we were simply pro-woman."[135]

The WP's constitutive force, nonetheless, was bound up with its instrumental successes. For example, the Democratic State Central Committees of Arizona and Idaho endorsed woman suffrage, as did many state Republican committees.[136] The WP's ultimate coup, however, was pressuring the Democratic National Convention to endorse woman suffrage. Section 20 of the party's platform said, "We recommend the extension of the franchise to the women of the country by the States upon the same terms as men."[137] Although the plank recommended a state-by-state strategy, it represented the first time the Democratic Party officially endorsed woman suffrage. Moreover, Jeannette Rankin of Montana secured a Republican seat in the House with two thousand more votes than her Democratic opponent.[138] To the CUWS, Rankin's triumph as the first woman elected to the US Congress symbolized the growing success of the woman suffrage movement and was a reflection of its efforts to mobilize Montana women to vote.[139] Constructing the WP as a force in national politics coupled with the growing presence of women in such spaces thus motivated the CUWS to escalate its militant maneuverings after the 1916 elections.

CONCLUSION: A TURN TOWARD THE PRESIDENCY

In sum, the anti-Democratic campaign strategies that the CUWS employed between 1913 and 1916 helped constitute women's citizenship identities by mobilizing US white women to participate in a national movement through the mimetic adoption of third-party politics. While the campaign helped form the group's militant identity, it also worked against such a "militant" label because their members engaged the rituals of party politics. Nonetheless, toward the end of 1916, when the Democratic Party was losing favor in Congress, the CUWS would turn its militant campaign toward the newly re-elected Democratic president.

The anti-Democratic campaign shaped a militant identity by casting it as an extension of the militant tradition in the woman suffrage movement. For example, prior to the envoys' dispatch in 1915, Gail Laughlin likened the CUWS campaign to Susan B. Anthony's militant refusal to pay a hundred-dollar fine for voting in the 1872 presidential election. She concluded, "When you hear something called 'militant' condemned, you will remember that nothing worth while has ever been won except by those who are willing to sacrifice freedom, labor or love for it."[140] Laughlin took pride in the organization's militant acts as she considered resistance to the CUWS part of the process toward achieving women's full citizenship rights.

Some suffragists, however, resisted embracing a militant identity. In 1915, Clara Ueland, a Minnesota suffragist, argued: "I do not consider them 'militant.' It is not militant to send delegations to congressmen and to the president. These are entirely legitimate methods."[141] Her inclination to eschew a militant label suggested that many, even supporters of the CUWS, considered militancy a more threatening approach toward achieving woman suffrage. Throughout the campaign to agitate Congress, the CUWS often positioned itself as a nonthreatening or "legitimate" organization, which helped broaden its social appeal and gain institutional support. The CUWS, however, did not shy away from directly challenging the limits placed on women's political participation, particularly as it committed sensational acts of citizenship and worked to position itself as a threat to the Democratic Party. Thus, the militant-driven campaign encouraged women to participate in the suffrage movement, and yet to resist doing so as self-proclaimed militants. As the CUWS continued its fight for woman suffrage in late 1916 and throughout 1917, this resistance to militancy translated into greater resistance to the organization's more ardently militant protest strategies.

Whether or not the CUWS openly committed acts in the name of militancy, its anti-Democratic campaign faced vociferous opposition from other suffrage leaders. Former NAWSA president Carrie Chapman Catt, for example, felt that the CUWS jeopardized the state-by-state campaigns of the NAWSA. She said, "What is good for one part of the country may not be good for the other. . . . [The CUWS's] only purpose is to create a disturbance, [and] it will be absolutely impossible for us to accomplish any good work."[142] Perhaps reflecting the prominence of third-party politics in the current political context, Catt compared the CUWS to a group of defective party members. She argued: "The division of a party almost invariably means the victory of the other at election and history has proved this so many times that they know what they are about when they are pleased at the division in the opposing ranks. What is true about political parties is even more true of a reform movement like ours. Our strength lies in a united band of women demanding the same thing."[143]

Catt's opposition showed that the identity of the CUWS as a third party did not represent the woman suffrage movement as a whole. Moreover, Catt's criticism reinforced the ideological differences between the CUWS and the NAWSA. The militant campaign of the CUWS worked to defeat the election or reelection of congressmen instead of focusing on the more moderate approach of winning state referenda or electing pro-suffrage candidates. The militancy of the CUWS, however, was motivated by the notion that these moderate approaches did not expedite social change.

To an extent, Catt's reservations were justified. Because the CUWS aimed to agitate the Democratic Party as a whole, its campaign threatened the election or reelection of many suffrage-supporting Democrats in 1914 and 1916. As such, some suffragists considered its work counterproductive. A Colorado suffragist accused the CUWS of being "very hostile" to a suffrage-supporting Democrat, US Senator Charles Thomas, and creating "a vicious fight" for his reelection.[144] Harriot Taylor Upton of Ohio argued that the 1914 CUWS campaign had contributed to the defeat of the state's suffrage referendum.[145] Similarly, Emma Haley Frazelle blamed "the foolishness of the Congressional Union and the Woman's Party" for dividing Oregon women between presidential candidates Hughes and Wilson, and thereby, "deffinately [*sic*] injuring the cause of suffrage."[146] Considering the more militant approach of the CUWS toward social change, such backlash was to be expected.

Within suffrage circles, others credited the militant campaign for mobilizing and uniting US women toward a federal amendment. For example, Clara Ueland wrote about her decision to "co-operate with the Congressional Union" instead of with the NAWSA: "I am bound to say that the young women who are working for the Congressional Union here have done, in a vigorous and direct way, some very effectual suffrage work. In about two weeks they have visited ten counties and more than fifteen towns, holding parlor and street meetings, and have formed deputations to visit three of our Congressmen."[147]

Here, the efforts of the CUWS to mobilize US women were perceived as more "effectual" than those of the NAWSA. Moreover, these "vigorous and direct" efforts were identified as "parlor and street meetings" and visits with congressmen—all acts that moved masses of women into public and political spaces, thus expanding women's citizenship identities within the nation-state beyond the domestic sphere. This recognition of these public tactics helped to feminize these masculine spaces and to push toward the possibility of a national suffrage amendment.

The growing legitimacy of the CUWS must be understood, at least in part, as a derivative of the CUWS members' privileged identities as mostly white, upper- and middle-class women. Considering that most political parties at that time—even parties centered on empowering marginalized groups—were led by white males, the CUWS with its WP could more easily transition into US party politics and be received as a legitimate political presence due to the whiteness of its members.[148] Although many disempowered and marginalized groups participated in organized movements, many lacked the racial privilege to compete as their own political parties. The perceived racial inferiority of these groups also contributed to their oppressed and marginalized position in US society, which in turn, helps explain why most of them did not possess state-level suffrage at this time. Thus, without the "whiteness" associated with ideal US citizenship, these marginalized groups faced opposition toward earning state- and federal-level suffrage and the authority to enter national party politics. Omitting discussion of African American women's rights in their discourse during these campaign years most likely helped increase the legitimacy of the CUWS, but, again, demonstrated the organization's limited and expedient vision of citizenship rights.

Due, in part, to the somewhat privileged position of the CUWS in US politics, the organization's formation of a political party challenged the limits of women's political participation in the nation-state and represented a legitimate threat to the Democratic Party. The CUWS's assumption of political power not only motivated the formation of the WP, but inspired women to agitate members of Congress between 1913 and 1916. As a reflection of its militancy, the CUWS aimed to rhetorically unite western white women with disenfranchised women, to mobilize white women in every US congressional district, and to participate as members of a political party. Taken together, these rhetorical strategies worked to empower US white women to assert their political agency and redefine their citizenship identities as independent national citizens.

Nonetheless, the organization's battle for a woman suffrage amendment was not over. The reelection of President Wilson in 1916 represented a large defeat for the CUWS, as he was the only presidential candidate to not publicly endorse national woman suffrage. Wilson won the electoral votes in all but two suffrage states, and, more so, these wins were attributed to women's support of Wilson's neutral position on the war.[149] However, the organization was encouraged by the Democrats' loss of the majority in the House and loss of two Senate seats. Given that the Republicans now represented the majority in the House, the focus of the CUWS on agitating Democratic members of Congress almost seemed futile.[150] The demonstrated strength and influence of President Wilson, however, encouraged the CUWS to direct most of its militant efforts toward the office of the presidency.

4

Mimesis and the Rhetorical Presidency

The Silent Sentinels

The Congressional Union for Woman Suffrage (CUWS) waged a militant campaign against Democratic members of Congress between 1913 and 1916 in a national effort to pressure Democrats to support a federal woman suffrage amendment. Through its mimetic adoption of third-party strategies and the subsequent formation of the Woman's Party, the CUWS worked to constitute US women as political actors and provide a reenvisioning of women's roles in the nation-state.

Following the 1916 elections, the suffragists celebrated the return of a Republican majority to the House of Representatives, but faced the intransigence of the Democratic Party in the Senate and in the presidential office. The simultaneous reelection of a Democratic president and the election of eighteen Republican members of Congress suggested that Wilson was able to engage the US electorate in a way that defied party loyalties.[1] While many attribute Wilson's reelection to his promise to keep the United States out of World War I, it could also be attributed to the enhanced dialogue initiated by Wilson as he helped transition the presidency from a constitutional office to a more rhetorical one.

Wilson's "rhetorical presidency" emerged as presidents, more so than their nineteenth-century counterparts, began going over the heads of Congress and targeting the American people with persuasive appeals in the process of promoting their own political agendas.[2] Within the context of the Progressive Era, the rhetorical presidency, in part, empowered and constituted the political voice of the American people. As such, President Wilson transformed his presidential role into a speaker and activist for the people as

FIGURE 4.1. The "Silent Sentinels" at the White House gates (1917). Reproduced courtesy Harris & Ewing Collection, Library of Congress, LC-DIG-hec-07526.

he also worked to craft a unified nationalist identity. Wilson's efforts were undergirded by his progressive beliefs; he sought to undo the abuses sustained by industrialization and political machinery by regenerating a participatory democracy and Anglo-Saxon culture.[3] In the process, Wilson ushered forth a more empowering model of US citizenship.

Scholars have noted the paradox of Wilson's simultaneous promotion of a unified nationalist identity and restriction of citizenship rights for women, African Americans, American Indians, and immigrants. Wilson's centrist progressivism perpetuated a homogenous construction of the ideal citizen as white (preferably of western or northern European descent) and of course male.[4] Considering that Wilson once argued that immigrants "poured the poison of disloyalty into the very arteries of our national life . . . [and] must be crushed out," it might not be surprising that he agreed to the restricted employment of African Americans in the federal government and banned Chinese and Japanese immigrants from the "Asiatic Barred Zone" during World War I.[5] Addressing the "threat" posed by immigrants, who represented one-third of the nation's hundred million inhabitants, Wilson endorsed educational programs that "Americanized" and disciplined immigrants to abandon their national and cultural heritages.[6] Despite Wilson's continued resistance to a federal woman suffrage amendment, suffragists—particularly white activists—began to see the political potential for expanding Wilson's empowered and homogenous construction of citizenship to include women.

As Wilson promoted himself as the leader of his party and the United States, the CUWS began shifting its energies toward agitating the president. In the later stages of the 1916 presidential and congressional elections, the CUWS and the Woman's Party began transforming their anti-Democratic stance into an anti-Wilson campaign. In September, for instance, Alva Belmont twice referred to the Democrats as "Mr. Wilson and his party" in a letter to another CUWS member. Similarly, the *Suffragist* declared that "the effort of the Woman's Party will be directed toward the defeat of Mr. Wilson and the national Democratic ticket."[7] The pressure of the CUWS on Wilson was motivated partly by Charles Evans Hughes's endorsement of woman suffrage in the 1916 election. The Republican Party's presidential candidate was the first major-party candidate to endorse the measure (former president Roosevelt had endorsed a federal suffrage amendment as the Progressive Party's candidate in 1912). Hughes's support then compelled Alice Paul to instigate "an equally vigorous [campaign] upon the President and the democratic leaders" to endorse woman suffrage.[8] Thus, the turn of the CUWS toward agitating the president could be considered a reflection of the increased viability of presidential support, as well as a response to the rise of the rhetorical presidency. Consequently, in early 1917, the CUWS initiated an intensified anti-Wilson campaign by merging with its Woman's Party, which collectively became the National Woman's Party (NWP).[9]

This chapter traces how the NWP agitated President Wilson and constituted women's citizenship identities in the nation-state through its mimetic adoption of Wilson's presidential authority between 1917 and 1919. In addition to the ritualistic and traditional rhetorics of political mimesis discussed in previous chapters, this analysis finds that the NWP protests exhibited the mimetic forms of parody and quotation in these latter stages of its campaign. Specifically, the NWP parodied the president's appeals to the US public through silent protest, and, through the mimetic form of quotation, the NWP espoused Wilson's citizenship ideals as their own, and more particularly, as those of soldiers liberating the oppressed. This discussion of women's citizenship identities is guided by the theoretical and historical underpinnings of gendered nationalism and gendered militarism.

GENDER, NATION, AND WAR

As the president worked to shape a nationalist identity, he conceptualized the nation in gendered terms. From the time of the Revolutionary War, nationalist ideals have been sustained by gender ideologies that simultaneously constrained women's contributions to the nation-state from within the domestic sphere and conflated ideal citizenship behavior with men's participation in the public-political sphere.[10] Moreover, women were the legal and social dependents of men, thus restricting their abilities to assert their citizenship rights in order to fully contribute to the nation. Thus, maleness and masculinity were associated with democracy, strength, and independence while femaleness and femininity were typically associated with weakness and dependence.[11] While such gendered associations were loosening by the early twentieth century, particularly as women's political participation expanded during the Progressive Era, the era's revival of Anglo-Saxon ideals reified the white male as the model citizen. Wilson's tasks of uniting the nation and negotiating the threat of an international conflict shaped the gendered ways in which he constructed the nation.

Wilson's Gendered Nationalism

As Wilson addressed the US citizenry in his nationalist treatise *The New Freedom*, he relied on a gendered understanding of independence and dependence. He wrote: "If any part of our people want to be wards, if they want to have guardians put over them, if they want to be taken care of, if they want to be children, patronized by the government, why, I am sorry, because it will sap the manhood of America. But I don't believe they do. I believe they want to stand on the firm foundation of law and right and take care of themselves. I, for my part, don't want to belong to a nation, I believe that I do not belong to a nation that needs to be taken care of by guardians. I want to belong to a nation, and I am proud that I do belong to a nation, that knows how to take care of itself."[12] Wilson advocated a more decentralized government by arguing that a centralized government would threaten "the manhood of America," aligned here with "law and right" and independence, or the ability "to take care of itself." Following Wilson's logic, the citizens of such an overbearing government would be treated as "wards" and "children"—those in society who held the same dependent and disempowered status as women. Such a gendered framework provided Wilson with the vocabulary to articulate his economic policy as part of America's project to sustain its independence.

Rhetorically, such gendered principles shape nationalist discourse, particularly as leaders of the nation need to promote measures to "protect" the nation or to vilify others as a "threat" to the nation. Often nations acquire a gendered identity, most significantly as a woman—as something pure, to be cherished and protected. Seeing the nation as "mother" positions the nation's people as children, who, in times of danger, need to be protected at all costs.[13] The nation can also be constructed as a male—"as a father who is virile and represents authority, and must be obeyed even to the point of sacrificing one's life."[14] Such gendering helps justify protective measures, including violence and war, as duty and honor to one's family. Considering the nation in familial and specifically gendered terms is nothing new. As Jean Bethke Elshtain and others have noted, citizenship offers membership to a national community or family.[15] In fact, along with modern conceptualizations of nations as cultural communities bound by the imagination, scholars have pointed to some nations that are primordial communities comprised of the descendents of peoples bound by geographical location.[16] While the United States is not a primordial community, the idea that the nation is an extended family is a key rhetorical construct in nationalist discourse.

Gendering the nation often naturalizes women's subordinated and disenfranchised status. Because women biologically reproduce the nation, they come to symbolize a nation's culture, or symbolize "carriers of the collectivity's 'honour' and as its intergenerational reproducers of culture."[17] When women's roles as mothers become glorified, their bodies come to signify their reproductive abilities; thus, an attack on a woman is equated to an attack on a nation.[18] In this sense, women become like the nation—the protected property of men. Further, once these properties have been trespassed or violated, violence and aggression in response are justified. The irony here, however, is that while women are considered sacred to a nation and worthy of defense, they are not necessarily considered worthy of the citizenship rights needed to defend themselves. Furthermore, considering women only for their ability to reproduce a nation highlights a fundamental belief that poses the greatest challenge to acquiring women's full citizenship rights: "Women are determined by biology, men by their free wills."[19] As such, the collusion of Wilson's rhetorical presidency and his gendered constructions worked against the NWP's goal of empowering women to assert their political voices and citizenship rights.

Gendered Militarism and World War I

The gendered dimensions of nation and citizenship become most prominent in the context of war. In his discussion of how an individual's identity is bound to national identity, Otto Bauer said that "the idea of nation is bound up with the idea of my ego."[20] Because citizenship has primarily been defined in male terms, this "ego" is similarly masculine. Tamar Mayer argues, "It is men who are generally expected to defend the 'moral consciousness' and the 'ego' of the nation. . . . Their own 'ego' becomes at stake in national conflicts."[21] As such, war becomes an arena in which national and gendered identities are threatened, contested, and violently defended. The military, Betty A. Reardon argues, becomes "the unchecked manifestation of patriarchy as the *overt* and *explicit* mode of governance."[22] As such, the military is the means through which a nation maintains and exerts control over others and defends the male "ego" of America.[23]

In light of the masculine ego of war and nation, soldiers become the embodiment of "military manhood" or "heroic masculinity" and are thus, constructed in opposition to womanhood and femininity.[24] Such dichotomous logic promotes the use of the "protection myth" or the notion that the man-soldier must protect women and children from "the Other." Ironically, as J. Ann Tickner argues, 90 percent of war casualties are women and children.[25] Moreover, as the protection myth relies on the construction of weak women, the act of rape comes to symbolize the violation of a nation's purity.[26] The threat of rape can also be used to vilify an enemy. In World War I, reports of German soldiers mutilating, raping, and killing Belgian and French civilians circulated throughout the United States; eventually, Germany's invasion was described as "the rape of Belgium" and depicted through posters of German soldiers dragging women out of burning villages by their hair.[27] While these constructions worked to demonize an enemy, they reified the masculinity of war by conflating women and nations as the weak and vulnerable properties of men.[28]

The masculine/feminine dichotomies endemic to war discourse (protector/protected; invader/invaded; penetrator/penetrated) help link traditional gender roles to the preservation of the nation's security. Erika A. Kuhlman argues that during World War I "conventional images of weak, vulnerable femininity and strong, protective masculinity reverberated throughout all levels of American society . . . in the halls of Congress, within the pages of the press, among circles of progressive reformers, and even among pacifists who earlier had recorded their fundamental opposition to war."[29] These gendered ideals were visible earlier, during the Spanish-American War, which, according to Kristin L. Hoganson, solidified the construction of the soldier as the embodiment of male physical prowess.[30] War, however, is often a time when gender roles are in flux; women often take up jobs in the absence of men and are mobilized to contribute to the domestic war effort as though they were soldiers. Women's enhanced social and political participation during the Progressive Era exacerbated this fluctuation in traditional gender roles. Such gender complexities were reflected in World War I propaganda posters, which "depicted women as ethereal angels of liberty or as mothers sacrificing for their sons" while they also "showed uniformed women as active participants in war (although, significantly, never in combat)."[31] These shifting gendered identities "produced widespread anxiety among men and women" as the nation geared up for war.[32]

Such anxieties persisted in the early twentieth century despite the long history of women engaging in combat and serving integral roles in the military. Typically, women's military duties were often limited to those of nurses, laundresses, and cooks—occupations that were considered in line with feminine roles.[33] Beliefs in women's natural mothering abilities often provided women the means to enter the hyper-masculine sphere of war and the military as mothers protecting their children.[34] In many US wars, however, women fought alongside their male family members or even passed as male soldiers.[35] In World War I, twenty-five thousand American women participated as members of the Navy (as "Yeomanettes") and the Marines, and in numerous relief capacities. These women performed more duties than women in previous wars—as physicians, nurses, dentists, therapists, interpreters, translators, decoders, and statisticians. Although most women remained stateside, ten thousand nurses served in England and France, while others traveled to the Balkans, Russia, and the Near East.[36]

As he negotiated the gendered anxieties of war and citizenship, President Wilson eventually endorsed federal woman suffrage as a reward for women's contributions to the war.[37] Historically war allowed minority groups to demonstrate their loyalty to the nation. Revolutionary War veterans who were otherwise ineligible to vote were granted the franchise; similarly, arguments for the Fifteenth Amendment were motivated by the soldiering efforts of African American men.[38] Such precedents empowered women to assert their citizenship rights in ways that resisted the construction of women as caretakers and mothers. In her study of women in World War I, Kimberly Jensen argues that women at arms "claimed fuller female citizenship" and "challenged the traditional gender bargain of men as the Protectors and women as the Protected: women armed to defend the state could defend themselves against the violence of invasion and also domestic violence."[39] Women physicians and nurses also made arguments for equal citizenship rights in order to challenge the masculine hostility of the military and to foster solidarity with female war victims abroad.[40]

Women also made arguments for fully enfranchised citizenship rights based on their domestic war efforts. Most of these efforts were extensions of women's increased participation in the political, social, and reform movements of the Progressive Era, which, as Jensen argues, "provided strong credentialing for the participatory thread of citizenship."[41] Hundreds of thousands of working-class women took factory jobs to produce war supplies and munitions, enduring long hours, accidents, and even deathly explosions.[42] The sharp increase in women factory workers motivated the creation of the Women's Division of the US Department of Labor, which functioned to protect women from poor working conditions. Middle- and upper-class women formed relief organizations, such as the Vacation War Relief Committee, the Surgical Dressings Committee, the National Patriotic Relief Society, and the National League for Women's Service.[43] The government formed the Committee on Women's Defense Work as part of the Council of National Defense, and the committee worked, in part, to recruit southern African American women into the war trades and to help replace some of the jobs left by the three hundred sixty-eight thousand African American men serving in the war.[44] African American women ran multiple volunteer organizations to support the war, including the Women's Volunteer Aid Society, the African American YWCA, the Woman's Loyal Union, and booster clubs throughout the nation.[45]

Thus, while the war perpetuated and challenged traditional gender roles and identities, it also provided US women the grounds to demand equal citizenship rights. Women's domestic war service could easily be justified as extensions of women's domesticity or as a temporary, wartime necessity. Women's participation in the military, however, represented a gender paradox that often resulted in hostility and resistance. As women asserted their identities as soldiers, they obfuscated the premise upon which men took to battle. If women could defend themselves, why did men need to fight? Resistance to soldiering women in World War I resulted in men "challenging, denigrating, and demonizing the woman warrior."[46] The woman soldier ideal was not limited to women serving in the military, however; thousands of American women at home joined defense clubs, such as the Women's Defense Club of Maine, and trained as soldiers "to shoot, and shoot straight."[47]

Although these women never engaged in combat, a "grassroots movement to promote the female use of guns during the First World War" took hold as gun manufacturers and rifle associations argued that "self-defense is part of national defense."[48] As such, the empowering forces of the Progressive Era, the liberating potential of wartime gender roles, and the onset of war hysteria offered the NWP the rhetorical resources to assert their citizenship rights and to mimic war discourses that glorified the male soldier's fight for democracy abroad.

President Wilson and the NWP

On March 4, 1917, the NWP protested against President Wilson on the day of his second inauguration ceremony. Unlike the NWP's 1913 parade held the day before Wilson's first inauguration ceremony, the parade's marchers concluded by circling the White House ten times.[49] Despite freezing rain and high winds, the "business women, labor women, socialist women, and many professions, trades and orders," did not relent; the president, however, refused to acknowledge the women at his gates.[50] Perhaps the reelected president had grown weary of the NWP's pointed protests. Four months earlier, on December 4, 1916, a few NWP members disrupted Wilson's annual message to Congress. A yearly report describes the scene: "At the last moment in President Wilson's speech when he was discussing the rights of the Philippines and the Porto [*sic*] Ricans, [we] dropped over the rail a gleaming yellow banner bearing the words: 'Mr. President, what will you do for woman suffrage?'"[51] Heckling the president marked a new chapter in the NWP's militant campaign for woman suffrage.[52]

Since 1913, Alice Paul and Lucy Burns had recognized President Wilson's potential to command the Democratic Party's support of the suffrage movement. An article in the *Suffragist* argued, "The President has demonstrated that he is more than a 'titular' leader of his party. The party responds to his leadership."[53] By 1915, members of Congress similarly recognized this power. Sen. Asle J. Gronna (R-ND) instructed the NWP: "Turn your guns on President Wilson. He is the real center of power."[54] In fact, the president had established a reputation for being able to push progressive legislation through Congress with great expediency.[55] In 1914, for example, after the passage of the Underwood Tariff Act, the Federal Reserve Act, and the Panama Canal tolls repeal act, the NWP argued that Wilson "not only initiated legislation, but has actually forced it through when it was in actual contradiction to a plank in the Democratic platform. . . . What the President has done in all these matters, he can do with regard to Suffrage. He has greater power than any other person or group of persons to secure the passage of the Suffrage amendment."[56] Similarly, the NWP asserted that woman suffrage was consistent with Wilson's progressive legislative program as he pushed for the Adamson eight-hour workday act, the Keating-Owen Child Labor Act, the Rural Credits Act, and the Workingmen's Compensation Act.[57]

Despite the empowering potential of Wilson's rhetorical and progressive leadership, he remained ambivalent about endorsing a federal woman suffrage amendment. Such ambivalence could be informed by Wilson's personal dispositions toward women. NWP members may not have been surprised to learn that, in 1884, Wilson attended a Woman's Congress meeting of the Association for the Advancement of Women in Baltimore and reported the following to his wife: "Barring the chilled, scandalized feeling that always overcomes me when I see and hear women speak in public, I derived a good deal of whimsical delight . . . from the proceedings."[58] Here, Wilson voiced the commonly held notion that when women spoke in public, they violated their duties binding them to the private sphere. The next year, Wilson voiced similarly traditional views in another letter to his wife; he argued that if a woman "cannot preserve her individuality in the family . . . she simply has no individuality worth preserving."[59] Thus, in Wilson's view, a woman best flourished and asserted her "individuality" in a familial context.

Scholars have attributed Wilson's early views on women to his adoption of the "the culture and mores of the South," since he was born in Staunton, Virginia, and was raised in Augusta, Georgia.[60] He married Ellen Axson on June 24, 1885, with whom he had three daughters, Jessie, Eleanor, and Margaret. While he spoke highly of his wife and loved his children, Wilson biographer Arthur S. Link writes that, at home, "Wilson was unquestionably lord and master, but he ruled with love, and his family literally worshipped him."[61] Outside of the home, Wilson developed a close relationship with Mary Peck, whom he met in the late 1890s while vacationing in Bermuda without his family. Wilson repeatedly visited Peck, sparking rumors of an affair, although the extent of their relationship is not clear.[62]

As a professor, Wilson first taught at Bryn Mawr College, an all-women's school. He went on to teach at Wesleyan University in Middletown, Connecticut, before he landed at Princeton University in 1890 as a "leader of professors."[63] Wilson served as the university's president between 1902 and 1910, when he left after an administrative fallout. Wilson was elected governor of New Jersey in November 1910 and to the presidency in November 1912.[64] Sadly, Ellen enjoyed only a brief stint as first lady before she died of kidney failure in August 1914. Ellen's death was considered "the greatest blow of Wilson's first term," as many close friends and political allies observed Wilson's deep grief.[65] In March of the next year, however, Wilson became enamored with Edith Bolling, a wealthy and independent D.C. socialite. The two were married in December, despite concerns from Wilson's inner circles that a hasty remarriage might threaten his reelection.[66]

Edith played an active role in Wilson's presidential affairs. Her assertive personality shone as she drove her own car and "prided herself on being the first Washington woman to indulge such a daring."[67] Such independence challenged Wilson's previously articulated gender beliefs. Wilson's love for Edith was so strong that some thought that his desire to write her multiple letters a day interfered with his presidential correspondence.[68] Moreover, Wilson sought Edith's input on policy matters as he often sent her copies of official correspondence. And, throughout 1919, after Wilson suffered a stroke, Edith functioned as Wilson's surrogate or "the sole conduit between the president and the rest of the world."[69] Despite Edith's acute political abilities, she remained a staunch opponent to woman suffrage. On September 8, 1916, regarding a speech Wilson delivered at a suffrage meeting in Atlantic City, she wrote: "The only speech of my Precious One that I ever failed to enjoy, but I hated the subject so it was acute agony."[70] Edith's biographer, Alden Hatch, attributes this "violent opposition" to her identity as a southern woman. Nonetheless, Edith's active role in her husband's political life suggested that Wilson personally believed in women's political abilities.[71]

Similarly, one of Wilson's daughters, Margaret, became increasingly involved in women's rights activism. In 1913, as a member of the General Federation of Women's Clubs (GFWC) and as vice chair of the National Social Centre Legislative Committee, she worked to turn public schools into centers for political meetings.[72] Regarding her efforts to facilitate political deliberation in public spaces, Margaret said, "the matter of first importance is to see to it that the citizens' forum is properly constituted."[73] Much later, in 1921, Margaret spoke at an NWP national convention.[74] Wilson often claimed that he personally believed in woman suffrage, but was constrained by party politics. Thus, it seemed that Wilson upheld the public-private sphere doctrine he espoused early in his career as his political decisions seemed unaffected by the marked examples of empowered women in his personal life.

While the NWP was not privy to Wilson's personal beliefs regarding women's citizenship rights, he nevertheless demonstrated an ability to codify progressive legislation; his reshaped role as an engaged leader of the American people prompted the NWP to send multiple delegations of women to meet with the president between 1913 and 1916. However, NWP members and other women found that Wilson's willingness to listen functioned as a substitute for political action. In November 1913, for example, seventy-three New Jersey women who had supported Wilson's 1912 presidential election gathered in Washington, D.C., to call upon the president.[75] When the women gathered at NWP headquarters before marching to the White House, however, they found their meeting with President Wilson "without date."[76] According to the *Suffragist,* Paul phoned the president's secretary and warned, "The deputation is starting immediately for the White House. . . . The women have come prepared to stay a month if necessary, but they intend to see the President."[77] Upon their arrival, the women were met at the White House gates and led to an office, where President Wilson awaited them. Leaders of the delegation pleaded their case to the president, who promised to give it his "earnest attention."[78]

Shortly thereafter, the president addressed Congress and failed to mention the woman suffrage amendment. NWP and NAWSA members were infuriated—so much so, that the president's omission was the focus of the national convention of the NAWSA, hosted by the NWP in Washington D.C. At the close of the convention, Paul organized a deputation of fifty-five women, led by Dr. Anna Howard Shaw, to march to the White House.[79] In her remarks to the president, Shaw appealed to his empowering ideals. She said, "Recognizing your splendid stand on the liberties and rights of the people, we appeal to you because we believe you will bring to our question that same spirit of justice which you have manifested toward all other great questions."[80] The president admitted that he personally believed in woman suffrage, but that he could only endorse legislation based on the will of his party, "for whom," he said, "I am a spokesman."[81]

Two years later, in December 1915, the NWP's cross-country envoys, Sara Bard Field and Francis Joliffe, concluded their reception at the Capitol by marching with at least three hundred women to the White House where the president awaited their arrival. Field's address to the president asked that woman suffrage "be made a national matter" and be included as part of his upcoming message to Congress.[82] Wilson rehearsed the argument that he was "always restrained . . . by the consciousness that [he] must speak for others," and added the particularly condescending claim that woman suffrage crowded his congressional agenda. He said, "I have the habit—perhaps the habit of a teacher—of confining my utterances to one subject at a time, for fear that two subjects might compete with one another for prominence."[83]

The NWP inspired and mobilized other groups of women to direct their grievances to the president. In February 1914, the NWP hosted the first group of wage-earning women to meet with the president. Margaret Hinchey, a member of the Laundry Workers Union of New York City, Rose Winslow, a former factory worker, and Rose Sneidermann, vice president of the Women's Trade Union League (WTUL), led "laundresses, seamstresses, corset-makers, factory girls, business women, storekeepers, office women, stenographers, and printers" in a silent march to the White House.[84] A few months later, prominent NWP member and noted journalist Rheta Childe Dorr led five hundred members of the GFWC to meet with Wilson. She asked Wilson to use his "powerful influence with Congress to have the Bristow-Mondell Suffrage amendment passed in this session." This time the president made a states' rights argument regarding voting laws and reiterated his duties as party leader.[85] Wilson maintained these lines of argument as other delegations of women continued to meet with him throughout 1915 and 1916.[86]

Although Wilson once argued that universal suffrage lay "at the foundation of every evil in this country," he began to show signs of support for woman suffrage in late 1916.[87] In addition to voting for the New Jersey state measure in 1915, many members of Wilson's cabinet voted for woman suffrage at the state level.[88] Moreover, in September 1916, Wilson stood on stage next to Carrie Chapman Catt and Anna Howard Shaw at a NAWSA convention and said, "I have not come to fight anybody, *but with somebody.* We feel the tide; we rejoice in the strength of it; and we shall not quarrel in the long run as to the method of it."[89] Here Wilson refrained from upholding the state-by-state method of achieving woman suffrage, suggesting he was open to a federal amendment.

Such progress, however, was not enough for the NWP, particularly since the president was reelected without putting a federal woman suffrage amendment on his platform. Thus, the NWP aimed to press woman suffrage into Wilson's consciousness, by first heckling him during an address to Congress in the aftermath of his reelection. According to the *Suffragist,* after the NWP members unfurled the banner, "[t]he President looked up, hesitated a moment, then went on," while members of Congress "were turning wildly in every direction, and a buzz of whispered comment swept the floor." The women made no comment, nor did they protest when a page secured the banner or when they were escorted out of the gallery. They believed "a comment was not needed; the yellow banner had raised the suffrage issue in Congress."[90] This marked the first instance that the NWP felt its demands were best made through silence.

The fall of 1916 proved pivotal for the NWP, particularly as members grieved the loss of Inez Milholland Boissevain, prominent suffragist, lawyer, and international activist. Despite grave illness, she spent her final days speaking for the anti-Democratic campaign of the NWP throughout the fall. Paul arranged to hold a memorial service for Milholland on Christmas Day in the Capitol rotunda—the first ever held for a nonmember of Congress.[91] Other NWP members considered Milholland a martyr, "a crusader," and "a torch that illuminated the rank and file and had the rare power of dramatizing a cause to the multitude."[92] Milholland best personified these characteristics as she led the 1913 national suffrage parade wearing a flowing white gown, riding atop a white horse, upholding a golden bugle.

Milholland's death helped galvanize NWP members into an anti-Wilson campaign; they argued that Milholland "symbolized the whole daily sacrifice that hundreds of women have made and are making for the sake of political freedom."[93] Shortly after the suffragists heckled Wilson during his address to Congress, the *Suffragist* said: "But it is warfare in which women will not be worsted. If the President is determined to ignore women suffrage, women are equally determined that it will not be ignored; and that the attention of the Congress, of the press and of the people of the United States will be perpetually directed to the fact that woman suffrage is an issue clamoring for attention."[94] Just as the United States prepared to enter World War I, the NWP prepared to declare war on President Wilson.

THE RHETORICAL PRESIDENCY AND THE SILENT SENTINELS

On January 9, 1917, members of the NWP departed the White House after another disheartening meeting with President Wilson. One member recalled his parting words: "Ladies, concert public opinion on behalf of woman suffrage."[95] After crossing Lafayette Square to their headquarters, the dejected NWP members brainstormed their next move. Harriot Stanton Blatch hatched a plan. Her words were recorded in the *Suffragist.* She declared: "We must go to him every day, we must have a continuous delegation to the President of the United States, if he is to realize the never-ceasing, insistent demand of women that he take action where he is responsible. We may not be admitted within the doors, but we can at least stand at the gates. We may not be allowed to raise our voices and speak to the President, but we can address him just the same, because our message to him will be inscribed upon the banners which we will carry in our hands. Let us post our silent sentinels at the gates of the White House."[96] The following day at 10:00 A.M., a dozen

FIGURE 4.2. "College Day" on the picket line at the White House (February 1917). Reproduced courtesy Library of Congress, LC-USZ62–31799.

women planted themselves before the White House gates, stood silently, and upheld banners, which asked, "Mr. President, What Will You Do for Woman Suffrage?" and "Mr. President, How Long Must Women Wait for Liberty?" (see fig. 4.2).[97] After years of tireless activism, the NWP emerged with silent strength to bolster the fight for woman suffrage.

The "Silent Sentinels," as the protesters were christened by the NWP, stood firmly day after day throughout 1917.[98] While most of these protesters were dressed in proper ladies' attire—long sleeves, long skirts, and hats—they all wore sashes bearing the party's colors of purple, gold, and white.[99] NWP delegations of about twelve to fifteen protesters took turns at the picket line, representing different states and different professions, such as teachers and factory workers.[100] Some women held flag-like banners with stripes of the NWP's colors, and others held banners with messages to President Wilson, which read: "Mr. President, You Say Liberty Is the Fundamental Demand of the Human Spirit" and "Democracy Should Begin at Home."[101] Thus, while the protesters stood in silence, their critiques of President Wilson and demands for liberty were clearly displayed.

The rhetorical presidency allowed the Sentinels' protest to function as a symbolic response to Wilson's refashioning of presidential leadership. As citizens answering their leader's call, the Sentinels identified themselves as politically active members of Wilson's democracy. At the same time, the rhetorical presidency functioned as a model of direct communication with the American public. In fact, the Sentinels credited Wilson for the strategy: "The President asked us to concert public opinion before we could expect anything of him; we are concerting it."[102] Thus, the Sentinels made complex rhetorical appeals to President Wilson as worthy citizens with political voices to the American public as they mimicked Wilson's move to appeal directly to public opinion. The rhetorical presidency, therefore, not only facilitated the Sentinels' development of direct and indirect appeals to President Wilson, but it also allowed them to assert political voice and realize their citizenship identities.

Reflecting Wilson's vision of the presidency that hailed the American people as principal actors in the enactment of democratic precepts, the NWP responded by performing ideal citizenship behavior and addressed their concerns to their president. The *Suffragist* stated, "the women of the nation are holding [President Wilson] responsible for the non-passage of the federal suffrage amendment," which clearly shows that the Sentinels considered the protest a legitimate call for dialogue with their nation's leader.[103] The Sentinels' banners directly asked Wilson, "How Long Must Women Wait for Liberty?," which simultaneously recognized the power of the president to grant liberty while empowering the Sentinels with the political voice to question the president. Moreover, as a way to put President Wilson's proverbial foot in his mouth, the *Suffragist* published an excerpt of the former professor's work, *Constitutional Government,* entitled, "A Word to Agitators." The passage read: "Agitation is certainly of the essence of a constitutional system."[104] Here the Sentinels legitimized their protest as the constitutional behavior Wilson valued.

The protest of the Sentinels can also be considered as a mimetic performance of Wilson's rhetorical presidency, demonstrating a nuanced use of the rhetoric of political mimesis. Prior to the protest, the mimetic strategies of the NWP empowered members as political actors engaged in political rituals and activities typically reserved for men, thus serving the constitutive function of helping members see themselves as such actors. By mimicking Wilson's appeals to the US public, the NWP's rhetoric of political mimesis took a parodic form, as it not only offered a representation or likeness of Wilson's rhetorical presidency, but it also worked to establish a "critical ironic distance" from Wilson.[105] Linda Hutcheon's theory of parody turns to the Greek root of the term to expose its functional (and, I would argue, constitutive) range—from "respectful admiration to biting ridicule."[106] She argues: "The prefix *para* has two meanings, only one of which is usually mentioned—that of 'counter' or 'against.' Thus parody becomes an opposition or contrast between texts. . . . However, *para* in Greek can also mean 'beside,' and therefore there is a suggestion of an accord or intimacy instead of a contrast."[107] The Sentinels' parodying of the rhetorical presidency, like the NWP's previous mimetic enactments, exhibited a degree of "accord or intimacy" with the president; in so doing, the protesters magnified the "opposition or contrast" between their citizenship values and Wilson's stance on woman suffrage.

Because parody relies on irony's "refusal of semantic univocality," the Sentinels' protest established "a critical distance" in which "this irony can be playful as well as belittling; it can be critically constructive as well as destructive."[108] Margaret Rose similarly emphasizes the polysemic range of parody: "Both by definition and structurally, parody is ambivalently critical and sympathetic towards its target."[109] Parody offers a multiplicity of meanings that differentiates it from satire, which relies on irony to represent a distorted reality and almost always serves to mock and ridicule.[110] Thus, like mimesis, parody held the potential to empower the NWP as it performed the multiple functions of establishing political similarity and difference; however, parodic forms of mimesis specifically accentuate *difference,* a function that constitutively and strategically became more and more necessary in order for the NWP to expose the hypocrisies of Wilson's presidential, international, and citizenship ideals. In short, parodying the president allowed the Sentinels to—as Rose says—"unmask and deflate."[111]

As the Sentinels stood in front of the White House, turned away from the president's door and, rather, facing the US public, their parodic performance literally and symbolically positioned the women upon a national stage. This positioning helped the NWP reach a national audience as the Silent Sentinels garnered weekly coverage from publications such as the *Philadelphia Press,* the *Chicago Evening Post,* the *Seattle Post-Intelligencer,* and the *New York Evening Post.*[112] Upon such a national stage, the Sentinels established "critical distance" from Wilson as they reinscribed the power relationships embedded in Wilson's rhetorical presidency and created their own pulpit of public influence in the suffrage drama.

As self-constituted national leaders, the Sentinels' hailed forth an empowered political response from the public, which in turn reified their parodying of the president and further constituted American women as citizens. One NWP supporter wrote, "I believe the work you women are doing down in Washington is the best 'bit' of real *advance work* being done in the country. You can never know the *joy* it is to me to have this share in this special moment. . . . I believe that each day those banners are unfolded visualizing woman's demand for 'liberty' there [are] being released through that simple act great spiritual forces which are sweeping our country from coast to coast."[113] Like the Sentinels' empowered response to Wilson, US women responded to the Sentinels as national suffrage leaders. Here the Sentinels managed to turn the president's shift to consulting public opinion into a source of power as they carried on as leaders of the American public and established political voice for American women. In this parodic appeal to their fellow citizens, the Sentinels worked to decentralize Wilson in the suffrage drama, while the appeal also pointed to Wilson's inability to include women in his democratic vision. Here, the Sentinels' likeness to the president magnified the president's promotion of differentiated citizenship.

The Sentinels' silence also functioned parodically. Specifically, their silent protest parodied Wilson's silent resistance to woman suffrage—or what the NWP considered Wilson's "weapon of silence."[114] Again, the Sentinels performatively established a likeness to Wilson (by symbolically and literally ignoring their perceived agitator) as a critique of the women's relative powerlessness. In addition to this parodic turn, the Sentinels' silence was particularly strategic because it represented a dynamic rhetorical shift in the woman suffrage movement. Certainly the Sentinels maintained the NWP's tradition of creating a spectacle to attract attention and publicity.[115] Yet, the shift was marked by the Sentinels' move toward silence as the primary strategy of suffrage agitation. For almost seventy years prior to the Sentinels, numerous suffrage leaders and organizations literally raised their voices through conventions, petitions, parades, lobbying, soapbox speeches, and weekly organs. In 1916, for instance, Carrie Chapman Catt, president of the NAWSA, pledged "to keep so much 'suffrage noise' going on all over the country" by lobbying at state and federal levels.[116] Other suffrage and anti-suffrage organizations raised their voices within the suffrage drama of 1917.[117] The shift to silence proved politically strategic, however, because, as Barry Brummett maintains, "the expectations it violates are strongly established and rigidly upheld."[118] Thus, such silence helped drum up publicity as a new rhetorical strategy in the national suffrage movement and drew attention to the NWP's efforts to sway public opinion as a means to influence Wilson's response to the NWP's campaign.[119]

The Sentinels, representing politically voiceless women, parodied the rhetorical presidency to appeal to both Wilson and the American public. First, the enactment of the rhetorical presidency registered as a response to Wilson's instantiation of the bully pulpit. Next, when considered an act of parody, the protest invited a look at Wilson's continued resistance to suffrage and to the limits of his democratic vision. As one *Suffragist* article reported, "Pickets dramatized *for the country* from coast to coast the truth that women . . . are waiting upon a reactionary President for democracy."[120]

Here, "the country" was the Sentinels' audience, but ultimately, it was the president's attention they demanded. The Sentinels' White House location, banners addressed to "Mr. President," and philosophy of agitation all functioned as direct appeals to presidential power. Although Wilson seemed to be the Sentinels' greatest opponent, he was also their greatest potential ally. As such, parodying the rhetorical presidency facilitated the generation of direct and indirect appeals to President Wilson.

The Silent Sentinels' parodying of the rhetorical presidency also strengthened their militant identity as empowered US citizens. The Sentinels demonstrated their rhetorical acuity by challenging presidential power and appealing to the public's political influence. These appeals revealed a complex understanding of power relationships. Although the presidency shaped the NWP's militant philosophies and tactics, the Sentinels demonstrated that they were not victims of structural forces—they summoned the agency to crowd the president on his public platform and take ownership in his rhetorical presidency as a means to empower their campaign for woman suffrage. The Sentinels thus shaped and were shaped by the structural power of the presidency as the protesters both agitated and reinforced Wilson's authority over the suffrage issue. Ultimately the ideological potency of the rhetorical presidency allowed the Sentinels to act as citizens influencing their leader, and as leaders joining forces with their fellow citizens to alter national policy. This layered appeal facilitated an exchange of power that strengthened the Sentinels' militant identity as citizens and further constituted their political voice.

US MILITARISM AND THE "SILENT SENTINELS"

The "Silent Sentinels" strengthened their identity and justified sacrifice through America's wartime ideology. The protesters most obviously reflected US militarism by identifying themselves as sentinels—those who keep watch or stand guard. However, this sense of vigilance was not fully realized until the more violent chapters of the Sentinels' protest began. Shortly after the United States entered World War I, onlookers, police, and soldiers did not take the Sentinels' protests on President Wilson lightly. In fact, between June and November 1917, the Sentinels endured physical and psychological harm, such as beatings, arrests, imprisonment, and force-feedings, creating the exigency to harden their militant identity and remain steadfast in the fight for woman suffrage. As George Lakey argued, "One way in which the militants set themselves off from the larger suffrage movement was by pointing to their strength."[121] Often this strength was conceived in militaristic terms. As one protester said, "This sense of comradeship always comes from suffering and toiling together."[122] Thus, Wilson's militaristic ideology provided the Sentinels with the necessary rhetorical resources to mimetically represent themselves as soldiers joining the fight for democracy. In this chapter of its protests, the NWP's rhetoric of political mimesis took the form of quotation as the Sentinels literally appropriated Wilson's war discourses into their own.

By the spring of 1917, the US entrance into World War I seemed inevitable. Following the sinking of the *Lusitania* in 1915, which caused the deaths of 128 Americans, Wilson embarked on a preparedness campaign, during which he maintained that the United States would not enter the war, but would need to be prepared if attacked by enemy nations. However, in the early months of 1917, the threat of attack became more imminent with the Zimmerman telegram's proposal to bring German forces to the Mexico-US border and the monthly destruction of more than six hundred thousand tons of Allied and neutral goods by German submarines. Wilson delivered his war message on April 2, followed by the passage of the war resolution on April 4. Wilson signed a draft bill on May 18, initiating the training of approximately two million soldiers to serve as the American Expeditionary Force and to help—in Wilson's words—secure "a universal domination of right."[123]

Wilson's rhetorical leadership soared as commander in chief. Binkley argues: "During the war years President Wilson produced an almost hypnotic effect by his felicitous phrasing of the ideological common denominators of the Great Crusade, and he obtained hitherto unknown unity that transcended party and became national."[124] Wilson's remarkable ability to solidify a unified national identity by constructing the war as a project to bring US democracy to the world magnified Wilson's potential as the NWP's greatest ally. The NWP argued that woman suffrage strengthened Wilson's democratic program by empowering women to help with the war effort. It declared: "American women ask to be enrolled in the citizenry of the United States so that they may do their utmost in the service of their country."[125] Additionally, Wilson's war ethos helped the Sentinels endure repeated abuses as soldiers sacrificing in the service of liberation.

The Sentinels' heightened militarism also reflected a wartime shift in gender ideology. As Nira Yuval-Davis argues, "Personal identities and modes of interpersonal and intergendered behaviour cannot but spill over into the civil society once the military gains prominence in society."[126] The prominence of US militarism, particularly as the country began its participation in

World War I, expanded women's participation in the public sphere through national service. The Sentinels' campaign for woman suffrage incorporated this ideological expansion into their rhetoric of just cause. An article in the *Suffragist* said, "The conviction spreads that it is irrational to keep women disenfranchised when their work has grown more obviously necessary than ever before to the continued existence of the nation."[127] Part of this "work" included cultivating families with great civic virtue as a way of making a political contribution to America's democratic society. As Miriam Cooke and Angela Woollacott argue, "War transforms motherhood from a social to a political factor."[128] While the NWP never supported the war effort, in part because of many members' participation in the peace movement, it argued that if women were considered integral to the nation's unity and democratic identity, then they should be given true democratic power.

Through the mimetic form of quotation, the Sentinels' banners most prominently mimicked Wilson's militarism and exploited the empowering potential of wartime gender roles. The Sentinels' direct quotation of Wilson's discourse functioned in tandem with their parodic performance of Wilson's rhetorical presidency. Hutcheon's theory of parody treats quotation as one way in which meanings are "trans-contextualized" in the effort to establish difference via similarity.[129] Similarly, Herman Meyer argues, "The gentlest form of contrast is found in the tension which results when the quoted words as such are used in the original sense but, through their *context,* collide with meanings of an opposite sort and are themselves dragged over into a contrary sense. . . . The quoted words themselves are given a meaning that is conditioned by the new context and deviates from their original meaning."[130] "Drag[ging] over" words from one context to another signals a "participation in the riches of the Western cultural tradition" and thus, "guarantees [the audience] a certain community of general cultural horizons."[131] The Sentinels' direct quotation of Wilson's discourse thus reified their participation in the Western cultural traditions of democratic representation, leadership, and citizenship as refashioned by Wilson's rhetorical presidency. However, in the context of their militant, anti-Wilson protest, Wilson's words took on "meanings of an opposite sort" that magnified the gap between Wilson's democratic ethos and the protesters' citizenship rights.

The Sentinels' banners exploited the mimetic form of quotation after four months of protesting without incident and shortly after the United States entered WWI in early April 1917. The Sentinels upheld an inflammatory banner (see fig. 4.3) that read: "To the Russian Envoys: President Wilson and Envoy Root are deceiving Russia. They say, 'We are a democracy. Help

FIGURE 4.3. The "Silent Sentinels" upholding a banner addressing "the Russian envoys," speaking as political leaders and fully enfranchised US citizens (1917). Reproduced courtesy Harris & Ewing Collection, Library of Congress, LC-DIG-hec-09043.

us win a world war so that democracies may survive.' We, the Women of America, tell you that America is not a democracy. Twenty million American Women are denied the right to vote. President Wilson is the chief opponent of their national enfranchisement. Help us make this nation really free. Tell our government that it must liberate its people before it can claim free Russia as an ally."[132] Empowered by wartime necessity, the Sentinels' quotation worked to adopt Wilson's authority as commander-in-chief and reversed the assumption that "the Women of America" were examples of liberty. The Sentinels quoted Wilson's call upon Russian allies in order to call upon Russian women. The Sentinels further identified themselves as an army twenty million strong, positioned to fight Wilson as the United States fought the enemies of democracy. Moreover, the Sentinels' banner created an alliance with Russian women, who had recently been granted the right to vote. As this alliance paralleled the US wartime alliance with Russia, it poignantly stressed the inconsistent application of Wilson's democratic values to American women.[133] Reflecting such sentiments, another banner (see fig. 4.4) quoted Wilson: "'We Shall Fight for the Things Which We Have Always Held Dear to Our Hearts—for Democracy, for The Right of Those Who Submit to Authority to Have a Voice in Their Own Governments.' President Wilson's War Message, April 2nd 1917."[134]

Quoting Wilson's war message unmasked the hypocrisy of Wilson's call to uplift politically voiceless people in other nations. As such, the banner allowed the Sentinels to adopt Wilson's voice to pronounce the NWP's own militaristic philosophy toward securing political voice for American women.

Appropriating the contours of US militarism became more necessary as violence against the protesters peaked. First, it is noteworthy that the Sentinels maintained the protest over the course of a year, with delegations of women standing in winter snow, summer heat, and "in the face of bitter wind and driving rain."[135] Many women fell ill, acquired frostbite, and found "the sockets of their arms aching from the strain" of holding banners for hours on end.[136] The real wounds, however, were not sustained because of the weather or exhaustion, but because of the attacks of police and bystanders. As arrests increased and the Sentinels remained at the White House gates, passersby began to expect confrontation: "The police made no attempt to disperse the crowd, but directed their attack upon the women marching[;] . . . the majority, taking their attitude from the police, also attacked the women, snatch-

FIGURE 4.4. The Silent Sentinels using quotation in a banner to expose the hypocrisy of President Wilson's democratic discourse (April 1917). Reproduced courtesy Harris & Ewing Collection, Library of Congress, LC-DIG-hec-08299.

ing their flags."[137] By November, a total of 218 women had been arrested, often for "obstructing traffic," 97 of whom went to the District prison or to the Occoquan workhouse, incurring notable abuses from the wardens.[138] NWP leader Lucy Burns's hands were shackled above her head one night.[139] Mobs and sailors attacked returning Sentinels, throwing eggs and tomatoes at them, and, worse, hitting, choking, and dragging them.[140] Those who remained imprisoned endured smothering temperatures in the sewing rooms and freezing temperatures into the winter months.[141] Alice Paul, after being dragged for a block by a sailor, was sentenced to seven months in solitary confinement.[142]

As the violent stages of the protest continued, the Sentinels' identities shifted from mimetic representations of the nation's leader to soldiers engaged in battle.[143] Constituting their identities as such seemed necessary for the women to endure violent reactions to their mimetic performance of political leaders. The *Suffragist*'s construction of the Sentinels was shaped by military metaphors, identifying the women as "chivalrous," aligned in "squads," and as "comrades patrolling the same beat."[144] Following the first six arrests for "inciting to unlawful assembly and riot," the *Suffragist* reported that these women remained in a "spirit of revolt, of rebellion."[145] By late August after many more arrests, the *Suffragist* constructed the Sentinels as soldiers maintaining their post, and standing "brave in the sunshine, flanked by the worn standards that have become the battle flags of suffrage."[146] By mid-October, eighteen Sentinels were imprisoned in the District jail, where they mimicked the survival techniques of Allied soldiers: "In spite of the dampness and chill of the old stone building, which forces the women to wrap themselves in newspapers, a practice borrowed from the trenches in Europe, their spirit is undaunted."[147] Paul embodied the sacrificial character of a soldier as she defiantly broke a window with a book of Elizabeth Browning's poems to save the lives of a few elderly women by restoring air ventilation.[148] Paul was ultimately placed in the psychopathic ward, where she endured force-feedings—and subsequent vomiting and dizziness—three times daily.[149]

Although wartime allows for the fluctuation of gender roles, the NWP's battle stance was perceived as too great a violation of womanly behavior and of wartime allegiance to the president. Just as women at arms were perceived as a threat to the heroic masculinity of the nation's ego, the Sentinels' soldiering threatened to destabilize the protector/protected myth fundamental to the logic of war. Thus, like enemy nations, the Sentinels were to be conquered, dominated, physically violated, and even symbolically raped through force-feedings. Specifically, the president and other political elites attempted to recover social control of the Sentinels through censorship, political maneuvering, and physical domination. As early as July, the unjust conditions of the women's imprisonment were brought to Wilson's attention. Gilson Gardner, a journalist whose wife was placed in the Occoquan workhouse, warned Wilson that arresting "women of prominence and refinement like Charles A. Dana'[s] daughter, and the daughter of former Senator and secretary of State Bayard" was a sign of "political unwisdom."[150] That same month, Dudley Field Malone, who Wilson had appointed as collector of the Port of New York, presented the president with a well-documented case of the suffragists' abuses. Perhaps these appeals worked, as Wilson pardoned eleven suffragists on July 20. Christine A. Lunardini and Thomas J. Knock argue that the pardons were motivated less by sympathy and more by Wilson's fear of controversy.[151] Either way, the suffragists considered the pardons an empty gesture. One of the pardoned picketers, Alison Turnbull Hopkins, wife of the chairman of the New Jersey Progressive Party, wrote Wilson: "[I] do not desire your presidential benevolence, but American justice."[152]

Wilson's personal dislike of the Sentinels strongly suggested that the pardons were acts of political appeasement. That month, he wrote that the Sentinels were "doing a great deal of damage to the cause they are trying to promote," and, in a letter to his daughter Jessie, he described the picketers as "obnoxious."[153] Moreover, the Sentinels repulsed Edith Wilson, who referred to them as "disgusting creatures" and "those detestable suffragists." Edith felt Wilson's pardoning of "those devils in the workhouse" was "a mistake." On July 17, when Edith learned that Malone supported the protesters, she wrote, "My Precious One did not come home from the office until six-thirty and was so weary it broke my heart to look at him. He loved Dudley and said he felt like someone had died."[154] As though a traitor, Malone became the subject of a Secret Service investigation for the following six weeks, during which his suffrage activities "abruptly ended."[155] Later Malone resigned his position and became counsel to the NWP.[156]

By August, the Sentinels' soldier identities pushed the president beyond his willingness to appease and pardon the women; as though engaged in war, Wilson began to fight back. Ironically, Wilson attempted to silence the protesters. Wilson and Arthur Brisbane, editor of the *Washington Times,* agreed to limit newspaper coverage of the protests as a way to cut off the NWP's lifeline—national publicity. Wilson wrote to Brisbane, "My own suggestion would be that nothing that they do should be featured with headlines or put on the front page but that a bare colorless chronicle of what they do should be all that was printed."[157] Brisbane agreed, although Lunardini and Knock conducted a check of newspaper headlines and concluded that "editors were loathe to pass up a good story," and that "the Wilson administration openly or covertly approved of purposeful distortion of news that concerned the militant suffragists."[158]

Considering Wilson's continued correspondence and support of the NAWSA's suffrage efforts, it seemed that Wilson's attempts to silence the Sentinels were motivated less by his resistance to woman suffrage and more by his rejection of the NWP's militant methods. For instance, Helen Hamilton Gardener of the NAWSA successfully persuaded Wilson to help create a House Committee on Woman Suffrage in September.[159] That same month, Wilson publicly supported state suffrage campaigns and pledged to urge Democrats to support them as well.[160] In fact, in October, Wilson extended his support to the NAWSA's New York suffrage campaign. His dislike of the NWP was made clear in a letter to the NAWSA's Carrie Chapman Catt: "May I not say that I hope that no [New York] voter will be influenced in his decision with regard to this great matter by anything the so-called pickets may have done here in Washington?"[161]

As the NWP's militaristic campaign persisted, Wilson was nearly forced to address the question of the prison abuses, particularly as reports circulated of Alice Paul's and Rose Winslow's daily force-feedings. Instead, however, this exigency gave Wilson the opportunity to escalate institutional efforts of social control. In early November, Wilson sent Dr. William Alanson White and William Gwynn Gardiner, a commissioner of the District of Columbia, to assess "the exact conditions at the District Jail" and to "examine if necessary Miss Paul and Miss Winslow." Gardiner's subsequent report to Wilson stood in sharp contrast to the suffragists' personal testimonies regarding their treatment in prison. The report thus functioned as a tool of bureaucratic corroboration as it helped justify the continued physical domination over the imprisoned women. To begin, the report noted that the food and service were "all that could be expected," that the picketers' quarters were in "sanitary condition," and that the broken windows and peeling paint were the suffragists' own doing. In opposition to Paul's testimony, the doctors who performed the force-feedings described them as "an every-day occurrence" without "ill effect." Similarly, Dr. James Alonzo Gannon said that Paul and Winslow "took the tube" and "swallowed willingly, there being no force or persuasion used upon either of them." Reinforcing Wilson's previous attempts to quash the controversy, Gardiner advised Wilson to "remain silent" on the question of the women's imprisonment.

He argued that the "guards and matrons" behaved in "good order and discipline" and warned that the suffragists "plan[ned] to violate every rule" of these institutions."[162] Despite these multiple efforts to smother the women's demands for citizenship rights, Rep. John Baer (R-ND) launched a congressional investigation of the women's treatment. Before the investigation was underway, Wilson commuted Paul's and the other prisoners' sentences in late November; with Gardiner's report in hand, Wilson denied ever knowing of the abuses.[163]

Although the Sentinels endured violent reactions to their demands, the protesters' relative privilege may have protected them from more severe abuses during a time of war hysteria. According to Haig A. Bosmajian, "it cannot be ignored that it was the practice of selective enforcement which resulted in the Espionage Act never being applied to the women pickets. . . . Socialists, anarchists, were being sentenced to ten- and fifteen-year prison sentences for saying less."[164] Linda J. Lumdsen argues that the Sentinels' femininity and whiteness protected them from more extreme punishment.[165] To an extent, the NWP reproduced Wilson's progressive senses of homogeneity and racial exclusion as African American women were notably absent throughout the Sentinels' year-long protest.[166] The Sentinels' white identities may also have worked in conjunction with the complexities of wartime gender roles to protect the women. Although the Sentinels' masculine soldier identities represented a threat to Wilson's gendered war logic, their whiteness resonated with the concurrent glorification of the white woman-as-mother. Thus, paradoxically, controlling the Sentinels' bodies worked to discipline the women's transgression of gender roles while it also represented a violation of the nation's purity. Moreover, women's increased political and social participation in the domestic war effort may have helped justify the white women's demands as a way to prove their national allegiance.

CONCLUSION

The NWP considered the protest of the "Silent Sentinels" integral toward agitating Wilson and constituting their citizenship identities. At an NWP conference held in late 1917, party member Mabel Vernon identified four effects of the picketing. First, it generated publicity. Of the Sentinels' debut appearance, Vernon argued: "If our pickets had not done anything more, . . . through the press millions and millions of people were reached on that one day to think of national woman suffrage." Second, the Sentinels forced woman suffrage into Wilson's consciousness. Vernon asked, "Was it not worth even going to prison for, to have national woman suffrage daily in the mind of the President?" Third, the picketing and banners "kept alive the woman suffrage question in the war session of Congress." Last, the NWP believed the Sentinels allowed them to enact their rights as citizens. Vernon concluded: "[C]ertainly we can go on demonstrating, giving right here in Washington the visualization of all this sentiment which does exist, we know it exists, in all parts of our country."[167] Vernon pointed out that, through the act of protest, the Sentinels realized their militant strength and "sentiment"—the basis of their shared identities as national citizens.

In the same way that the Sentinels parodied Wilson's rhetorical presidency, they quoted and adopted the president's wartime ethos and fought for suffrage as liberators of oppressed citizens. With this key turn, the militaristic, nationalist, and gender ideological forces specific to wartime America collided to empower the Sentinels during their most trying episodes. Marc W. Steinberg argues that marginalized groups will often "seize upon silences and contradictions in moral justifications of domination and negate or reverse those points in the dominant discourse." Through political mimesis, the Sentinels parodied Wilson's symbolic silence and militaristic ideology "to legitimize their claims within the existing ideology of domination and to subvert some of the powerholders' justifications."[168] The NWP's parodying of the rhetorical presidency may have resonated with Wilson's "ideology of domination" and, through quotation, worked to expose the inconsistencies in his war ethos, so much so that bystanders, police, the press, bureaucrats, and Wilson himself sought to engage the Sentinels as though at war with them. Just as with soldiers engaged in battle, the Sentinels' suffering worked to strengthen a militant identity that further motivated their campaign for full citizenship rights.

5

Mimesis and US Internationalism

Statue Protests and the "Watch Fires of Freedom"

On January 9, 1918, less than two months after the Sentinels were released from prison, President Wilson advised a committee of Democrats to vote for the federal woman suffrage amendment "as an act of right and justice."[1] The following day, two key deliberative moments took place: the House of Representatives passed the woman suffrage amendment, and Wilson delivered "Conditions of Peace" to a joint session of Congress. Wilson's speech outlined his "Fourteen Points" and advocated for "a general association of nations."[2] The coupling of these events—one advocating legislation for women's full citizenship rights and the other specifying Wilson's "programme of the world's peace"—cannot be separated from the democratizing exigencies of the war.[3] Certainly the Sentinels' militaristic protests mimicked the soldiering efforts of US troops and may well have provided Wilson with the exigency to pressure fellow Democrats to endorse the amendment. The war similarly prompted Wilson to press his internationalist agenda, in which the United States would rally non-imperialist nations to "fight and continue to fight" until "open covenants of peace" were established.[4] Thus, it is not surprising that, as Wilson shifted his support toward federal woman suffrage, he linked the issue to his international agenda. In doing so, Wilson preserved his war ethos yet offered the NWP extended leverage for holding the president and Democrats accountable for actualizing America's democratization project. Throughout the latter months of 1918 and into the spring of 1919, the NWP's activism resonated with US efforts to spread democracy throughout the world as the NWP forged alliances with French revolutionaries and French suffragists, held the US Senate and Wilson accountable to

Wilson's program of democracy, and spread democracy through its "Watch Fires of Freedom."

WILSON'S US INTERNATIONALISM

Wilson's rhetorical presidency and his nativist nationalism resonated well with the rising tide of US internationalism. On May 24, 1915, at the Pan-American Financial Conference, for example, Wilson addressed "the bonds between the Americas," arguing: "We cannot know each other unless we see each other; we cannot deal with each other unless we communicate with each other. So soon as we communicate and are upon a familiar footing of intercourse with one another, we shall understand one another."[5] Wilson's insistence on communicating with and understanding foreign countries was, in part, driven by the rise of US internationalism, wherein America grew as a symbol of military and democratic strength. The expansion of American influence in foreign affairs can be traced back to the Monroe Doctrine in 1823 through the turn of the twentieth century when President William McKinley promoted the nation's participation in the Spanish-American War. Shortly thereafter, President Roosevelt added a "Corollary" to the Monroe Doctrine, which positioned the United States as an "international police power."[6]

President Wilson's refashioned citizenship ideals helped further the nation's expansion into the international arena. As James Andrews argues, "Wilson's rhetorical restructuring had transformed the long-held vision of America as a shining example of liberty for the world to emulate to its embodiment as the self-sacrificing defender of liberty."[7] Part of this sacrificial character led to the US participation in World War I. Although Wilson was criticized both for entering the war and for not entering it soon enough, Wilson justified America's entrance in part by saying that "[t]he world must be made safe for democracy" by fighting "for the rights and liberties of small nations."[8] Expanding Wilson's model of empowered US citizenship into the international arena constructed such "small nations" as dependent citizens of the worldwide democracy Wilson envisioned. Like Wilson's progressive efforts to "civilize" immigrants in the United States, America's role in the war could also be understood as the perpetuation of "the 'manifest destiny' of Americans to spread white civilization to more barbaric races around the globe by ruling them as subjects in tutelage, not citizens."[9] Thus, Wilson fashioned an international model of citizenship in which the president and the United States enacted ideal citizenship behavior by spreading democracy throughout the world. As Wilson declared in his second inaugural address, Americans were now "citizens of the world."[10]

MAKING THE WORLD SAFE FOR WOMAN SUFFRAGE

Amidst Wilson's promotion of "a nationalism of internationalism," Wilson fashioned a model of international citizenship in which the peoples of the world united toward the proliferation of democracy.[11] Such a citizenship ideal, however, assumed that US citizens were the natural leaders of democratic expansion, ultimately exporting America's citizenship hierarchies into the international arena. Wilson's progressive glorification of western European cultures resounded with the nation's wartime alliances with France and England.[12] Fostering solidarity with these nations and their heritages helped mobilize an international war effort. This international model of citizenship colluded with the growing internationalism of the woman suffrage movement and provided the means for the NWP to assert woman suffrage as a right of international citizenship.

Wilson's model of international citizenship resonated well with woman suffragists, as they saw the liberating potential of establishing a community that transcended national citizenship. The words of author and noted feminist Virginia Woolf best capture the sentiment: "I have no country. As a woman I want no country. As a woman my country is the whole world."[13] The explosion of women's rights movements in North America, South America, Europe, Australia, Asia, and Africa shaped this international consciousness.[14] Kumari Jayawardena and Ida Blom tie many of these movements to revolutionary overthrows and postcolonial nation-building projects in which women were empowered by wartime necessity or by participation in the establishment of new governments.[15] Thus, as women worldwide worked to constitute their national citizenship identities, their political consciousnesses acquired a heightened sense of internationalism.

By the early twentieth century, women's rights movements had established international ties and formed international organizations such as the International Woman Suffrage Association (IWSA) founded in 1902 and the International Congress of Women (ICW) founded in 1904.[16] In the second decade of the twentieth century, England's militant suffrage organization, the Women's Social and Political Union (WSPU), had established strong ties to the international socialist movement, which helped inspire women's militancy throughout much of the world. In Ireland, for example, Hanna Sheehy-Skeffington organized the Irish Women's Franchise League, which heckled politicians and broke windows to ultimately gain the support of the Irish Labour Party. In Nanking, China, members of the Woman Suffrage Alliance, a socialist organization, stormed the parliament three days in a row, demanding that woman suffrage be taken seriously. In Argentina, suffragists organized the Partido Feminista Nacional, a militant organization modeled after the WSPU, determined to expand upon women's limited suffrage rights.[17] Women across nations formed coalitions to organize national-level movements. In 1917, for example, the Women's Indian Association was formed in India by Margaret Cousins (a leader in the Irish suffrage movement), English activist Annie Besant, and by Dorothy Jinarajadasa, a Hindu leader from India.[18]

International suffrage alliances were reinforced by the internationalism of the peace and settlement house movements.[19] Women's demands for peace were typically perceived as less threatening than women's demands for equal rights because of the gendered construction of war; in other words, it was thought that war represented the domain of men and that peace functioned as the sphere of influence for women. Even so, women's participation in international peace movements empowered women to demand suffrage in order to spread peace beyond the "domestic" borders of the nation. In 1914, Rosika Schwimmer, a working-class Hungarian immigrant, became a leading figure in the antiwar movement, centered at Lillian Wald's Henry Street Settlement house in New York City. She helped form the Woman's Peace Party alongside Jane Addams in 1915 and also served as secretary of the IWSA.[20]

Egalitarian notions of citizenship, however, did not necessarily motivate international women's rights and peace-keeping movements. Just as Wilson fashioned a model of international superiority, the white women leaders of these international movements purported to enlighten, civilize, and democratize women of "uncivilized" nations. To illustrate, white Australian women, who were enfranchised in 1902, constructed themselves as pioneers of women's national suffrage and addressed American audiences regularly on how to win woman suffrage. Marilyn Lake argues that these white women "saw themselves as members of the same (extended) family as white British and American women: their sense of themselves was constituted in these years around the turn of the century within an imperialist framework, in terms of the dichotomies drawn between the 'civilised' and 'primitive.'"[21] Like Wilson, these suffragists' progressive efforts sustained racist and nativist constructions of citizenship as they also expanded the suffrage movement across national boundaries. Moreover, many of these white suffragists referred to each other as family members and as "sisters," thereby naturalizing white women's superiority and excluding nonwhite women from their vision of women's citizenship.[22] Many feminist scholars argue that assuming such international solidarity erased women's local and national identities and undermined the overall feminist project of recognizing and understanding the complexities of women's identities.[23] As such, the international woman suffrage movement reflected the empowering and disempowering contours of Wilson's move to spread democracy throughout the world.

Statue Protests and International Revolutionaries

Following Wilson's endorsement of federal woman suffrage in January 1918, he began pressuring senators to support the measure as part of the war effort. In May 1918, for instance, he appealed to the sense of national and Democratic loyalty of Sen. Josiah Wolcott (D-DE): "Will you forgive the leader of your party if he begs that you will vote for the suffrage amendment? . . . A crisis has come such as the world never faced before. In that crisis the world depends upon the United States. Unless the Administration is sustained throughout the war by real friends it cannot meet that responsibility successfully. The next Congress must be controlled by genuine dependable friends; and we may lose it,—I fear we shall lose it,—if we do not satisfy the opinion of the country on this matter now."[24] Wilson's appeal relied on his position as leader of his party and worked to position himself as a leader of world democracy. Wilson also voiced his fear of a Republican takeover in the upcoming midterm elections; thus, while Wilson's endorsement helped elevate woman suffrage to a matter of international, national, and party politics, it also served as an expedient strategy toward enhancing the nation's international prominence.

Throughout the spring and summer of 1918, Wilson exerted his influence on both Democratic and Republican senators, although he had had yet to do so in a formal address to the Senate. Perhaps more significantly, Wilson had yet to effectively convert any one senator's position on the suffrage controversy.[25] Additionally, as the president secured other pieces of legislation related to the war (for example, the Wire Control Bill on July 13), the NWP wondered why Wilson did "nothing effective to insure victory for the suffrage amendment."[26] The NWP's patience grew thin as the exigencies of war intensified throughout the rest of the summer, particularly after the American Expeditionary Force (AEF) arrived in France.[27] Rhetorically, however, by working to link woman suffrage to the war effort, Wilson offered woman suffrage a degree of international significance. In light of the country's wartime alliance with France, the NWP sought unity with French revolutionaries and suffragists.

In early August 1918, the NWP launched its last chapter of militant protest by invoking the collective memories of French revolutionaries Marquis de Lafayette and Jean-Baptiste Donatien de Vimeur, comte de Rochambeau.[28] Lafayette and Rochambeau were respected military leaders in France and served under Gen. George Washington in the American Revolution. The two united with Washington for the ultimate defeat of Lord Cornwallis in 1781 and returned home as heroes.[29] In light of the growing internationalism of the United States in the early twentieth century, Lafayette's and Rochambeau's international military leadership helped legitimize efforts to spread democracy abroad. Shortly after the Spanish-American War in 1902, for example, Theodore Roosevelt unveiled Rochambeau's statue in Lafayette Square across the street from the White House. In early September 1918, Wilson attended a ceremony at Lafayette's statue in the square to honor the 161st anniversary of the general's birth, and the following December, during a trip to France, Wilson laid a wreath upon Lafayette's grave as "a fellow servant of liberty."[30] The NWP similarly tapped into Lafayette's and Rochambeau's collective memories as they marched in line to the generals' statues in Lafayette Square, where members upheld banners, climbed the statues, and delivered speeches.[31]

The NWP held protests at the Lafayette and Rochambeau statues in order to align its woman suffrage campaign with America's revolutionary legacy. For the NWP, Lafayette and Rochambeau represented the nation's revolutionary principles yet also offered the NWP's campaign international legitimacy. Regarding the NWP's first statue protest, held on August 8, 1918, the NWP aimed to "come into living contact with the best traditions of their country's past . . . to ask for the thing these men fought for—freedom in the United States."[32] As integral leaders in America's struggle for independence and "freedom," the generals were also conflated with the birth of American democracy. As such, the NWP appealed to Lafayette and Rochambeau as "women, who need the weapon of democracy to help win a war for democracy."[33] Here the NWP placed Lafayette's and Rochambeau's historical legacies in their arsenal to help win their "war for democracy" through a federal suffrage amendment. This appeal rehearsed Wilson's war program; it could be said that he, too, used "the weapon of democracy to help win a war for democracy" abroad. By tapping into the collective memories of Lafayette and Rochambeau, the NWP rehearsed Wilson's rhetorical strategies to enhance public opinion for the suffrage amendment and to place added pressure on Wilson to instill his democratic values at home.

The NWP adopted Lafayette's and Rochambeau's revolutionary motives to help legitimize their protest against the US government. In the *Suffragist*'s description of "these two heroic Frenchmen," the NWP noted their "unselfish idealism, their distinguished rank, and their impetuous courage," which helped the United States "become a strong and just republic."[34] By likening itself to Lafayette and Rochambeau, the NWP inherited the "idealism" and "courage" necessary to fortify the nation's democratic principles. The NWP's mimetic assumption of Lafayette's and Rochambeau's revolutionary spirit also constructed their protests as acts of rebellion in which sacrifice was justified. The *Suffragist* noted that "Lafayette defied his King and his government to put his sword at the service of the young republic," while Rochambeau "trained French battalions to the aid of the hard-pressed American colonies, battling for independence."[35] Like Lafayette's defiance, the NWP justified their protests against President Wilson as acts of allegiance to "the young republic." The NWP also used Rochambeau's selflessness as a means to accentuate their sacrifice to liberate American women as they "battl[ed] for independence." Inheriting Lafayette's and Rochambeau's senses of self-sacrifice helped construct the suffrage protesters as revolutionary martyrs. The NWP invoked the memory of its own martyr, Inez Milholland, to help forge a symbolic alliance with the generals. In fact, the NWP's first statue protest was conducted in honor of Milholland's spirit of "rebellion against injustice."[36]

Drawing upon the collective memories of Lafayette and Rochambeau helped the NWP levy its criticism of Wilson's resistance as a betrayal of the generals' revolutionary vision. Recalling their Sentinels' protests, the NWP said, "The women, who for long months of the past year stood with their golden suffrage banners before the gates of the White House, silently appealing for the right of self-government, thought often, as they looked across at the soldierly bronze figures facing them, what these pure-hearted lovers of liberty would have thought [of] the refusal of America to deal generously with the liberties of its own people."[37] Similarly, the cover of the August 10 issue of the *Suffragist* featured a cartoon of Lafayette asking Rochambeau, "Does the Republic we fought for deny liberty to its own citizens?"[38] In both instances, the NWP insinuated that Wilson obstructed the same "liberties" for which the generals fought and the nation seemingly symbolized. Moreover, the NWP drew a comparison between the military ethos of Lafayette and Rochambeau, and Wilson's role as commander in chief, and thus indi-

FIGURE 5.1. NWP members, one reading a speech, at Lafayette's statue (1918). Reproduced courtesy Harris & Ewing Collection, Library of Congress, LC-DIG-hec-11380.

rectly criticized Wilson's abilities to lead the nation in war. Such a critique was particularly salient considering Wilson's reluctance to enter the war in the first place.

The NWP's invocation of Lafayette's and Rochambeau's legacies also resonated with the wartime alliances between France and the United States, particularly with the AEF's concurrent battles in France. The NWP argued that just as "Rochambeau was commissioned by France" to fight in the American Revolution, American troops were sent to France to help defeat Germany. In turn, the NWP called upon Lafayette to help the suffragists' campaign for democracy. In a September protest, NWP member Bertha Arnold addressed the general: "Will you ask the great leader of democracy to look upon the failure of our beloved country[?] . . . Let that outstretched hand of your[s] pointing to the White House, recall to him his words and promises, his trumpet call for all of us, to see that the world is made safe for democracy. As our army now in France spoke to you there, saying, 'Here we are to help your country fight for liberty,' will you not speak here and now for us, a little band with no army, no power but justice and right, no strength but in our Constitution and in the Declaration of Independence."[39] Arnold called upon Lafayette not to fight, but to "speak" on behalf of the suffragists and to "ask" President Wilson why he had not yet granted woman suffrage. Through this representation of Lafayette, the NWP attempted to trap Wilson in his democratic promises and magnify the inconsistencies of his internationalist ideology.

Invoking Lafayette's and Rochambeau's collective memories, however, pointed to complexities of asserting political agency amidst institutional forces. For example, Lafayette and Rochambeau functioned as symbols of key democratic principles; however, such principles have historically been the foundation for the exclusion and restriction of citizenship rights. The NWP's appeals to Lafayette, for instance, as "a little band with no army, no power" reified US women's disempowered citizenship status and rehearsed the process through which women have appealed to privileged white men throughout US history for their rights. Lafayette's statue, in fact, features a partially robed woman at its base, lifting a sword up to the general. Addressing Lafayette, Bertha Arnold said that NWP members were "condemned like the bronze woman at your feet, to a silent appeal. She offers you a sword. Will you not use the sword of the spirit, mightier far than the sword she

FIGURE 5.2. Crowds gathering to see the NWP's protest at Lafayette's statue (1918). Reproduced courtesy Harris & Ewing Collection, Library of Congress, LC-DIG-hec-11566.

holds out to you."[40] In this scene, the NWP members placed themselves below Lafayette, in a position of powerlessness, from which they symbolically extended to him a weapon to help fight for woman suffrage. However, from this subordinate position, this woman—or the NWP—authorized the use of the weapon. Thus, this representation of Lafayette symbolized the power struggle between the NWP and President Wilson in which the NWP positioned Wilson as the primary change agent for woman suffrage, yet asserted its political agency in the process of participating in his presidential vision.

International Militant Leaders

While the NWP's statue protests may have invoked the paternalistic relationship between the US government and disenfranchised women, the NWP also sought solidarity with French suffragists who demanded equal citizenship rights in their own country. In 1918, both the US and French suffrage movements were endorsed by their presidents but faced resistance from their legislative bodies.[41] Seeking an alliance with French suffragists to help liberate women worldwide paralleled Wilson's international efforts to "liberate" oppressed nations. Ironically, as the NWP's international alliance with France attempted to increase pressure on President Wilson, it also worked to reify Wilson's growing role as the leader of world democracy. The reach of Wilson's rhetorical leadership extended beyond national borders and eventually influenced the French government's position on suffrage, which in turn, subverted the NWP's efforts to unite with French women in a common state of disenfranchisement. Nonetheless, the NWP reenvisioned the national limits of US women's citizenship rights by mimicking Wilson's international campaign and forging unity with French suffragists.

As early as 1913, the NWP recognized the international character of the movement; its national parade featured a section representing nations that had already granted women fully enfranchised citizenship rights. In its 1916 anti-Democratic campaign, the NWP declared, for example, "This is the century of the awakening consciousness of women. In every nation of the earth, women are sacrificing for the advancement of other women."[42] In fact, throughout 1917 and 1918, the *Suffragist* provided weekly reports on the women's rights movements in countries such as Great Britain, Italy, Denmark, France, Hungary, Switzerland, Turkey, India, Sweden, Norway, Canada, Russia, Austria, Uruguay, Bohemia, Moravia, Silesia, Austria, Jamaica, and Ireland.[43] This growing awareness motivated the NWP's campaign for

US women's rights, while it also helped construct the vote as a way to empower women in other nations.

In light of the Progressive Era's reprisal of US nationalism and nativism, the NWP's efforts to form an alliance with French suffragists also reflected the need to establish dominance over other nations. Thus, after Germany enfranchised women in late 1918, the NWP said, "[T]he United States of America is put in the humiliating position of lagging behind Germany."[44] However, the NWP also positioned itself as the leader of the woman suffrage movement among Allied nations. In early 1918, the NWP said of the French government's resistance to enfranchising women: "For a progressive and enlightened democracy, such a record on a 'fundamental' question is almost disconcerting as was the studious neglect of politicians in this country, so recently forced to a position more in keeping with its war for democracy abroad."[45] In light of the timing, it can be inferred that the NWP considered itself the driving force behind Wilson's shift toward supporting a federal woman suffrage amendment in January 1918. Moreover, the NWP placed itself in a superior position as it constructed the French woman suffrage movement as a lesser challenge. As such, the NWP constructed itself as a leader in the worldwide woman suffrage movement, just as Wilson did in the international movement for democracy.

Through the *Suffragist*'s coverage of the French woman suffrage movement, the NWP worked to create alliances with French women and reify its position as leader in the international suffrage movement. In May 1918, Jeanne Mélin, leader of her newly formed French militant organization Comité d'action, wrote to Pierre-Etienne Flandin, leader of the Commission of Universal Suffrage, in protest of his recent revisions to the suffrage bill. The amendments specified that French women could not vote until they were twenty-five, unlike men who could vote at twenty-one, and that women elected at the municipal level could not help elect senators.[46] Regarding this development, the NWP wrote: "Just as in England and in this country, there have been groups of suffragists who have become impatient of the old slow methods of suffrage propaganda and have insisted upon immediate recognition, the same sort of group has arisen in France. . . . [Comité d'action's] letter sounds like a protest from the National Woman's Party to the Senate. The dissatisfaction of women with conservative government is not, however, confined to this country and is finding expression in other countries in the same way as in this country."[47] Here the NWP worked to create a sense of solidarity with England's suffrage movement, where Paul and Burns earned their militant training. Moreover, the NWP constructed Comité d'action as a mimetic formation of itself—as "the same sort of group [which] has arisen in France." Specifically, the NWP inferred that the letter of protest from the Comité d'action mimicked the NWP's rhetoric of protest. The NWP, however, elided any reference to itself as a mimetic formation of England's Women's Social and Political Union (WSPU). The WSPU is often credited for disseminating militant suffrage activism all over the world.[48] Additionally, the NWP's rendition of the French suffrage movement suggested that militancy had just taken hold in France, when an organized militant movement had been active since January 1914. In fact, Mélin's Comité d'action only represented about 150 women, who worked in concert with the dominant militant suffrage organization, the Ligue francaise pour le droit des femmes.[49] Thus, the NWP's strategic construction of the French suffrage organization as a mimetic formation of itself helped elevate the NWP as a leader in the international suffrage movement, while it worked to forge a sense of unity among British, American, and French suffragists.

Just as the NWP worked to position itself as a leader of the international suffrage movement, Wilson's support of French suffragists worked to position the United States as a leader in world democracy. In fact, while touring Europe in June 1918, President Wilson addressed France's more moderate suffrage organization, the Union francais pour le suffrage des femmes (UFSF). Like the NWP's report on the militant suffrage organization, Wilson's support of French national suffrage helped reify the United States as the leader of world democracy. Relayed to the UFSF through Carrie Chapman Catt, Wilson said of French women: "The war could not have been fought without them, or its sacrifices endured. It is high time that some part of our debt of gratitude to them should be acknowledged and paid, and the only acknowledgement they ask is their admission to suffrage. Can we justly refuse it? As for America, it is my earnest hope that the Senate of the United States will give an unmistakable answer to this question by passing the suffrage amendment to our federal constitution before the end of this session."[50] Like his arguments for US woman suffrage, the president supported French woman suffrage as a debt to war service. Moreover, as Wilson took the opportunity to pressure the US Senate to pass the amendment, he implied that French leaders should model his democratic efforts, thereby positioning the United States as the premier example of democratic policy. It should be noted, however, that most prominent politicians in France supported woman suffrage, including the leaders of France's two major parties and France's wartime president, Raymond Poincaré.[51] Their support thus suggested that Wilson's endorsement was motivated perhaps less by his concern for French women and more by his efforts to bolster America's international standing, particularly as US woman suffrage potentially offered the president greater political capital as he sought to implement his postwar peace plan.

Wilson's address to the UFSF also represented an extension of the rhetorical presidency, particularly as Wilson worked to establish an international alliance of nations. In this expansion of the rhetorical presidency, Wilson appealed to the people of another nation in such a way that reified his international and national agenda. Shortly after Wilson addressed the UFSF, the NWP reported that "wide publicity has been given [in Paris] to President Wilson's statement in favor of woman suffrage. . . . As a result, the Socialist group in the French Chamber of Deputies will ask for the appointment of a committee to consider the question and make a report."[52] A few months later, the UFSF happily wrote Wilson: "As we hoped, your opinion on woman suffrage has made a deep impression in France and has exercised a favorable influence on our deputies." Embittered by the successful reach of Wilson's rhetorical presidency, the *Suffragist* said: "We are glad to hear that the expressions of the President's opinion ha[ve] had so beneficial an effect upon the French deputies. Up to the present it has not [had] any visible effect on any American Senator."[53] While the NWP pointed to Wilson's unwillingness to support US woman suffrage, Wilson's endorsement of French suffrage worked as part of his internationalist program, which held the potential to bolster US woman suffrage. Ideally, Wilson's efforts would help compel US senators to endorse woman suffrage in order to further establish the United States as a democratizing force in the international arena. Typical of the NWP's militant sense of immediacy, the group wasted no time adopting Wilson's international ethos and putting pressure on US senators to support America's democratic efforts abroad.

Senate Protests and International Democracy

The NWP's efforts to forge an international alliance with French revolutionaries and suffragists mimicked and helped reify President Wilson's international leadership. Strengthening Wilson's leadership was crucial in the fall of 1918 as the war neared its conclusion and Wilson prepared to shape a peacetime alliance of nations. Despite Wilson's public support for the UFSF, he had yet to make a public appeal to the US Senate to pass the suffrage measure. The NWP's continued statue protests throughout September and October only intensified after Wilson's rhetorical leadership bolstered woman suffrage in France. In light of these exigencies, Wilson made a formal address to the US Senate on September 30, 1918, in which he argued for woman suffrage as part of his international agenda.

In this address to the Senate, Wilson not only argued that woman suffrage was "vitally essential to the successful prosecution of the great war of humanity in which we are engaged," but he linked woman suffrage to US internationalism.[54] He said, "We cannot isolate our thought or our action in such a matter from the thought of the rest of the world. We must either conform or deliberately reject what they propose and resign the leadership of liberal minds to others."[55] Wilson seemed most concerned with preserving the nation's emerging role as the leader of world democracy as he began supporting women's fully enfranchised political rights. Not surprisingly, then, when Wilson further argued for woman suffrage, he rehearsed the traditional construction of women as morally superior beings rather than grounding his argument in equal rights ideologies. Regarding women's roles in postwar reconstruction, he said, "[W]e shall need . . . the sympathy and the insight and clear moral instinct of the women of the world."[56] Although Wilson promoted woman suffrage for women worldwide, he did so in such a way that de-emphasized women's political participation.

With Wilson's support of woman suffrage throughout 1918, particularly as part of his war program, the NWP expected the president to flex his rhetorical leadership and effectively sway the Democratic vote in the Senate. By early fall, however, such hopes had not been actualized. Earlier, on May 10, the Senate failed to pass the amendment by three votes, and on June 27 the measure failed by two votes, prompting the NWP to argue that "the President could have won [these votes] if he had put forth a fraction of his strength."[57] After Wilson's September 30 address, the Senate was still two votes shy of passing the amendment. Shifting away from the president, the NWP vowed to "make it so uncomfortable for the Senate that they will be glad to have [woman suffrage] out of the way," promising that its "demonstrations will go on at whatever cost of humiliation, pain, even life to these women."[58] Thus, throughout October and November 1918, the NWP turned their attention to the Senate as the chief opponent to woman suffrage.

Consistent with the NWP's previous protests, the militant women adopted the president's wartime authority and pressured the Senate to pass the woman suffrage amendment as a necessary war measure. Moreover, the NWP's protest against Democratic senators fashioned a wartime alliance with the president while it also positioned the women as loyal citizens of Wilson's United States. As such, the NWP's appeals constructed the thirty-four "wilful [*sic*] senators" as disloyal opponents to the war. Similar to the

FIGURE 5.3. Mildred Gilbert of California, Pauline Floyd of Washington D.C., and Vivian Pierce of California picketing the Russell Senate Office Building (1918). Reproduced courtesy Harris & Ewing Collection, Library of Congress, LC-DIG-hec-05533.

"Silent Sentinels," delegations of women took to the steps of the Capitol and to the entrance of the Senate Office Building and stood silently with banners in hand. One banner declared that the senators had "obstructed the war program of the President. They have lined up the Senate with Prussia by denying self government to the people."[59] This banner compared the Senate to an antidemocratic imperialist government. However, armed with Wilson's explicit endorsement, the NWP's accusation mimicked Wilson's own efforts to pressure contrary senators and worked to legitimize the women's protest as part of their wartime allegiance.

The NWP's alliance with the president was strengthened by the war service of many of the protesters. For example, munitions factory workers participated in the NWP's line-up.[60] Earlier that year, munitions workers pled for suffrage rights in a testimony to Congress. They argued: "[W]e face the risk of injury and death as soldiers face it. . . [We] will be recognized as citizens of the government we are working to defend and equals of the men who fight with the arms we make for them."[61] Similar to the Sentinels, these women identified themselves as soldiers, reflecting the growing recognition that citizenship rights were earned through war service. Red Cross workers also joined the NWP that fall after 106 Red Cross women protested against the president in May.[62] Some NWP protesters declared that they were mothers and sisters of soldiers fighting overseas.[63] Reifying the protesters' patriotism, the *Suffragist* reported that "sailors on Pennsylvania Avenue gravely salut[ed] the [US] flag at the head of the [NWP's] line."[64] Unlike the Sentinels, who protested well before the AEF landed in France, many of these women possessed the necessary war ethos to help legitimize their protest as part of the war effort.

NWP members also mimicked the president's role of commander in chief as they assumed the authority to question the senators' patriotism. The NWP assailed the war ethos of Sen. James W. Wadsworth Jr. (R-NY), who had served in the Spanish-American War. With their mimetic adoption of Wilson's war authority and as loyal US citizens, the protesters demanded that the senator consistently participate in Wilson's international and domestic war efforts. The NWP's banner said: "Senator Wadsworth's Regiment Is Fighting for Democracy Abroad; Senator Wadsworth Left his Regiment and Is Fighting against Democracy in the Senate; Senator Wadsworth Could Serve His Country Better by Fighting with His Regiment Abroad than by Fighting Women."[65] Wadsworth's war experience allowed the NWP to constitute the deliberative space of the US Senate as an arena of war in which senators needed to fight for woman suffrage as soldiers fought for democracy abroad. In declaring the Senate a battlefield, the NWP symbolically expanded the reach of the war and thus worked to extend women's participation and authority in the nation-state. Cooke and Woollacott explain: "To the extent that boundaries between home and front can be deconstructed, unprecedented modes of gendered thinking become possible."[66] By reconstituting the wartime battlefield, the NWP created even greater exigency for expanding wartime gender roles and women's citizenship rights.

Despite the pressing exigencies of the war, the endorsement of the president, and the NWP's continued agitation, the war ended, and the Senate adjourned on November 21 without passing the woman suffrage amendment. When the armistice was signed on November 11, signaling the war's end, the NWP lost the symbolic force of Wilson's war rhetoric and thus construed the president as a traitor to his own war program and democratic mission. Even though the NWP felt particularly betrayed as the president campaigned for the reelection of Democratic senators,[67] they were heartened by the defeat of many of those same Democratic senators.[68] Moreover, the NWP considered Wilson's campaign to form a peacetime alliance at the upcoming peace conference in Paris the necessary leverage to hold the president accountable for extending citizenship rights at home. Thus, in late November, the NWP prepared to hold President Wilson to the fire.

"Watch Fires of Freedom"

Before Congress reconvened in December 1918, and before Wilson jettisoned to Europe to promote the League of Nations, the NWP announced: "We demand that the President put all his strength into seeing that when Congress meets in December, this measure is passed before any other is considered. We demand that before the President leaves to promote democracy for Europe at the peace table, he devote all his power to establishing self-government for the people at home. Until the Senate passes this measure, America must . . . enter the Peace Conference with unclean hands."[69] In his December 2 address to Congress, Wilson placed woman suffrage on his legislative program; unfortunately, the Democratic chairman of the Rules Committee did not put the measure on the docket.[70] Enraged, the NWP argued that Wilson "had so long formulated, defended, and thus encouraged and solidified" the Senate's opposition.[71] In December, the NWP regrouped during its Conference of the National Advisory Council, and devised a strategy to force a vote on woman suffrage in the Senate before it adjourned in four months. The conference boasted attendance from enfranchised women all over the world and women from every congressional district in the nation. As the NWP had done many times before, the women marched to the Senate and presented each senator with a suffrage resolution.[72] However, the conference concluded with the introduction of a new protest strategy; three hundred NWP members marched to Lafayette's statue with an urn and copies of Wilson's speeches that promoted democracy in Europe. Page by page, the women consigned Wilson's words to flames.[73]

The NWP officially activated the "perpetual Watch Fire of Freedom" on January 1, 1919, intending to burn Wilson's speeches as he delivered them in Europe.[74] As soon as reports of a speech reached the women, they rang a "liberty bell" at the NWP headquarters and marched to the park to set fire to a copy of the text.[75] NWP member, Lucy Branham, attributed the practice to "the ancient fights for liberty [when] the crusaders for freedom symbolized their protest against those responsible for injustice by consigning their hollow phrases to the flames."[76] Like the NWP's silent protests, these women identified themselves as "crusaders of freedom"; however, by extinguishing Wilson's words in a live flame, the NWP intensified its attack on Wilson by literally and symbolically reducing his words to ashes, further accentuating the hypocrisy between his words abroad and at home. Thus, through the "Watch Fires," the NWP attempted to pressure Wilson to actualize his democratic commitments at home.

The NWP's "Watch Fires" reflected the ways in which Wilson's war discourse drew upon the naturalizing power of fire metaphors. Jason C. Flanagan argues that fire metaphors helped Wilson transition the nation into war.[77] Wilson often constructed Europe as site of eminent threat, or a place "ablaze with terrible war."[78] During his preparedness campaign in 1916, the president said, "The world is on fire and there is tinder everywhere. The sparks are liable to drop anywhere, and somewhere there may be material which we can not prevent from bursting into flame."[79] Shortly before the United States entered the war, Wilson transformed fire from a threatening agent to a purifying and regenerative agent: "We are being forged into a new unity amidst the fires that now blaze throughout the world. In their ardent heat we shall, in God's providence, let us hope, be purged of faction and division, purified of the errant humours of party and of private interest, and shall stand forth in the days to come with a new dignity of national pride and spirit."[80] The malleability of fire metaphors helped Wilson justify the country's belated entrance into the war as a natural and necessary step toward freedom.

The NWP naturalized its attacks on the president through the literal and symbolic meanings of fire. The NWP's use of fire helped construct woman suffrage as an inevitable victory, as it constructed fire as an invincible and relentless force. For instance, not only did the flames survive the law enforcement's fire extinguisher, they also resisted the extinguishing power of another natural force—rain. Mildred Morris wrote: "Rain falls and the flames dance as full and red as ever! Indomitable flames—as indomitable as the women who guard them! All night the rain falls but the watchfire of freedom keeps burning on!"[81] Although Rose Conlan, Alice Paul, Julia Emory, and Edith Ainge were arrested for attempting to light another fire, the fire continued to burn all day and night. Elizabeth Kalb linked the fire's endurance to that of the suffragist, writing of "[t]hat watch fire, which, however many times it be extinguished, always flames up again, lit by the unfailing hope and determination in women's hearts."[82] So long as the women remained as extraordinarily steadfast as the flames, they would win the fight for woman suffrage.

Additionally, the fires symbolized the ubiquitous threat of woman suffrage. Just like the expanding reach of the war, the "Watch Fires of Freedom" would ideally bring suffrage to women. For example, on January 7, 1919, when the NWP attempted to burn a speech Wilson had just delivered in Turin, Italy, the police attempted to put out the NWP's fire. The *Suffragist* reported: "Suddenly from the mysterious darkness came the order to stop the fire, which the police did very effectively. No sooner was the fire quite dead, however, till they awakened to the fact that a second fire was flaming all about the base of Lafayette statue. . . . Here, there, everywhere the flames arose; the whole District seemed to be burning with indignation against the President who has so completely forgot the demands of his own country."[83] Here the NWP translated the ubiquity and resilience of the fire to the suffragists themselves, thus creating the sense that NWP members, who were "burning with indignation," were also agents of fire consuming "the whole District." Matilda Young reinforced the NWP's threat by promising, "The women of the country will keep the flame of liberty ablaze until complete victory is assured and the words of the President are translated into reality."[84] Like Wilson, the NWP used fire to symbolize the natural spread of democracy.

The NWP reinforced the ubiquity of the woman suffrage movement by conducting "Watch Fire" protests in Boston and New York, within close proximity to the president as he promoted the League of Nations. On February 24, NWP members created a "Watch Fire" on the Boston Common to greet the president upon his return from Europe. Shortly after the Boston protest, NWP members headed to New York and created a "Watch Fire" in front of the Metropolitan Opera House. Inside the Met, one member recorded Wilson's words as he said them and then sneaked her notes outside to Elsie Hill, who burned them with her torch.[85] Burning the president's words in front of the Met represented the instantaneous defeat of Wilson's ideological program, as NWP members attempted to suck the life out of his words as soon as he uttered them. Moreover, as both of these "Watch Fires" took place near the president, they magnified the bodily threat posed by the fires.

Thus, as a ubiquitous and immediate threat, the fire functioned as another strategy to empower the NWP's anti-Wilson campaign. By burning the president's words, the NWP emphasized their emptiness and, in a way, rendered the president silent and powerless. The NWP escalated these efforts to symbolically silence the president on February 9, when the women burned the president in effigy. The *Suffragist* described it as "a final protest against the threatened shame and disgrace to the Administration and to America." About two thousand people gathered to witness the hundred women protest in "a drama of freedom."[86] By burning the effigy, the "Watch Fire" functioned as a crucible purifying the NWP's campaign of the "shame and disgrace" obstructing the women's freedom. Moreover, the fire created a site of power where the NWP controlled the president's fate and symbolically killed his opposition to suffrage. This act mimicked the president's attempts to silence US women, deny them full citizenship rights, and condone acts of physical domination. At the same time, burning the president's words and the president in effigy worked to delegitimize his peacetime campaign and draw attention to his hypocrisy.

The NWP continued its "Watch Fire" protests through May, though burning Wilson in effigy was its most volatile and direct form of attack on the president. The women never took to initiating physical violence or destroying public property, but their symbolic execution of the president represented the height of the NWP's militancy and its final mimetic performance of Wilson's resistance to woman suffrage. Through its statue protests, Senate protests, and "Watch Fires," the NWP worked to mimic and expose the hypocrisy of Wilson's international and wartime authority and thus empower women's full citizenship rights in the national and international arenas. These protest strategies also positioned the NWP in close proximity to the president in an attempt to force him to debate the issue, while also elevating their own political authority. In light of the Senate's passage of the amendment in early June 1919, the NWP's last chapter of militant protest must be considered a key factor in securing woman suffrage.

CONCLUSION: SUFFRAGE SUCCESS AND BACKLASH

In May 1919, Senator William J. Harris (D-GA) declared his intent to support the woman suffrage amendment, providing the measure its sixty-fourth vote and the necessary two-thirds majority to submit it to states for ratification. By this time, Congress had adjourned, thus prompting the NWP to hold daily protests at the Lafayette statue demanding a special session.[87] The special session met on May 19, and on June 4 at 5:15 P.M., House Joint Resolution 1 passed through the Senate.[88]

The Senate's ultimate passage of the federal woman suffrage amendment can be partly attributed to Wilson's expedient endorsement of woman suffrage. When he called upon the special session of Congress to pass the woman suffrage amendment, he said, "I, for one, covet for our country the distinction of being among the first to act in a great reform."[89] Although many other countries had granted women national voting rights by this time, Wilson's support for the measure worked to promote the United States as a leader among democratic nations. In fact, Wilson persuaded Senator Harris to support the movement at a meeting in Paris, where the president was engaged in forming the League of Nations.[90] Thus, the exigencies of postwar international relations and party loyalty cannot be separated from the amendment's success. So although Harris's support signaled a victory for the suffragists, it can also be considered a victory for Wilson's League.

The NWP's protests between 1918 and 1919 mimicked Wilson's rhetorical leadership and his capacity as a wartime president, which helped reify his political role and power in the woman suffrage debate. More significantly, the NWP's rhetorical acts of political mimesis empowered US women to assert their political agency and redefine their roles in the nation-state. In the process, they positioned themselves in the coveted spaces of the nation, exerting their own authority to bring public opinion to the side of suffrage.

To an extent, however, the NWP's rhetoric of political mimesis was perceived as a threat to presidential and congressional power. The NWP's statue protests, Senate protests, and "Watch Fires" provoked significant backlash similar to the acts of social control exacted against the "Silent Sentinels." The statue protests resulted in particularly brutal arrests. The *Suffragist* noted, "When released [from police headquarters] the women appeared with tears streaming down their faces, bruised throats, swollen, twisted wrists, and sprained fingers." Other women testified to being "thrown upon the tables and choked" while detained.[91] The women who were imprisoned suffered nauseating odors and stifled air.[92] The NWP's protests on the Senate provoked the Capitol police to tear and retrieve the women's banners, detain them in the Capitol's guard room for hours, and throw the women down the front steps of the building, knocking one protester, Annie Arneil, unconscious.[93] At the "Watch Fires," NWP members were mobbed and arrested daily. For example, shortly after Sue White and Gabrielle Harris dropped Wilson's effigy into the flames, thirty-nine women were arrested. [94] Moreover, the NWP members who protested Wilson in New York "were beaten and dragged and trampled under foot by the police, aided by a mob of soldiers and sailors."[95]

While these acts of physical domination often worked to render the women physically powerless, such acts of institutional resistance most significantly attempted to deny the women their citizenship identities. For example, the sixteen women arrested at the Boston "Watch Fire" endured little physical abuse but they were symbolically rendered powerless as their individual identities were erased in the court hearings. The judge argued that their names "were of no consequence," and, as documented in the *Suffragist,*

"Some of the [women's] names were known. Some were not. Some were tried under wrong names, some were tried several times under different names, some were tried under the name of Jane Doe; in fact there was quite a family of Jane Does in the Boston Court that morning."[96] Clearly, the women were being tried *as women* who had overstepped the boundaries of appropriate citizenship behavior by entering the spaces of politics, particularly the spaces of the presidency. Yet, the NWP members forged a shared identity as members of "a family of Jane Does," turning their site of oppression into a site of empowerment. The use of the family metaphor reified the naturalizing construction of women as domestic beings, but it also created a sense of strength in the face of physical and symbolic oppression.

Unlike the Sentinels' protests in 1917, however, the protests between 1918 and 1919 were protected by greater institutional legitimacy. During the Senate protests, the NWP's lawyer appealed to Judge Frederick L. Siddons, who determined that holding the women inside the Capitol building and seizing the women's banners was unlawful.[97] The protesters received further support from Judge Benjamin Barr Lindsey, who had recently returned from a six-month visit in Europe as a member of the Committee on Public Information—the propaganda arm of the Wilson presidency. Concerned with how the nation was perceived by other nations, Lindsey argued that "the authorities responsible for the arrest of the women ought to be indicted for aiding German propaganda against our country."[98] Moreover, the day after the New York protests, "sailors, privates, and officers both military and naval, continued to come into the office of Suffrage Headquarters to apologize for the conduct of men in uniform."[99] By May 1919, when the NWP protested at the Lafayette statue in demand of a special session of Congress, civil and military police stood guard to protect them from attack. Thus, the NWP helped expand the citizenship rights of women by expanding the boundaries of social change.[100]

Like the Sentinels, NWP members were protected by their privileged identities as mostly white women. During the statue protests, for example, Matthew O'Brien, counsel to the NWP, refuted the charges against women for "climbing upon the monument," by arguing: "It cannot be that well-dressed, well-educated, well-conducted women could be regarded as a disfigurement to a monument."[101] More significantly, as the exigencies of war were replaced by the exigencies of peace, the women's protests seemed to resonate with the international push for women's national rights. Once Wilson returned from the peace conference in Paris, the women's protests for a special session of Congress incurred little institutional and social resistance.

Throughout this latter chapter of the NWP's militant protests, the NWP helped fashion an international model of woman citizenship that reinforced the growing internationalism of the movement. However, this model also perpetuated an Anglo-Saxon citizenship ideal reflective of Wilson's progressive program of nativist nationalism. The NWP forged alliances with the predominantly white leaders of British and French suffragist movements. And although the *Suffragist* featured weekly reports on suffrage movements led by non-Anglo-Saxon women in Asia, South America, and Africa, the NWP rarely sought to create solidarity with any women of color. African American women were excluded from the NWP's protests and discursive constructions of suffrage unity. Indicative of the NWP's latent racism, Maud Younger delivered a speech in late 1918 and referred to resistant senators as the "Ten Little Nigger Boys"—the subjects of a children's nursery rhyme that depicted ten African American boys who, one by one, were killed through their own mischievous behavior.[102] The reference demonstrated that the NWP promoted the same exclusionary ideologies that worked against women, thus exposing the limits of the NWP's campaign for equal rights.

As such, the NWP's rhetorical acts of political mimesis between 1918 and 1919 can be considered artifacts of the Progressive Era's empowering and disempowering potential. Wilson's fashioning of the rhetorical presidency and the rise of US internationalism similarly shaped the NWP's final stages of militancy in its fight for a federal woman suffrage amendment. The NWP mimicked Wilson's internationalist strides by aligning woman suffrage with America's democratizing efforts worldwide. By June 1919, the NWP had helped make the world safe for woman suffrage and thus shifted its energies toward securing the ratification of the thirty-six states needed to write the amendment into the US Constitution.

Afterword

"Suffrage Leaders"

By August 1920, Tennessee and North Carolina were the suffragists' last hopes for ratification—and a majority of North Carolina's representatives stood in opposition to the woman suffrage amendment. A Supreme Court decision allowed Tennessee's Democratic governor, Albert H. Roberts, to call a special legislative session on August 9. On the morning of August 18, after last-minute shifts in suffrage allegiances, Tennessee legislators tied in a vote on a motion to table the woman suffrage amendment.[1] Following the tie, members were to vote on the woman suffrage measure itself. All eyes turned to a twenty-four-year-old representative, Harry Burn. As a junior representative of an anti-suffrage district, many expected Burn to oppose the amendment. But a message from his suffrage-supporting mother that morning said: "Don't forget to be a good boy and help Mrs. [Carrie Chapman] Catt put 'Rat' in Ratification." Burn voted in the affirmative. Similarly, Rep. Banks Turner changed his vote to the affirmative, ratifying the measure with 49 to 47 votes, signaling the passage of a federal woman suffrage amendment.[2]

Upon Tennessee's ratification of the Nineteenth Amendment, National Woman's Party Political Chairman Abby Scott Baker and the Democratic presidential nominee, Gov. James A. Cox, posed for a celebratory photograph. When a reporter asked Baker whom she credited for the suffrage success, Baker recognized the strength of key political endorsements. She said, "Individual men have helped splendidly and we thank them heartily." Baker's assertion of her political agency shone through, however, when she added: "But the American women can take to themselves the happy assurance that it was the women themselves who won their enfranchisement."[3] Baker's statement symbolized the empowering thrust of the seven-year fight for woman suffrage: by engaging "individual men" and mimicking the rituals of male political power, "it was the women themselves" of the National Woman's Party (NWP) who constituted their citizenship identities and asserted their political agency in the pursuit of enfranchisement.

This book's focus on how the NWP's rhetoric of political mimesis helped effect the passage of the Nineteenth Amendment offers multiple historical and theoretical implications. Historically, the impact of the NWP's mimetic adoption of political strategies is made visible when considering the national prominence of the NWP during the ratification campaign, the promotion of suffrage as part in parcel to Wilson's democratic vision, and the unity and disunity of suffrage communities before and after ratification. The NWP's campaign also exhibits the theoretical contributions of political mimesis as it empowered the NWP and US women to constitute their citizenship identities and assert political agency as they engaged in the rituals and rhetorics of politics. Consequently, the campaign of the NWP showed that members of the US polity could participate in and take part ownership of the rhetorical presidency. Such participation helped the NWP contribute to the normalization of women's presence in political spaces, nationalize the suffrage movement, and reenvision the gendered nation-state. Such mimetic rhetorics thus facilitated the performance of both traditional and militant acts of political protest, the latter of which engendered severe backlash.

IMPACTING NATIONAL AND SUFFRAGE COMMUNITIES

Most scholars agree that the combination of the militant strategies of the NWP and the more moderate strategies of the National American Woman Suffrage Associations (NAWSA) helped effect the passage of the Nineteenth Amendment.[4] This study, however, deepens our appreciation of the contributions of the NWP to US political culture in the early twentieth century in a number of ways. First, the mimetic campaign of the NWP earned the organization a prominent position in national politics and in the mediated spotlight. The political legitimacy the NWP earned between 1913 and 1919 culminated the organization's recognition as a key player in the state ratification campaign, which exhibited many of the militant and more traditional campaign strategies employed prior to 1919. Specifically, the NWP's ratification campaign focused on state work as subordinate to national work, targeted protests at national parties, and developed close ties with presidential candidates. Next, the NWP's rhetorical campaign that linked Wilson's brand of democracy and woman suffrage together paved the way for future national leaders to envision US women as political actors. Last, as the NWP worked to unite women along international, labor, and regional lines, it also worked to divide women along race lines. Such unity and disunity shaped the ways in which women asserted their political agency after the passage of the Nineteenth Amendment.

"Suffrage Leaders"

The state ratification campaign of the NWP demonstrated the organization's successful insinuation into national-level politics, the normalization of women in political and national spaces, and forced a rhetorical exchange between the NWP and political leaders. The success of the ratification campaign rested on the extension of the group's previous philosophy and tactics. For example, as was emblematic of the representation of state suffrage organizations in the NWP's 1913 parade, the NWP treated state ratification campaigns as subordinate but integral to national enfranchisement. After the Senate passed House Joint Resolution 1 on June 4, 1919, Alice Paul said, "Ratification work is not to take the form of numerous independent state campaigns, but of a great national movement receiving support from every state, including those that have already ratified, and serving to intensify special work in those particular states that may present difficulties."[5] "Intensifying special work" in those "difficult" states is just what the NWP did. NWP scholar Christine A. Lunardini notes that the NWP relied on its "excellent state organizations. . . . Their lobbying techniques, honed to razor-sharpness on the national legislators, were now applied with equal vigor and results to the state legislators."[6] For example, when the Tennessee legislature was called into special session, the NWP immediately set up six different headquarters in Nashville alone.[7] From these locations, the NWP dispatched members to visit almost all Tennessee legislators in their homes.[8] Politicking at the state level yet remaining focused on enfranchisement at the national level reflected the militant push of the NWP to nationalize citizenship rights.

Much like the adaptation by the NWP of third-party strategies, the NWP targeted political parties as the key change agents in the final months of the ratification campaign. By July 1920, the NWP had—in Paul's words—conducted a "campaign of unparalleled intensity," helping to earn the ratification of thirty-five states.[9] Although legislatures of twenty-nine of the thirty-five states held Republican majorities, the Republican Party had not effectively pressured governors Percival Clement of Vermont or Marcus Holcomb of Connecticut to call special sessions. Such resistance prompted two hundred NWP members to stage a silent protest at the Republican National Convention in Chicago just like that of the "Silent Sentinels" protest staged outside the White House throughout 1917. On the third day of the convention, prominent Republican women unfurled a banner over a balcony ledge, which asked, "Why Does the Republican Party Block Suffrage? We Do Not Want Planks. We Demand the 36th State."[10] Just as the NWP had previously intruded into the halls of the US Capitol and state capitol buildings, group members inserted themselves within the deliberative spaces of national politics to engage Republican Party leaders, assert their citizenship rights, and help generate national attention to the suffrage cause.

The NWP's targeting of presidential nominees during the 1920 election cycle exhibited the group's more traditional strategies. After centering its militant campaign of opposition on President Wilson for years, NWP members ventured to do the same to presidential nominees Gov. James A. Cox and Sen. Warren G. Harding. Unlike its relationship with Wilson, however, the NWP cultivated working relationships with both Cox and Harding through careful politicking. For example, in a telegram to the chairman of the Harding-Coolidge campaign, the NWP exploited the oppositional politics of the presidential campaigns. The NWP said: "Democrats intend to put through [the] amendment and then claim credit for it with the women all over the United States and will attempt to put [the] Republicans in [a] bad light politically. We think it absolutely imperative that you vote for [the] amendment and urge others to do so."[11] Needing Harding's endorsement, the NWP did not protest the leader, but rather positioned itself as his ally by preying upon the Republicans' fear of another Democratic presidency. Further demonstrating the political savvy of the NWP, Paul appealed to the candidates' need for the women's electoral power. She said, "It is not too much to say that whether or not women vote next November rests with the Presidential nominees and their efforts for ratification."[12] The NWP's many years of targeting President Wilson as the leader and speaker of his party prepared the organization to target Cox and Harding as leaders of their parties in 1920. Pursuing Cox and Harding also reflected the earlier efforts of the NWP to parody the rise of the rhetorical presidency and constitute citizenship voices therein. Wilson's turn to support woman suffrage, however, helped position the next president as a supporter of woman suffrage, facilitating a less adversarial relationship between the NWP and the presidential candidates.

From a more privileged political position, Paul was able to call in political favors to pressure resistant politicians. For example, Edgar B. Stewart, a state senator from West Virginia (the thirty-fourth state to ratify), arranged a meeting between Paul and Cox "through a close friend," Judge Ansbery. Demonstrating the effectiveness of these networks, Stewart then told Paul, "[Ansbery] told my friend in a telephone conversation [that he'd] had from my office, that he had taken up the matter two or three days before with Governor Cox and had his assurances that he would leave nothing undone to swing Tennessee into line for ratification. . . . It would seem, therefore, that such pressure as can be had from that source will be made."[13] Paul and Stewart thus were keenly aware that applying "such pressure" from a key "source" would help effect positive change for woman suffrage.

The increased access of NWP leaders to the presidential candidates further positioned them as powerful political leaders in their own right. Most prominently, Abby Scott Baker, Political Chairman of the NWP, helped place the NWP in the mediated spotlight during the final months of the ratification campaign. She developed close relationships with Cox and Harding by maintaining a grueling travel schedule between the candidates' headquarters in Tennessee and Ohio.[14] On August 5, for example, Baker held a conference with Senator Harding before whisking off to a dinner with Governor Cox.[15] Much like the NWP's sensational acts of citizenship, in which women canvassed the United States to agitate members of Congress, Baker's tireless travels attracted press attention and helped normalize women's presence in political spaces. A front-page article in the *Washington Post,* for instance, noted that Baker was "in constant touch with Gov. Cox on the Tennessee situation."[16] The *New York Times* credited Baker with persuading Cox and Harding to send telegrams to resistant Tennessee legislators.[17] Another *Post* article depicted Baker's last-ditch efforts as revolutionary heroism by reporting that Baker "made a sort of midnight ride of Paul Revere to Marion last night to make a last minute plea to Senator Harding."[18] Baker's popular press coverage demonstrated the NWP's successful ingratiation into national politics, and, compared to Wilson's severe resistance to the NWP, Cox's and Harding's willingness to engage Baker signaled a shift toward the acceptance of women in party politics and political spaces.[19]

The NWP's use of such militant and traditional strategies helped position the organization as the leading force behind the ratification campaign. The *New York Times* reported exclusively on Paul's and Baker's campaign efforts when reporting on the "suffrage leaders" in Tennessee.[20] As such, the NWP was often constructed as *the* change agent for woman suffrage.[21] One *New York Times* article, for instance, exclusively noted the NWP's efforts: "With just one week ahead of the Tennessee Legislature's convening in special session to act on the Federal suffrage amendment, the National Woman's Party is making a strong drive to capture the ten votes needed in the House and the six votes they are short in the Senate."[22] In fact, the front-page article in the *Times* announcing the official proclamation of the amendment's ratification reported: "Woman's Party Jubilant."[23]

While the NAWSA and other suffrage-supporting organizations also earned national press coverage, the NWP swiftly secured a prominent position in national politics through its militant campaign for woman suffrage.[24] After its inception in 1913, the organization grew from just three members to fifty thousand and raised enough funds to spend $150,000 on the ratification campaign alone.[25] Although the circulation of the *Suffragist* dwindled from twenty thousand copies in 1917 to twenty-eight hundred copies in 1920, one quarter of these remaining subscribers were news agents, thus demonstrating the focus of the NWP on generating national-level attention.[26] In light of its historical impact, the success of the NWP's campaign can be attributed, at least in part, to its rhetoric of political mimesis, which helped insert NWP members within the privileged spaces of politics, normalize women's presence in national politics, and keep the suffrage conversation going through national media attention.

World Democracy and Woman Suffrage

The prominent role of the NWP in the woman suffrage movement can also be attributed to its rhetorical campaign to link woman suffrage to President Wilson's internationalist ideology. As the nation slowly shifted away from the democratic optimism of the Progressive Era into postwar discontent, the efforts of the NWP to keep woman suffrage at the forefront of US politics paid off as Wilson eventually came to actively support the amendment. Participating in and parodying Wilson's rhetorical presidency helped incorporate woman suffrage into the nation's democratic program. The NWP's "Silent Sentinels," statue protests, and "Watch Fires" proved so strong that even as Wilson's League of Nations failed, both presidential candidates, Cox and Harding, envisioned women voters as key supporters of their internationalist programs.

Despite the strength of Wilson's rhetorical leadership, he returned to a disillusioned nation after signing the Treaty of Versailles. Postwar inflation took hold and disempowered laborers went on strike. Additionally, the Red Scare prompted some vigilante groups to terrorize those perceived to be communist while the Justice Department and the attorney general had detained and deported some four thousand immigrants by 1920. Similarly, Wilson exacerbated racial tensions by tacitly supporting Postmaster General Albert S. Burleson's segregationist policies. Moreover, following the St. Louis riots in 1917, Chicago witnessed two weeks of racially motivated riots leaving thirty-eight dead and others injured and homeless.[27]

Many Americans were simply dissatisfied with the Treaty of Versailles and accused "the Big Four" of attempting to solidify power among the United States, France, Italy, and England. The treaty was formally presented to the Senate on July 10, 1919, prompting long hearings and debates throughout the summer. Simultaneously, Wilson welcomed Republican senators and members of the Senate Foreign Relations Committee to the White House to push the proposed League of Nations as a way to prevent future conflicts of such magnitude. The majority of the Senate was prepared to ratify the treaty, but only with amendments to Article 10, which would guarantee "the political independence and territorial integrity of member nations."[28] But by mid-August, Wilson recognized that he needed to mobilize the forces of public opinion. Thus, in early September, he embarked upon an intense train tour throughout the midwstern and western states. Wilson historian Arthur S. Link describes Wilson's efforts as "matchless oratory," writing that "[w]esterners had never seen such an outpouring of approval for a public leader."[29] This stunning enactment of the rhetorical presidency, however, took its toll on the president. Due to blinding headaches, Wilson cut short the tour, and he suffered a stroke after returning to Washington. Next month the Senate voted against the treaty.[30]

Even with the left side of his brain paralyzed, Wilson continued to marshal support for his international policies. After many attempts to sway the Republican opposition, the treaty was defeated on March 19, 1920. By the end of that summer, however, the Democratic ticket, comprised of Governor Cox and a young Franklin Delano Roosevelt, vowed to carry out Wilson's plans for the League. However, the Democratic Party's vision of the nation and its internationalist philosophies were soundly defeated. The nation voted largely Republican, electing Senator Harding as president—the candidate who supported a more "purified" League. Wilson ended his presidency quietly and even won a Nobel Peace Prize in December 1920. His health never recovered and he died in February 1924.[31]

Amidst Wilson's political and physiological turmoil, the NWP's exploitation of his hypocritical stance on woman suffrage had taken hold and, in part, motivated Wilson to pressure reluctant governors and legislators to support woman suffrage. For example, in August 1918, the *New Republic* reported that "English, French, German, and Russian radicals" questioned if a "nation capable of such flagrant hypocrisy could not be equally capable of arming to safeguard the world for democracy and then using the resulting increase of power."[32] The NWP's mimetic adoption of Wilson's war and peace rhetorics magnified the hypocritical proliferation of Wilson's democratic ideals, creating the exigency for Wilson to adopt woman suffrage as part of his internationalist peace program. Christine A. Lunardini argues that, throughout his campaign for the League of Nations, Wilson needed to help pass woman suffrage "in order to maintain public trust in the integrity of the United States both home and abroad."[33] Demonstrating his commitment to the measure, Wilson sent messages to the Kentucky, Oklahoma, West Virginia, Louisiana, Delaware, North Carolina, and Tennessee legislatures, urging them to call special sessions. He also sent telegrams to every southern governor.[34]

The rhetorics of democratic proliferation and woman suffrage were so inextricably fused that even after Wilson's League of Nations failed to pass muster with the Senate, both Governor Cox and Senator Harding addressed newly enfranchised US women as key supporters of their international planks. Shortly after news of Tennessee's ratification reached Democratic headquarters, the Woman's Bureau of the Democratic National Committee wrote to Wilson: "The women of the Democratic Party are proud of their political relationship with you, and will go confidently forward into a campaign in which their ideals for world peace may at last find full expression."[35] Similarly, Sen. Key Pittman (D-NV) claimed, "An overwhelming majority of the women of this country are going to vote the Democratic ticket in the fall, because they want to see the League of Nations ratified and [see] this country join with the other nations to prevent a recurrence of war."[36] The Republican Party made similar appeals to women. Mrs. Charles H. Sabin, wife of the vice-chairman of the Republican Ways and Means Committee, called women voters to "band together in a mighty effort" and help the Republican Party bring "pre-war order out of post-war chaos."[37]

The campaign of the NWP for woman suffrage as part of America's democratic ethos evidenced the NWP's parodic fashioning of the rhetorical presidency, which helped empower women as a force in the US electorate. Link reminds us of Wilson's faith in the rhetorical presidency, as Wilson nearly died appealing to the US public during his western tour: "[Wilson] knew the massive power of public opinion in a democracy. He had seen it force a reluctant Senate to consent to tariff and banking reform years before. The people had never failed to respond in crises in the past."[38] The NWP worked to elevate the "massive power" of US women as more than just respondents to the president's appeals, but rather as empowered political agents who forced the president to respond to crises. Expanding the rhetorical presidency as a site of rhetorical exchange between the nation's leader and the nation's people thus holds great constitutive potential for otherwise disempowered members of the nation-state. As such, US women were better able to envision themselves as participating members of the nation-state even before citizenship rights were conferred through the Nineteenth Amendment. Likewise, US women were better able *to be recognized* as political agents once they were granted the right to vote. Reflecting the legacy of such political and rhetorical power, Will Hays, chairman of the Republican National Committee, said on the day of ratification: "With the constitutional right given to the millions of American women, we will liberate a body of public opinion upon the campaign and its issues which will prove itself one of our greatest national assets."[39]

Unity and Disunity

The impact of the NWP's campaign for woman suffrage can also be explored by looking at the ways in which it fostered unity along international, class, and regional lines, yet simultaneously reinforced the otherization of African American women. The expanse and the limits of the NWP's impact on solidifying a community of empowered American women voters are exposed by looking at the ways in which the NWP members asserted themselves in US politics after 1920.

The NWP played a key role in establishing a growing community of politically empowered women worldwide. The NWP itself was mimetic of a militant English organization, and was then in turn mimicked by militant suffragists in other countries, such as France. In the decades following World War I, nation-building projects helped enfranchise women in many nations, such as in Germany, Austria, Great Britain, and the United States. Ellen Carol DuBois argues, however, that the war actually delayed woman suffrage in France, Italy, Denmark, and Iceland. She adds that neutral nations, such as the Netherlands and Sweden, enfranchised women for reasons unrelated to the war.[40] Even so, Alice Paul played an increasingly prominent role in the women's rights movements worldwide. Throughout the 1920s, for example, Paul worked with Japan's leading suffragist, Ichikawa Fusae, to help enfranchise women in Japan. Paul has also been noted for inspiring suffrage movements in China and the Philippines.[41] Also, in 1938, Paul founded the World Woman's Party (WWP), which focused on equal rights for women around the globe.[42]

The participation of the NWP in the international women's rights movement was also a reflection of the group's alliance with the labor movement. Throughout the 1920s and 1930s, national suffrage movements were more successful in South American, Middle Eastern, and Asian nations, a trend that has been attributed to the simultaneous working-class movements in these countries.[43] The NWP helped solidify the alliance between the international women's rights and labor movements by building upon the emerging worldwide militant socialist movement and uniting working-class and upper-class white women. Specifically, the NWP's close relationship with Harriot Stanton Blatch helped its 1913 national parade represent socialist women, working-class women, and women from multiple nations. The NWP maintained these associations throughout its campaign for woman suffrage. In the July 1920 issue of the *Suffragist,* for example, the NWP reported on the "First International Congress of Working Women" and "Women in Industry" worldwide.[44] After the passage of the Nineteenth Amendment, most women who remained in politics fought for the rights of working-class women and children, reinforcing the link between the woman suffrage and labor movements.[45]

In addition to helping unite white working-class women nationally and internationally, the NWP's campaign for woman suffrage helped unite women across regions of the United States. Most remarkably, many southern women became ardent suffrage supporters. The *Suffragist* reported that in the final stages of the suffrage campaign, southern women underwent an "overnight transformation," as evidenced by the public support of southern newspapers in Kentucky, Florida, Tennessee, Virginia, North Carolina, and Georgia.[46] Southern support, however, may have also worked to solidify racist fears of empowering African Americans' voting rights. Marjorie Spruill Wheeler notes that southern suffragists "shared many of the ideas of Southerners of their race and class. . . . Even the most progressive believed that white political supremacy was necessary, at least until African-Americans 'advanced' and were more 'qualified' for the vote."[47] In light of the NWP's history of expedient racism, its members viewed its coalition with white southern women as a welcome boost in the ratification campaign despite the limits such views placed on the NWP's longer-term goals of sex equality.

Reflecting patterns of inclusion and exclusion in social movements, the NWP continued to embrace a racist position toward African American women's rights. In fact, as the Nineteenth Amendment neared ratification, the NWP became more poignantly focused on enhancing white women's rights. In 1919, Paul told the *New York World:* "Negro men cannot vote in South Carolina and therefore negro women could not if women were to vote in the nation. We are organizing white women in the South." Paul added defensively that the NWP had "heard of no activity or anxiety among the negresses."[48] In response, African American women allied with the National Association for the Advancement of Colored People (NAACP) and passed a resolution against Paul's statement in the NAACP's *Branch Bulletin.* Paul responded that she felt "a sincere regret" for being criticized by "the negro, whose enfranchisement women helped to win."[49] Walter White of the NAACP then met with Paul and reported back to Mary Church Terrell: "Just as you say . . . all of them are mortally afraid of the South and if they could get the Suffrage Amendment through without enfranchising colored women, they would do it in a moment."[50]

The NWP's expedient racism was shared by the NAWSA. In 1919, Sen. Andrieus Aristieus Jones (D-NM) proposed a states' rights amendment to the suffrage resolution; consequently, African American women felt it would be used to exclude them from national suffrage rights. Though the amendment did not pass, some women of the Northeastern Federation of Women's Clubs (NFWC) of the National Association of Colored Women (NACW) sought cooperative membership in the NAWSA to force the organization to take a stand on African American women's voting rights. Carrie Chapman Catt implored Ida Husted Harper to discourage the president of the NFWC, Elizabeth C. Carter, from implementing this plan. In response to the NAWSA's similarly expedient arguments, Paula Giddings argues: "White women simply were willing to let Black women go down the proverbial drain to get the vote for themselves."[51]

Expedient racism in the suffrage movement not only exposed the constitutive limits of the NWP's rhetoric, but it also cost the NWP support. During the final days of ratification in Tennessee, Paul appealed to the NAACP for help. NAACP president Mary White Ovington wrote to Paul that white women had "ruined any chance for their receiving support from the colored people in the suffrage fight. I know it has been the determined policy of the suffragists to ignore the colored question in the South."[52] Even at the NWP's February 1921 meeting to launch a campaign for women's equality, Paul refused to place African American women's rights on the agenda. After leaders of the NAACP and the NACW protested, Paul allowed their resolution to be heard, although it was ultimately voted down. Addie Hunton of the NAACP, however, celebrated the efforts to "get the resolution on the floor" and to send "a large deputation of colored women [to] prove that they were alert to the situation," exhibiting the enhanced political agency of African American women during this period as well.[53]

The racist attitude of the NWP toward African American women was first exposed in its 1913 national suffrage parade, when it harnessed the support of southern white suffragists and relegated a contingent of women from Howard University to the back of the parade. Such racism also pervaded the Senate's debate over the amendment in June 1919. For example, Sen. Byron Patton Harrison (D-MS) made a motion to restrict the vote to white women. Senators Ellison Smith (D-SC) and James A. Reed (D-MO) also made explicitly racist arguments; Reed conceded that he only endorsed the measure to maintain the Democratic Party's power.[54] Nonetheless, African American women continued to assert their political agency, particularly within the rise of the Harlem Renaissance in the 1920s. Nikki Brown and Giddings maintain that during this decade, African American women increasingly participated in national party politics and helped promote interracial cooperation, even in the South.[55]

The NWP's participation in the suffrage movement also worked to divide white women after the passage of the Nineteenth Amendment as many white women actually resisted asserting their right to vote throughout the 1920s. Suffrage scholars explain that prior to enfranchisement women held diverse political views, but that they united temporarily to pursue the Nineteenth Amendment. Once women were enfranchised, women more freely pursued their own political interests and actually increased their volunteer activities.[56] Even so, women were typically relegated to minority roles in party politics, demonstrating the way in which the momentum of social and political change can quickly slow.

To an extent, however, the NWP helped women explore their political and social independence after 1920. In fact, before the 1920 elections, NWP adviser Dudley Field Malone presciently told the *New York Times,* "[T]he militant spirit of the women alone has won the victory and this same spirit will prevent them from being herded into any party."[57] As Paula Baker argues, the 1920s "represented the endpoint of nineteenth-century womanhood," and thus women "rejected domesticity as an ideal."[58] Asserting such political independence, the NWP held a small conference to discuss the future of the organization immediately following ratification.[59] While many NWP members retired and many others declared their utter exhaustion, the NWP's rank-and-file leaders entertained the idea of becoming a third party. Instead they elected to pursue a program of women's constitutional equality.

The NWP first proposed the Equal Rights Amendment (ERA) in 1923, hoping to amend the Constitution to ensure women's full legal equality beyond the right to vote.

The ERA campaign of the NWP similarly worked to divide and unite the women's rights community. Throughout the 1920s and 1930s, for example, the ERA faced colossal opposition from the well-established women's labor movement, which argued that the ERA would nullify state-level protections for working-class women. However, upon the emergence of the women's rights movement in the late 1950s and early 1960s, the ERA came to symbolize women's social, political, and economic equality. By the time the ERA passed through both houses of Congress in 1972, the amendment was supported by organizations representing women across race and class lines. Nonetheless, the ERA expired in 1982 without the required ratification of thirty-six states.[60] In the case of the woman suffrage campaign of the NWP, however, the NWP helped solidify national and international alliances between white working-class and upper-class women; in the process of building such alliances, however, it publicly and privately excluded African American women from its vision of women's equality—a pattern that likewise reemerged in subsequent campaigns for equality as well. Thus, just as the NWP mimicked the political activities of the British suffragists in 1913, the aftermath of such mimetic activities continued to circulate well beyond the commencement of the woman suffrage debate.

THE RHETORIC OF POLITICAL MIMESIS

In addition to considering the strength and limits of the campaign of the NWP within its historical and rhetorical context, this study invites a look at how political mimesis helps effect social and political change as strategies of militancy and tradition. More specifically, this study points to how the rhetoric of political mimesis empowered the NWP and US women to constitute citizenship identities and expand their roles in the nation-state as it simultaneously limited the potential of women's political equality.

Political Mimesis as Political Strategy

Through its rhetoric of political mimesis, the NWP helped US women enact full citizenship rights as they asserted their political agency and envisioned themselves as participating members in the nation-state. By mimicking the more traditional rituals of politics—marching in national parades, petitioning Congress, lobbying legislators, holding conventions, engaging in campaign politics, meeting with political leaders, fashioning a political party, and appealing to the US public—NWP members transformed themselves into political change agents with an authority that sought to rival that of the nation's top political leaders. In so doing, the NWP helped legitimize women's presence in the political sphere. Significantly, politicians validated the mimetic efforts of the NWP to normalize women's political agency—not simply by supporting woman suffrage, but by adopting the rhetorical strategies of the NWP that linked woman suffrage and US democracy. Such political legitimacy demonstrated that the NWP helped US women see themselves as political change agents, which represented a key constitutive process that enhanced the ability of others to see them as full-fledged members of the nation-state.

Thus, the process of mimicking the rhetorical strategies of party politics and political activism was just as important as the NWP's end goal of enfranchising US white women. Throughout its seven-year militant campaign, the NWP constituted its members' identities as fully capable members of the US citizenry. In fact, on the day of the ratification of the Nineteenth Amendment, NWP secretary Emma Wold wrote: "We hope that the Woman's Party will continue as an agency for removing discriminations that still exist against women—a group of the sort of awakened women that our social structure so sorely needs."[61] Such constitutive efforts are also visible in the 1920 elections during which six NWP members sought seats in Congress.[62] Thus, white women had to be envisioned as political leaders and as fully contributing citizens before they could be granted the same civic rights as the male citizenry.

This mimetic process of social and political change begs the questions of agent and agency, particularly since the militant campaign of the NWP targeted President Wilson and members of Congress in a dialectical exchange over woman suffrage. Most certainly, these men functioned as gatekeepers of the institutional legitimacy sought by the NWP. But it was the women themselves who initiated the necessary rhetorical dialogue toward acquiring fully enfranchised citizenship rights. NWP members did not wait on the due process of political change to take effect; rather, they mimicked the rituals of politics as though they already possessed fully enfranchised citizenship rights. They entered the restricted spaces of political activity and consulted the US citizenry as if they held the same presidential and congressional authority as their political rivals. Without such a strong sense of empowerment, NWP members would not have enacted their citizenship rights and would not have inspired those with political power to recognize and legitimize women's political rights.

The NWP's rhetoric of political mimesis also helped nationalize the suffrage movement and force a national debate on woman suffrage. By mimicking rituals of *national* politics, the NWP worked to elevate suffrage as a nationwide issue and compelled national political leaders to respond to their grievances, which sustained discussion of the issue even during the contestations of war. More specifically, the NWP forced a nationwide debate on woman suffrage by sending mass delegations of women and its cross-country envoys to meet with US and state congressmen, by dispatching its "Silent Sentinels" to the White House gates, and by inspiring women in other nations to address President Wilson. The more the NWP engaged political leaders on the issue of woman suffrage, the more political legitimacy members earned as participatory citizens in the nation-state. Through political mimesis, thus, these militant women refused to be ignored and persisted in keeping the issue of suffrage among the nation's most pressing public issues.

Similarly, the NWP's rhetoric of political mimesis helped the NWP earn national press attention, which represented another key component in nationalizing the suffrage debate. Adopting the ethos of the nation's political leaders often violated the gendered boundaries of citizenship and thus worked to sensationalize the woman suffrage movement and earn front-page headlines. Additionally, enacting citizenship rights in national spaces, such as the streets of Washington, D.C., the Capitol, and the front of the White House, attracted attention from national media outlets. Thus, the NWP's rhetoric of political mimesis held a national audience, which consequently helped shape woman suffrage as a national issue. In so doing, the NWP elevated questions of citizenship rights beyond state-level politics, countering the states' rights backlash of the Fifteenth Amendment. By helping to turn suffrage into a political issue with national consequences, the NWP helped force Congress and the president to take a stand on woman suffrage and to debate the issue in the formal deliberative spaces of the nation-state.

Political Mimesis and Social Change

In light of the masculine construction of the US nation-state and of US citizenship, the NWP's mimetic assumption of citizenship rights helped re-envision the gendered imagination of the nation-state and allowed women to participate more fully in national politics from that point forward. The NWP's enactment of women's citizenship rights and the ultimate passage of the Nineteenth Amendment thus helped erode the masculine construction of ideal US citizen and of the nation. The flux in wartime gender roles further allowed US women and the NWP to participate in and contribute to the nation in ways traditionally reserved for men. This participation not only allowed women to demand citizenship rights based on an expanded notion of wartime service, but it also offered the NWP the rhetorical resources to demand the right to vote as part of President Wilson's internationalization of democracy. This rhetorical strategy took hold as Wilson and other prominent politicians rehearsed the same argument as they campaigned for the League of Nations. Reflecting women's expanded roles in political and public matters, Governor Cox said: "[Women] helped win the war, and they are entitled to a voice in the readjustment now at hand. . . . [T]heir unquestioned progressive spirit will be helpful in problems that require public judgment."[63]

The intrusion of the NWP into political spaces reflects the ways in which political mimesis facilitated the dialectical process of social change. Mimicking political rituals reified the more traditional means of effecting change, such as campaigning, lobbying, petitioning, and debating. These practices helped buffer the NWP from critique as its members played by the accepted rules of political engagement. At the same time, however, such actions declared the militancy of the NWP, which attracted increased scorn and consternation as its members carried on as political leaders. The NWP's assertion of political authority in spaces where its members debated elected officials represented a militant act given women's historical exclusion from the public sphere and the restrictions against women's public speech. Thus, these women asserted their political agency and reconstituted their identities as fully enfranchised members of the nation, which in turn helped reenvision the gendered nation in ways that exhibited a more inclusive citizenry. Ultimately, political mimesis enhanced the authority of NWP leaders as national political leaders through traditional and militant means.

Asserting citizenship rights in political spaces through mimesis, however, engendered severe backlash, which suggested just how militant such acts were often perceived and just how entrenched such masculine authority had become. Certainly, as its campaign evolved, the NWP increased in militancy, particularly with the more threatening acts of burning Wilson's speeches and his image in effigy. Even during its state ratification campaign, the NWP admitted it pressured legislators "by putting fear into the hearts of old party leaders."[64] The militancy of such political mimesis was most evident by the acts of social control that such intrusions precipitated, including the forcible removal from public spaces, censorship, force-feedings, and beatings. Thus, the nation-state responded to such mimicking of political rituals with force and violence as a means to control these women's voices, their bodies, and their actions, and ultimately to restrict women's citizenship rights.

Resistance to the militancy of the NWP appears most vivid when compared to the acceptance of the moderate strategies of the NAWSA. Rhetorically, the NAWSA made similar arguments to the NWP, but did so through less confrontational means. Much like the NWP, the NAWSA appealed to Wilson's international ideology. Helen Hamilton Gardener of the NAWSA wrote to Wilson: "It is unthinkable that the United States Senate can now vote to range itself on the side of Germany and Hungary, who, alone of all the warring countries, have denied to women the ballot since this [war] began." Gardener continued to advise Wilson to "appeal to the Senate . . . and handle [suffrage] as a vital war measure."[65] Much like the NWP, Gardener and the NAWSA appealed to Wilson's refashioned role as the leader of world democracy, particularly as she flattered Wilson, "to whom," she said, "the world is looking for leadership in a matter of self-determination of the nations."[66] Accentuating the different strategies between the NAWSA and the NWP, the NAWSA made such arguments in personal appeals to Wilson—not through protests that intruded upon reserved political spaces or that deliberately exposed his hypocritical promotion of democracy. Moreover, Gardener deferred to Wilson's authority as she said: "I have always believed that it was only a question of the right time to do it when you would make the country understand clearly that a fight for democracy did not, and could not, exclude women."[67] Militants, however, refused to wait on "the right time" for woman suffrage to come around; through their mimetic assertion of citizenship rights in the political sphere, the NWP worked to expand women's roles in the nation-state, and consequently made itself the target of social control.

Efforts to physically and symbolically control the transgression of the NWP into the political sphere can also be explained as a reaction to its mimetic appropriation of power. Matthew Potolsky argues that "mimetic desire invites rivalry, and rivalry leads to conflict and strife."[68] Moreover, Rene Girard argues that "when two or more partners try to prevent one another from appropriating the object they all desire," violence typically ensues.[69] Potolsky also explains that such acts of social control produced by governments and other institutions help relieve "the community of the angst produced by mimetic rivalries."[70] In the gendered context of Wilson's rhetorical presidency and World War I, the nation was certainly uneasy with the assertion of citizenship rights by the NWP, particularly in such politicized spaces. Forcibly removing these women from such spaces offered the masculinized national (and international) community relief from such public wrangling of power.

Although the NWP's mimetic assertion of political power generated such backlash, the rhetorical agency of the NWP as political leaders in their own right helped redefine the spaces of national politics, generate national media attention to woman suffrage, force leaders to debate the issue, and earn them the right to vote. Unlike other suffrage organizations, the NWP engaged the president and other politicians as empowered political leaders and US citizens.

The Limitations of Political Mimesis

Despite its empowering potential, political mimesis can also work to limit the egalitarian promise of political and social change. First, the NWP's assumption of equal political power with President Wilson and members of Congress did not mean they were equals, even though the NWP ultimately helped facilitate the achievement of women's equal voting rights. In a study on "egalitarian mimesis" in which homosexual men earned equal political rights with heterosexual men in France, Marie-Jo Bonnet argues that mimesis actually prevented "any debate on equality between the sexes." She admits that by performing the rituals of heterosexual men, homosexual men earned some degree of "equal" rights, but she contends that it preempted the necessary dialogue regarding the basis of their perceived inequality. As Bonnet says, such "institutional logic" "implies a recognition of the other as Other, and not merely as an equal."[71] Similarly, while the NWP's rhetoric of political mimesis helped force the US government to recognize women's equal voting rights, it did not engender substantive discussion regarding women's social inequality and further magnified their potential contributions to the nation-state as *gendered* citizens, not as citizens proper.

The NWP's rhetoric of political mimesis also worked to liken the mostly white NWP constituency to white males of political privilege, thus excluding African American and non-Anglo-Saxon women from its vision of political equality. Moreover, because the campaign of the NWP successfully helped enfranchise US white women, the NWP contributed to the notion that white women were the ideal woman-citizens. Thus, just as mimetic strategies can liberate, they can simultaneously serve a discriminatory function by reifying the oppressive ideologies of the nation-state, drawing attention away from the ongoing feminist project of liberating all women from patriarchy. For some, mimesis as a social and political strategy of acquiring equal rights has been criticized as "a strategy of avoidance" that can result in greater resistance and backlash; it both fails to address the roots of inequality and continues to oppress and exclude certain groups from participating in its liberatory potential.[72] To a large extent, the NWP's rhetoric of political mimesis encouraged members to overstate the contributions of the NWP to equal citizenship rights. As early as 1915, Annie G. Porritt declared: "It is one of the most obvious aspects of the suffrage movement, that it has broken down class and race distinctions and has brought women together in a manner that was unprecedented in human history."[73] As the NWP's history of expedient racism demonstrated, however, political mimesis actually encouraged identification with those of racial privilege—mirroring the racism and nativism that gripped the nation in the first decades of the new century.

In all, the brief but intense militant campaign of the NWP for woman suffrage offers a study in the ways in which a disempowered group asserted its citizenship rights through a rhetoric of political mimesis. While the campaign of the NWP was crucial toward securing the passage of the Nineteenth Amendment, it also provided the means through which US women could empower themselves as political change agents, earn political legitimacy, and reenvision white women's roles the nation-state. The campaign of the NWP also offers political mimesis as a vocabulary for understanding how a disempowered group can rhetorically insinuate itself into the privileged rhetorics and spaces of political power to constitute citizenship identities and enhance citizenship rights. Consider the following letter to Alice Paul from Mrs. C. L. Roberts, a Texas woman, written two days after US women were enfranchised: "I can smile, and smile now, when some 'moss-back' of a man attempts to point out to me why women should not vote. [I] have just been asked by one, 'what would a woman congress do, should they become "pregnant" about the time of some important issue.' It was too disgusting to answer, and I was glad I could smile in the knowledge that we can vote—and are no longer under hateful domineering males such as he."[74]

Abbreviations

AEF	American Expeditionary Force
AERA	American Equal Rights Association
AWSA	American Woman Suffrage Association
CUWS	Congressional Union for Woman Suffrage
ERA	Equal Rights Amendment
GFWC	General Federation of Women's Clubs
ICW	International Congress of Women
IWSA	International Woman Suffrage Association
NAACP	National Association for the Advancement of Colored People
NACW	National Association of Colored Women
NAOWS	National Association Opposed to Woman Suffrage
NFWC	Northeastern Federation of Women's Clubs
NLU	National Labor Union
NWP	National Woman's Party
NWSA	National Woman Suffrage Association
UFSF	Union Française pour le Suffrage des Femmes
WCTU	Woman's Christian Temperance Union
WFL	Women's Franchise League
WP	Woman's Party
WSPU	Women's Social and Political Union
WTUL	Women's Trade Union League
WWA	Working Women's Association
WWCTU	World's Woman's Christian Temperance Union
WWP	World Woman's Party

Notes

INTRODUCTION

1. "President Asked to Open Second Term with Action on Suffrage," *Suffragist,* March 10, 1917, National Woman's Party Papers, reel 151, 7, University of Maryland, College Park McKeldin Library; hereafter, NWPP. Comma was added for syntactical clarity.

2. Ibid., 8.

3. Ibid., 7.

4. Ibid., 7–9. Quotation on 7.

5. Ibid., 7.

6. Ibid.

7. "50,000 See Inauguration," *New York Times,* March 6, 1917, 1. See also "Await Inaugural in Solemn Mood," *New York Times,* March 4, 1917, 1; "President Takes the Oath Today," *New York Times,* March 5, 1917, 1; "Wilson Sounds a Solemn Note," *New York Times,* March 6, 1917, 1.

8. The *Suffragist* noted that one thousand marchers participated, while the *New York Times* reported four hundred women. To avoid exaggeration, I use the smaller number. See "Suffragists Girdle White House in Rain," *New York Times,* March 5, 1917, 3.

9. In the Senate chambers, three NWP members unfurled a banner that read, "Mr. President, what will you do for woman suffrage?" "Report for 1916," January 1917, NWPP, reel 2, 13.

10. Jennifer L. Borda, "Woman Suffrage in the Progressive Era: A Coming of Age," in *Rhetoric and Reform in the Progressive Era,* ed. J. Michael Hogan, vol. 6 of *A Rhetorical History of the United States: Significant Moments in American Public Discourse,* ed. Martin J. Medhurst (East Lansing, Mich.: Michigan State University Press, 2003), 358.

11. Linda G. Ford, "Alice Paul and the Triumph of Militancy," in *One Woman, One Vote: Rediscovering the Woman Suffrage Movement,* ed. Marjorie Spruill Wheeler (Troutdale, Ore.: New Sage Press, 1995), 283.

12. Ibid., 292.

13. "Discourse," for the purpose of this project, reaches beyond the realm of the written or spoken word and encompasses all acts that may be valued for their ability to carry symbolic meaning. These texts include spoken and written discourse, but also symbolic acts such as protesting, parading, chanting, heckling, and passive resistance. Studying these texts will reveal the NWP's ideological standpoint. Maurice Charland argues, "The power of the text is the power of an embodied ideology. The form of an ideological rhetoric is effective because it is within the bodies of those it constitutes as subjects." Maurice Charland, "Constitutive Rhetoric: The Case of the Peuple Québécois," *Quarterly Journal of Speech* 73 (1987): 143.

Additionally, this book pulls on the *Suffragist,* correspondence, pamphlets, campaign booklets, financial reports, scrapbooks, newspaper clippings, and ephemera. All NWP papers are compiled under the "National Woman's Party Papers: The Suffrage Years," on microfilm at the University of Maryland McKeldin Library, in College Park. Further, Thomas C. Pardo offers a meticulous guide to the papers: *The National Woman's Party Papers, 1913–1974: A Guide to the Microform Edition* (Sanford, N.C.: Microfilming Corporation of America, 1979). Firsthand accounts of NWP protests also enrich our historical understanding of the NWP's role in the suffrage movement: Inez Haynes Irwin, *The Story of Alice Paul and the National Women's Party* (Fairfax, Va.: Denlinger's Publishers, 1977); Caroline Katzenstein, *Lifting the Curtain: The State and National Woman Suffrage Campaigns in Pennsylvania as I Saw Them* (Philadelphia: Dorrance, 1955); Doris Stevens, *Jailed for Freedom: American Women Win the Vote,* ed. Carole O'Hare (Troutdale, Ore.: New Sage Press, 1995).

14. For a full discussion of the inception of the rhetorical presidency, see Jeffrey K. Tulis, *The Rhetorical Presidency* (Princeton, N.J.: Princeton University Press, 1987). Nonetheless, Mel Laracey contends that presidents used different forms of media to appeal to the American public throughout the nineteenth century. Mel Laracey, *Presidents and the People: The Partisan Story of Going Public* (College Station: Texas A&M University Press, 2002). Also, David Zarefsky argues that presidents have appealed to the American people since George Washington's time in office. David Zarefsky, "The Presidency Has Always Been a Place for Rhetorical Leadership," in *The Presidency and Rhetorical Leadership,* ed. Leroy G. Dorsey (College Station: Texas A&M University Press, 2002), 20–41.

15. For a thorough discussion of Woodrow Wilson's rhetorical presidency and how Wilson used the rhetorical presidency to shape an American identity, see Mary E. Stuckey and Frederick J. Antczak, "The Rhetorical Presidency: Deepening Vision, Widening Exchange," *Communication Yearbook* 21 (1998): 405–41; Mary E. Stuckey, "'The Domain of Public Conscience': Woodrow Wilson and the Establishment of a Transcendent Political Order," *Rhetoric & Public Affairs* 6 (2003): 1–24.

16. The scholarly debate regarding the rhetorical presidency stems from differing views on rhetoric. See James W. Caesar, Glen E. Thurow, Jeffrey Tulis, and Joseph M. Bessette, "The Rise of the Rhetorical Presidency," *Presidential Studies Quarterly* 11 (Spring 1981): 158–71; Martin J. Medhurst, "A Tale of Two Constructs: The Rhetorical Presidency versus Presidential Rhetoric," in *Beyond the Rhetorical Presidency,* ed. Martin J. Medhurst (College Station, Texas A&M University Press), xii–xiii; Jef-

frey K. Tulis, "Revising the Rhetorical Presidency," in *Beyond the Rhetorical Presidency,* 4.

17. Stuckey and Antczak, "The Rhetorical Presidency," 415.

18. Tulis, *The Rhetorical Presidency,* 19. For more on Roosevelt's rhetorical presidency, see Michael Nelson, "Theodore Roosevelt's and William Howard Taft's Theories of Presidential Power," in *The Evolving Presidency: Addresses, Cases, Essays, Letters, Reports, Resolutions, Transcripts, and Other Landmark Documents, 1787–1998,* ed. Michael Nelson (Washington, D.C.: Congressional Quarterly Press, 1999), 93–94. Also, for a thorough discussion of Theodore Roosevelt's presidency and how he became "The Personalized President," see David H. Burton, *The Learned Presidency: Theodore Roosevelt, William Howard Taft, Woodrow Wilson* (Cranbury, N.J.: Associated University Presses, 1988); Lewis L. Gould, *The Modern American Presidency* (Lawrence: University Press of Kansas, 2003); Lewis L. Gould, *The Presidency of Theodore Roosevelt* (Lawrence: University Press of Kansas, 1991); Sidney M. Milkis and Michael Nelson, *The American Presidency: Origins and Developments: 1776–1998,* 3rd ed. (Washington, D.C.: Congressional Quarterly Press, 1999).

19. Theodore Roosevelt, "Debate on Proper Scope of Presidential Power and Leadership," in *The Evolving Presidency,* 95. It should also be noted that President McKinley is credited for framing the modern presidency and setting up Theodore Roosevelt's ability to treat the role of president as activist. Gould, *The Modern American Presidency,* 7–10.

20. Tulis, *The Rhetorical Presidency,* 18. Additionally, Wilson's approach toward Congress and the American public set a few rhetorical precedents. He was the first chief executive since John Adams to deliver his Annual Message before Congress rather than sending a written message, he used the motion picture and the mass media industries for political ends, and he was the first to institute an official wartime propaganda program that targeted domestic audiences in particular (Committee on Public Information).

21. James Andrews, "Presidential Leadership and National Identity: Woodrow Wilson and the Meaning of America," in *The Presidency and Rhetorical Leadership,* 132.

22. Tulis, *The Rhetorical Presidency,* 125.

23. Stuckey, "'The Domain of Public Conscience,'" 5.

24. Ibid., 3.

25. Wilfred E. Binkley, *President and Congress* (New York: Alfred A. Knopf, 1947), 205.

26. See Mary E. Stuckey, *Defining Americans: The Presidency and National Identity* (Lawrence: University Press of Kansas, 2004), 152. Also, contemporary scholars on American Indian identity prefer the use of "American Indian" to "Native American" to refer to Native populations in North America known as American Indian, Indigenous, and Natives. See Eva Marie Garroutte, *Real Indians: Identity and the Survival of Native America* (Berkeley: University of California Press, 2003); *Natives and Academics: Writing about American Indians,* ed. Devon Mihesuah (Lincoln: University of Nebraska Press, 1998); *Studying Native America: Problems and Prospects,* ed. Russell Thornton (Madison: University of Wisconsin Press, 1998); and

Jason Edward Black, *"Words True to Both Hearts": Merging Native-U.S. Rhetoric in the Removal and Allotment of American Indians* (Tuscaloosa: University of Alabama Press, forthcoming).

27. J. Michael Hogan problematizes the driving forces of the Progressive Era, noting that progressivism was used to justify competing and contradictory social and political goals. J. Michael Hogan, "Introduction: Rhetoric and Reform in the Progressive Era," in *Rhetoric and Reform in the Progressive Era,* ix–xxiv. Also see Richard Hofstadter, *The Age of Reform: From Bryan to F.D.R.* (New York: Alfred A. Knopf, 1968); Hofstadter, *The Progressive Movement, 1900–1915* (Englewood Cliffs, N.J.: Prentice-Hall, 1963).

28. Hofstadter, *The Progressive Movement,* 1–2.

29. Ibid.; Milkis and Nelson, *The American Presidency,* 193.

30. Hofstadter, *The Age of Reform,* 5–7.

31. Many historians eschew the notion that Roosevelt was a "progressive" president (1901–1909) and agree that he did not adopt a progressive platform until 1912. Leroy G. Dorsey, however, argues that "in a rhetorical sense, Roosevelt was the consummate Progressive: a reformer with a strong faith in the power of rhetoric to shape public opinion and in the power of public opinion, in turn, to bring about meaningful social reform." Nonetheless, Roosevelt's presidency did not explicitly advocate a progressive platform. Leroy G. Dorsey, "Preaching Morality in Modern America: Theodore Roosevelt's Rhetorical Progressivism," in *Rhetoric and Reform in the Progressive Era,* 49. Also see the following historical works regarding Theodore Roosevelt's presidency: H. W. Brands, *T. R.: The Last Romantic* (New York: Basic Books, 1997); Gould, *The Presidency of Theodore Roosevelt;* Richard Hofstadter, *The American Political Tradition and the Men Who Made It* (New York: Vintage Books, 1954); Nathan Miller, *Theodore Roosevelt: A Life* (New York: William Morrow, 1992); George E. Mowry, *The Era of Theodore Roosevelt and the Birth of Modern America, 1900–1912* (New York: Harper and Row, 1958); Mowry, *Theodore Roosevelt and the Progressive Movement* (New York: Hill and Wang, 1946); Henry F. Pringle, *Theodore Roosevelt: A Biography* (New York: Harcourt, Brace, 1931). In 1912, Theodore Roosevelt lost the Republican Party presidential nomination to Pres. Howard Taft. He then founded the Progressive Party and ran as the party's presidential nominee. Ultimately, Roosevelt and Taft split the GOP vote, and the Democratic nominee, Woodrow Wilson, took the presidency. Although Wilson ran for the Democratic Party, he represented the democratic progressives. Wilson's win was a coup for the Democratic Party as the party also secured control of both houses of Congress. Gould, *The Modern American Presidency,* 43.

32. Rogers M. Smith, *Civic Ideals: Conflicting Visions of Citizenship in U.S. History* (New Haven: Yale University Press, 1997), 411.

33. Ibid., 413–14. Smith attributes many of Wilson's progressive ideals to Herbert Croly, an intellectual and political figure of the time.

34. Woodrow Wilson, "An Inaugural Address," in *The Papers of Woodrow Wilson,* hereafter *PWW,* ed. Arthur S. Link (Princeton, N.J.: Princeton University Press, 1978), 27: 151.

35. Ibid.

36. Woodrow Wilson, "An Address to a Joint Session of Congress," *PWW,* 41: 525.

37. Geoffrey R. Stone, *Perilous Times: Free Speech in Wartime: From the Sedition Act of the 1790s to the War on Terrorism* (New York: W. W. Norton, 2004), 146. Also see James Magee, *Freedom of Expression* (Westport, Conn.: Greenwood Press, 2002).

38. J. Michael Sproule, *Propaganda and Democracy: The American Experience of Media and Mass Persuasion* (Cambridge, UK: Cambridge University Press, 1997), 10.

39. Stone, *Perilous Times,* 146; Magee, *Freedom of Expression.*

40. Stone, *Perilous Times,* 186.

41. Fear of German immigrants was so strong that some communities banned German-language teaching and German-language books. Also, Attorney General Gregory sought the help of volunteer citizen groups, such as the American Protective League, to report suspicious activity on behalf of German Americans. These groups engaged in wiretaps, ransacking of homes, tarring and feathering, and even murder. Stone, *Perilous Times,* 155–57. For a thorough discussion of the court cases brought about under the Espionage Act of 1917, see Zechariah Chafee Jr., *Free Speech in the United States* (Cambridge: Harvard University Press, 1954).

Further complicating the formation of an American identity was the massive influx of European immigrants and their pursuit of US citizenship. The diversity of languages, religious practices, and ethnic traditions confronted the homogeneity of the ideal American citizen. Further, immigrants' abilities to adopt an American identity were limited by exclusive citizenship laws and an obligation to city bosses for work. Wilson reconciled the potential threat immigrants posed to a unified American identity by supporting the popular notion that the United States was a "melting pot" in which immigrants' identities could be sterilized into a more pure American identity. In 1908, "The Melting Pot" was a popular play in which a Russian immigrant exalted the cleansing power of assimilating to American identity. Israel Zangwill, "The Melting Pot," in *From the Ghetto to the Melting Pot: Israel Zangwill's Jewish Plays, Three Manuscripts,* ed. Edna Nahshon (Detroit: Wayne State University Press, 2006); Andrews argues that the melting pot metaphor "undergirded Wilson's vision and maintained rhetorical respectability well into the twentieth century." Andrews, "Presidential Leadership," 137.

42. Haig A. Bosmajian, "The Abrogation of the Suffragists' First Amendment Rights," *Western Journal of Speech Communication* 38 (1974): 218–32. In his extensive account of World War I opponents, Stone lists pacifists and internationalists, such as Jane Addams; socialists, such Eugene V. Debs of the Socialist Party; and anarchists, such as Emma Goldman and Mollie Steimer. Stone, *Perilous Times,* 140–46.

43. *Tinker v. Colwell,* 193 U.S. 473 (1904).

44. Smith, *Civic Ideals,* 457–58.

45. The 1907 Expatriation Act states: "That all children born outside the limits of the United States who are citizens thereof in accordance with the provisions of section nineteen hundred and ninety-three of the Revised Statutes of the United States and who continue to reside outside the United States shall, in order to receive the protection of this Government, be required upon reaching the age of eighteen years to

record at an American consulate their intention to become residents and remain citizens of the United States and shall be further required to take the oath of allegiance to the United States upon attaining their majority." 1907 Act of March 2, 1907, Section 6, 34 Stat. 1228, 1229. Having won the vote in 1911, California women were able to push the act to appeal in 1912, although to no avail. Smith, *Civic Ideals,* 456–57.

46. *Muller v. Oregon,* 208 U.S. 412 (1908).

47. Smith, *Civic Ideals,* 459; *Muller v. Oregon,* 208 U.S. 412 (1908).

48. Hofstadter, *The Progressive Movement,* 5.

49. At this time, political party machines were funded by "big business," such as railroads, utilities, and insurance companies. Referenda allowed state voters to reject state laws. Similarly, recall measures allowed the people to remove public officials from office. Thus, referenda and recalls allowed people to challenge and undermine the political power held by big businesses. Hofstadter, *The Progressive Movement,* 4, 9–10. Kathleen E. Kendall demonstrates how 1912 marked the beginning of the contemporary primary, during which public speaking and mass communication were integral ways to connect presidential candidates to the American public. Kathleen E. Kendall, *Communication in the Presidential Primaries: Candidates and the Media: 1912–2000* (Westport, Conn.: Praeger Publishers, 2000), 6.

50. Hofstadter, *The Progressive Movement,* 5. See also Hofstadter, *The Age of Reform,* 185–96. For a discussion of how the muckrakers were perceived by Pres. Theodore Roosevelt, and about their role in the progressive movement, see Stephen E. Lucas, "Theodore Roosevelt's 'The Man with the Muck-Rake': A Reinterpretation," *Quarterly Journal of Speech* 59 (1973): 452–63.

51. Hogan, "Introduction," xiv.

52. Christine A. Lunardini and Thomas J. Knock suggest a link between the rise of the rhetorical presidency and suffragists' move to target President Wilson as a potential ally in winning woman suffrage. However, their study focuses on the combined efforts of the NAWSA and the NWP to persuade Wilson to support suffrage. More importantly, their study focuses on Wilson's integral role in helping to pass the Nineteenth Amendment. Christine A. Lunardini and Thomas J. Knock, "Woodrow Wilson and Woman Suffrage: A New Look," *Political Science Quarterly* 95 (1980–1981): 655–71. Additionally, Sally Hunter Graham demonstrates how the NWP's 1917 protests provoked Wilson to censor the suffragists and manipulate the press. Her study, however, focuses on assessing Wilson's motives for his eventual endorsement of the Nineteenth Amendment, not on discussing the NWP's protest in the context of the rhetorical presidency. Sally Hunter Graham, "Woodrow Wilson, Alice Paul, and the Woman Suffrage Movement," *Political Science Quarterly* 98 (1983–1984): 665–79.

Histories of the NWP include Sidney Roderick Bland, "Techniques of Persuasion: The National Woman's Party and Woman Suffrage, 1913–1919" (PhD diss., George Washington University, 1972); Linda G. Ford, *Iron-Jawed Angels: The Suffrage Militancy of the National Woman's Party, 1912–1920* (Lanham, Md.: University Press of America, 1991); Inez Haynes Irwin, *The Story of Alice Paul;* and Christine A. Lunardini, *From Equal Suffrage to Equal Rights: Alice Paul and the National Woman's Party, 1910–1928* (New York: New York University Press, 1986). Ford's

Iron-Jawed Angels was recently made into an HBO film, *Iron-Jawed Angels* (Home Box Office, 2004).

Studies that center on Alice Paul's leadership include Jean Baker, *Sisters: The Lives of America's Suffragists* (New York: Hill and Wang, 2005); Linda G. Ford, "Alice Paul and the Politics of Nonviolent Protest," in *Votes for Women: The Struggle for Suffrage Revisited,* ed. Jean H. Baker (Oxford: Oxford University Press, 2002), 174–88; Ford, "Alice Paul and the Triumph of Militancy," 277–94; Borda, "Woman Suffrage in the Progressive Era." Moreover, Alice Paul is considered a central character in the inception of the debate over the Equal Rights Amendment. See Susan D. Becker, *The Origins of the Equal Rights Amendment: American Feminism between the Wars* (Westport, Conn.: Greenwood Press, 1981); Amy E. Butler, *Two Paths to Equality: Alice Paul and Ethel M. Smith in the ERA Debate, 1921–1926* (Albany: State University of New York Press, 2002).

For other studies on the NWP's militancy, see Linda Lumsden, "Suffragist: Making of a Militant," *Journalism & Mass Communication Quarterly* 72 (1995): 525–38; Belinda A. Stillion Southard, "Militancy, Power, and Identity: The Silent Sentinels as Women Fighting for Political Voice," *Rhetoric & Public Affairs* 10 (2007): 399–417.

53. Stuckey and Antczak, "The Rhetorical Presidency," 413.

54. Ford, "Alice Paul and the Triumph of Militancy," 279.

55. Elizabeth Cady Stanton argued for woman suffrage at the Woman's Rights Convention at Seneca Falls in 1848; however, she was met with great resistance from Lucretia and James Mott, among others. The ninth resolution of the Declaration of Sentiments, drafted at the convention, asked for woman's enfranchisement—and was the only resolution that did not pass.

56. Marjorie Spruill Wheeler, "Editor's Introduction," introduction to Linda G. Ford's essay, "Alice Paul and the Triumph of Militancy," in Wheeler, *One Woman, One Vote,* 278.

57. In early 1914, the Congressional Committee became the independent Congressional Union for Woman Suffrage (CUWS) and then the National Woman's Party in 1917. Wheeler, "Editor's Introduction," 278. From this point forward, the introduction will refer to the National Woman's Party, in all stages of its organization, as the NWP.

58. For a complex discussion of agency, see Karlyn Kohrs Campbell, "Agency: Promiscuous and Protean," *Communication and Critical/Cultural Studies* 2 (2005): 1–19. Also, this book adopts a constitutive understanding of rhetoric. As James Jasinski has argued, rhetoric should be appreciated for its power to constitute identity. This book considers the NWP's campaign as a "text" that reflects the symbolic values of the prevailing ideological forces. James Jasinksi, "A Constitutive Framework for Rhetorical Historiography: Toward an Understanding of the Discursive (Re)Constitution of 'Constitution' in *The Federalist Papers,*" in *Doing Rhetorical History: Cases and Concepts,* ed. Kathleen J. Turner (Tuscaloosa: University of Alabama Press, 1998), 74–75. Additionally, this study argues that identity is formed through the intersection of multiple ideological forces. As Nira Yuval-Davis contends, "Studying citizenship, however, can throw light on some of the major issues which are involved in the complex relationships between individuals, collectivities and the state,

and the ways gender relations (as well as other social divisions) affect and are affected by them." Nira Yuval-Davis, *Gender & Nation* (London: Sage Publications, 1997), 69. Last, this study's use of the term "identity" resists the implication that an identity is a singular, stabilized presentation of self; rather, this study uses the term "identity" to refer to the multiple elements that contribute to the construction of one's overall identity. As Geoff Eley and Ronald Grigor Suny argue, "The multiplicity, fluidity, contextual, and contested qualities of identities that studies of gender have highlighted have undermined any notion of a single all-embracing primary identity to which all others must be subordinated at all times and costs." Consequently, this study's use of "identity" does not imply a primary or particularly privileged element of one's identity, bur rather a reflection of the composite fragments of one's overall identity. Geoff Eley and Ronald Grigor Suny, "Introduction: From the Moment of Social History to the Work of Cultural Representation," in *Becoming National: A Reader,* eds. Geoff Eley and Ronald Grigor Suny (New York: Oxford University Press, 1996), 10.

59. Daniel Druckman, "Nationalism, Patriotism, and Group Loyalty: A Social Psychological Perspective," *Mershon International Studies Review* 38 (1994): 44.

60. Anthony D. Smith, "The Nation: Real or Imagined?" in *People, Nation & State: The Meaning of Ethnicity and Nationalism,* ed. Edward Mortimer (London: I. B. Tauris Publishers, 1999), 37.

61. Benedict Anderson, *Imagined Communities: Reflections on the Origin and Spread of Nationalism* (London: Verso, 1991), 6.

62. Otto Bauer, "The Nation," *Mapping the Nation,* ed. Gopal Balakrishnan (London: Verso, 1996), 39–77.

63. Ibid.

64. E. J. Hobsbawm, *Nations and Nationalism since 1780: Programme, Myth, Reality,* 2nd ed. (Cambridge, UK: Cambridge University Press, 1992), 102–9. Hobsbawm identifies two significant eras in the history of nationalism: 1830–1870 and 1880–1914. Within the first era, he argues, a number of European nations were formed following revolutions; the term "nationalism" meant the establishment of a sovereign nation-state. "Nationalism" in the second era took on a more symbolic meaning, wherein "*any* body of people considering themselves a 'nation' claimed the right to self-determination." Hobsbawm, *Nations,* 102; Smith, *Civic Ideals,* 411.

65. Rogan Kersh, *Dreams of a More Perfect Union* (Ithaca, N.Y.: Cornell University Press, 2001), 262, 267.

66. Ibid., 268.

67. Theodore Roosevelt, *The New Nationalism* (New York: Outlook Company, 1910).

68. Eley and Suny, "Introduction," 10.

69. Katherine Verdery argues that scholarship on the concept of "nation" "should treat nation as a symbol and any given nationalism as having multiple meanings, offered as alternatives and competed over by different groups manoeuvring [*sic*] to capture the symbol's definition and its legitimizing effects." Katherine Verdery, "Whither 'Nation' and 'Nationalism'?" in *Mapping the Nation,* 228; Josep R. Llobera, *Foundations of National Identity: From Catalonia to Europe* (New York: Berghahn Books, 2004), 190.

70. Kersh, *Dreams of a More Perfect Union,* 16.

71. M. Lane Bruner, *Strategies of Remembrance: The Rhetorical Dimensions of National Identity Construction* (Columbia: University of South Carolina Press, 2002), 1.

72. Erwin C. Hargrove, *The President as Leader: Appealing to the Better Angels of Our Nature* (Lawrence: University Press of Kansas, 1998), vii. Quotation marks surrounding "teach reality" were part of the original text.

73. Vanessa B. Beasley, *You, the People: American National Identity in Presidential Rhetoric* (College Station: Texas A&M University, 2004), 22.

74. Stuckey, *Defining Americans,* 8.

75. Ibid., 9.

76. Beasley, *You, the People,* 5.

77. Verdery, "Whither 'Nation' and 'Nationalism,'" 227.

78. Prasenjit Dura, "Historicizing National Identity, or Who Imagines What and When," in *Becoming National,* 163.

79. Bauer, "The Nation," 56.

80. Verdery, "Whither 'Nation' and 'Nationalism,'" 230.

81. Campbell, "Agency: Promiscuous and Protean," 3.

82. Ibid.

83. The presentation of these categories may appear reductive, but the author recognizes that each of these senses of citizenship involve competing and complicated understandings of citizenship. Further, these categories are thought to overlap and interact with each other. Smith, *Civic Ideals,* 6. Further, Robert Alejandro identifies at least six senses of citizenship: (1) citizenship as universality and legal construction, (2) citizenship as neutrality, (3) citizenship as communality and participation, (4) citizenship as amelioration of class conflicts, (5) citizenship as self-sufficiency, and (6) citizenship as hermeneutical endeavor. Alejandro, *Hermeneutics, Citizenship, and the Public Sphere,* 9–38.

84. Evelyn Nakano Glenn, *Unequal Freedom: How Race and Gender Shaped American Citizenship and Labor* (Cambridge: Harvard University Press, 2002), 20–21; Uday S. Mehta, "Liberal Strategies of Exclusion," *Politics and Society* 18 (1990): 436–37; Smith, *Civic Ideals,* 3; Iris Marion Young, "Polity and Group Difference: A Critique of the Ideal of Universal Citizenship," in *Feminism and Politics,* ed. Anne Phillips (Oxford: Oxford University Press, 1998), 401–29.

85. Smith, *Civic Ideals,* 2. Full US citizenship has historically been denied based on race and nationality, in addition to sex. This project's focus on the woman suffrage movement limits its discussion of citizenship to its gendered aspects, but remains committed to recognizing how race, nationality, and sex, as a confluence of factors, have been the bases of denying US citizenship rights. Also, see Eithne Luibheid, *Entry Denied: Policing Sexuality at the Border* (Minneapolis: University of Minnesota Press, 2002), Eithne Luibheid, *Migrations: Sexuality, U.S. Citizenship, and Border Crossings,* eds. Eithne Luibheid and Lionel Cantu (Minneapolis: University of Minnesota Press, 2005), for a discussion of the how citizenship rights have been denied to immigrants based on sexuality.

86. Smith, *Civic Ideals,* 2.

87. Ibid., 6.

88. Alejandro, *Hermeneutics, Citizenship, and the Public Sphere,* 1.

89. Pnina Werbner and Nira Yuval-Davis, "Introduction," in *Women, Citizenship and Difference,* eds. Nira Yuval-Davis and Pnina Werbner (London: Zed Books, 1999), 4. On "differentiated citizenship," see Young, "Polity and Group Difference." Similarly, T. H. Marshall's central work, *Citizenship and Social Class,* argues that ideally citizenship means "full membership in a community" on the civil, political, and social levels. T. H. Marshall, *Citizenship and Social Class* (Cambridge, UK: Cambridge University Press, 1950), 14.

90. Werbner and Yuval-Davis, "Introduction," 5. Charles Tilly similarly argues that citizenship is relational, cultural, historical, and contingent. Charles Tilly, "Citizenship, Identity and Social History," *International Review of Social History* 40 (1995): 1–17.

91. Robert Asen contends that citizenship should be considered as a "mode of public engagement" and not as "as set of rights, condition of membership, or allegiance to a cultural tradition." While this book is somewhat amenable to Asen's discourse theory of citizenship by considering the ways in which "people enact citizenship through their own agency" regardless of possessing the right to vote, it also recognizes that the right to vote symbolizes full membership in a political community. NWP members in particular enacted citizenship as they engaged the political system in their pursuit of enfranchisement, yet still sought recognition of this citizenship status by the nation-state. Robert Asen, "A Discourse Theory of Citizenship," *Quarterly Journal of Speech* 90 (2004): 203, 204.

92. Kathleen B. Jones, "Citizenship in a Woman-Friendly Polity," in *The Citizenship Debates: A Reader,* ed. Gershon Shafir (Minneapolis: University of Minnesota Press, 1998), 222.

93. Ibid.

94. Ibid.

95. Shafir, "Introduction," 23.

96. Yuval-Davis, *Gender & Nation,* 24.

97. Ibid. For example, "rules, regulations, and policies" pertaining to abortion, maternity leave, right to wages, divorce, and child custody highlight the tension between the particular and the universal nature of women's citizenship.

98. Malcolm O. Sillars, "Defining Movements Rhetorically: Casting the Widest Net," *Southern Speech Communication Journal* 46 (1980): 21, 29. The rhetorical study of social movements has progressed from considering how social movements develop in a linear fashion to considering how social movements use particular symbolic resources throughout a relational process to achieve social and political change. In a foundational study, for example, Leland M. Griffin identified three phases to a social movement: inception, development, consummation. Leland M. Griffin, "The Rhetoric of Historical Movements," *Quarterly Journal of Speech* 38 (1952): 185. Robert S. Cathcart offers a rhetorical definition opposed to Griffin's historical approach: "All discussion about movements centers around the tokens, symbols, and transactions which unite or separate people who organize to produce change. Movements are carried forward through language, both verbal and nonverbal, in strategic forms that bring about identification of the individual with the movement." Rob-

ert S. Cathcart, "New Approaches to the Study of Movements," *Western Speech* 36 (1972): 86. Still, Cathcart's view was considered to be too linear, in that he argued that a social movement progresses from confrontation to transformation to transcendence. Cathcart, "Movements: Confrontation as Rhetorical Form," *Southern Speech Communication Journal* 48 (1978): 243. In 1980, Sillars identified four problems with social movement studies: they assume movements are linear phenomena, they focus on a cause-effect process, they stress intent, and they prescribe rigid definitions. Malcolm O. Sillars, "Defining Movements Rhetorically," 19.

99. Complicating earlier social movement literature, which discussed movements in either-or terms, contemporary theorists reconsider social change as a dialectical process. Examples of this either-or characterization can be found in Herbert W. Simons's "Requirements, Problems, and Strategies: A Theory of Persuasion for Social Movements," *Quarterly Journal of Speech* 56 (1970): 1–11. Simons argues that "[t]he core characteristic of militant strategists is that they seek to change the actions of their primary targets as a precondition for change in attitudes. By means of direct action techniques and verbal polemics, militants threaten, harass, cajole, disrupt, provoke, intimidate, coerce" (8). Similarly, Robert S. Cathcart distinguishes between "managerial" and "confrontational" rhetorics—the former of which is used to "uphold and re-enforce the established order" and the latter to "reject the system, its hierarchies and its values." See Cathcart, "Movements," 237. Charles Conrad, for example, suggests that social movement philosophies lie between the militant/moderate, radical/reformist, or visionary/pragmatic extremes, wherein the polar elements of both are negotiated. See Charles Conrad, "The Transformation of the 'Old Feminist' Movement," *Quarterly Journal of Speech* 67 (1981): 284.

100. J. Michael Hogan, "Managing Dissent in the Catholic Church: A Reinterpretation of the Pastoral Letter on War and Peace," *Quarterly Journal of Speech* 75 (1989): 401.

101. Gail Collins, *America's Women: Four Hundred Years of Dolls, Drudges, Helpmates, and Heroines* (New York: Harper Collins, 2004), 311.

102. Martin Duberman, *Left Out: The Politics of Exclusion: Essays, 1964–1999* (New York: Basic Books, 1999), 152.

103. Jean L. Cohen, "Strategy or Identity: New Theoretical Paradigms and Contemporary Social Movements," *Social Research* 52 (1985): 692.

104. According to Gregg, "the ego-function of rhetoric has to do with *constituting* self-hood through expression; that is, with establishing, defining, and affirming one's self-hood as one engages in a rhetorical act." Richard B. Gregg, "The Ego-Function of the Rhetoric of Protest," *Philosophy & Rhetoric* 4 (1971): 75.

105. Jasinski, "A Constitutive Framework," 74–75.

106. Charland, "Constitutive Rhetoric," 143. Similarly, Cohen argues, "The access of interpretation to identity is through the interrogation of forms of consciousness. This procedure can take the form of an examination so long as the theories in question are those of the participants, produced for movements and, to an extent, within movements. While rarely up to the level of systematic social science, such theories or 'ideologies' receive their importance precisely to the extent to which they help the crystallization of already-emergent identities." Cohen, "Strategy or Identity,": 665–66.

107. Cathcart, "Movements," 243.

108. Mari Boor Tonn, "Militant Motherhood: Labor's Mary Harris 'Mother' Jones," *Quarterly Journal of Speech* 82 (February 1996): 2. Also, Leonard B. Wuthman argues that Daniel O'Connell's negotiation of militant and moderate strategies was effective toward coercing Parliament to meet Catholic demands. Leonard B. Wuthman, "The Militant-Moderate Agitator: Daniel O'Connell and Catholic Emancipation in Ireland," *Communication Quarterly* 30 (1982): 225–31.

109. Campbell, "Agency," 3.

110. Arlene Elowe MacLeod, "Hegemonic Relations and Gender Resistance: The New Veiling as Accommodating Protest in Cairo," *Signs* 17 (1992): 534.

111. Rhys H. Williams, "Constructing the Public Good: Social Movements and Cultural Resources," *Social Problems* 42 (1995): 129.

112. For a thorough reading of the evolution of mimesis and its historical contexts, see Gunter Gebauer and Christoph Wulf, *Mimesis: Culture, Art, & Society,* trans. Don Reau (Berkeley: University of California Press, 1995). Also, most theorists point to Erich Auerbach's *Mimesis: The Representation of Reality in Western Literature,* trans. Willard R. Trask, 50th anniversary ed. (Princeton, N.J.: Princeton University Press, 2003) as a starting point for contemporary discussions regarding mimesis.

113. On Plato's notion of mimesis, see *Plato: The Collected Dialogues,* eds. Edith Hamilton and Huntington Cairns, trans. A.E. Taylor (Princeton, N.J.: Princeton University Press, 1989). For commentary, see Hayden W. Ausland, "On Reading Plato Mimetically," *American Journal of Philology* 118 (1997): 371–416; Elizabeth Belfiore, "A Theory of Imitation in Plato's Republic," *Transactions of the American Philological Association* 114 (1984): 121–46; Willem Jacob Verdenius, *Mimesis: Plato's Doctrine of Artistic Imitation and its Meaning to Us* (Leiden, Holland: E. J. Brill, 1962). Anne Duncan offers a useful overview of the relationship between Platonic and Aristotelian views on mimesis and drama in *Performance and Identity in the Classical World* (Cambridge, UK: Cambridge University Press, 2006), 13–15. Other instructive sources include Richard McKeon's "Literary Criticism and the Concept of Imitation in Antiquity," *Modern Philology* 34 (1936): 1–35; G. Else, "Imitation in the 5th Century," *Classical Philology* 53 (1958): 73–90; Goran Sörbom, *Mimesis and Art: Studies in the Origin and Early Development of an Aesthetic Vocabulary* (Stockholm: Svenska Bokforlaget, 1966); Edward Corbett, "The Theory and Practice of Imitation in Classical Rhetoric," *College Composition and Communication* 22 (1971): 243–50; Dale Sullivan, "Attitudes toward Imitation: Classical Culture and the Modern Temper," *Rhetoric Review* 8 (1989): 5–21; Dale Sullivan, "The Decline of Imitation in Eighteenth and Nineteenth Century Rhetoric," *Platte Valley Review* 20 (1992): 45–62; Michael Leff, "Hermeneutical Rhetoric," in *Rhetoric and Hermeneutics in Our Time: A Reader,* ed. Walter Jost and Michael J. Hyde (New Haven: Yale University Press, 1997), 196–214. On mimesis and literature, see John D. Boyd, *The Function of Mimesis and its Decline* (New York: Fordham University Press, 1980).

114. Francis Wolff, "The Three Pleasures of Mimesis According to Aristotle's *Poetics,*" in *The Artificial and the Natural: An Evolving Polarity,* eds. Bernadette Bensaude-Vincent and William R. Newman (Cambridge: MIT Press, 2007). The sources pertaining to Aristotle's view of mimesis are plentiful, but for a clear review of

Aristotle's view of mimesis as it relates to understanding and knowledge, see Stavros Tsitsiridis, "Mimesis and Understanding: An Interpretation of Aristotle's *Poetics* 4.1448B–19," *Classical Quarterly* 55 (2005): 435–46.

115. The medieval understanding of *imitatio* differed from that of the Renaissance, however. For a swift summary, see François Rigolot, "The Renaissance Crisis of Exemplarity," *Journal of the History of Ideas* 59 (1998): 561.

116. See Tom Huhn's discussion of mimesis in *Imitation and Society: The Persistence of Mimesis in the Aesthetics of Burke, Hogarth, and Kant* (University Park: Pennsylvania State Press, 2004).

117. Deborah Jenson, *Trauma and its Representations: The Social Life of Mimesis in Post-Revolutionary France* (Baltimore, Md.: Johns Hopkins University Press, 2001), 6. Emphasis in original.

118. Samuel Ijsseling, *Mimesis: On Appearing and Being* (Kampen, Netherlands: Kok Pharos, 1997), 21, 29.

119. Arne Melberg, *Theories of Mimesis* (Cambridge, UK: Cambridge University Press, 1995), 1.

120. Michael Taussig, *Mimesis and Alterity: A Particular History of the Senses* (New York: Routledge, 1993), *xiii–xiv.*

121. Ibid., *xiii.*

122. Gebauer and Wulf, *Mimesis,* 21.

123. Ibid., 22.

124. Jensen, *Trauma and its Representations,* 7.

125. See Taussig, *Mimesis and Alterity;* Homi K. Bhabha, *The Location of Culture* (London: Routledge, 2004); Ana María Manzanas and Jesús Benito, *Intercultural Mediations: Hybridity and Mimesis in American Literatures* (Münster, Germany: Die Deutsche Bibliothek, 2003); Poonam Trivedi, "'Bananas on a Mango Tree': Colonial Mimesis, Hybridity and Modern Indian Theatre," in *Refiguring Mimesis: Representation in Early Modern Literature,* eds. Jonathan Holmes and Adrian Streete (Hertfordshire: University of Hertfordshire Press, 2005).

126. Gebauer and Wulf, *Mimesis,* 5.

127. Ibid., 24.

128. Barbara Fuchs, *Mimesis and Empire: The New World, Islam, and European Identities* (Cambridge, UK: Cambridge University Press, 2001), 3, 4.

129. Teresa L. Ebert, "Gender and the Everyday: Toward a Postmodern Materialist Feminist Theory of Mimesis," in *"Turning the Century": Feminist Theory in the 1990s,* ed. Glynis Carr (Cranbury, N.J.: Associated University Presses, 1992), 107.

130. Ellen Carol DuBois, "Working Women, Class Relations, and Suffrage Militance: Harriot Stanton Blatch and the New York Woman Suffrage Movement, 1894–1909," *Journal of American History* 74 (1987): 34–58.

CHAPTER 1

1. According to *History of Woman Suffrage,* Gen. William Howe "issued his celebrated proclamation offering amnesty and protection to all who, within sixty days, should declare themselves peaceable British subjects, and bind themselves to

neither take up arms nor encourage others to do so." *History of Woman Suffrage,* eds. Elizabeth Cady Stanton, Susan B. Anthony, and Matilda Joslyn Gage, 6 vols. (New York, 1881–1922), 1: 442–44.

2. See Linda Grant De Pauw, *Fortunes of War: New Jersey Women in the American Revolution* (Trenton: New Jersey Historical Commission, 1975); Sophie H. Drinker, "Votes for Women in 18th-Century New Jersey," *Proceedings of the New Jersey Historical Society* 80 (1962): 34–42; Irwin N. Gertzog, "Female Suffrage in New Jersey, 1790–1807," *Women & Politics* 11 (1990): 47–58; Judith Apter Klinghoffer and Lois Elkis, "'The Petticoat Electors': Women's Suffrage in New Jersey, 1776–1807," *Journal of the Early Republic* 12 (1992): 159–93; Richard P. McCormick, *The History of Voting in New Jersey: A Study in the Development of Election Machinery, 1664–1911* (New Brunswick, N.J.: Rutgers University Press, 1953); Mary Philbrook, "Woman's Suffrage in New Jersey Prior to 1807," *Proceedings of the New Jersey Historical Society* 57 (1939): 87–98; J. R. Pole, "Suffrage Reform and the American Revolution in New Jersey," *Proceedings of the New Jersey Historical Society* 74 (1956): 173–93; Edward Raymond Turner, "Women's Suffrage in New Jersey: 1790–1807," *Smith College Studies in History* 1 (1916): 165–87.

3. See Mary Beth Norton, *Founding Mothers and Fathers: Gendered Power and the Forming of American Society* (New York: Alfred A. Knopf, 1996); Mary Beth Norton, *Liberty's Daughters: The Revolutionary Experience of American Women, 1750–1800* (Ithaca, N.Y.: Cornell University Press, 1996); Mary Beth Norton, "The Evolution of White Women's Experience in Early America," *American Historical Review* 89 (1984): 593–619; Joan Hoff Wilson, "The Illusion of Change: Women and the American Revolution," in *The American Revolution: Explorations in the History of American Radicalism* (DeKalb: Northern Illinois University Press, 1976), 383–445. Regarding republican motherhood, see Ruth H. Bloch, "American Feminine Ideals in Transition: The Rise of the Moral Mother, 1785–1815," *Feminist Studies* 4 (1978): 100–126; Ruth H. Bloch, "The Gendered Meanings of Virtue in Revolutionary America," *Signs* 13 (1987): 37–58; Linda K. Kerber, "The Republican Ideology of the Revolutionary Generation," *American Quarterly* 37 (1985): 474–95; Linda K. Kerber, *Women of the Republic: Intellect and Ideology in Revolutionary America* (Chapel Hill: University of North Carolina Press, 1980); Jan Lewis, "The Republican Wife: Virtue and Seduction in the Early Republic," *William and Mary Quarterly* 44 (1987): 689–721.

4. Karlyn Kohrs Campbell argues that throughout both waves of the women's rights movement, women have had to assert themselves as change agents through rhetoric. Karlyn Kohrs Campbell, "The Rhetoric of Women's Liberation: An Oxymoron," *Quarterly Journal of Speech* 59 (1973): 74–86. Also, Kathleen J. Turner argues that "rhetorical history seeks to understand the context through messages that reflect and construct that context," showing how women's rights arguments are enmeshed with the contextual and ideological forces of the time; Kathleen J. Turner, "Introduction: Rhetorical History as Social Construction," in *Doing Rhetorical History: Concepts and Cases,* ed. Kathleen J. Turner (Tuscaloosa: University of Alabama Press, 1998), 2.

5. Smith introduces the notion of ascriptive inegalitarianism as a way to consider citizenship as a system of inequities. See Rogers M. Smith, *Civic Ideals: Conflicting Visions of Citizenship in U.S. History* (New Haven: Yale University Press, 1997), 6.

6. Paula Baker, "The Domestication of Politics: Women and American Political Society, 1780–1920," *American Historical Review* 89 (1984): 620–47; Norton, *Founding Mothers and Fathers;* Norton, "The Evolution of White Women's Experiences"; Smith, *Civic Ideals,* 50–51.

7. Smith, *Civic Ideals,* 52–53. Regarding subjectship and independence, see Joan R. Gundersen, "Independence, Citizenship, and the American Revolution," *Signs* 13 (1987): 60.

8. My use of the concept of a colonial identity is informed by E. J. Hobsbawm's discussion of "proto-nationalism," which he defines as "the consciousness of belonging or having belonged to a lasting political entity." He characterizes proto-nationalism as a necessary precursor to the development of a nation and patriotic nationalism, however it is not a determining factor in the establishment of nations or a shared, national identity. E. J. Hobsbawm, *Nations and Nationalism since 1780: Programme, Myth, Reality,* 2nd ed. (Cambridge, UK: Cambridge University Press), 73–78.

9. For a discussion of Britain's conceptualization of republicanism, see Michael Schudson, *The Good Citizen: A History of American Civic Life* (New York: Free Press, 1998), 28; Kerber, "Republican Ideology," 475–80; Gordon S. Wood, *The Creation of the American Republic, 1776–1787* (Chapel Hill: University of North Carolina Press, 1969), 47–53.

10. For a history of the complicated relationship between British authorities and the multiple groups of settlers, American Indians, and Africans, see Smith, *Civic Ideals,* 54–67.

11. Of these eligible men, only about 10–40 percent voted in colonial elections. Christopher Collier, "The American People as Christian White Men of Property: Suffrage and Elections in Colonial and Early National America," in *Voting and the Spirit of American Democracy: Essays on the History of Voting and Voting Rights in America,* ed. Donald W. Rogers (Urbana: University of Illinois Press, 1990), 21–23. Also see Robert J. Dinkin, *Voting in Provincial America: A Study of Elections in the Thirteen Colonies, 1689–1776* (Westport, Conn.: Greenwood Press, 1977); Alexandar Keyssar, *The Right to Vote: The Contested History of Democracy in United States* (New York: Basic Books, 2000).

12. For scholarship pertaining to the voting rights of African Americans and American Indians, as well as restrictions based on age, residency, religion, and property, see Collier, "The American People," 22, 24; Dinkin, *Voting in Provincial America,* 30–40; Smith, *Civic Ideals,* 65–66. Records indicate that some Massachusetts widows with significant property voted, as well as New York widows in 1737. Also, Delaware, Georgia, and South Carolina specified that voters must be male. In 1762, a Virginia statute explicitly stated that women (among a long list of others) could not vote. Dinkin, *Voting in Provincial America,* 29–30. See also Mary S. Benson, *Women in Eighteenth Century America: A Study of Opinion and Social Usage* (New York: Columbia University Press, 1935), 244–49; Marchette Chute, *The First Liberty: A History of the Right to Vote in America, 1619–1850* (New York: Dutton, 1969); Chilton Williamson, *American Suffrage: From Property to Democracy, 1760–1860* (Princeton, N.J.: Princeton University Press, 1960).

13. Scholars have argued that colonial women were more liberated than their nineteenth century counterparts—see Elisabeth Anthony Dexter, *Colonial Women of Affairs: Women in Business and the Professions in America before 1776,* 2nd ed. (New York: A. M. Kelley, 1972); Gerda Lerner, "The Lady and the Mill Girl: Changes in the Status of Women in the Age of Jackson," *American Studies* 10 (1969): 5–15; Herbert Moller, "Sex Composition, and Correlated Culture Patterns of Colonial America," *William and Mary Quarterly* 2 (1945): 113–53; Richard B. Morris, *Studies in the History of American Law, with Special Reference to Seventeenth and Eighteenth Centuries,* 2nd ed. (New York: Octagon Books, 1959); Julia Cherry Spruill, *Women's Life and Work in the Southern Colonies* (Chapel Hill: University of North Carolina Press, 1938); Roger Thompson, *Women in Stuart England and America: A Comparative Study* (London: Routledge, 1974)—but recent scholarship argues otherwise. See Norton, "The Evolution of White Women's Experiences"; Norton, *Founding Fathers and Mothers;* Wilson, "The Illusion of Change." For more on women in colonial times, see Louise M. Young, "Women's Place in American Politics: The Historical Perspective," *Journal of Politics* 38 (1976): 295–335.

14. Joan R. Gunderson, "Independence, Citizenship, and the American Revolution." *Signs* 13 (1987), 60. For more on property law and women in colonial times, see Nancy F. Cott, "Divorce and the Changing Status of Women in Eighteenth Century Massachusetts," *William and Mary Quarterly* 33 (1976): 586–614; James Kettner, "The Development of American Citizenship in the Revolutionary Era: The Idea of Volitional Allegiance," *American Journal of Legal History* 18 (1974): 208–12; Marylynn Salmon, *Women and the Law of Property in Early America* (Chapel Hill: University of North Carolina Press, 1986); Robert J. Steinfeld, "Property and Suffrage in the Early Republic," *Stanford Law Review* 41 (1998): 335–76.

15. Smith, *Civic Ideals,* 68–69. In the seventeenth century, Chesapeake-area women were often widowed due to the high mortality rate; as such, they were given more legal power than New England widows, who remained married longer and were widowed less often. Chesapeake Bay women married younger and were widowed younger. As such, men in the area left widows more land than in New England. Additionally, widows were granted the right to change their husband's will if they were left less than the stated minimum. Conversely, northeastern settlers experienced low mortality rates and thus women remained married longer and patriarchy took a stronger hold on society. Wilson, "The Illusion of Change," 598–99.

16. All colonies except Connecticut and Massachusetts allowed women to have separate estates from husbands, so they could exercise economic independence after marriage, and, upon widowhood, they did not lose property to their sons. Further, in a Maryland county, widows possessed the right to challenge their husbands' wills in court; in South Carolina, 40 percent of women with separate estates won sole control of property and 28 percent of wives shared equal power over estates with husbands. Ibid., 605–6.

17. Norton, "White Women's Experiences," 603. Daughters often received about half as much as sons and what they did receive was in movable goods because it was assumed that they would marry and take their inheritance with them.

18. Smith, *Civic Ideals,* 68–69.

19. Bloch, "American Feminine," 102–3.

20. Norton, "White Women's Experiences," 604–5.

21. Bloch, "American Feminine," 102–3.

22. Norton, "White Women's Experiences," 596; 607–9; Wilson, "The Illusion," 408–9.

23. Smith, *Civic Ideals,* 68.

24. See John Locke, *Two Treatises of Government,* 2nd ed., Peter Laslett, ed. (London: Cambridge University Press, 1967); Locke, *An Essay Concerning Human Understanding,* Kenneth P. Winkler, ed. (Indianapolis: Hackett Publishing, 1996).

25. On the ways in which Locke's ideas were blended with classical republicanism, see Louis B. Hartz, *The Liberal Tradition in America: An Interpretation of American Political Thought since the Revolution* (New York: Harcourt, Brace, & World, 1955); James T. Kloppenberg, "The Virtues of Liberalism: Christianity, Republicanism, and Ethics in Early American Political Discourse," *Journal of American History* 74 (1987): 9–33; J. G. A. Pocock, *The Machiavellian Moment: Florentine Political Thought and the Atlantic Republican Tradition* (Princeton, N.J.: Princeton University Press, 1975); J. G. A. Pocock, *Virtue, Commerce, and History: Essays on Political Thought and History, Chiefly in the Eighteenth Century* (Cambridge: Harvard University Press, 1985); Katharine M. Rodgers, "Republicanism: The Career of a Concept," *Journal of American History* 79 (1992): 11–38; Robert E. Shalhope, "Toward a Republican Synthesis: The Emergence of an Understanding of Republicanism in American Historiography," *William and Mary Quarterly* 29 (1972): 49–80; Robert E. Shalhope, "Republicanism in Early American Historiography," *William and Mary Quarterly* 39 (1982): 334–56; Wood, *The Creation of the American Republic,* 46–90.

26. Smith, *Civic Ideals,* 83.

27. Ibid., 74.

28. Collier, "The American People," 23. Regarding Catholics, Jews, and free slaves, see Keyssar *The Right to Vote,* 20; Eric Foner, "From Slavery to Citizenship: Blacks and the Right to Vote," in Rogers, *Voting and the Spirit of American Democracy,* 55–56; Charles H. Wesley, "Negro Suffrage in the Period of the Constitution," *Journal of Negro History* 32 (1947): 143–68.

29. William Blackstone, *Commentaries on the Laws of England: A Facsimile of the First Edition, 1765–1769* (Chicago: University of Chicago Press, 1979). For a look at the voting rights of different minority groups, see Keyssar, "Table A.1, "Suffrage Requirements: 1776–1790," *The Right to Vote;* and Kirk Harold Porter's "Table I: Property Qualifications Just before the Revolutionary War," and "Table II: Property Qualifications Immediately after the Revolutionary War," in his dissertation, *A History of Suffrage in the United States,* 2nd ed. (New York, AMS Press, 1971), 12–13; Marc Kruman, *Between Authority and Liberty: State Constitution Making in Revolutionary America* (Chapel Hill: University of North Carolina Press, 1997), 92–95.

30. Norton, "White Women's Experiences," 617. Also, Rosemarie Zagarri traces "rights talk" from revolutionary through postrevolutionary America and the ways in which differing senses of rights, Lockean liberalism, and republicanism were used to

deny women rights. Rosemarie Zagarri, "The Rights of Man and Woman in Post-Revolutionary America," *William and Mary Quarterly* 55 (1998): 203–30.

31. Abigail Adams to John Adams, March 31, 1776, *Adams Family Correspondence,* ed. L. H. Butterfield (Cambridge: Harvard University Press, 1965), 1: 369–70, 382. Also, shortly after, John Adams wrote a letter to James Sullivan expressing his fear of women voting: "Depend upon it, Sir, it is dangerous to open so fruitfull a Source of Controversy and altercation; as would be opened by attempting to alter the Qualifications of Voters. There will be no End of it. New Claims will arise. Women will demand a Vote. Lads from 12 to 21 will their Rights not enough attended to, and every Man, who has not a Farthing, will demand an equal Voice with any other in all Acts of State." May 26, 1776, *Papers of John Adams,* ed. Robert J. Taylor et al. (Cambridge: Harvard University Press, 1979), 4: 208–13.

32. Kerber, *Women of the Republic,* 159–84; Norton, "White Women's Experiences," 614–15. See also Cott, "Divorce and the Changing Status of Women."

33. For example, in 1764, James Otis of Massachusetts asserted that women should possess the right to vote. James Otis, "The Rights of the British Colonies Asserted and Proved, (1764)" in *Pamphlets of the American Revolution, 1750–1776,* ed. Bernard Bailyn (Cambridge: Harvard University Press, 1965), 1: 420–21.

34. Smith, *Civic Ideals,* 110–11; Melissa A. Butler, "Early Liberal Roots of Feminism: John Locke and the Attack on Patriarchy," *American Political Science Review* 72 (1978): 135–50; Carole Pateman, *The Disorder of Women: Democracy, Feminism, and Political Theory* (Stanford: Stanford University Press, 1989); Hilda L. Smith, *Reason's Disciples: Seventeenth Century English Feminists* (Urbana: University of Illinois Press, 1982), 56–59.

35. Gundersen, "Independence," 65–76; For more on coverture and how it contradicts basic republican and liberal principles, see Kerber, *Women of the Republic,* 139–55.

36. Norton, "White Women's Experiences," 421–23.

37. Ibid., 424; Wilson, "The Illusion," 396–97.

38. Collier, "The American People," 25; Keyssar, *The Right to Vote,* 14–15.

39. Wilson, "The Illusion," 397–98, 421–22.

40. Kerber, "The Republican Ideology" 484–85. Also see Kerber, *Women of the Republic;* Rosemarie Zagarri, "Morals, Manners, and the Republican Mother," *American Quarterly* 44 (1992): 192–216.

41. Kerber, *Women of the Republic,* 229.

42. Bloch, "The Gendered Meanings," 57–58.

43. Norton, "White Women's Experiences," 618; Keith Melder, *The Beginnings of Sisterhood: The American Women's Rights Movement, 1800–1850* (New York: Schocken Books, 1977), 1–11. For scholarship regarding the Greek roots of separate spheres, see Gershon Shafir, "Introduction," in *The Citizenship Debates: A Reader,* ed. Gershon Shafir (Minneapolis: University of Minnesota Press, 1998), 1–28.

44. Gundersen, "Independence," 76.

45. Kerber, *Women of the Republic,* 229; Lewis, "The Republican Wife."

46. Glenna Matthews, *The Rise of the Public Woman* (New York: Oxford University Press, 1992), 70; Kerber, *Women of the Republic,* 189–231.

47. Lori D. Ginzberg, *Women and the Work of Benevolence: Morality, Politics, and Class in the 19th-Century United States* (New Haven: Yale University Press, 1990); Norton, "White Women's Experiences," 616.

48. Wilson, "The Illusion," 429–30.

49. Kerber, *Women of the Republic,* 284, 285. In 1790, Judith Sargent Murray wrote under the penname Constantia in the essay "On the Equality of the Sexes." Judith Sargent Murray, "On the Equality of the Sexes," *Massachusetts Magazine* 2 (March 1790): 132–35, (April 1790): 223–26.

50. Smith, *Civic Ideals,* 88–89. Scholarship on the Anti-Federalists is expansive, but the following sources provide a thorough explanation of the Anti-Federalists' arguments and primary documents: Christopher M. Duncan, *The Anti-Federalists and Early American Political Thought* (DeKalb: Northern Illinois University Press, 1995); Herbert J. Storing, *The Complete Anti-Federalist* (Chicago: University of Chicago Press, 1981); *The Essential Federalist and Anti-Federalist Papers,* David Wootton, ed. (Indianapolis: Hackett Publishing, 2003). Regarding the Federalists, see Smith, *Civic Ideals,* 123–25. Also see Roger H. Brown, *Redeeming the Republic: Federalists, Taxation, and the Origins of the Constitution* (Baltimore: Johns Hopkins University Press, 1993); Linda K. Kerber, *Federalists in Dissent: Imagery and Ideology in Jeffersonian America* (Ithaca, N.Y.: Cornell University Press, 1970); Wilson Carey McWilliams and Michael T. Gibbons, eds., *The Federalists, the Antifederalists, and the American Political Tradition* (New York: Greenwood Press, 1992); David J. Seimers, *Ratifying the Republic: Antifederalists and Federalists in Constitutional Time* (Stanford: Stanford University Press, 2002).

51. Keyssar, *The Right to Vote,* 22–24. The US Constitution, article 1, section 2, says: "The House of Representatives shall be composed of Members chosen every Year by the People of the several States, and the Electors in each State shall have the Qualifications requisite for Electors of the most numerous Branch of the State Legislature." Also, the US Constitution, article 2, section 1, says that each state legislature has the right to determine the "manner" in which presidential electors will be selected, while article 4 says that the federal government must "guarantee to every State in this Union a Republican Form of Government."

52. The US Constitution mentions citizenship three times as a requirement to hold federal office (see US Constitution, article 1, sections 2 and 3; and article 2, section 1). The Constitution also gave Congress the power to "establish an uniform Rule of Naturalization [*sic*]" (article 1, section 8), but not explicitly a rule regarding citizenship. The Constitution also referred to citizens when assigning jurisdiction to the federal courts (article 3, section 2), and in a "Privileges and Immunities cause" pertaining to extradition (article 4, section 2).

53. Smith, *Civic Ideals,* 24. Political agency, as discussed in the introduction, reaches beyond a state-sanctioned right to vote and can be asserted through identification with a group of oppressed people and by confronting political institutions and demanding rights. Also, many scholars have discussed the rhetorical force of "the people," including Richard Buel Jr., *Securing the Revolution: Ideology in American Politics, 1789–1815* (Ithaca, N.Y.: Cornell University Press, 1972); Maurice Charland, "Constitutive Rhetoric: The Case of the Peuple Québécois," *Quarterly Journal of*

Speech 73 (1987): 133–51; Michael C. McGee, "In Search of 'The People': A Rhetorical Alternative," *Quarterly Journal of Speech* 61 (1975): 235–49; Edmund S. Morgan, *Inventing the People: The Rise of Popular Sovereignty in England and America* (New York: Norton, 1988); Schudson, *The Good Citizen,* 49–51; Wood, *The Creation of the American Republic,* 344–89. Moreover, the issue of slavery empowered state governments to shape the livelihoods of America's largest minority population. As a measure of compromise, the Constitution left slavery in the hands of state governments and even created measures to preserve the South's economic dependence on slavery. The Constitution prohibited the abolition of the African slave trade for at least twenty years; every state was required to return fugitive slaves; and the three-fifths clause gave southern states more electoral votes in national elections. Foner, "From Slavery to Citizenship," 57.

54. For scholarship on the rise of the two-party system in American politics, see Jean H. Baker, *Affairs of Party: The Political Culture of Northern Democrats in the Mid-Nineteenth Century* (Ithaca, N.Y.: Cornell University Press, 1983); Lee Benson, *The Concept of Jacksonian Democracy: New York as a Test Case* (Princeton, N.J.: Princeton University Press, 1961); Ronald P. Formisano, *The Birth of Mass Political Parties: Michigan, 1827–1861* (Princeton, N.J.: Princeton University Press, 1970); Harry L. Watson, *Jacksonian Politics and Community Conflict: The Emergence of the Second American Party System in Cumberland County, North Carolina* (Baton Rouge: Louisiana State University Press, 1981). For scholarship on the centrality of party politics to civic life, see Donald W. Rogers, "Introduction: The Right to Vote in American History," in Rogers, *Voting and the Spirit of American Democracy,* 9–10; Schudson, *The Good Citizen,* 94.

55. Jacob Katz Cogan, "The Look Within: Property, Capacity, and Suffrage in Nineteenth-Century America," *Yale Law Journal* 107 (1997): 477–78; Keyssar, *The Right to Vote,* 35, 68–70; Smith, *Civic Ideals,* 165–96; Wilentz, "Property and Power," 35–36; Wood, *The Radicalism of the American Revolution* (New York: Vintage Books, 1991), 311–18; Wilentz, "On Class and Politics in Jacksonian America," *Reviews in American History* 10 (1982): 45–63. For more on voter turnout during the early nineteenth century, see Ronald P. Formisano, "Deferential-Participant Politics: The Early Republic's Political Culture," *American Political Science Review* 68 (1974): 473–87; Ronald P. Formisano, "Toward a Reorientation of Jacksonian Politics: A Review of the Literature, 1959–1975," *Journal of American History* 63 (1976–77): 42–65; Paul Kleppner, *Who Voted? The Dynamics of Electoral Turnout, 1870–1980* (New York: Praeger, 1982); Richard P. McCormick, "Ethno-Cultural Interpretations of Nineteenth-Century American Voting Behavior," *Political Science Quarterly* 89 (1974): 351–77; Richard P. McCormick, "New Perspectives on Jacksonian Politics," *American Historical Review* 65 (1956–60): 288–301.

56. Michael McGerr, "Political Style and Women's Power, 1830–1930," *Journal of American History* 77 (1990): 866–67. Also see Angela G. Ray, "The Permeable Public: Rituals of Citizenship in Antebellum Men's Debating Clubs," *Argumentation & Advocacy* 41 (2004): 1–16.

57. By 1860, all states required voters to be US citizens. Paul Kleppner, "Defining Citizenship," 45.

58. Schudson, *The Good Citizen,* 94.

59. Keyssar, *The Right to Vote,* 59. Also see Cogan, "The Look Within"; Rowland Berthoff, "Conventional Mentality: Free Blacks, Women, and Business Corporations as Unequal Persons, 1820–1870," *Journal of American History* 76 (1989): 753–84.

60. Ann M. Boylan, "Women and Politics in the Era before Seneca Falls," *Journal of the Early Republic* 10 (1990): 363.

61. Massachusetts did so in 1835; Mississippi in 1839; New York and Pennsylvania in 1848. Melder, *The Beginnings of Sisterhood,* 5; Albie Sachs and Joan Hoff Wilson, *Sexism and the Law: A Study of Male Beliefs and Legal Bias in Britain and the United States* (New York: Free Press, 1979), 78.

62. Keyssar, *The Right to Vote,* 175.

63. Sharon Harley, "Northern Black Female Workers: Jacksonian Era," in Sharon Harley and Rosalyn Terborg-Penn, eds., *The Afro-American Woman: Struggles and Images* (Port Washington, N.Y.: Kennikat Press, 1978), 5–16.

64. Norma Basch, "Equity vs. Equality: Emerging Concepts of Women's Political Status in the Age of Jackson," *Journal of the Early Republic* 3 (1983): 318.

65. Melder, *The Beginnings of Sisterhood,* 5–6. Also see Toby L. Ditz, "Ownership and Obligation: Inheritance and Patriarchal Households in Connecticut, 1750–1820," *William and Mary Quarterly* 47 (1990): 235–65; Sachs and Wilson, *Sexism and the Law,* 77–78.

66. Baker, "The Domestication of Politics," 631.

67. Cogan, "The Look Within"; Keyssar, *The Right to Vote,* 175.

68. Keyssar, *The Right to Vote,* 54.

69. Baker, "The Domestication of Politics," 631; Smith, *Civic Ideals,* 146–47.

70. On the tension between women as citizens and women as women in the early nineteenth century, Gundersen, "Independence"; Virginia Sapiro, "Women, Citizenship, and Nationality: Immigration and Naturalization Policies in the United States," *Politics & Society* 13 (1984): 1–26.

71. Kerber, *Women of the Republic,* 283.

72. Kerber argues that the definition of citizenship in the early republic should be expanded to recognize the ways in which women were politically engaged: "If we broaden the discussion and recognize that citizenship involves wide-ranging issues of claims and rights and of political behavior, as well as matters of allegiance, support, and analysis, then it is not difficult to find many occasions when women addressed political matters." Linda K. Kerber, "The Paradox of Women's Citizenship in the Early Republic," *American Historical Review* 97 (1922): 354–55.

73. See John C. Baker, "Women, Language, and the Argument for Education Reform in Antebellum Ladies' Magazines," *Women & Language* 20 (1997): 49–52.

74. For a discussion on the impact of Wollstonecraft's *Vindication* in the United States, see Zagarri, "The Rights of Man," 205–11.

75. Melder, *The Beginnings of Sisterhood,* 16.

76. Eleanor Flexner and Ellen Fitzpatrick, *Century of Struggle: The Woman's Rights Movement in the United States* (Cambridge: Harvard University Press, 1996), 24–25.

77. Ginzberg, *Women and the Work of Benevolence,* 17. For more scholarship on how religion influenced women's activism in the early nineteenth century,

see Nancy A. Hewitt, "Feminist Friends: Agrarian Quakers and the Emergence of Women's Rights in America," *Feminist Studies* 12 (1986): 27–49; Nancy Isenberg, *Sex and Citizenship in Antebellum America* (Chapel Hill: University of North Carolina Press, 1998), 41–74.

78. Barbara Welter's hallmark article, "The Cult of True Womanhood: 1820–1860," *American Quarterly* 18 (1966): 151–74, has invited much commentary and criticism regarding the women in early- to mid-nineteenth-century America. Most notably, Welter has been criticized for not acknowledging the privileges of the "true woman," along race and class lines. For more scholarship on "true woman" ideals, see Inga Bryden and Janet Floyd, eds., *Domestic Space: Reading the Nineteenth-Century Interior* (Manchester, UK: Manchester University Press, 1999); Joan Landes, *Women and the Public Sphere in the Age of the French Revolution* (Ithaca, N.Y.: Cornell University Press, 1988); Bonnie Smith, *Changing Lives: Women in European History* (Lexington, Mass.: D. C. Heath, 1989); Bonnie Smith, *Ladies of the Leisure Class: The Bourgeoises of Northern France in the Nineteenth Century* (Princeton, N.J.: Princeton University Press, 1981); Nancy M. Theriot, *Mothers and Daughters in Nineteenth-Century America: The Biosocial Construction of Femininity* (Lexington: University Press of Kentucky, 1996); Martha Vicinus, *Suffer and Be Still: Women in the Victorian Age* (Bloomington: University of Indiana Press, 1977). Scholarship that challenges and refines Welter's conceptualization of true womanhood include: Mary M. Cronin, "Redefining Woman's Sphere: New England's Antebellum Female Textile Operatives' Magazines and the Response to the 'Cult of True Womanhood,'" *Journalism History* 25 (1999): 13–25; Ann Douglas, *The Feminization of American Culture* (New York: Anchor Press/Doubleday, 1977); Ellen Carol DuBois, Mari Jo Buhle, Temma Kaplan, Gerda Lerner, and Carroll Smith-Rosenberg, "Politics and Culture in Women's History: A Symposium," *Feminist Studies* 6 (1980): 26–64; Caroll Smith-Rosenberg, "Beauty, the Beast, and the Militant Woman: A Case Study in Sex Roles and Social Stress in Jacksonian America," *American Quarterly* 23 (1971): 562–84.

79. The Female Benevolence Society was one of the most prominent of these organizations. Baker, "The Domestication of Politics," 632–34.

80. Boylan, "Women and Politics," 365.

81. Ibid., 365–72.

82. Alisse Portnoy, *Their Right to Speak: Women's Activism in the Indian and Slave Debates* (Cambridge: Harvard University Press, 2005), 54; Also see Alisse Theodore, "'A Right to Speak on the Subject': The U.S. Women's Antiremoval Petition Campaign, 1829–1831," *Rhetoric & Public Affairs* 5 (2002): 601–24.

83. Ibid. Also see Melder, *The Beginnings of Sisterhood,* 31; Carroll Smith-Rosenberg, "The Female World of Love and Ritual: Relations between Women in Nineteenth-Century America," *Signs* 1 (1975): 1–29.

84. Boylan, "Women and Politics," 372–76; Smith-Rosenberg, "Beauty, the Beast, and the Militant Woman," 563–64.

85. Ginzberg, *Women and the Work of Benevolence,* 25.

86. Boylan, "Women and Politics," 378.

87. Ibid., 364; Smith-Rosenberg, "Beauty, the Beast and the Militant Woman"; Melder, *The Beginnings of Sisterhood,* 55; Mary P. Ryan, "The Power of Women's

Networks: A Case Study of Female Moral Reform in Antebellum America," *Feminist Studies* 5 (1979): 66–85.

88. Ellen Carol DuBois, "Outgrowing the Compact of the Fathers: Equal Rights, Woman Suffrage, and the United States Constitution, 1820–1878," *Journal of American History* 74 (1987): 837. Further, the labor movement of the 1820s and 1830s did not provide the opportunities or rhetorical resources to argue for women's rights as much as the abolition movement; DuBois attributes this to the more masculinized aspects of class issues. Ibid., 840.

89. Wright had such a profound effect on the role of women in social reform that woman's rights advocates throughout the nineteenth century were often pejoratively labeled "Fanny Wrightists." Flexner and Fitzpatrick, *Century of Struggle,* 25–26.

90. See Hewitt, "Feminist Friends"; Blanche Glassman Hersh, *The Slavery of Sex: Feminist Abolitionists in America* (Urbana: University of Illinois Press, 1978); Gerda Lerner, "Black and White Women in Interaction and Confrontation," in *Prospects: An Annual of American Cultural Studies,* vol. 2, ed. Jack Salzman (New York: Burt Franklin, 1976): 193–208.

91. See Stephen Howard Browne, *Angelina Grimké, Rhetoric, Identity, and the Radical Imagination* (East Lansing: Michigan State University Press, 1999).

92. See Susan Zaeske, *Signatures of Citizenship: Petitioning, Antislavery, and Women's Political Identity* (Chapel Hill: University of North Carolina Press, 2003).

93. These women were Sarah Mapps Douglass, Sarah Forten, Margaretta Forten, and Harriet Forten. Rosalyn Terborg-Penn, "Discrimination against Afro-American Women in the Woman's Movement, 1830–1920," in Harley and Terborg-Penn, eds., *The Afro-American Woman,* 18.

94. Discrimination against African American women did not stop in the 1860s but African American women became a stronger, organized force after that time. Ibid., 20. Also see Rosalyn Terborg-Penn, "African American Women and the Woman Suffrage Movement," in *One Woman, One Vote: Rediscovering the Woman Suffrage Movement,* ed. Marjorie Spruill Wheeler (Troutdale, Ore.: New Sage Press, 1995), 137–39.

95. Carla Peterson, "A 'Sign unto This Nation': Sojourner Truth, History, Orature, and Modernity," in *Black Women's Intellectual Traditions: Speaking Their Minds,* eds. Kristin Waters and Carol B. Conaway (Burlington: University of Vermont Press, 2007), 161. For a critical look at differing accounts of this text, see *With Pen and Voice: A Critical Anthology of Nineteenth-Century African-American Women,* ed. Shirley Wilson Logan (Carbondale: Southern Illinois University Press, 1995).

96. Flexner and Fitzpatrick, *Century of Struggle,* 58.

97. Ginzberg, *Women and the Work of Benevolence,* 85. Also, Zagarri argues that discourse on revolutionary and equality ideals about women circulated just as much as republican mother ideals. Further, she claims, "This discourse concerning women's rights provides a crucial intellectual link between the Revolutionary era and the first feminist movement of the 1830s and 1840s." Zagarri, "The Rights of Man and Woman," 228.

98. Boylan, "Women and Politics," 363.

99. The Fifteenth Amendment, which was ratified in 1870, says: "The right of citizens of the United States to vote shall not be denied or abridged by the United

States or by any State on account of race, color, or previous condition of servitude." U.S. Constitution, amendment 15, section 1.

100. Foner, "From Slavery to Citizenship," 57.

101. In 1855, the Know-Nothings won control of all New England states except Maine and Vermont; they emerged as the leading opposition to Democrats in the mid-Atlantic states, California, and slave states; and, in 1856, the Know-Nothing presidential candidate, Millard Fillmore, polled over 21 percent, still the largest percentage of a third-party candidate with the exception of Theodore Roosevelt in 1912. Kleppner, "Defining Citizenship," 46–52; Keyssar, *The Right to Vote,* 83–87.

102. Elisabeth Griffith, *In Her Own Right: The Life of Elizabeth Cady Stanton* (New York: Oxford University Press, 1984), 35–39.

103. See Jacob Katz Cogan and Lori D. Ginzberg, "1846 Petition for Woman's Suffrage, New York State Constitutional Convention," *Signs* 22 (1997): 427–39.

104. Flexner and Fitzpatrick, *Century of Struggle,* 60, 68; Judith Wellman, *The Road to Seneca Falls: Elizabeth Cady Stanton and the First Woman's Rights Convention* (Urbana: University of Illinois Press, 2004), 153.

105. Flexner and Fitzpatrick, *Century of Struggle,* 68–69.

106. Stanton et al., eds., *History of Woman Suffrage,* 1:67; Griffith, *In Her Own Right,* 55.

107. Wellman, *The Road to Seneca Falls,* 194–96.

108. Flexner and Fitzpatrick, *Century of Struggle,* 71.

109. Three days before the Seneca Falls Convention, Stanton met with McClintock and her oldest daughters to revise Stanton's draft of what would become the "Declaration of Sentiments." During this meeting, it was agreed upon that the draft would be "a second Declaration of Independence." Wellman, *The Road to Seneca Falls,* 191–92.

110. Ellen Carol DuBois, "Introduction: The Invention of Women's Rights," in *Elizabeth Cady Stanton, Susan B. Anthony: Correspondence, Writings, Speeches,* eds. Gerda Lerner and Ellen Carol DuBois (New York: Schocken Books, 1981), 2.

111. "Declaration of Sentiments," cited in Karlyn Kohrs Campbell, *Man Cannot Speak for Her,* vol. 2 (Westport, Conn.: Praeger, 1989), 34.

112. Ibid., emphasis added.

113. Stephen E. Lucas, "The Rhetorical Ancestry of the Declaration of Independence," *Rhetoric & Public Affairs* 1 (1998): 151.

114. For more on the women's rights conventions of the 1850s, see DuBois, "Outgrowing the Compact of Our Fathers," 841–44; Isenberg, *Sex and Citizenship,* chapters 1–2; Keyssar, *The Right to Vote,* 176–77.

115. For more on these arguments and debates, see Dianne Avery and Alfred S. Konefsky, "The Daughters of Job: Property Rights and Women's Lives in Mid-Nineteenth-Century Massachusetts," *Law and History Review* 10 (1992): 323–56; Norma Basch, "Invisible Women: The Legal Fiction of Marital Unity in Nineteenth-Century America," *Feminist Studies* 5 (1979): 346–66; Norma Basch, "Relief in the Premises: Divorce as a Woman's Remedy in New York and Indiana, 1815–1870," *Law and History Review* 8 (1990): 1–24; Conrad, "The Transformation," 284–97; DuBois, "Outgrowing the Compact of Our Fathers," 843–44; Isen-

berg, *Sex and Citizenship,* ch. 6; Carole Pateman, *The Sexual Contract* (Stanford: Stanford University Press, 1988); B. Zorina Kahn, "Married Women's Property Laws and Female Commercial Activity: Evidence from United States Patent Records, 1790–1895," *Journal of Economic History* 56 (1996): 360–65; Carole Shammas, "Re-assessing the Married Woman's Property Acts," *Journal of Women's History* 6 (1994): 9–30; Amy Dru Stanley, "Conjugal Bonds and Wage Labor: Rights of Contract in the Age of Emancipation," *Journal of American History* 75 (1988): 471–500; Reva B. Siegel, "Home as Work: The First Woman's Rights Claims Concerning Wives' Household Labor, 1850–1880," *Yale Law Journal* 103 (1994): 1073–1217.

116. Conrad, "The Transformation."

117. See Kirt H. Wilson, *The Reconstruction Desegregation Debate: The Politics of Equality and the Rhetoric of Place, 1870–1875* (East Lansing: Michigan State University Press, 2002).

118. In 1865, Congress ratified the Thirteenth Amendment, which was designed to abolish slavery and economic boundaries that oppressed African Americans. The following year, Pres. Andrew Johnson reinstated a few measures that helped empower the southern planter class and subjugated newly freed blacks to yearly labor contracts with weighty violation codes. However, in response, the Republican Congress enacted the Civil Rights Act of 1866, which offered in greater detail the specific rights held by freed African Americans. The act declared: "All persons born in the United States and not subject to any foreign power, excluding Indians not taxed, are hereby declared to be citizens of the United States; and such citizens, of every race and color, without regard to any previous condition of slavery or involuntary servitude, . . . shall have the same right, in every State and Territory in the United States, to make and enforce contracts, to sue, be parties, and give evidence, to inherit, purchase, lease, sell, hold, and convey real and personal property, and to full and equal benefit of all laws and proceedings for the security of person and property, as is enjoyed by white citizens." Almost more significantly, states were prohibited from violating the act. Rogers, "Introduction," 60; "An Act to protect all Persons in the United States in their Civil Rights, and furnish the Means of their Vindication," ch. 31, sec. 1, U.S. Statutes at Large 14 (1866): 27.

119. Section 1 of the Fourteenth Amendment says: "All persons born or naturalized in the United States, and subject to the jurisdiction thereof, are citizens of the United States and of the State wherein they reside. No State shall make or enforce any law which shall abridge the privileges or immunities of citizens of the United States; nor shall any State deprive any person of life, liberty, or property, without due process of law; nor deny to any person within its jurisdiction the equal protection of the laws." U.S. Constitution, amendment 14, section 1.

120. See *Scott v. Sandford,* 60 U.S. 393 (1857). Also see Ellen Carol DuBois, "Taking Law into Their Own Hands: Voting Women During Reconstruction," in Rogers, *Voting and American Democracy,* 70; DuBois, "Taking the Law Into Our Own Hands: *Bradwell, Minor,* and Suffrage Militance in the 1870s," in Wheeler, *One Woman, One Vote,* 82–98; *Dred Scott v. Sandford* 60 U.S. 393 (1857).

121. Keyssar, *The Right to Vote,* 92.

122. Rogers, "Introduction," 62.

123. Keyssar, *The Right to Vote,* 95–101.

124. Baker, "The Domestication of Politics," 636–37.

125. Terborg-Penn, "African American Women," 139.

126. Flexner and Fitzpatrick, *Century of Struggle,* 155.

127. Terborg-Penn, "African American Women," 140.

128. Ibid, 157–58.

129. On the conflicts that lead to the creation of the NWSA and the AWSA, see Andrea Moore Kerr, "White Women's Rights, Black Men's Wrongs: Free Love, Blackmail, and the Formation of the American Woman Suffrage Association," in *One Woman, One Vote,* 61–80.

130. Flexner and Fitzpatrick, *Century of Struggle,* 145–46.

131. Keyssar, *The Right to Vote,* 104.

132. Ellen Carol DuBois, *Feminism and Suffrage: The Emergence of an Independent Women's Movement in America, 1848–1869* (Ithaca, N.Y.: Cornell University Press, 1978), 126–37.

133. Quoted in Flexner and Fitzpatrick, *Century of Struggle,* 161.

134. *Minor v. Happersett* 88 U.S. 162 (1875).

135. Flexner and Fitzpatrick, *Century of Struggle,* 162.

136. US Representatives William Loughridge (R-IA) and Benjamin F. Butler (R-MA) produced the minority report. Karlyn Kohrs Campbell, *Man Cannot Speak for Her,* vol. 1 (Westport, Conn.: Praeger, 1989), 107–8.

137. Flexner and Fitzpatrick, *Century of Struggle,* 147.

138. Ibid., 157–58; DuBois, "Taking Law into Their Own Hands," 74.

139. DuBois, "Taking Law into Their Own Hands," 77.

140. Keyssar, *The Right to Vote,* 182.

141. For a discussion of how these women's actions constituted their citizenship identities, see Angela G. Ray, "The Rhetorical Ritual of Citizenship: Women's Voting as Public Performance, 1868–1875," *Quarterly Journal of Speech* 93 (2007): 1–26.

142. DuBois, "Taking Law into Their Own Hands," 74–76.

143. On the four stages of the Reconstruction Era, see Smith, *Civic Ideals,* 289–90. See also Wilson, *The Reconstruction Desegregation Debate.*

144. McGerr, "Political Style," 868.

145. Keyssar, *The Right to Vote,* 186.

146. On state suffrage campaigns, see Holly J. McCammon, "Stirring Up Suffrage Sentiment: The Formation of State Woman Suffrage Organizations, 1866–1914," *Social Forces* 80 (2001): 449–80; Holly J. McCammon and Karen E. Campbell, "Winning the Vote in the West: The Political Successes of the Women's Suffrage Movements, 1866–1919," *Gender & Society* 15 (2001): 55–82. McCammon and Campbell contend Alan Grimes's (1967) *The Puritan Ethic and Woman Suffrage* (New York: Oxford University Press, 1967), which argued that the West gave women the right to vote because they thought it would expedite the spread of white, puritan values and lifestyle. Alternatively, they argue that "gendered and political opportunities worked together with the ways in which suffragists mobilized to convince male lawmakers and male electorates to extend democracy to women." McCammon and Campbell, "Winning the Vote in the West," 57. Also see Holly J. McCammon, Karen E. Campbell, Ellen M. Gran-

berg, and Christine Mowery, "How Movements Win: Gendered Opportunity Structures and U.S. Women's Suffrage Movements, 1866–1919," *American Sociological Review* 66 (2001): 49–70; Rebecca J. Mead, *How the Vote Was Won: Woman Suffrage in the Western United States, 1868–1914* (New York: New York University Press, 2004).

147. Baker, "The Domestication of Politics," 637–38. Regarding Willard's rhetoric, see Ruth Bordin, *Women and Temperance: The Quest for Power and Liberty, 1873–1900* (Philadelphia: Temple University Press, 1981); Carolyn De Swarte Gifford, "Home Protection: The WCTU's Conversion to Woman Suffrage," in *Gender, Ideology, and Action: Historical Perspectives on Women's Public Lives,* ed., Janet Sharistanian (Westport, Conn.: Greenwood Press, 1986), 95–120; Bonnie J. Dow, "The 'Womanhood' Rationale in the Woman Suffrage Rhetoric of Frances E. Willard," *Southern Communication Journal* 56 (1991): 298–307; Amy R. Slagell, "The Rhetorical Structure of Frances E. Willard's Campaign for Woman Suffrage, 1876–1896," *Rhetoric & Public Affairs* 4 (2001): 1–23.

148. Ellen Carol DuBois, "Woman Suffrage Around the World: Three Phases of Suffragist Internationalism," in *Suffrage and Beyond: International Feminist Perspectives,* eds., Caroline Daley and Melanie Nolan (New York: New York University Press, 1994), 257, 259.

149. Sandra Stanley Holton, "'To Educate Women into the Rebellion': Elizabeth Cady Stanton and the Creation of a Transatlantic Network of Radical Suffragists," *American Historical Review* 99 (1994): 1112–33. See also Sandra Stanley Holton, "From Anti-Slavery to Suffrage Militancy: The Bright Circle, Elizabeth Cady Stanton and the British Women's Movement," in Daley and Nolan, *Suffrage and Beyond,* 213–33.

150. Keyssar, *The Right to Vote,* 194–96.

151. Schudson, *The Good Citizen,* 146.

152. Keyssar, *The Right to Vote,* 112–65. On the Chinese Exclusion Act of 1882, see Roger Daniels, "Chinese Exclusion: Causes and Consequences, 1882–1943," in *Who Belongs in America? Presidents, Rhetoric, and Immigration,* ed. Vanessa B. Beasley (College Station: Texas A&M University Press, 2006), 89–106.

153. On Grover Cleveland's discussion of immigrants, see Mary E. Stuckey, *Defining Americans: The Presidency and National Identity* (Lawrence: University Press of Kansas, 2004), 129. On Theodore Roosevelt's use of the "good citizen" construct, see Theodore Roosevelt, *The Strenuous Life* (New York: Century, 1901); John Paulson, "Theodore Roosevelt and the Rhetoric of Citizenship: On Tour in New England, 1902," *Communication Quarterly* 50 (2002): 123–34.

154. McGerr, "Political Style," 869–70.

155. For a discussion of the inception of the rhetorical presidency and Roosevelt's innovative use of the office, see Jeffrey K. Tulis, *The Rhetorical Presidency* (Princeton, N.J.: Princeton University Press, 1987).

156. On McKinley's speaking tours, see Lewis L. Gould, *The Modern American Presidency* (Lawrence: University Press of Kansas, 2003), 7–10. See also Richard Hofstadter, *The Progressive Movement, 1900–1915* (Englewood Cliffs, N.J.: Prentice-Hall, 1963), 6–7.

157. Regarding Catt's rhetorical work, see Susan Schultz Huxman, "Perfecting the Rhetorical Vision of Woman's Rights: Elizabeth Cady Stanton, Anna Howard

Shaw, and Carrie Chapman Catt," *Women's Studies in Communication* 23 (2000): 307–36.

158. McCammon, "Stirring Up," 453–54.

159. On woman suffrage in the West, see Mead, *How the Vote Was Won;* Thomas A. Larson, "Dolls, Vassals, and Drudges: Pioneer Women in the West," *Western Historical Quarterly* 3 (1972): 5–16; Thomas A. Larson, "Woman Suffrage in Western America," *Utah Historical Quarterly* 38 (1970): 7–19; Beverly Beeton, *Women Vote in the West: The Woman Suffrage Movement, 1869–1896* (New York: Garland, 1986); Beverly Beeton, "How the West Was Won for Woman Suffrage," in Wheeler, *One Woman, One Vote,* 99–116; Sandra L. Myres, "Suffering for Suffrage: Western Women and the Struggle for Political, Legal, and Economic Rights," in *Westering Women and the Frontier Experience, 1800–1915,* ed. Sandra L. Myres (Albuquerque: University of New Mexico Press, 1982), 213–36; Rebecca Edwards, "Pioneers at the Polls: Woman Suffrage in the West," in *Votes for Women,* ed., Jean Baker (New York: Oxford University Press, 2002), 151–74.

160. Keyssar, *The Right to Vote,* 197–200.

161. Regarding the ways in which western suffragists employed scientific racism, see Gail Bederman, *Manliness and Civilization: A Cultural History of Gender and Race in the United States, 1880–1917* (Chicago: University of Chicago Press, 1995); Louise Michele Newman, *White Women's Rights: The Racial Origins of Feminism in the United States* (New York: Oxford University Press, 1999), 132–57; Nancy Leys Stepan, "Race, Gender, Science and Citizenship," *Gender and History* 10 (1998): 26–52; Jane Rendall, "Citizenship, Culture, and Civilisation: The Languages of British Suffragists, 1866–1874," in Daley and Nolan, *Suffrage and Beyond,* 127–50. For literature on anti-Chinese racism, see Alexander Saxton, *The Indispensable Enemy: Labor and the Anti-Chinese Movement in California* (Berkeley: University of California Press, 1971); Roger Daniels, *Asian America: History of Chinese and Japanese in the United States since 1850* (Seattle: University of Washington Press, 1988); Sucheng Chan, "The Exclusion of Chinese Women, 1870–1943," in *A Heritage of Her Own: Toward a New Social History of American Women,* eds. Nancy F. Cott and Elizabeth H. Pleck (New York: Simon and Schuster, 1979), 75–125; Sucheng Chan, ed., *Entry Denied: Exclusion and the Chinese Community in America, 1882–1943* (Philadelphia: Temple University Press, 1991). Last, on constructions of American Indian identity, see Gail H. Landsman, "The 'Other' as Political Symbol: Images of Indians in the Woman Suffrage Movement," *Ethnohistory* 39 (1992): 247–84; Wendy Wall, "Gender and the 'Citizen Indian,'" in *Writing the Range: Race, Class, and Culture in the Women's West,* eds. Elizabeth Jameson and Susan Armitage (Norman: University of Oklahoma Press, 1997), 202–29; Margaret D. Jacobs, "Resistance to the Rescue: The Indians of Bahapki and Mrs. Annie E. K. Bidwell," in Jameson and Armitage, *Writing the Range,* 230–51.

162. On African American women's involvement in the suffrage movement and in clubs, see Sarah Deutsch, "Landscape of Enclaves: Race Relations in the West, 1865–1990," in *Under Open Sky: Rethinking America's Western Past,* eds. William Cronon, George Miles, and Jay Gitlin (New York: W. W. Norton, 1992), 110–31; National Association of Colored Women's Clubs (NACWC), *A History of the Club*

Movement among the Colored Women of the United States of America (Washington, D.C.: NACWA, 1902); Lawrence B. deGraaf, "Race, Sex, and Region: Black Women in the America West, 1850–1920," *Pacific Historical Review* 49 (1980): 309–11; Ann D. Gordon, ed., *African American Women and the Vote, 1837–1965* (Amherst: University of Massachusetts Press, 1997); Rosalyn M. Terborg-Penn, *African-American Women in the Struggle for the Vote, 1850–1920* (Bloomington: Indiana University Press, 1998), 54–106; Bettina Aptheker, *Woman's Legacy: Essays on Race, Sex, and Class in American History* (Amherst: University of Massachusetts Press, 1982), 63–66.

163. Terborg-Penn, "African American Women," 142. Also see Shirley Wilson Logan's discussion of Harper in *"We Are Coming": The Persuasive Discourse of Nineteenth-Century Black Women* (Carbondale: Southern Illinois University Press, 1999).

164. See Patricia A. Schechter, *Ida B. Wells-Barnett and American Reform, 1880–1930* (Chapel Hill: University of North Carolina Press, 2001).

165. Terborg-Penn, "African American Women," 143.

166. See Logan, "We Are Coming," 98–126.

167. Smith, *Civic Ideals*, 387.

168. Baker, "The Domestication of Politics," 641. See also Karen J. Blair, *The Clubwoman as Feminist: True Womanhood Redefined, 1868–1914* (New York: Holms and Meier, 1980); J. C. Croly, *The History of the Women's Club Movement in America* (New York: Henry B. Allen, 1898); Marilyn Gittell and Teresa Shtob, "Changing Women's Roles in Political Volunteerism and Reform of the City," *Signs* 5 (1980 supplement): S69.

169. Keyssar, *The Right to Vote*, 206–207.

170. Mead, *How the Vote Was Won*, 2.

171. Keyssar, *The Right to Vote*, 209.

172. On the innovations of the woman suffrage campaign during this time, see Jennifer L. Borda, "The Woman Suffrage Parades of 1910–1913: Possibilities and Limitations of an Early Feminist Rhetorical Strategy," *Western Journal of Communication* 66 (2002): 25–52; Sara Hunter Graham, "The Suffrage Renaissance: A New Image for a New Century, 1896–1910," in Wheeler, *One Woman, One Vote*, 157–78; Keyssar, *The Right to Vote*, 206. On suffrage parades and other strategies, see Holly J. McCammon, "'Out of the Parlors and into the Streets': The Changing Tactical Repertoire of the U.S. Women's Suffrage Movements," *Social Forces* 81 (2003): 787–818; Susan G. Davis, *Parades and Power: Street Theatre in Nineteenth-Century Philadelphia* (Philadelphia: Temple University Press, 1986).

173. Keyssar, *The Right to Vote*, 208–10.

174. Maryjo Wagner, "Farms, Families, and Reform: Women in the Farmers' Alliance and Populist Party" (PhD diss., University of Oregon, 1986); Marilyn P. Watkins, *Rural Democracy: Family Farmers and Politics in Western Washington, 1890–1925* (Ithaca, N.Y.: Cornell University Press, 1995); Julie Roy Jeffrey, "Women in the Southern Farmers' Alliance: A Reconsideration of the Role and Status of Women in the Late Nineteenth-Century South," *Feminist Studies* 3 (1975): 72–91; Michael Lewis Goldberg, *An Army of Women: Gender and Politics in Gilded Age Kansas*

(Baltimore: Johns Hopkins University Press, 1997); Michael Lewis Goldberg, "Non-Partisan and All-Partisan: Rethinking Woman Suffrage and Party Politics in Gilded Age Kansas," *Western Historical Quarterly* 25 (1994): 21–44.

175. On women in the labor movement, see Nancy Schrom Dye, *As Equals and as Sisters: Feminism, the Labor Movement, and the Women's Trade Union League of New York* (NY: Columbia University Press, 1980); Meredith Tax, *The Rising of the Women: Feminist Solidarity and Class Conflict, 1880–1917* (Urbana: University of Illinois Press, 1991).

176. Mead, *How the Vote Was Won,* 9–11. Although marginally, women participated in political parties in the last decades of the nineteenth century. See Rebecca Edwards, *Angels in the Machinery: Gender in American Party Politics from the Civil War to the Progressive Era* (New York: Oxford University Press, 1997).

177. Mead, *How the Vote Was Won,* 11. See also Ann Schofield, "Rebel Girls and Union Maids: The Woman Question in the Journals of the AFL and IWW, 1905–1920," *Feminist Studies* 9 (1983): 335–58; Alice Kessler-Harris, "Women, Work, and the Social Order," in *Liberating Women's History,* ed. Berenice A. Carroll (Urbana: University of Illinois Press, 1976), 330–43; Heidi Hartmann, "Capitalism, Patriarchy, and Job Segregation by Sex," *Signs* 1 (1976): 137–69; Susan Levine, *Labor's True Woman: Carpet Weavers, Industrialization, and Labor Reform in the Gilded Age* (Philadelphia: Temple University Press, 1984); Mari Jo Buhle, *Women and American Socialism, 1870–1920* (Urbana: University of Illinois Press, 1981).

178. Ellen Carol DuBois, "Working Women, Class Relations, and Suffrage Militance: Harriot Stanton Blatch and the New York Woman Suffrage Movement, 1894–1909," *Journal of American History* 74 (1987): 34–39. For more on working women in the Northeast during this time, see Mary Blewett, *We Will Rise in Our Might: Workingwomen's Voices from Nineteenth-Century New England* (Ithaca, N.Y.: Cornell University Press, 1991); Ardis Cameron, *Radicals of the Worst Sort: Laboring Women in Lawrence, Massachusetts, 1860–1912* (Urbana: University of Illinois Press, 1993); Christine Stansell, *City of Women: Sex and Class in New York, 1789–1860* (Urbana: University of Illinois Press, 1982).

179. DuBois, "Working Women," 40–41. Towards the end of her life, Stanton embraced a severe individualist perspective on natural rights, despite the elitism she exhibited when advocating for literacy tests. On Stanton's individualistic philosophy, see Karlyn Kohrs Campbell, "Stanton's 'The Solitude of Self': A Rationale for Feminism," *Quarterly Journal of Speech* 66 (1980): 304–12.

180. DuBois, "Working Women," 45. See also Ellen Carol DuBois, *Harriot Stanton Blatch and the Winning of Woman Suffrage* (New Haven: Yale University Press, 1997); Elinor Lerner, "Immigrant and Working Class Involvement in the New York City Woman Suffrage Movement, 1905–1917: A Study in Progressive Era Politics" (PhD diss., University of California, Berkeley, 1981).

181. DuBois, "Working Women," 41–46.

182. Gittell and Shtob, "Changing Women's Roles," S69–S71.

183. Baker, "The Domestication of Politics," 637.

184. Gittell and Shtob, "Changing Women's Roles," S70–S71.

185. DuBois, "Working Women," 50–57.

186. DuBois, "Woman Suffrage," 260. See also Marilyn J. Boxer and Jean H. Quataert, *Socialist Women: European Socialist Feminism in the Nineteenth and Early Twentieth Centuries* (New York: Elsevier, 1978); Richard J. Evans, *Comrades and Sisters: Feminism, Socialism and Pacifism in Europe, 1870–1945* (New York: St. Martin's Press, 1987); Charles Sowerwine, "Socialism, Feminism, and the Socialist Women's Movement from the French Revolution to World War II," in *Becoming Visible: Women in European History,* 3rd ed., eds. Renate Bridenthal, Merry E. Wiesner, and Susan Mosher Stuard (Boston: Houghton Mifflin, 2006); Jane Slaughter and Robert Kern, eds., *European Women on the Left: Socialism, Feminism, and the Problems Faced by Political Women, 1880 to the Present* (Westport, Conn.: Greenwood Press, 1981); Richard J. Evans, *The Feminists: Women's Emancipation Movements in Europe, America, and Australasia, 1840–1920* (New York: Barnes & Noble, 1977).

187. DuBois, "Woman Suffrage," 265.

188. Ibid. For more on the WSPU and its militancy, see DuBois, "Woman Suffrage," 265–67; Susan Kingsley Kent, *Sex and Suffrage in Britain, 1860–1914* (Princeton, N.J.: Princeton University Press, 1987); Andrew Rosen, *Rise Up, Women! The Militant Campaign of the Women's Social and Political Union, 1903–1914* (London: Routledge & Kegan Paul, 1974); Cheryl R. Jorgensen-Earp, *The Transfiguring Sword: The Just War of the Women's Social and Political Union* (Tuscaloosa: University of Alabama Press, 1997).

189. DuBois, "Woman Suffrage," 267–69.

190. Keyssar, *The Right to Vote,* 205–6.

CHAPTER 2

1. Rogers M. Smith, *Civic Ideals: Conflicting Visions of Citizenship in U.S. History* (New Haven: Yale University Press, 1997), 424. See also Kathleen E. Kendall, *Communication in the Presidential Primaries: Candidates and the Media: 1912–2000* (Westport, Conn.: Praeger Publishers, 2000).

2. Mary E. Stuckey, *Defining Americans: The Presidency and National Identity* (Lawrence: University Press of Kansas, 2004), 151.

3. Ibid., 152.

4. Ibid., 152–53.

5. *Plessy v. Ferguson* 163 U.S. 537 (1896). For a summary of Jim Crow laws, see Smith, *Civic Ideals,* 448–52.

6. Ian F. Haney López, *White by Law: The Legal Construction of Race* (New York: New York University Press, 1996), 44.

7. Vanessa B. Beasley discusses the growth of racist and nativist organizations and scientific arguments in the late nineteenth century. Vanessa B. Beasley, *You, the People: American National Identity in Presidential Rhetoric* (College Station: Texas A&M University, 2004), 69–70.

8. For example, in 1906, Congress adopted the major Naturalization Act intended to severely limit the naturalization of immigrants by establishing standardized procedures and imposing penalties for fraudulent naturalizations. The act also created the Division of Naturalization, which greatly enhanced federal power in the process

of mitigating the extension of citizenship rights to outsiders, with the exception of northern European immigrants. Additionally, Congress passed the 1907 Immigrant Act, which increased immigrant head taxes and lead to the creation of the US Immigration Commission, which produced a forty-two-volume report on the "evils" of immigration. Smith, *Civic Ideals,* 429, 442, 446.

9. The intersection of progressivism and US internationalism resulted in what Smith considers a four-part hierarchical structure of citizenship laws. At the lowest level, immigrants such as Filipinos and Chinese laborers were denied entry or expelled due to ethnicity alone; next, territorial inhabitants considered racially inferior, such as those from Guam, were conferred colonial subjectship, but were ineligible for citizenship; at the next level, women, Puerto Ricans, blacks, and some American Indians were granted second-class citizenship, wherein certain citizenship rights were denied based on perceived incapability; and last, those "white" enough, including nonaboriginal peoples from Hawaii and Alaska, were granted full citizenship rights. Even the Fourteenth Amendment was used to reinforce these citizenship hierarchies when Justice Melville Fuller argued that one's citizenship should remain the nation of birth. Ibid., 429–30, 440.

10. Alexandar Keyssar, *The Right to Vote: The Contested History of Democracy in United States* (New York: Basic Books, 2000), 207.

11. Kirt Wilson, *The Reconstruction Desegregation Debate: The Politics of Equality and the Rhetoric of Place, 1870–1875* (East Lansing: Michigan State University Press, 2002), 160.

12. Ibid.

13. US Constitution, amendment 14, section 1.

14. For more on the regional and ideological differences between the North and South following the Civil War and the Reconstruction era, see Monroe Lee Billington, *The Political South in the Twentieth Century* (New York: Scribner, 1975); Thomas D. Clark, *The South since Reconstruction* (Indianapolis: Bobbs-Merrill, 1973); Richard N. Current, *Northernizing the South* (Athens: University of Georgia Press, 1973); John Hope Franklin, *Reconstruction after the Civil War,* 2nd ed. (Chicago: University of Chicago Press, 1994); David M. Potter, *The South and the Sectional Conflict* (Baton Rouge: Louisiana State University Press, 1968); Howard N. Rabinowitz, *The First New South* (Arlington Heights, Ill.: Harlan Davidson, 1992).

15. Jacqueline Glass Campbell, "Seeking a Moral Economy of War: Confederate Women and Southern Nationalism in Civil War North Carolina," in *Women Shaping the South: Creating and Confronting Change,* eds. Angela Boswell and Judith N. McArthur (Columbia: University of Missouri Press, 2006), 96. Also see H. E. Gulley, "Women and the Lost Cause: Preserving a Confederate Identity in the American Deep South," *Journal of Historical Geography* 19 (1993): 125–41.

16. Campbell, "Seeking a Moral Economy," 95–96.

17. Keyssar, *The Right to Vote,* 194–95. For more on women in the South during this time, see Marjorie Spruill Wheeler, *New Women of the New South: The Leaders of the Woman Suffrage Movement in the Southern States* (New York: Oxford University Press, 1993).

18. Keyssar, *The Right to Vote,* 206–9. Also see Elna C. Green, *Southern Strategies: Southern Women and the Woman Suffrage Question* (Chapel Hill: University of North Carolina Press, 1997); Ann D. Gordon, ed., *African American Women and the Vote: 1837–1965* (Amherst: University of Massachusetts Press, 1997); Smith, *Civic Ideals,* 455–56.

19. Rosalyn Terborg-Penn, "African American Women and the Woman Suffrage Movement," in *One Woman, One Vote: Rediscovering the Woman Suffrage Movement,* ed. Marjorie Spruill Wheeler (Troutdale, Ore.: New Sage Press, 1995), 149; Wheeler, *New Women of the New South,* 101–2, 104, 110, 113–25.

20. Paula Giddings, *When and Where I Enter: The Impact of Black Women on Race and Sex in America* (New York: W. Morrow, 1996), 128. Also see Kenneth R. Johnson, "Kate Gordon and the Woman-Suffrage Movement in the South," in *History of Women in the United States: Historical Articles on Women's Lives and Activities,* ed. Nancy Cott (Munich, 1992), vol. 19, part 1: 226–52; B. H. Gilley, "Kate Gordon and Louisiana Woman Suffrage," in Cott, *History of Women in the United States,* 19: 254–71.

21. Keyssar, *The Right to Vote,* 195–96.

22. See chapter 1, note 161, for readings on how western suffragists employed racist arguments.

23. See Holly J. McCammon, Karen E. Campbell, Ellen M. Granberg, and Christine Mowery, "How Movements Win: Gendered Opportunity Structures and U.S. Women's Suffrage Movements, 1866–1919," *American Sociological Review* 66 (2001): 49–70; and Rebecca J. Mead, *How the Vote Was Won: Woman Suffrage in the Western United States, 1868–1914* (New York: New York University Press, 2004).

24. Terborg-Penn, "African American Women," 147–49.

25. Giddings, *When and Where I Enter,* 126–27.

26. Terborg-Penn, "African American Women," 147–49.

27. Keyssar, *The Right to Vote,* 210; Smith, *Civic Ideals,* 456. On anti-suffrage, see Manuela Thurner, "'Better Citizens Without the Ballot': American Anti-suffrage Women and Their Rationale During the Progressive Era," *Journal of Women's History* 5 (Spring 1993): 33–60. Regarding suffrage failures in the South: In 1912, Virginia voted against a suffrage amendment, 88–12; Louisiana rejected a bill that would have granted suffrage in the Democratic primaries as well as a proposal for school suffrage; and although Arkansas approved a suffrage referendum, it never went to the people. Keyssar, *The Right to Vote,* 210. See also David Morgan, *Suffragists and Democrats: The Politics of Woman Suffrage in America* (East Lansing: Michigan State University Press, 1972).

28. In 1912, referenda failed in Ohio, Wisconsin, and Michigan; in 1913, they failed in North Dakota, South Dakota, Nebraska, Mississippi, Ohio, and Michigan; and in 1914, they failed in New York, New Jersey, Pennsylvania, and Massachusetts. Keyssar, *The Right to Vote,* 208.

29. Molly Ladd-Taylor, "Hull House Goes to Washington: Women and the Children's Bureau," in *Gender, Class, Race, and Reform in the Progressive Era,* eds. Noralee Frankel and Nancy S. Dye (Lexington: University Press of Kentucky, 1991), 111.

30. Eileen Boris, "Reconstructing the 'Family': Women, Progressive Reform, and the Problem of Social Control," in Frankel and Dye, *Gender, Class, Race, and Reform,* 82.

31. Nancy A. Hewitt, "Politicizing Domesticity: Anglo, Black, and Latin Women in Tampa's Progressive Movements," in Frankel and Dye, *Gender, Race, Class, and Reform,* 25–38; quotation on 38.

32. Sharon Harley, "When Your Work is Not Who You Are: The Development of a Working-Class Consciousness among Afro-American Women," in Frankel and Dye, *Gender, Race, Class, and Reform,* 42–55.

33. Jacqueline A. Rouse, "Atlanta's African-American Women's Attack on Segregation, 1900–1920," in Frankel and Dye, *Gender, Race, Class, and Reform,* 10–23.

34. Christine A. Lunardini, *From Equal Suffrage to Equal Rights: Alice Paul and the National Woman's Party, 1920–1928* (New York: New York University Press, 1986), 37.

35. Susan Kingsley Kent, *Sex and Suffrage in Britain, 1860–1914* (Princeton, N.J.: Princeton University Press, 1987), 197; Sandra Stanley Holton argues that the militant tradition in England grew from a number of radical traditions and campaigns, including the abolition movement, the Anti-Corn League, and women's tax resistance. Sandra Stanley Holton, "From Anti-Slavery to Suffrage Militancy: The Bright Circle, Elizabeth Cady Stanton and the British Women's Movement," eds., Caroline Daley and Melanie Nolan, *Suffrage and Beyond: International Feminist Perspectives* (New York: New York University Press, 1994), 229.

36. Ibid.

37. Andrew Rosen, *Rise Up, Women! The Militant Campaign of the Women's Social and Political Union, 1903–1914* (London: Routledge & Kegan Paul, 1974), 49–53.

38. Kent, *Sex and Suffrage,* 198–204.

39. For a complete analysis of the rhetorical strategies of the WSPU and discussion of how the organization segued from leading a campaign for woman suffrage to leading a war support campaign, see Cheryl R. Jorgensen-Earp, *"The Transfiguring Sword": The Just War of the Women's Social and Political Union* (Tuscaloosa: University of Alabama, 1997).

40. Jennifer L. Borda, "Woman Suffrage in the Progressive Era: A Coming of Age," in *Rhetoric and Reform in the Progressive Era,* ed. J. Michael Hogan, vol. 6 of *A Rhetorical History of the United States: Significant Moments in American Public Discourse,* ed. Martin J. Medhurst (East Lansing: Michigan State University Press, 2003), 370.

41. On New Year's Eve 1906, Wells organized the first open-air meeting held in the United States for the woman suffrage movement. Blatch followed Wells's example, and organized open-air meetings in May 1908 in upstate New York. Ellen Carol DuBois, "Working Women, Class Relations, and Suffrage Militance: Harriot Stanton Blatch and the New York Woman Suffrage Movement, 1894–1909," *Journal of American History* 74 (1987): 53–54.

42. Holly J. McCammon, "'Out of the Parlors and into the Streets': The Changing Tactical Repertoire of the U.S. Women's Suffrage Movements," *Social Forces*

81 (2003): 793. See also Susan G. Davis, *Parades and Power: Street Theatre in Nineteenth-Century Philadelphia* (Philadelphia: Temple University Press, 1986).

43. DuBois, "Working Women," 53–54. Sharon Hartman Strom demonstrates that the suffrage parade as a tactic may have originated in a Massachusetts campaign waged in the spring of 1909. See Sharon Hartman Strom, "Leadership and Tactics in the American Woman Suffrage Movement: A New Perspective from Massachusetts," *Journal of American History* 62 (1975): 296–315.

44. Borda, "Woman Suffrage," 370–72.

45. McCammon, "'Out of the Parlors,'" 789.

46. DuBois, "Working Women," 57.

47. Ibid., 56.

48. Ellen Carol DuBois, *Harriot Stanton Blatch and the Winning of Woman Suffrage* (New Haven: Yale University Press, 1997), 186.

49. Rheta Childe Dorr, "Mrs. Pankhurst: The Personality and Meaning of England's Great Suffrage Leader," *Suffragist,* November 22, 1913, 14–15.

50. Amy E. Butler, *Two Paths to Equality: Alice Paul and Ethel M. Smith in the ERA Debate, 1921–1926* (Albany: State University of New York Press, 2002), 40–45.

51. Ibid., 40.

52. Nancy F. Cott, *The Grounding of Modern Feminism* (New Haven: Yale University Press, 1987), 53.

53. Lunardini, *From Equal Suffrage,* 18–19.

54. Jorgensen-Earp, "*The Transfiguring Sword,*" 10.

55. Ibid., 23–25; Rosen, *Rise Up, Women!,* 49.

56. Hilary Frances describes this component of militancy, although the Women's Freedom League was a "non-violent" militant group: "One way of developing non-violent militancy was to choose significant representational targets as focus for action. Thus, the point at which the individual negotiates mechanisms of state, that is, legal, economic, bureaucratic and political institutions, was used to highlight the injustices suffered by woman as citizens without the vote. Lawcourts, the tax system, the census count, the ballot box became sites for symbolic demonstrations which, being neither violent nor destructive, helped increase strategic possibilities." Hilary Frances, "'Dare to be Free!': The Women's Freedom League and its Legacy," eds., June Purvis and Sandra Holton, *Votes for Women* (London: Routledge, 2000), 186. See also chapter 5, "The Law," in Susan Kingsley Kent, *Sex and Suffrage in Britain, 1860–1914* (Princeton, N.J.: Princeton University Press, 1987), 140–56. Kent catalogs all of the women's reform measures presented in Parliament over the course of the early women's movement in England. She also discusses the ways in which the Pankhurst sisters and other feminist activists targeted members of Parliament in their militant suffrage campaign.

57. Rosen, *Rise Up, Women!,* 308. "Militancy," as it is cataloged in Rosen's index, cites page numbers for "arson," "miscellaneous," and "window-breaking," but never a page that provides a definition of militancy. Jorgensen-Earp, "*The Transfiguring Sword,*" 16.

58. Rosen, *Rise Up, Women!,* 53. Emphasis in original.

59. Borda, "Woman Suffrage in the Progressive Era," 357.

60. Lunardini, *From Equal Suffrage,* 20–22. See also Inez Haynes Irwin, *The Story of Alice Paul and The National Woman's Party* (Fairfax, Va.: Denlinger's Publishers, 1977), 12–13.

61. Irwin, *The Story of Alice Paul,* 13, 19.

62. Lunardini, *From Equal Suffrage,* 24.

63. Irwin, *The Story of Alice Paul,* 19–20.

64. DuBois, *Harriot Stanton Blatch,* 182–85; Irwin, *The Story of Alice Paul,* 23–24.

65. Alice Paul to Harriot Stanton Blatch, March 21, 1914, National Woman's Party Papers, reel 1, University of Maryland, College Park, McKeldin Library: hereafter, NWPP.

66. Cott, *The Grounding,* 53–55. Regarding Eastman, Beard, and Lewis, see also Lunardini, *From Equal Suffrage,* 22–24.

67. While, for the most part, women of different classes worked harmoniously for the Committee, class issues did cause some tension in the organization. For example, in 1914, after the Committee's sensational first year as a woman suffrage organization, Alva (Mrs. O. H. P) Belmont joined the executive board. She had suffered a horrendous divorce from William Vanderbilt, which left her embittered but quite wealthy. Despite founding the Political Equality League on behalf of garment workers in New York, her tyrannical personality made her more of a liability than an asset. In fact, she was blacklisted among domestic workers in New York. Further, her wealth alone repelled potential Committee members with labor movement backgrounds. However, Belmont's connections and resources were too good to pass up. Cott, *The Grounding,* 55–56.

68. Ibid., 56–58.

69. For a brief history of Paul's relationship with African American suffragists, see Terborg-Penn, "African American Women," 148–51.

70. Karlyn Kohrs Campbell and Kathleen Hall Jamieson, *Presidents Creating the Presidency: Deeds Done in Words* (Chicago: University of Chicago Press, 2008), 29, 30.

71. Washington's inauguration ceremonies took place in New York. Nonetheless, on Washington's inaugural parade, see Clarence Winthrop Bowen, ed., *The History of the Centennial Celebration of the Inauguration of George Washington as First President of the United States* (New York: D. Appleton, 1892), 21–60; James Thomas Flexner, *George Washington and the New Nation (1783–1793)* (Boston: Little, Brown, 1970), 185; Douglas Southall Freeman, *George Washington: A Biography,* vol. 6 (New York: Charles Scribner's Sons, 1954), 188.

72. Campbell and Jamieson, *Deeds Done in Words,* 30. On presidential oaths, see Matthew A. Pauley, *I Do Solemnly Swear: The President's Constitutional Oath* (Lanham, Md.: University Press of America, 1999); Gunter Gebauer and Christoph Wulf, *Mimesis: Culture, Art, and Society,* trans. Don Reau (Berkeley: University of California Press, 1995), 5.

73. Dominic Bryan, *Orange Parades: The Politics of Ritual, Tradition and Control* (London: Pluto Press, 2000), 16.

74. Ibid., 8.

75. Mikhail Bakhtin, *Rabelais and His World* trans. Helene Iswoldsky (Cambridge: MIT Press, 1968), 5.

76. Ibid., 7.

77. Ibid., 5.

78. Ibid., 10.

79. Ibid., 10–11.

80. Catherine Allgor, *Parlor Politics: In Which the Ladies of Washington Help Build a City and a Government* (Charlottesville: University Press of Virginia, 2000), 104.

81. Ibid., 86.

82. Ibid., 119.

83. For a discussion regarding the expansion and restriction of women's participation in the public sphere during the second decade of the twentieth century, see Vanessa B. Beasley, "Engendering Democratic Change: How Three U.S. Presidents Discussed Female Suffrage," *Rhetoric & Public Affairs* 5 (2002): 79–103; quotation on 84. See also Sara Hayden, "Negotiating Femininity and Power in the Early Twentieth Century West: Domestic Ideology and Feminine Style in Jeannette Rankin's Suffrage Rhetoric," *Communication Studies* 50 (1999): 83–102.

84. A group of women marched from New York to Washington, D.C., to participate in the parade. They were led by "General" Rosalie Jones and called themselves "pilgrims." For coverage of these women, as well as coverage on the arrival of marchers by train and automobile, see: "Throngs Greet Pilgrims' Entry," *Washington Post,* March 1, 1913, 1, 3, 12; "Pilgrim Hikers Take City by Storm," *Washington Post,* March 1, 1913, 3; "Suffragists Take City for Pageant," *Washington Post,* March 2, 1913, 1, 3, 6–7; "Five Thousand of Fair Sex Ready to Parade," *Washington Post,* March 3, 1913, 1–2; "Cardinal Scores Women Hikers," *Daily Picayune,* March 2, 1913, 1; "Suffragists to Have Fete To-Day," *Daily Picayune,* March 3, 1913, 2; "Suffrage Invasion Is on in Earnest," *New York Times,* March 2, 1913, 15; "Women Await Order to Fall in Line," *New York Times,* March 3, 1913, 7.

85. See the "Pageant Outline," 1913, NWPP, reel 1, as well as relevant photographs noted throughout.

86. Campbell and Jamieson, *Presidents Creating the Presidency,* 31.

87. According to the "Pageant Outline," there were two separate banners. According to the "Official Program of the Woman's Suffrage Procession," this section was entitled "The Seventy-Five Years' Struggle for Freedom or Justice Conquering Prejudice." Because the outline specifically identifies banners and the program only offers this as a title, I'm treating the discourse as two separate banners. "Pageant Outline," 3; "Official Program of the Woman's Suffrage Procession," March 13, 1913, Printed Ephemera Collection, portfolio 208, folder 16, Library of Congress, Washington, D.C.

88. "Official Program," 7.

89. The women performing the tableau wore silken, flowing robes as they canvased the palladium façade of the building, creating a striking and mythical aesthetic. One by one, the characters fled down the first tier of the steps to join Columbia, who held a golden spear in her hand. Justice carried a sword while accompanied

by women holding unfurled scrolls. Charity was accompanied by young girls wearing togas, girls whom she sheltered underneath an umbrella of fabric. Liberty and a group of young girls descended the steps gesturing their arms in celebration. Hope and many young girls ran down the steps carrying golden balloons. Last, after releasing a dove, Peace walked with young girls carrying olive branches and flowers. Much detail regarding the allegory can be ascertained from the "Official Program," 15, 17. Also see "Told the Story of the Ages," *New York Times,* March 4, 1913, 5. Also, the following photos in the NWP digital photo archives depict many scenes of the allegory: (1) "German actress Hedwig Reicher dressed as 'Columbia' standing in front of the Treasury Building during the suffrage tableau held in conjunction with the pre-inaugural suffrage parade in Washington, D.C. on March 3, 1913," Harris and Ewing, March 3, 1913, P1249, Digital ID: SB000559; (2) "German actress Hedwig Reicher dressed as 'Columbia' standing in front of the Treasury Building during the suffrage tableau held in conjunction with the pre-inaugural suffrage parade in Washington, D.C. on March 3, 1913," Harris and Ewing Publication, March 3, 1913, P1221, Digital ID: SB000560; (3) "'Charity,' on the steps of the Treasury Building, part of the suffrage tableau held in conjunction with the pre-inaugural suffrage parade in Washington, D.C. on March 3, 1913," Harris and Ewing Publication, March 3, 1913, P1248, Digital ID: SB000561; (4) "'Charity,' on the steps of the Treasury Building, part of the suffrage tableau held in conjunction with the pre-inaugural suffrage parade in Washington, D.C. on March 3, 1913," Harris and Ewing Publication, March 3, 1913, P1247, Digital ID: SB000562; (5) "Hedwig Reicher dressed as 'Columbia' with other suffrage pageant participants standing in background in front of the Treasury Building during the parade held in Washington, D.C. on March 3, 1913," Harris and Ewing Publication March 3, 1913, P1249, Digital ID: SB000563; (6) "'Charity,' on the steps of the Treasury Building, part of the suffrage tableau held in conjunction with the pre-inaugural suffrage parade in Washington, D.C. on March 3, 1913," Harris and Ewing Publication, March 3, 1913, P1246, Digital ID: SB000564; (7) "Florence Fleming Noyes, dressed as 'Liberty,' with her group in front of the Treasury Building during the suffrage tableau held in conjunction with the pre-inaugural suffrage parade in Washington, D.C. on March 3, 1913," Harris and Ewing Publication, March 3, 1913, P1232, Digital ID: SB000565; (8) "Florence Fleming Noyes, dressed as 'Liberty,' with her attendants in front of the Treasury Building during the suffrage tableau held in conjunction with the pre-inaugural suffrage parade in Washington, D.C. on March 3, 1913," Harris and Ewing Publication, March 3, 1913, P1252, Digital ID: SB000566; (9) "Part of the suffrage tableau held on the steps of the Treasury Building in conjunction with the pre-inaugural suffrage parade in Washington, D.C. on March 3, 1913," Harris and Ewing Publication, March 3, 1913, P1231, Digital ID: SB000567; (10) "German actress Hedwig Reicher dressed as 'Columbia' summons 'Justice' in front of the Treasury Building during the suffrage tableau held in conjunction with the pre-inaugural suffrage parade in Washington, D.C. on March 3, 1913," Harris and Ewing Publication, March 3, 1913, P1244, Digital ID: SB000568; (11) "The group representing 'Hope' descend[s] the steps of the Treasury Building, part of the suffrage tableau held in conjunction with the pre-inaugural suffrage parade in Washington, D.C. on March 3, 1913," Harris and Ewing

Publication, March 3, 1913, P1923, Digital ID: SB000569; (12). "'Peace' [—] the final episode of the suffrage tableau held on the steps of the Treasury Building in conjunction with the pre-inaugural suffrage parade held in Washington, D.C. on March 3, 1913," Harris and Ewing Publication, March 3, 1913, P1243 Digital ID: SB000570.

90. On the evolution of the name "Columbia," see Albert H. Hoyt, "The Name 'Columbia,'" *New England Historical and Genealogical Register* 40 (1886): 310–13.

91. Phillis Wheatley's "To His Excellency General Washington" can be found in Phillis Wheatly, *Complete Writings,* ed. Vincent Carretta (New York: Penguin Books, 2001).

92. Thomas J. Steele, "The Figure of Columbia: Phillis Wheatley Plus George Washington." *New England Quarterly* 54 (1981): 266.

93. John Locke wrote, "[B]eing all equal and independent, no one ought to harm another in his life, health, liberty, or possessions." John Locke, *The Second Treatise of Government,* originally published 1690 (New York: Barnes & Noble Publishing, 2004), 4.

94. Ellen Carol DuBois, "Introduction: The Invention of Women's Rights," in *Elizabeth Cady Stanton, Susan B. Anthony: Correspondence, Writings, Speeches,* ed., Ellen Carol DuBois (New York: Schocken Books, 1981), 2.

95. "Pageant Outline," 4. A quotation by Abraham Lincoln in the "Official Program" makes a similar point: "I go for all sharing the privilege of the government who assist in bearing its burdens, by no means excluding women" (page 3).

96. See chapter 1, note 159, for sources on the suffrage movement in western states.

97. "Official Program," 9, 11. These delegations were included in the third and fourth sections of the parade.

98. Linda K. Kerber, *Women of the Republic: Intellect and Ideology in Revolutionary America* (Chapel Hill: University of North Carolina Press, 1980), 189–231. Also see Ann Firor Scott, *Making the Invisible Woman Visible* (Urbana: University of Illinois Press, 1984), 39.

99. "Pageant Outline," 4.

100. "Woman's Beauty, Grace, and Art Bewilder the Capital," *Washington Post,* March 4, 1913, 10.

101. "Pageant Outline," 4.

102. See the following photograph: "'Women of the Bible Lands' float in the March 3, 1913 suffrage parade held in Washington, D.C. March 3, 1913," P1226, Digital ID: SB000325.

103. "Official Program, 7." Neither the parade's program nor the photograph of this float specify which New Testament women were represented.

104. Ibid., 13.

105. "Pageant Outline," 4.

106. "Trained nurses in uniform in the March 3, 1913 suffrage parade held in Washington, D.C. March 3, 1913," P1175, Digital ID: SB000274.

107. For a definitive source on Florence Nightingale, see Cecil Blanche Fitz Gerald Woodham-Smith, *Lonely Crusader: The Life of Florence Nightingale, 1890–1910* (New York: Whittlesey House, 1951).

108. Campbell and Jamieson, *Presidents Creating the Presidency,* 31.

109. Regarding the constitution of the "people" as a national community, see Maurice Charland, "Constitutive Rhetoric: The Case of the Peuple Québécois," *Quarterly Journal of Speech* 73 (1987): 133–50; Michael C. McGee, "In Search of 'The People': A Rhetorical Alternative," *Quarterly Journal of Speech* 61 (1975): 235–49.

110. See United States Constitution, amendment 14, section. 1.

111. "The 'Great Demand' banner in the suffrage parade held in Washington, D.C. on March 3, 1913," Harris and Ewing Publication, P1172, Digital ID: SB000355.

112. Both the Pageant Outline and the Official Program list delegations from sixteen nations in this first section. "Pageant Outline," 1–2; "Official Program," 5, 7.

113. "Official Program," 13. The program says that this "first convention" took place in Rochester, New York, which is where the leaders of the convention originally met to plan the convention. The "first convention," held in "1848" was most certainly held in Seneca Falls. The "Pageant Outline" does not include this float, and rather includes two other floats which do not appear in the Official Program. While most of the outline and the program coincide, my assumption is that the published program is the definitive source on which floats appeared in the parade. See "Pageant Outline," 7.

114. See Judith Wellman, *The Road to Seneca Falls: Elizabeth Cady Stanton and the First Woman's Rights Convention* (Urbana: University of Illinois Press, 2004), 191–92. Also, regarding the story of the first women's rights convention, see Elizabeth Cady Stanton, Susan B. Anthony, and Matilda Joslyn Gage, eds., *History of Woman Suffrage,* 6 vols. (New York: Source Book Press, 1889), 1:67–69.

115. "Official Program," 13; "Pageant Outline," 7.

116. See the following photo of the float: "March 3, 1913 suffrage parade held in Washington, D.C., when police failed to keep Pennsylvania Avenue clear for the procession, March 3, 1913," P1147, Digital ID: SB000360.

117. According to the Pageant Outline, the banner appeared as such: "NO COUNTRY CAN EXIST HALF SLAVE AND HALF FREE Abraham Lincoln." I've changed to title case and added a comma for syntactical clarity. "Pageant Outline," 8.

118. The banner misquotes President Lincoln. In his "House Divided" speech, he said, "I believe this government cannot endure permanently half slave and half free." Moreover, this speech was not delivered while he was president, but after he received the Republican nomination for senator in 1858.

119. Campbell and Jamieson, *Presidents Making the Presidency,* 38.

120. On Lincoln's reuniting efforts, see Gary Wills, *Lincoln at Gettysburg: The Words That Remade America* (New York: Touchstone, 1992).

121. "Pageant Outline," 9.

122. Harriot Stanton Blatch to Lucy Burns, February 10, 1913, NWPP, reel 1; Procession Committee to Harriot Stanton Blatch, February 23, 1913, reel 1, NWPP.

123. Harriot Stanton Blatch to Alice Paul, April 3, 1913, NWPP, reel 1, 1.

124. Erika A. Kuhlman, *Petticoats and White Feathers: Gender Conformity, Race, and the Progressive Peace Movement, and the Debate Over War, 1895–1919* (Westport, Conn.: Greenwood Press, 1997), 25.

125. Beasley, *You, the People,* 28.

126. Bryan, *Orange Parades,* 8.

127. Teresa L. Ebert, "Gender and the Everyday: Toward a Postmodern Materialist Feminist Theory of Mimesis," in *"Turning the Century": Feminist Theory in the 1990s,* ed. Glynis Carr (Cranbury, N.J.: Associated University Presses, 1992), 105–7.

128. Alexander Keyssar offers chronologies of these differing citizenship and voting laws and tends to laws which set up property, tax paying, literacy, and residency requirements, and exclusions based on race, class, criminal offense, and sex. See "Appendix: State Suffrage Laws, 1775–1920," Keyssar, *The Right to Vote,* 324–90. For histories of American Indian citizenship rights, see David E. Wilkins, *American Indian Sovereignty and the Supreme Court: The Masking of Justice* (Austin: University of Texas Press, 1997); and Brian Dippie, *The Vanishing American: White Attitudes and U.S. Indian Policy* (Lawrence: University of Kansas Press, 1991).

129. See note 9 for a summary of what Smith considers a four-part hierarchy of citizenship.

130. "Official Program," 15.

131. Harriot Stanton Blatch to Alice Paul, January 31, 1913, NWPP, reel 1; Procession Committee to Harriot Stanton Blatch, February 8, 1913, NWPP, reel 1.

132. "Procession battles its way up unpoliced Pennsylvania Avenue during the pre-inaugural suffrage parade in Washington, D.C. on March 3, 1913," P1202, Digital ID: SB000366.

133. "Official Program," 9, 11.

134. Ibid., 11.

135. "Delegates in the March 3, 1913 suffrage parade held in Washington, D.C., wait for the procession to begin," Edmonston, Washington, D.C., March 3, 1913, P1190, Digital ID: SB000290.

136. "Official Program," 13, 15.

137. One photo from the parade features members of the Louisiana delegation. See "Delegation of suffragists from Louisiana participated in the March 3, 1913 suffrage parade held in Washington, D.C.," March 3, 1913, P1314, Digital ID: SB000284.

138. Regarding the organization of the Illinois, Kentucky, and Louisiana delegations, the seventh section of the "Official Program" shows these delegations in very close proximity along the left side of a cluster of seventeen states plus Washington, D.C. "Official Program," 15.

139. Giddings, *When and Where,* 127.

140. Kate Gordon and Laura Clay were most resistant to black women marching in the parade, and formed the Southern States Woman Suffrage Conference. DuBois, *Harriot Stanton Blatch,* 186. Also see Lunardini, *From Equal Suffrage,* 26–27; Giddings, *When and Where,* 128.

141. DuBois, *Harriot Stanton Blatch,* 186. Also see Cott, *The Grounding,* 68–70.

142. Lunardini, *From Equal Suffrage,* 27.

143. Terborg-Penn, "African American Women," 147.

144. "Illinois Women Feature Parade," *Chicago Daily Tribune,* March 4, 1913.

145. Anne Meis Knupfer, *Toward a Tenderer Humanity and a Nobler Womanhood: African American Women's Clubs in Turn of the Century Chicago* (New York:

New York University Press, 1996), 52. Also see Roger Streitmatter, *Raising Her Voice: African-American Woman Journalists Who Changed History* (Lexington: University Press of Kentucky, 1994), 60.

146. "Marches Despite Protests," *Chicago Defender,* March 8, 1913. For more on Wells-Barnett's continued protests against white suffragists, see Patricia Ann Schechter, *Ida B. Wells-Barnett and American Reform, 1800–1930* (Chapel Hill: University of North Carolina Press, 2001), 200–202.

147. See note 84 for a sampling of newspaper articles relating to the parade.

148. Harriot Stanton Blatch to Lucey [*sic*] Burns, February 17, 1913, NWPP, reel 1.

149. "5,000 Women March, Beset by Crowds," *New York Times,* March 4, 1913, 5.

150. Ibid.

151. "Parade Protest Arouses Senate," *New York Times,* March 5, 1913, 8.

152. Ibid.

153. Ibid.

154. "5,000 Women March," 5.

155. "Suffragists Odious," *New York Times,* March 9, 1913, 42.

156. "Parade Protest," 8.

157. Ibid.

158. See *Report of the Committee on the District of Columbia, United States Senate, Pursuant to Resolution 499 of March 4, 1913, Directing Said Committee to Investigate the Conduct of the District Police and the Police Department of the District of Columbia in Connection With the Woman Suffrage Parade on March 3, 1913,* 63rd Congress, 1st Sess., Senate Report No. 53 (May 29, 1913).

159. Lunardini, *From Equal Suffrage,* 29–30.

160. The day after the suffrage parade and the day of Wilson's inauguration, the front page of the *Washington Post* was split between covering these two events. See "Woman's Beauty, Grace, and Art Fill the Capital" and "Woodrow Wilson Arrives to Become Nation's Head Today," *Washington Post,* March 4, 1913, 1. Also, the front page of the *Daily Picayune* featured the following two articles: "Woodrow Wilson Grasps Taft Hand in White House" and "Pageant Failure Because Rowdies Assault Women," March 4, 1913, 1. The suffrage parade was reported as part of Wilson's inauguration festivities in the *New York Times.* See "Wilson Takes Office To-Day as 28th President," March 4, 1913, 1–2. See also "5,000 Women March," 5.

161. Alice Paul to Harriot Stanton Blatch, August 8, 1913, NWPP, reel 1, 1–2.

162. Harriot Stanton Blatch to Alice Paul, August 26, 1913, NWPP, reel 1, 1–2.

163. Gebauer and Wulf, *Mimesis,* 5.

CHAPTER 3

1. Mary Morris Lockwood to Mrs. Charles Boughton Wood, July 19, 1913, reel 1, National Woman's Party Papers, University of Maryland, College Park, McKeldin Library hereafter, NWPP.

2. The *Suffragist* says the CUWS was "formed with the object of assisting the work of the Congressional Committee of the National American Woman Suffrage As-

sociation, the committee which is working to secure a Federal suffrage amendment." "The Congressional Union for Woman Suffrage," *Suffragist*, November, 15, 1913, 2. Also see Inez Haynes Irwin, *The Story of Alice Paul and The National Woman's Party* (Fairfax, Va.: Denlinger's Publishers, 1977), 37–38. The organization was officially formed in April 1913, because the Committee's finances were still being handled in tandem with the NAWSA, and the Committee wished to raise funds exclusively for its work. Much detail about the process through which the CUWS established itself as a separate organization from the NAWSA is provided by Christine A. Lunardini, *From Equal Suffrage to Equal Rights: Alice Paul and the National Woman's Party, 1920–1928* (New York: New York University Press, 1986), 32–36.

3. Under "Methods," the WSPU constitution says: "1) Action entirely independent of political parties. 2) Opposition to whatever Government is in power until such time as the franchise is granted. 3) Vigorous agitation upon lines justified by the position of outlawry to which women are presently condemned." Emmeline Pethick-Lawrence, *The Meaning of the Woman's Movement*, pamphlet, (n.d.), Sophia Smith Collection, Smith College.

4. Ibid.; Steven Rosenstone, Roy L. Behr, and Edward H. Lazarus, *Third Parties in America: Citizen Response to Major Party Failure* (Princeton, N.J.: Princeton University Press, 1984), 6.

5. Pethick-Lawrence, *The Meaning of the Woman's Movement*, emphasis added.

6. More specifically, the WSPU campaign escalated to acts of terrorism and property destruction, while the CUWS never instigated acts of violence. Jorgensen-Earp attributes the WSPU "escalation of militant strategies" to "the need to make the movement visible." While the NWP escalated its militant strategies to create visibility, it embraced *antiviolent* strategies. Donna M. Kowal argues that specific political and historical elements made the more definitively militant approach of the WSPU and the more "adjustive" approach of the NWP each appropriate for ingratiating them with opposing institutions. See Cheryl R. Jorgensen-Earp, *"The Transfiguring Sword": The Just War of the Women's Social and Political Union* (Tuscaloosa: University of Alabama, 1997); Donna M. Kowal, "One Cause, Two Paths: Militant v. Adjustive Strategies in the British and American Women's Suffrage Movements," *Communication Quarterly* 48 (2000): 242.

7. Pethick-Lawrence, *The Meaning of the Woman's Movement.*

8. Vanessa B. Beasley, "Engendering Democratic Change: How Three U.S. Presidents Discussed Female Suffrage," *Rhetoric & Public Affairs* 5 (2002): 84; Sara Hayden, "Negotiating Femininity and Power in the Early Twentieth Century West: Domestic Ideology and Feminine Style in Jeannette Rankin's Suffrage Rhetoric," *Communication Studies* 50 (1999): 85–87.

9. Tamar Mayer, "Gender Ironies of Nationalism: Setting the Stage," in *Gender Ironies of Nationalism: Sexing the Nation*, ed. Tamar Mayer (London: Routledge, 2000), 13.

10. Floya Anthias and Nira Yuval-Davis, "Introduction," in *Woman-Nation-State*, eds. Nira Yuval-Davis and Floya Anthias (New York: St. Martin's Press, 1989), 11.

11. Andrew Rosen, *Rise Up, Women! The Militant Campaign of the Women's Social and Political Union, 1903–1914* (London: Routledge & Kegan Paul, 1974), xviii.

12. In the 1860s, the socialist First International attracted "an unusually large number of [American] women" to voice their demands for both class and sex emancipation. Mari Jo Buhle, *Women and American Socialism, 1870–1920* (Urbana: University of Illinois Press, 1981), xiv.

13. Sherry J. Katz, "A Politics of Coalition: Socialist Women and the California Suffrage Movement, 1900–1911," in *One Woman, One Vote: Rediscovering the Woman Suffrage Movement*, ed. Marjorie Spruill Wheeler (Troutdale, Ore.: New Sage Press, 1995), 245–62.

14. Teresa L. Ebert, "Gender and the Everyday: Toward a Postmodern Materialist Feminist Theory of Mimesis," in *"Turning the Century": Feminist Theory in the 1990s*, ed. Glynis Carr (Cranbury, N.J.: Associated University Presses, 1992), 106.

15. Ibid., 95.

16. Kathleen A. Kendall, *Communication in the Presidential Primaries: Candidates and the Media, 1912–2000* (Westport, Conn.: Praeger, 2000), 6. For more on the presidential primary, see Charles E. Merriam and Louise Overacker, *Primary Elections* (Chicago: University of Chicago Press, 1928); Alan Ware, *The American Direct Primary* (Cambridge, UK: Cambridge University Press, 2002).

17. Kendall, *Communication in the Presidential Primaries*, 6; Stephen Ansolabehere, Shigeo Hirano, and James M. Snyder Jr., "What Did the Primary Do to Party Loyalty in Congress?" in *Party, Process, and Political Change in Congress, Volume 2: Further Perspectives on the History of Congress*, eds. David W. Brady and Mathew D. McCubbins (Stanford: Stanford University Press, 2007), 21.

18. Kendall, *Communication in the Presidential Primaries*, 7.

19. Michael McGerr, "Political Style and Women's Power, 1830–1930," *Journal of American History* 77 (1990): 866–67. On McKinley's speaking tours, see Lewis L. Gould, *The Modern American Presidency* (Lawrence: University Press of Kansas, 2003), 7–10. On Bryan's whistle-stop tour, see Richard Hofstadter, *The Progressive Movement, 1900–1915* (Englewood Cliffs, N.J.: Prentice-Hall, 1963), 6–7.

20. Donald R. Wolfensberger, *Congress and the People: Deliberative Democracy on Trial* (Washington, D.C.: Woodrow Wilson Center Press, 2000), 41–42.

21. Ibid., 42–46. Reed was Speaker of the House between 1889 and 1891, and also between 1895 and 1899.

22. Wolfensberger, *Congress and the People*, 48.

23. Ibid.; Ansolabehere et al., "What Did the Primary Do?" 32.

24. Ansolabehere et al., "What Did the Primary Do?" 32.

25. Wolfensberger, *Congress and the People*, 48–53. Majority Leader Oscar Underwood of Alabama was careful to consult House Democrats for "maximum party unity, discipline, and success." Ibid., 52.

26. See Rogers M. Smith, *Civic Ideals: Conflicting Visions of Citizenship in U.S. History* (New Haven: Yale University Press, 1997), 411.

27. Wolfensberger, *Congress and the People*, 52–53.

28. "Women and Congress," *Suffragist*, May 2, 1914, 7.

29. "Party Responsibility and Votes for Women," *Suffragist*, January 24, 1914, 4.

30. Rosenstone et al., *Third Parties in America*, 6.

31. "The Election Policy," *Suffragist,* September 26, 1914, 4.

32. For a history of third parties and single-issue parties, see John F. Bibby and L. Sandy Maisel, *Two Parties—or More?* (Boulder, Colo.: Westview Press, 2003); Howard P. Nash Jr., *Third Parties in American Politics* (Washington, D.C.: Public Affairs Press, 1959); Immanuel Ness and James Ciment, eds., *The Encyclopedia of Third Parties in America,* vols. 1–3 (Armonk, N.Y.: Sharpe Reference, 2000); Douglas E. Schoen, *Declaring Independence: The Beginning of the End of the Two-Party System* (New York: Random House, 2008).

33. Rosenstone et al., *Third Parties in America,* 4.

34. Ibid., 8–9.

35. Political scientists typically point to V. O. Key's theory of third parties in *Politics, Parties, and Pressure Groups,* 5th ed. (New York: Thomas Y. Crowell, 1964). J. David Gillespie adds a third category: the non-national significant other party, which takes hold on local and state levels. See J. David Gillespie, *Politics at the Periphery: Third Parties in Two-Party America,* 11–12.

36. Roosevelt earned 27.4 percent of the popular vote and 88 electoral votes, versus Taft's 23.2 percent of the popular vote and 8 electoral votes. *Guide to U.S. Elections,* 5th ed., vol. 1 (Washington, D.C.: CQ Press, 2005), 696, 781.

37. For works on the populist movement, see Peter H. Argersinger, *Populism and Politics: William Alfred Peffer and the People's Party* (Lexington: University of Kentucky Press, 1974); Gene Clanton, *Congressional Populism and the Crisis of the 1890s* (Lawrence: University of Kansas Press, 1998); Robert F. Durden, *The Climax of Populism: The Election of 1896* (Lexington: University of Kentucky Press, 1965); John D. Hicks, *The Populist Revolt: A History of the Farmers' Alliance and the People's Party* (Lincoln: University of Nebraska Press, 1961); Stanley B. Parsons, *The Populist Context: Rural versus Urban Power on a Great Plains Frontier* (Westport, Conn.: Greenwood Press, 1973); William A. Peffer, *Populism, Its Rise and Fall,* ed. Peter H. Argersinger (Lawrence: University of Kansas Press, 1992).

38. These causes included temperance, woman suffrage, labor, and agrarian radicalism. Buhle, *Women and American Socialism,* 88.

39. David Reynolds, *Democracy Unbound: Progressive Challenges to the Two Party System* (Boston: South End Press, 1997), 14.

40. On populism in Kansas, see Walter T. K. Nugent, *The Tolerant Populists: Kansas Populism and Nativism* (Chicago: University of Chicago Press, 1963). The formidable strength of the Democratic Party in the southern states, however, prevented the People's Party from making a significant showing in the region. Sample studies on populism in southern states include: Donna A. Barnes, *Farmers in Rebellion: The Rise and Fall of the Southern Farmers Alliance and People's Party in Texas* (Austin: University of Texas Press, 1984); Worth Robert Miller, *Oklahoma Populism: A History of the People's Party in the Oklahoma Territory* (Norman: University of Oklahoma Press, 1987).

41. For discussions of fusion in the populist movement, see Peffer, *Populism,* 72–89; Reynolds, *Democracy Unbound,* 16–17.

42. Reynolds, *Democracy Unbound,* 16.

43. Robert J. Spitzer, *The Right to Life Movement and Third Party Politics* (New York: Greenwood Press, 1987), 29.

44. Ibid., 1–28.

45. Some of these issues include governmental ownership of the railroads, postal savings banks, gradual income tax, the direct election of senators, and other progressive measures aimed at putting political power back in the hands of "the people." See Frank Smallwood, *The Other Candidates: Third Parties in Presidential Elections* (Hanover, N.H.: University Press of New England, 1983), 18.

46. Reynolds, *Democracy Unbound,* 17.

47. Gillespie, *Politics at the Periphery,* 11.

48. See William Best Hesseltine, *The Rise and Fall of Third Parties, from Anti-Masonry to Wallace* (Gloucester, Mass.: Public Affairs Press, 1957), 18.

49. See Gillespie, *Politics at the Periphery,* 9–10.

50. See Eric Thomas Chester, *True Mission: Socialists and the Labor Party Question in the United States* (London: Pluto Press, 2004); Reynolds, *Democracy Unbound,* 18–35.

51. Buhle, *Women and American Socialism,* 176–80.

52. Meredith Tax, *The Rising of the Women: Feminist Solidarity and Class Conflict, 1880–1917* (Urbana: University of Illinois Press, 2001), 236–40.

53. *Guide to U.S. Elections*, 5th ed., vol. I (Washington, D.C.: CQ Press, 2005), 696.

54. See "Putting Their Issue First," *Washington (D.C.) Times,* May 20, 1916, reprinted in the *Suffragist,* June 3, 1916, 10. Although women possessed the right to vote in twelve states, only eleven of them allowed women to vote for US senators and representatives.

55. At this time, April 1913, the CUWS had not officially formed, but for the sake of continuity, "CUWS" will be used to refer to the CUWS and the Congressional Committee.

56. See Lunardini, *From Equal Suffrage,* 32–49.

57. Mary Morris Lockwood, the *Suffragist,* November 15, 1913, 3.

58. Alice Paul to Mr. J. O. Spangler, November 6, 1913, NWPP, reel 1, 2.

59. Ibid.

60. According to the *Suffragist*'s financial reports, disbursements of the publication were counted in the following categories: "Addressograph lists," "Advertisers copies," "To branch headquarters," and "To organizers." In December 1917, copies disbursed totaled 20,828. Dorothy Bready, "Report of the Suffragist Office Department, Month of December, 1917," NWPP, reel 26.

61. Mabel Vernon to Alice Paul, September 11, 1914, NWPP, reel 1.

62. Lucy Burns, "National Convention at Washington," *Suffragist,* November 6, 1913, 31.

63. Helen Laura Sumner Woodbury, *Equal Suffrage: The Results of an Investigation in Colorado Made for the Collegiate Equal Suffrage League of New York State* (New York, 1909), 70, 114–17.

64. Paula Giddings, *When and Where I Enter: The Impact of Black Women on Race and Sex in America* (New York: W. Morrow, 1996), 107.

65. Rosalyn Terborg-Penn, "African American Women and the Woman Suffrage Movement," in *One Woman, One Vote,* 145–46.

66. Giddings, *When and Where,* 103–4, 129–30, 135.

67. On Jones's oratorical career, see Mari Boor Tonn, "Militant Motherhood: Labor's Mary Harris 'Mother' Jones," *Quarterly Journal of Speech* 82 (February 1996): 1–21; Dale Fetherling, *Mother Jones, the Miners' Angel: A Portrait* (Carbondale: Southern Illinois University Press, 1974); and Elliott J. Gorn, *Mother Jones: The Most Dangerous Woman in America* (New York: Hill and Wang, 2001).

68. Nancy Schrom Dye, *As Equals and As Sisters: Feminism, the Labor Movement, and the Women's Trade Union League of New York* (Columbia: University of Missouri Press, 1980), 90.

69. See Tax, *The Rising of the Women,* 241–75.

70. Dye, *As Equals and As Sisters,* 92–93, 125–26.

71. See Ellen Carol DuBois, *Harriot Stanton Blatch and the Winning of Woman Suffrage* (New Haven: Yale University Press, 1997).

72. The treasurer of the CUWS said: "We are sending organizers into every part of the United States, working on delegations to call upon the different Congressmen." Acting treasurer to Constance Drexel, July 31, 1915, NWPP, reel 1. Also, the *Suffragist* said, "Since March 1915, branches of the Congressional Union have been organized in twenty states." Doris Stevens planned to build up a committee of suffrage workers "in every Congressional district in the United States. There are four hundred and thirty-five Congressional districts." "Organization Work for 1916," *Suffragist,* January 15, 1916, 7.

73. "A Federal Amendment Now," *Suffragist,* November 15, 1913, 3. Emphasis added.

74. Buhle, *Women and American Socialism,* 57.

75. WTUL member (unnamed); Minutes, Meeting of the Regular Membership, Women's Trade Union League of New York, January 1913, Women's Trade Union League of New York Papers, State Labor Library, New York City.

76. Annie G. Porrit, "Nationalizing of Suffrage Work," *Suffragist,* February 6, 1915, 5.

77. Ibid.

78. See, for example, one of the resolutions adopted at the Salt Lake City convention on May 10, 1916, that begins: "Whereas, the women of Utah do not receive the protection of the United States Constitution as regards to their voting rights." Reprinted in "Convention in Salt Lake City Closes Western Trip," *Suffragist,* May 20, 1916, 4.

79. "Why a Woman's Party?" *Suffragist,* June 3, 1916, 10.

80. Ibid.

81. "Woman Voters' Convention Pledged to Anthony Amendment," *Suffragist,* September 25, 1915, 5.

82. Ibid.

83. Chicago's and Philadelphia's demonstrations had five thousand marchers; Boston's had nine thousand. See "The Greatest Suffrage Day," *Suffragist,* May 9, 1914, 2–3.

84. "The Greatest Suffrage Day," 2.

85. "Mayday from Ocean to Ocean," *Suffragist,* May 2, 1914, 4.

86. "The Will of the People," *Suffragist,* May 16, 1914, 6.

87. "Mayday from Ocean to Ocean," 4.

88. Rosen, *Rise Up, Women!,* xviii–xix.

89. Speech by Alice Paul, "The Program for 1914," *Suffragist,* January 17, 1914, 6.

90. No title, *New York Times,* January 8, 1914, 2.

91. No exact number of Maryland delegates was provided, but the photograph provided in the *Suffragist* indicated that there were at least thirty women who participated in the march. "Pilgrimage to the Opening of the Maryland Legislature," *Suffragist,* January 10, 1914, 7. A group of women from New Jersey participated in a similar pilgrimage to the 1913 national parade. "General" Rosalie Jones and her band of suffrage "pilgrims" marched from New Jersey to Washington, D.C., for the parade; they spoke along the way, and arrived en masse. See the following photos: "Rosalie Jones and her band of suffrage 'pilgrims,' who walked from New Jersey to Washington, D.C., speaking en route, arrive in Washington, D.C. For Pre-Inaugural Suffrage Parade on March 3, 1913," March 3, 1913, P1220, Digital ID Number: SB000312; "Rosalie Jones and her band of suffrage 'pilgrims,' who walked from New Jersey to Washington, D.C., speaking en route, arrive in Washington, D.C. For Pre-Inaugural Suffrage Parade on March 3, 1913," March 3, 1913, P1208, Digital ID Number: SB000313; Harris and Ewing, "Rosalie Jones and her band of suffrage 'pilgrims,' who walked from New Jersey to Washington, D.C., speaking en route, arrive in Washington, D.C. For Pre-Inaugural Suffrage Parade on March 3, 1913," March 3, 1913, P1183, Digital ID Number: SB000314.

92. The CUWS theory of agitation was based on the WSPU method of "[o]pposition to whatever Government is in power until such time as the franchise is granted." Pethick-Lawrence, *The Meaning of the Woman's Movement.*

93. "Congressional Union Deputation to Senator O'Gorman," *Suffragist,* May 8, 1915, 5.

94. Ibid.

95. See the following for details on these deputations: Photograph of the deputation on the cover of the *Suffragist,* May 18, 1915, and "Congressmen Interviewed During Maryland Convention," ibid., 5; "Delaware for Susan B. Anthony Amendment," *Suffragist,* May 22, 1915, 5; "South Carolina Congressman Receives Suffrage Deputation," *Suffragist,* July 3, 1915, 3; "Suffrage Deputations to United States Congressmen," *Suffragist,* November 20, 1915, 6–7; "Suffrage Deputations to United States Congressmen," *Suffragist,* November 27, 1915, 7–8; "Suffrage Deputations to United States Congressmen," *Suffragist,* December 4, 1915, 9; "Deputations to Congressmen," *Suffragist,* December 11, 1915, 11; "Deputation to Senator Thompson," *Suffragist,* March 11, 1916, 5.

96. For coverage of this event, see "Nation-Wide Demonstration," *Suffragist,* May 2, 1914, 5. For months preceding the demonstrations, the CUWS reported on the minute details of events to be held in all regions and states of the nation. For example, see "National Demonstration, May 2d and 9th," *Suffragist,* February 14,

1914, 3, for details on planning demonstrations in the Midwest, the West, and the South; see "Nation-Wide Demonstration, May 2d," *Suffragist,* February 21, 1914, 3, for details on demonstrations in New England and the mid-Atlantic states; and "The Nation-Wide Demonstration," *Suffragist,* April 11, 1914, 3, for details on demonstrations in Virginia, Maryland, Louisiana, Illinois, Ohio, Indiana, New Mexico, Wyoming, and Iowa.

97. "How Small Towns Celebrated," *Suffragist,* May 16, 1914, 3.

98. "National Demonstration, May 2d and 9th," *Suffragist,* February 14, 1914, 3.

99. Ibid.

100. "Nation-Wide Demonstration," *Suffragist,* May 2, 1914, 6. Although the CUWS orchestrated a number of demonstrations to Congress, this section focuses on the two demonstrations that originated in the states and journeyed toward the nation's capital. However it is worth noting that the CUWS employed the strategy of sending representatives from each congressional district to the Capitol prior to the May 9, 1914, demonstration and the 1915 journey of the envoys. For example, on April 7, 1913, the CUWS orchestrated a demonstration on Congress, which took place on the first day of a special session. This demonstration entailed bands, a mass meeting, guest speakers, and banners, and culminated in the delivery of resolutions and petitions to every member of the Senate and House of Representatives from women in every district in the nation. See, for example, Chairman Committee on Petitions to Mrs. Harriot Stanton Blatch, March 21, 1913, NWPP, reel 1; Chairman of Congressional Committee to Miss Mary Bentley Thomas, March 24, 1913, NWPP, reel 1. Also Series IV A Audits and Treasurer Reports, "Expenditures from December 7th, 1912, to December 31st, 1913," January 31, 1914, NWPP, reel 124, 1. The report specifies that the demonstration cost $674.49 for bands, theater, banners, and speaker. Delegates from each of the 435 Congressional districts marched to the Capitol and were then led into the Rotunda and filed through a receiving line of welcoming congressmen. The women then sat in the Senate and House galleries where they witnessed the readings of their petitions and the introduction of Senate Joint Resolution 1, a resolution for a federal woman suffrage amendment. See Lunardini, *From Equal Suffrage,* 36–37. Hearings on the resolution were scheduled for July 31, prompting the CUWS to orchestrate another pilgrimage to the Capitol composed of women from all over the country carrying petitions which had circulated throughout their home states. On July 31, these women gathered outside of Washington, D.C., in Hyattsville, Maryland, where they were met by CUWS members and placed into a fleet of automobiles. Members of the CUWS Senate Committee led the massive automobile procession, which proceeded to the Capitol building, where the women presented their petitions with over two hundred fifty thousand signatures to the Senate. See Irwin, *The Story of Alice Paul,* 39–40; Lunardini, *From Equal Suffrage,* 37–38. Also see "Expenditures from December 7th," 1. This demonstration cost $1028.86 for automobiles for the procession, banners, petitions, advertising, printing, and a banquet at Hotel Brighton. Also, during the CUWS convention on December 3, 1913, more than five hundred members attended a hearing before the Rules Committee of the House of Representatives, "representing Suffrage societies in all parts of the country," while

five hundred alternates stood by. See "Convention: National American Woman Suffrage Association," *Suffragist,* November 22, 1913, 10.

101. "Woman Voters' Convention Pledged to Anthony Amendment," *Suffragist,* September 25, 1915, 6.

102. "Bristow-Mondell Resolution Demanded by Thousands of Marchers," *Suffragist,* May 16, 1913, 7.

103. "The May Ninth Demonstration," *Suffragist,* April 18, 1914, 5.

104. "From San Francisco to Washington," *Suffragist,* October 9, 1915, 5.

105. "From Boston to New York," *Suffragist,* December 4, 1915, 5.

106. Quoted in paper dated January 1916, NWPP, reel 1, 10. Also see detailed account of the farewell in "The Farewell to the Woman Voters' Envoys," *Suffragist,* October 2, 1915, 5.

107. "Women Voters' Envoy in Utah," *Suffragist,* October 16, 1915, 5.

108. "Rousing Welcome Given Envoys of the Women Voters," *Suffragist,* November 6, 1915, 3.

109. See "Illinois Greets Women Voters' Envoy," *Suffragist,* November 13, 1915, 3.

110. For complete coverage of the envoys' travels, see "From San Francisco to Washington," *Suffragist,* October 9, 1915, 5; no title, dated "Jan. 1916," NWPP, 13; "Women Voters' Envoy in Utah," *Suffragist,* October 16, 1915, 5; "Eastern Journey of the Women Voters' Envoy," *Suffragist,* October 23, 1915, 5; "Woman Voters' Envoys Reach Unfree States," *Suffragist,* October 30, 1915, 3; "Rousing Welcome Given Envoys of the Women Voters," *Suffragist*, November 6, 1915, 3; "Illinois Greets Women Voters' Envoy," *Suffragist,* November 13, 1915, 3; "Women Voters' Envoys Reach the East," *Suffragist,* November 20, 1915, 3; and "The Women Voters' Envoy in the Eastern States," *Suffragist,* November 27, 1915, 3.

111. "Eastern Journey of the Women Voters' Envoy," *Suffragist,* October 23, 1915, 5.

112. Ibid.

113. Quoted in ibid.

114. Quoted in "Rousing Welcome."

115. Ibid.

116. "The Women Voters' Envoy in the Eastern States," *Suffragist,* November 27, 1915, 3.

117. Alice Paul to Mrs. Robert A. Morton, July 3, 1916, NWPP, reel 1, 2.

118. See "Now for the Woman's Party Convention," *Suffragist,* May 27, 1916, 7.

119. Alice Paul to Lucius Cuthbert, August 23, 1916, NWPP, reel 1, 2.

120. Alice Paul to Lucius Cuthbert, April 14, 1916, NWPP, reel 1.

121. This quotation is from a transcription of the Third Conference of the National Advisory Council on April 8 and 9, 1916. Report by Elizabeth Selden Rogers, "April 9, 1916," NWPP, reel 1, 2. This untitled report is dated April 9, 1916, but reports on events that took place after this date in late 1916, particularly Inez Milholland Boissevain's death, suggest that the date is incorrect and that the report is on the events of 1916.

122. Harriot Stanton Blatch to Alice Paul, March 7, 1916, NWPP, reel 1, 1–2.

123. "Suffrage in the Democratic Convention," *Suffragist,* June 24, 1916, 7.

124. The national political parties in 1916 were the Democratic, Prohibition, Republican, Socialist, and Socialist Labor Parties. For a complete reproduction of these parties' platforms, see Kirk H. Porter and Donald Bruce Johnson, comps., *National Party Platforms: 1840–1960* (Urbana: University of Illinois Press, 1961), 194–212.

125. Alice Paul to Mabel Vernon, September 16, 1914, NWPP, reel 1.

126. Harriot Stanton Blatch to Alice Paul, March 1, 1916, NWPP, reel 1, 1.

127. Blatch rebuked Paul and Burns many times for moving into New York and for competing with her state-level campaign. See, for example, Harriot Stanton Blatch to Lucy Burns, December 22, 1913, NWPP, reel 1, 1; Harriot Stanton Blatch to Alice Paul, October 5, 1914, NWPP, reel 1; Harriot Stanton Blatch to Alice Paul, December 24, 1914, NWPP, reel 1.

128. [Harriot Stanton Blatch] To Mr. W. H. Gates, Colorado State Headquarters, February 25, 1916, NWPP, reel 1, 1–2. Blatch did not sign the letter, but later wrote to Alice Paul that she had written to Gates. See Harriot Stanton Blatch to Alice Paul, March 1, 1916, NWPP, reel 1, 2. Emphasis in original.

129. Harriot Stanton Blatch to Alice Paul, March 7, 1916, NWPP, reel 1, 2.

130. Quotation taken from letter, Harriot Taylor Upton to Alice Paul, October 2, 1914, NWPP, reel 1.

131. "Putting Their Issue First."

132. Spencer Miller Jr., *San Francisco Bulletin,* September 18, 1915, reprinted in *Suffragist,* October 2, 1915, 4.

133. "Last Minute Activities of the Woman's Party," *Suffragist,* November 11, 1916, 4.

134. "The Results of the Election," *Suffragist,* November 11, 1916, 6.

135. Ibid. The article found that in Illinois, which was the only state where the women's vote was counted separately, seventy thousand more women voted against President Wilson than for him. They couldn't separate out votes in the eleven other states, but ten of them went to Wilson by "narrow margins." For statistics on the 1914 and 1916 congressional elections, see Michael J. Dubin, *United States Congressional Elections, 1788–1997: The Official Results of the Elections of the 1st through 105th Congress* (Jefferson, N.C.: McFarland, 1998), 397–418; for statistics on the 1916 presidential election, see *Guide to U.S. Elections,* vol. 1, 781–82.

136. See "Political Leaders of West Urge Congress to Pass Amendment," *Suffragist,* March 18, 1916, 8.

137. Porter and Johnson, *National Party Platforms,* 199.

138. See Katharine Rolston Fisher, "Our First Congresswoman," *Suffragist,* November 18, 1916, 5.

139. Ibid.

140. Speech, "Suffrage Tactics," reprinted in *Suffragist,* October 2, 1915, 3.

141. Clara Ueland to Mrs. Orton H. Clark, August 8, 1915, NWPP, reel 1, 2.

142. Carrie Chapman Catt to Mrs. Ellen Douglas Hope, April 11, 1914, NWPP, reel 1, 2–3.

143. Carrie Chapman Catt to Harriot Taylor Upton, April 19, 1915, NWPP, reel 1.

144. W. H. Gates of Colorado State Headquarters to Congressional Union for Woman Suffrage, February 15, 1915, NWPP, reel 1.

145. Harriot Taylor Upton of Ohio wrote: "The action of the Congressional Union nearly broke my heart because I knew that we could win if we had no special set backs and I knew that the Democratic people would be cross about this, and I doubt whether the defeating of one or two candidates was worth defeating a whole state." See Harriot Taylor Upton to Alice Paul, October 6, 1914, NWPP, reel 1; Upton also wrote, "I understand that Nebraska in its report will say that it was the action of the Congressional Union which lost them the state." See Harriot Taylor Upton to Alice Paul, February 15, 1915, NWPP, reel 1, 1.

146. Emma Haley Frazelle to Mrs. O. H. P. Belmont, September 30, 1916, NWPP, reel 1.

147. Clara Ueland to Henry Wade Rogers, August 3, 1915, NWPP, reel 1.

148. The Socialist Party, for example, has been noted for taking racist positions. See *Race, Ethnicity, and Gender in Early Twentieth-Century American Socialism,* ed. Sally M. Miller (New York: Garland Publishing, 1996).

149. Christine A. Lunardini and Thomas J. Knock, "Woodrow Wilson and Woman Suffrage: A New Look," *Political Science Quarterly* 95 (1980–1981): 663.

150. Republicans held 215 seats, while the Democrats held 214. Dubin, *United States Congressional Elections,* 418.

CHAPTER 4

1. Wilfred E. Binkley, *American Political Parties: Their Natural History* (New York: Alfred A. Knopf, 1962), 369–70.

2. See Jeffrey K. Tulis, "Revising the Rhetorical Presidency," in *Beyond the Rhetorical Presidency,* ed. Martin J. Medhurst (College Station: Texas A&M University Press, 1996), 4; David Zarefsky, "The Presidency Has Always Been a Place for Rhetorical Leadership," in *The Presidency and Rhetorical Leadership,* ed. Leroy G. Dorsey (College Station: Texas A&M University Press, 2002), 20–41; James R. Andrews, "Presidential Leadership and National Identity: Woodrow Wilson and the Meaning of America," in Dorsey, *The Presidency and Rhetorical Leadership,* 129–44; Glen E. Thurow, "Dimensions of Presidential Character," in Medhurst, *Beyond the Rhetorical Presidency,* 15–29.

3. In Wilson's first inaugural address, he considered the role of politicians as "spokesmen and interpreters" of the people. Woodrow Wilson, "An Inaugural Address," in *The Papers of Woodrow Wilson,* hereafter *PWW,* ed. Arthur S. Link (Princeton, N.J.: Princeton University Press, 1978), 27: 151. For a thorough discussion of Woodrow Wilson's rhetorical presidency, see Mary E. Stuckey and Frederick J. Antczak, "The Rhetorical Presidency: Deepening Vision, Widening Exchange," *Communication Yearbook* 21 (1998): 405–41; Mary E. Stuckey, "'The Domain of Public Conscience': Woodrow Wilson and the Establishment of a Transcendent Political Order," *Rhetoric & Public Affairs* 6 (2003): 1–24.

4. Rogers M. Smith, *Civic Ideals: Conflicting Visions of Citizenship in U.S. History* (New Haven: Yale University Press, 1997), 413–14; Stuckey, "'The Domain of Public Conscience,'" 8.

5. On Roosevelt's program of racial nationalism, see Gary Gerstle, *American Crucible: Race and Nation in the Twentieth Century* (Princeton, N.J.: Princeton University Press, 2001), particularly chapters 1 and 2. On Wilson's racist and nativist nationalism, see Robert H. Ferrell, "Immigration and the Red Scare," in *Who Belongs in America? Presidents, Rhetoric, and Immigration,* ed. Vanessa B. Beasley (College Station: Texas A&M Press, 2006); Woodrow Wilson, Ray Stannard Baker, Howard Seavoy Leach, and William E. Dodd, eds., *The Public Papers of Woodrow Wilson: The New Democracy* (New York: Harper & Bros., 1925), 1: 423–25; hereafter *PPWW;* Walter Millis, *Road to War: America, 1914–1917* (Boston: Houghton Mifflin, 1935), 237–39. Quotation from Woodrow Wilson, *A History of the American People,* vol. 4 (New York: Harper & Bros., 1902), 162.

6. Ferrell, "Immigration," 4.

7. Alva I. Belmont to Fellow-member, Correspondence, September 13, 1916, reel 1, National Woman's Party Papers, University of Maryland, College Park, McKeldin Library: hereafter, NWPP; "Policy of the National Woman's Party," *Suffragist,* September 30, 1916, 6.

8. Alice Paul [chair] to Mrs. Morton, August 7, 1916, NWPP, reel 1.

9. For simplicity, this chapter refers to all previous iterations of the organization, such as the Congressional Committee or the CUWS, as the NWP. On March 2, 1917, at the national convention of the CUWS, the organization announced, "At a time of national instability, it promises well for the future of the fight for women's political liberty in this country that these two organizations are now coming together to deliberate on the most vigorous means of carrying on the battle for the enfranchisement of women in spite of the distracted state of the public mind." "National Conventions," *Suffragist,* March 3, 1917, 12.

10. See Linda Kerber, *Women of the Republic: Intellect and Ideology in Revolutionary America* (Chapel Hill: University of North Carolina Press, 1980).

11. A good starting point for this discussion is Joan R. Gundersen, "Independence, Citizenship, and the American Revolution," *Signs* 13 (1987): 59–77.

12. Woodrow Wilson, *The New Freedom: A Call for the Emancipation of the Generous Energies of a People* (New York: Doubleday, Page, 1918), 65.

13. Josep R. Llobera, *Foundations of National Identity: From Catalonia to Europe* (New York: Berghahn Books, 2004), 47; Tamar Mayer, "Gender Ironies of Nationalism: Setting the Stage," in *Gender Ironies of Nationalism: Sexing the Nation,* ed. Tamar Mayer (London: Routledge, 2000), 10; Nira Yuval-Davis and Floya Anthias, "Introduction," in *Woman-Nation-State,* eds. Nira Yuval-Davis and Floya Anthias (New York: St. Martin's Press, 1989), 9–10.

14. Llobera, *Foundations of National Identity,* 47.

15. Jean Bethke Elshtain, "Antigone's Daughters," in *Feminism and Politics,* ed. Anne Phillips (Oxford: Oxford University Press, 1998), 371; Benedict Anderson, *Imagined Communities: Reflections on the Origin and Spread of Nationalism* (London: Verso, 1991), 6; Llobera, *Foundations of National Identity,* 47–48.

16. Nira Yuval-Davis, *Gender and Nation* (London: Sage Publications, 1997), 24.

17. Ibid., 67.

18. Mayer, "Gender Ironies," 18.

19. Jean Pickering and Suzanne Kehde, "Introduction," in *Narratives of Nostalgia, Gender, and Nationalism* (New York: New York University Press, 1997), 6.

20. Otto Bauer, "The Nation," in *Mapping the Nation,* ed. Gopal Balakrishnan (London: Verso, 1996), 63.

21. Mayer, "Gender Ironies," 6–7.

22. Betty A. Reardon, *Sexism and the War System* (New York: Teachers College Press, 1985), 15.

23. Ibid.; Mayer, "Gender Ironies," 5; Yuval-Davis, *Gender and Nation,* 97.

24. J. Ann Tickner, *Gendering World Politics: Issues and Approaches in the Post-Cold War Era* (New York: Columbia University Press, 2001), 57.

25. Ibid., 51.

26. Yuval-Davis, *Gender and Nation,* 107–111.

27. Kimberly Jensen, *Mobilizing Minerva: American Women in the First World War* (Urbana: University of Illinois Press, 2008), 29–30.

28. Tickner, *Gendering World Politics,* 57; Jensen, *Mobilizing Minerva,* 32. For more on rape in war, see Cynthia Enloe, *Maneuvers: The International Politics of Militarizing Women's Lives* (Los Angeles: University of California Press, 2000), 108–52 (chapter titled "When Soldiers Rape"); *Mass Rape: The War against Women in Bosnia-Herzegovina,* ed. Alexandria Stiglmayer (Lincoln: University of Nebraska Press, 1994); Susan Brownmiller, *Against Our Will: Men, Women, and Rape* (New York: Fawcett Columbine, 1993).

29. Erika A. Kuhlman, *Petticoats and White Feathers: Gender Conformity, Race, and the Progressive Peace Movement, and the Debate Over War, 1895–1919* (Westport, Conn.: Greenwood Press, 1997), 1–2.

30. Kristin L. Hoganson, *Fighting for American Manhood: How Gender Politics Provoked the Spanish-American and Philippine-American Wars* (New Haven: Yale University Press, 1998).

31. Kuhlman, *Petticoats and White Feathers,* 5.

32. Ibid., 2.

33. Tickner, *Gendering World Politics,* 57; Yuval-Davis, *Gender and Nation,* 101.

34. Yuval-Davis, *Gender and Nation,* 112.

35. On women fighting in the Revolutionary War, see Joan Hoff Wilson, "The Illusion of Change: Women and the American Revolution," in *The American Revolution: Explorations in the History of American Radicalism,* ed. Alfred F. Young (DeKalb: Northern Illinois University Press, 1976), 395; Mary Beth Norton, "The Evolution of White Women's Experience in Early America," *American Historical Review* 89 (1984): 421. On women fighting and serving in the Civil War and the Spanish-American War, see Dorothy Schneider and Carl J. Schneider, *Into the Breach: American Women Overseas in World War I* (New York: Viking Press, 1991), 7–8.

36. Jensen, *Mobilizing Minerva,* vii, ix; Schneider and Schneider, *Into the Breach,* 8–13.

37. For a full discussion of how President Wilson justified his endorsement of woman suffrage, see Vanessa B. Beasley, "Engendering Democratic Change: How Three U.S. Presidents Discussed Female Suffrage," *Rhetoric and Public Affairs* 5 (2002): 79–103.

38. See Alexandar Keyssar, *The Right to Vote: The Contested History of Democracy in United States* (New York: Basic Books, 2000), 20, 87–90.

39. Jensen, *Mobilizing Minerva,* ix.

40. Ellen Newbold La Motte published a memoir of her time as a Red Cross nurse in a French military hospital in Belgium and discussed how ill and injured soldiers accosted, insulted, and harassed women. Ellen Newbold La Motte, *The Backwash of War: The Human Wreckage of the Battlefield as Witnessed by an American Hospital Nurse* (New York: G. P. Putnam's Sons, 1934).

41. Ibid., x.

42. David Mitchell, *Women on the Warpath: The Story of the Women of the First World War* (London: Lowe and Brydone, 1965), 248. For more on women in factories in England during World War I, see Gareth Griffiths, *Women's Factory Work in World War I* (Wolfeboro Falls, N.H.: Alan Sutton, 1991); Deborah Thom, *Nice Girls and Rude Girls: Women Workers in World War I* (London: I. B. Tauris, 1998).

43. Schneider and Schneider, *Into the Breach,* 8.

44. William J. Breen, "Black Women and the Great War: Mobilization and Reform in the South," in *Women and War, vol. 15, History of Women in the United States,* ed. Nancy F. Cott (Munich: K. G. Saur, 1992); Nikki Brown, *Private Politics and Public Voices: Black Women's Activism from World War I to the New Deal* (Bloomington: Indiana University Press, 2006), 14. Also see Nancy A. Hewitt, "Politicizing Domesticity: Anglo, Black, and Latin Women in Tampa's Progressive Movements," in *Gender, Class, Race, and Reform in the Progressive Era,* eds. Noralee Frankel and Nancy S. Dye (Lexington: University Press of Kentucky, 1991).

45. Brown, *Private Politics,* 12–16.

46. Jensen, *Mobilizing Minerva,* x.

47. Ibid., 41–45.

48. Ibid., 47, 48.

49. "President Asked to Open Second Term with Action on Suffrage," *Suffragist,* March 10, 1917, 7.

50. "National Conventions."

51. "Report for 1916," January 1917, NWPP, reel 2, 13. Also see Report by Elizabeth Selden Rogers, "April 9, 1916," NWPP, reel 1, 2. This untitled report is dated April 9, 1916, but reports on events that took place after this date in late 1916, particularly Inez Milholland Boissevain's death, which suggests the date is incorrect and the report is on the events of 1916.

52. In 1915, a group of New York women linked to the CUWS were accused of heckling President Wilson as they waited in a lobby to request that he receive a deputation of New York women. Alice Paul and Alva Belmont denied that it was heckling. See the following correspondence for a discussion of the event between Carrie Chapman Catt, New York Board Members, and Alice Paul: To Alice Paul and Members of the Board of the Congressional Union from Carrie Chapman Catt, May 26, 1915,

NWPP, reel 1; To Members of the Executive Committee and Advisory Council of the Congressional Union from Eunice Dana Brannan and Elizabeth Selden Rogers, June 16, 1915, NWPP, reel 1; Alice Paul to Carrie Chapman Catt, June 24, 1915, NWPP, reel 1. Also see the account of the incident in the *Suffragist:* "'Heckling' the President," *Suffragist,* May 22, 1915, 4; "President Wilson and New York Women," *Suffragist,* May 29, 1914, 3.

53. *Suffragist,* December 6, 1913, 28.

54. Quoted in "Suffrage Deputations to United States Congressmen," *Suffragist,* December 4, 1915, 9.

55. "President Wilson and Suffrage," *Suffragist,* June 20, 1914, 4.

56. Ibid.

57. Christine A. Lunardini and Thomas J. Knock, "Woodrow Wilson and Woman Suffrage: A New Look," *Political Science Quarterly* 95 (4) (1980–1981): 663.

58. Wilson to Ellen Louise Axson, October 31, 1884, *PWW,* 3: 389.

59. Wilson to Ellen Axson, March 1, 1885, *PWW,* 4: 316–17.

60. Lunardini and Knock, "Woodrow Wilson," 656.

61. Arthur S. Link, *Woodrow Wilson: A Brief Biography* (Cleveland: World Publishing, 1963), 26.

62. Phyllis Lee Levin argues that Wilson and Peck's "correspondence reflects none of the urgency of Wilson's overt physical yearning for the women he married." Phyllis Lee Levin, *Edith and Woodrow: The Wilson White House* (New York: Scribner, 2001), 128. Later Wilson referred to his relationship with Peck as "the contemptible error and madness of a few months." Quotation from Letter to Edith Bolling Galt, Sept. 21, 1915. Quoted in H. W. Brands, *Woodrow Wilson,* American Presidents series (New York: Times Books, 2003). For more on the alleged affair, see Frances Wright Saunders, *Ellen Axson Wilson: First Lady between Two Worlds* (Chapel Hill: University of North Carolina Press, 1985), 187–88.

63. Link, *Woodrow Wilson,* 23–25; quotation on 25.

64. Ibid., 28–61.

65. Louis Auchincloss, *Woodrow Wilson* (New York: Penguin Group, 2000), 60; Brands, *Woodrow Wilson,* 64.

66. Auchincloss, *Woodrow Wilson,* 61; for more on Wilson and Edith Bolling, see Tom Shachtman, *Edith and Woodrow: A Presidential Romance* (New York: G. P. Putnam's Sons, 1981).

67. Brands, *Woodrow Wilson,* 65.

68. Ibid., 66.

69. Ibid., 67, 126.

70. Quoted in Alden Hatch, *Edith Bolling Wilson: First Lady Extraordinary* (New York: Dodd, Mead, 1961), 79.

71. Ibid., 79–80.

72. See "Miss Wilson's New Work," *New York Times,* February 17, 1913, 6; and "Miss Wilson on Social Centres," *New York Times,* March 28, 1913, 14.

73. Quoted in "Miss Wilson on Forums," *New York Times,* January 12, 1916, 4; for more on Wilson's other two daughters, see Saunders, *Ellen Axson Wilson,* 165–70.

74. "Women Plan Fight for Legal Equality," *New York Times,* February 5, 1921, 3.

75. "News Notes of the Week," *Suffragist,* November 15, 1913, 2; "New Jersey Delegation to President Wilson," *Suffragist* November 15, 1913, 5–6.

76. "Suffrage Deputation Interviews President Wilson," *Suffragist,* November 22, 1913, 13.

77. Ibid. Also see Irwin, *The Story of Alice Paul,* 41–42.

78. "Suffrage Deputation," *Suffragist,* 13.

79. Lunardini, *From Equal Suffrage,* 38; see also "National Convention at Washington," *Suffragist,* November 6, 1913, 31.

80. Anna Howard Shaw, quoted in "A Suffrage Delegation to the President," *Suffragist,* December 13, 1913, 37.

81. Woodrow Wilson, quoted in "A Suffrage Delegation to the President," 37.

82. No title, dated "Jan. 1916," NWPP, reel 1, 13–15.

83. "The Women Voters' Envoys Present Their Message to the President and to Congress," *Suffragist,* December 11, 1915, 5.

84. "Deputation to President Wilson," *Suffragist,* January 31, 1914, 4.

85. "President Refuses to Aid in Deputation," *Suffragist,* July 4, 1914, 4–5.

86. For instance, on January 6, 1915, 150 women of Democratic Party visited him. "Democratic Deputation to the President," *Suffragist,* January 9, 1915, 3. And on January 27, 1916, a deputation of New York women, including CUWS members, visited the president. See "Deputation of New York Women to President Wilson," *Suffragist,* February 5, 1916, 5.

87. Diary entry, June 19, 1876, *PWW,* 3: 143.

88. In 1915, Joseph P. Tumulty, his private secretary, and Secretary of War Lindley M. Garrison voted for woman suffrage in state referenda. Additionally, Treasury Secretary William Gibbs McAdoo, Wilson's son-in-law, and Secretary of Commerce William C. Redfield voted in New York, while Secretary of Labor William B. Wilson voted in Pennsylvania. Lunardini and Knock, "Woodrow Wilson," 662.

89. For full text, see *PPWW* 4: 297–300.

90. "'Mr. President, What Will You Do for Woman Suffrage?'" *Suffragist,* December 9, 1916, 7.

91. Alice Paul to Harriot Stanton Blatch, December 16, 1916, reel 1, NWPP. See also Alice Paul [National Chair] to Mrs. Blatch, December 18, 1916, NWPP, reel 1, 2.

92. Vivian Pierce, "Inez Milholland Boissevain," *Suffragist,* November 25, 1916, 7.

93. "A National Tribute to Inez Milholland," *Suffragist,* December 19, 1916, 5.

94. "Ignoring the Suffrage Issue," *Suffragist,* December 9, 1916, 6.

95. Quotation taken from a speech delivered by Mabel Vernon at the National Advisory Council Conference, December 7, 1917, "The Picketing Campaign Nears Victory: Speech of Mabel Vernon at National Advisory Council Conference, December 7," reprinted in *Suffragist,* December 22, 1917, 9–10.

96. Ibid., 9.

97. "Suffragists Wait at the White House for Action," *Suffragist,* January 17, 1917, 7. Commas were added to the text of the banners for syntactical clarity.

98. The Sentinels' picket line stopped at brief intervals when arrests began in June 1917, but continued throughout the summer months and into fall of 1917. The pickets stopped shortly after prisoners were freed in November 1917 and began again in the spring of 1918 when NWP members felt President Wilson had not pressured the Senate to pass the federal amendment.

99. The protesters' appearance is described based on the photos of the Sentinels provided in 1917 issues of the *Suffragist.*

100. The NWP had a chair and a delegation of members in each state at the time. Within the first two weeks of the pickets, for example, delegations from Maryland, the District of Columbia, New York, and Virginia protested Wilson. The *Suffragist* lists names of NWP members participating in the pickets, which range from about twelve to fifteen women per day, although the photos of these delegations suggest that more women participated. See "State Delegations Join the Picket Line at the White House," *Suffragist,* January 31, 1917, 4; "Suffrage Sentinels Still Wait at the White House," *Suffragist,* January 24, 1917, 4. For a sense of the different professions represented, see "Silent Watch at the White House Continues," *Suffragist,* February 17, 1917, 5, and "Labor Day on the Picket Line," *Suffragist,* February 24, 1917, 5.

101. "State Delegations," 4; "Woman Suffrage. Mrs. Swing, Picketing White House," Harris & Ewing Collection, Library of Congress, LC-DIG-hec-09020. Commas were added to the text of the banners for syntactical clarity.

102. "Suffragists Wait," 8.

103. "Suffrage Sentinels Still Wait," 4.

104. Woodrow Wilson, "A Word to Agitators," quoted in *Suffragist,* November 10, 1917, 7.

105. Linda Hutcheon, *A Theory of Parody: The Teachings of Twentieth-Century Art Forms* (New York: Methuen, 1985), 34.

106. Ibid., 16.

107. Ibid., 32.

108. Ibid., 54. On the differences between parody and satire, see Ziva Ben-Porat, "Method in Madness: Notes on the Structure of Parody, Based on MAD TV Satires," *Poetics Today* 1 (1979): 247–48.

109. Margaret Rose, *Parody/Metafiction* (London: Croom Helm, 1979), 34.

110. Ben-Porat, "Method in Madness," 247–48.

111. Rose, *Parody/Metafiction,* 34.

112. Beasley, "Engendering Democratic Change," 85. The named publications printed the following articles about the Silent Sentinels, which were reprinted in *Suffragist:* "Watchful Waiting," *Philadelphia Press,* January 18, 1917, reprinted in *Suffragist,* January 24, 1917, 11; "Women Understand," *Seattle Post-Intelligencer,* January 14, 1917, reprinted in *Suffragist,* January 31, 1917, 6; "Putting the White House on the Map," *Chicago Evening Post,* January 18, reprinted in *Suffragist,* January 31, 1917, 10; "The Evening Post Cautious but Encouraging," *New York Evening Post,* May 16, 1917, reprinted in *Suffragist,* May 26, 1917, 10. Throughout 1917, the *Suffragist* also reprinted articles and political cartoons from the following publications: *Bay City (Michigan) Tribune, Boston Journal, New York Tribune, Philadelphia Eve-*

ning Bulletin, Indianapolis News, Dallas News, Paducah Democrat, Augusta (Maine) Journal, Des Moines Tribune, New York Evening Mail, Birmingham News, Lowell Evening Citizen, and the *Washington Star.* This list is not exhaustive, which further demonstrates that the Sentinels' messages circulated throughout the United States.

113. V. Grice, February 8, 1917, NWPP, reel 2. Emphasis in original.

114. "Ignoring the Suffrage Issue," 6.

115. Susan D. Becker, *The Origins of the Equal Rights Amendment: American Feminism Between the Wars* (Westport, Conn.: Greenwood, 1981), 277.

116. Carrie Chapman Catt, "Report of Survey Committee to National Board of NAWSA," March 1916, Manuscript Division, Library of Congress.

117. Kristy Maddux argues that 1917 marked a powerful rhetorical transformation in the anti-suffrage movement. Kristy Maddux, "When Patriots Protest: The Anti-Suffrage Discursive Transformation of 1917," *Rhetoric & Public Affairs* 7 (2004): 283–310.

118. Barry Brummett, "Towards a Theory of Silence as a Political Strategy," *Quarterly Journal of Speech* 66 (1980): 295.

119. According to Eleanor Flexner and Ellen Fitzpatrick, "The technique of the 'Silent Sentinels' had been employed by the Women's Political Union in Albany in attempting to get a suffrage referendum bill before the New York legislature in 1912. However, picketing the White House was novel." Eleanor Flexner and Ellen Fitzpatrick, *Century of Struggle: The Woman's Rights Movement in the United States,* enlarged ed. (Cambridge: Belknap Press of Harvard University Press, 1996), 275.

120. *Suffragist,* November 27, 1917, 6. Emphasis added.

121. George Lakey, "Technique and Ethos in Nonviolent Action: The Woman Suffrage Cause," *Sociological Inquiry* 38 (1968): 41.

122. "Woman Suffrage in Wartime," *New Republic,* October 27, 1917, reprinted in *Suffragist,* November 24, 1917, 7.

123. See Robert H. Ferrell, *Woodrow Wilson and World War I: 1917–1921* (New York: Harper & Row, 1985), 3–18; Woodrow Wilson, "An Address to a Joint Session of Congress," April 2, 1917, *PWW,* 41: 526–27.

124. Wilfred E. Binkley, *American Political Parties: Their Natural History* (New York: Alfred A. Knopf, 1962), 70.

125. "Stop Hoping, Mr. President, and Act," *Suffragist,* July 6, 1918, 4.

126. Yuval-Davis, *Gender and Nation,* 106.

127. "Woman Suffrage in Wartime," *New Republic,* 7.

128. Miriam Cooke and Angela Woollacott, "Introduction," in *Gendering War Talk,* eds. Miriam Cooke and Angela Woollacott (Princeton, N.J.: Princeton University Press, 1993), xii.

129. Hutcheon, *A Theory of Parody,* 8.

130. Ibid., 44–45.

131. Herman Meyer, *The Poetics of Quotation in the European Novel* (Princeton, N.J.: Princeton University Press, 1968), 19–20.

132. "Suffrage Sentinels Arrested by the Government," *Suffragist,* June 30, 1917, 6.

133. After Czar Nicholas II was forced to abdicate, Russian women were granted the right to vote four days later on March 13, 1917.

134. "A Red-letter Week on the Picket Line," *Suffragist,* April 28, 1917, 4. Quotation marks are part of the original banner.

135. "President Asked to Open Second Term," 7.

136. Ernestine Evans, "An Hour on the Suffrage Picket Line," *Suffragist,* April 14, 1917, 5.

137. "The United States Convicts Eleven More Women for Demanding Democracy," *Suffragist,* July 14, 1917, 4.

138. Matilda Hall Gardner, "Occoquan," *Suffragist,* July 28, 1917, 5; Flexner and Fitzpatrick, *Century of Struggle,* 277.

139. "Prison Congress Asked to Investigate Occoquan," *Suffragist,* November 24, 1917, 10.

140. "A Congressional Investigation of the Lawless Attack on the Suffrage Picket Demanded," *Suffragist,* August 25, 1917, 5.

141. "President Onlooker at Mob Attack on Suffragists," *Suffragist,* August 18, 1917, 7.

142. "Seven Months in Jail for National Suffrage Leader," *Suffragist,* October 27, 1917, 4.

143. Prior to this, the NWP occasionally used militaristic metaphors throughout its anti-Democratic campaigns, but never to this degree. See "Pilgrimage to the Opening of the Maryland Legislature," *Suffragist,* January 10, 1914, 7; "The Nation-Wide Demonstration," *Suffragist,* April 11, 1914, 3; and "The Next Move on the West," *Suffragist,* March 18, 1916, 7.

144. "Suffrage Sentinels Still Wait," 4; "State Delegations," 4; "The Seventh Week," 5.

145. Lavinia Dock, "The Young Are at the Gates," *Suffragist,* June 30, 1917, 5.

146. "The Administration versus the Woman's Party," *Suffragist,* August 25, 1917, 7.

147. "Seven Months," 4.

148. Florence Brewer Boeckel, "Why They Put Alice Paul in Solitary Confinement," *Suffragist,* November 10, 1917, 7.

149. Ibid.

150. "A Memorandum by Gilson Gardner," July 17, 1917, *PWW,* 43: 201–202.

151. Lunardini and Knock, "Woodrow Wilson," 665.

152. "From Alison Low Turnbull Hopkins," July 20, 1917, *PWW,* 43: 235.

153. "To Dee Richardson," July 25, 1917, *PWW,* 43: 272–73; "To Jessie Woodrow Wilson Sayre," June 22, 1917, *PWW,* 42: 560.

154. Quoted in Hatch, *Edith Bolling Wilson,* 80.

155. Lunardini and Knock, "Woodrow Wilson," 670–71.

156. Malone was a vocal supporter of the NWP. In April 1918, he traveled with NWP leaders to Boston and to Portland, Maine, to raise money for the organization. He openly criticized anti-suffrage senators. See "Rousing Boston Meeting Voices Demand for Senate Action on Suffrage," *Suffragist,* April 6, 1918, 6–7; "Mr. Malone Not Defender in Victorica Case," *Suffragist,* June 15, 1918, 5.

157. Memorandum by Woodrow Wilson to Joseph P. Tumulty, undated, reel 209, Woodrow Wilson Papers, Library of Congress.

158. Brisbane instructed staff to "have nothing of the picketers *or* what they do in prison or anything else on the front page of the paper. Tell the news in two sticks . . . *never* display a head." Arthur Brisbane to Joseph P. Tumulty, November 9, 1917, case file 1215, Woodrow Wilson Papers, Library of Congress; Lunardini and Knock, "Woodrow Wilson," 672, 675–76.

159. Lunardini and Knock, "Woodrow Wilson," 664–65.

160. See, for example, Wilson's letter, "To Deborah Knox Livingston," September 4, 1917, *PWW,* 44: 144–45. Wilson offered his support to the Maine suffrage campaign.

161. "To Carrie Clinton Lane Chapman Catt," October 13, 1917, *PWW,* 44: 372.

162. "From William Gwynn Gardiner," November 9, 1917, *PWW,* 44: 559–61.

163. Rep. John Baer of North Dakota witnessed firsthand the attacks upon the Sentinels in front of the White House, sponsored a congressional investigation of the abuses, and introduced the "Baer resolution" on August 17, 1917. The full text of the resolution is reprinted in "A Congressional Investigation," 5. Lunardini and Knock speculate that during a late-night visit from David Lawrence, a journalist with ties to the Wilson administration, Wilson's plans for the suffrage amendment were relayed to Paul and perhaps motivated her to withdraw the picketing. That same week, the suffragists were released. Lunardini and Knock "Woodrow Wilson," 677–78; see also "The Government Releases Suffrage Prisoners," *Suffragist,* December 1, 1917, 9.

164. Haig A. Bosmajian, "The Abrogation of the Suffragists' First Amendment Rights," *Western Journal of Speech Communication* 38 (1974): 230.

165. Linda J. Lumsden, *Rampant Women: Suffragists and the Right of Assembly* (Knoxville: University of Tennessee Press, 1997), 149.

166. The *Suffragist*'s coverage of the protests throughout 1917 and 1918 makes no mention of any African American women's participation.

167. Vernon, "The Picketing Campaign," 9–10.

168. Marc W. Steinberg, "The Roar of the Crowd: Repertoires of Discourse and Collective Action among the Spitafields Silk Weavers in Nineteenth-Century London," in *Repertoires and Cycles of Collective Action,* ed. Mark Traugott (Durham, N.C.: Duke University Press, 1995).

CHAPTER 5

1. "President Wilson Comes Out for Federal Amendment," *Suffragist,* January 12, 1918, 8.

2. "An Address to a Joint Session of Congress," January 8, 1918, *PWW,* 45: 538.

3. Ibid., 536.

4. Ibid., 536, 538.

5. Woodrow Wilson, "A Welcome to the Pan-American Financial Conference," May 24, 1915, *PWW,* 32: 246.

6. Roosevelt employed the corollary to justify US intervention in the Philippines and in the Boxer Rebellion in China. "Message of the President of the United States,

Communicated to the Two Houses of Congress at the Beginning of the Third Session of the Fifty-Eighth Congress," Washington, December 6, 1904. Theodore Roosevelt, *Presidential Addresses and State Papers: April 7, 1904 to May 9, 1905,* vol. 3 (New York: Review of Reviews, 1910), 176.

7. James Andrews, "Presidential Leadership and National Identity: Woodrow Wilson and the Meaning of America," in *The Presidency and Rhetorical Leadership,* ed. Leroy G. Dorsey (College Station: Texas A&M University Press, 2002), 141.

8. Woodrow Wilson, "An Address to a Joint Session of Congress," *PWW,* 41: 525.

9. Rogers M. Smith, *Civic Ideals: Conflicting Visions of Citizenship in U.S. History* (New Haven: Yale University Press, 1997), 430.

10. Woodrow Wilson, "The Second Inaugural Address," March 5, 1917, *PWW,* 41: 334.

11. Smith, *Civic Ideals,* 421–22.

12. Ironically, the Allied forces worked to defeat Germany; thus, while Wilson glorified Anglo-Saxon culture, he also endorsed the restriction of immigrants' rights through the Alien Enemies Act, the Espionage Act of 1917, and the Sedition Act of 1918. See Robert H. Ferrell, *Woodrow Wilson and World War I: 1917–1921* (New York: Harper & Row, 1985), 207–8.

13. Virginia Woolf, *Three Guineas,* ed. Michele Barrett (Harmondsworth: Penguin, 1993), 234.

14. See P. Orman Ray, "The World-Wide Woman Suffrage Movement," *Journal of Comparative Legislation and International Law,* 3rd ser., 1 (1919): 220–38. Ray traces how countries, states, and provinces granted all increments of suffrage rights (tax-paying, widowed, single women, school elections, full) from the mid-nineteenth century to 1919.

15. Ida Blom, "Gender and Nation in International Comparison," in *Gendered Nations: Nationalisms and Gender Order in the Long Nineteenth Century,* eds., Ida Blom, Karen Hagemann, and Catherine Hall (Oxford: Berg, 2000), 3–26; Kumari Jayawardena, *Feminism and Nationalism in the Third World,* 2nd ed. (London: Zed Books, 1986); see also Sheila Rowbotham, *Women in Movement: Feminism in Social Action* (New York: Routledge, 1992), 184–200.

16. Andrew Parker, Mary Russo, Doris Sommer, and Patricia Yaeger, "Introduction," in *Nationalisms and Sexualities,* eds. Andrew Parker, Mary Russo, Doris Sommer, and Patricia Yaeger (New York: Routledge, 1992), 1–18.

17. Ellen Carol DuBois, "Woman Suffrage Around the World: Three Phases of Suffragist Internationalism, in *Suffrage and Beyond: International Feminist Perspectives,* eds. Caroline Daley and Melanie Nolan (New York: New York University Press, 1994), 267–68.

18. The organization was formed in 1917; also, in 1916, Indian women formed the All-India Muslim Women's Conference, and, in 1918, women formed the Indian National Conference. Rowbotham, *Women in Movement,* 199–200.

19. Francis A. Beer and Laura Brunell, "Women's Words: Gender and Rhetoric in the Gulf War Debate," in *Meanings of War and Peace,* ed. Francis A. Beer (College Station: Texas A & M University Press, 2001), 106–14; J. Ann Tickner, *Gendering World Politics: Issues and Approaches in the Post-Cold War Era* (New York: Colum-

bia University Press, 2001), 58–61; Sylvia Walby, "Woman and Nation," in *Mapping the Nation,* ed. Gopal Balakrishnan (London: Verso, 1996), 247; Pnina Werbner, "Political Motherhood and the Feminisation of Citizenship: Women's Activisms and the Transformation of the Public Sphere," in *Women, Citizenship and Difference,* eds. Nira Yuval-Davis and Pnina Werbner (London: Zed Books, 1999), 221–45; Nira Yuval-Davis, *Gender and Nation* (London: Sage Publications, 1997), 10.

20. David S. Patterson, *The Search for Negotiated Peace: Women's Activism and Citizen Diplomacy in World War I* (New York: Routledge, 2008); also see Frances H. Early, *A World without War: How U.S. Feminists and Pacifists Resisted World War I* (Syracuse: Syracuse University Press, 1997).

21. Marilyn Lake, "Between Old Worlds and New: Feminist Citizenship, Nation and Race, the Destabilisation of Identity," in Daley and Nolan, *Suffrage and Beyond,* 280.

22. Kathleen B. Jones, "Citizenship in a Woman-Friendly Polity," in *The Citizenship Debates: A Reader,* ed. Gershon Shafir (Minneapolis: University of Minnesota Press, 1998), 239–43. See also *Sisterhood Is Global: The International Women's Movement Anthology,* ed. Robin Morgan (New York: Feminist Press, 1996); *Sisterhood Is Forever: The Women's Anthology for a New Millennium,* ed. Robin Morgan (New York: Washington Square Press, 2003).

23. See Elsa Barkley Brown, "'What Has Happened Here': The Politics of Difference in Women's History and Feminist Politics," *Feminist Studies* 18 (1992): 295–312. Similarly, Chela Sandoval argues that historians must resist the hegemonic structure of US feminist theory and recognize women's varying experience in language, culture, ethnicity, race, class, and gender. Chela Sandoval, "U.S. Third World Feminism: The Theory and Method of Oppositional Consciousness in the Postmodern World," *Genders* 10 (1991): 1–24. See also Chandra Talpade Mohanty, ed. Anne Phillips (Oxford: Oxford University Press, 1998), "Feminist Encounters: Locating the Politics of Experience," in *Feminism and Politics,* 254–72. Furthermore, Sylvia Walby argues that, to an extent, women can create identification across national borders based on similar experiences of oppression, but that we should not overlook that feminism is created by local conditions. Walby, "Woman and Nation," 235–54.

24. "To Josiah Oliver Wolcot," May 9, 1918, *PWW,* 47: 577–78. For an earlier instance of how Wilson linked woman suffrage to the war effort, see "A Reply [to Vira Boarman Whitehouse of the New York State Woman Suffrage Party]," October 25, 1917, *PWW,* 44: 442.

25. In July 1918, Wilson made a similar appeal to Sen. David Baird (R-NJ). See "To David Baird," July 31, 1918, *PWW,* 49: 139–40.

26. "Suffrage Demonstration before White House Planned: Women Protest at Recess of Senate without Action on Suffrage: Call upon President to Demand Passage of Amendment," *Suffragist,* August 3, 1918, 5.

27. In fact, by March 1918, Allied forces reached a breaking point. The rise of Bolsheviks in the wake of the Russian revolution signaled the defeat and withdrawal of Russian troops. Thus, as Germany redeployed half a million troops to the western front, France faced almost certain defeat, particularly after the Germans initiated the highly effective strategy of infiltration. The American Expeditionary Forces (AEF), led

by General John Pershing, finally arrived in France in June 1918. By no means did the AEF secure a swift victory, but they helped win key battles at Aisne-Marne and St. Mihiel, as well as the epic battle at Meuse-Argonne, which lasted from September 26 until early November when Americans finally reached Sedan and blasted the railroad that supplied German troops. Ferrell, *Woodrow Wilson and World War I*, 65–83.

28. For a study on how public memory is constructed through the memorializing of revolutionary heroes, see Stephen H. Browne, "Remembering Crispus Attucks: Race, and the Politics of Commemoration," *Quarterly Journal of Speech* 85 (1999): 169–87.

29. Numerous histories of Lafayette's and Rochambeau's contributions to the American Revolution are available. For a good start, see James R. Gaines, *For Liberty and Glory: Washington, Lafayette, and Their Revolutions* (New York: W. W. Norton, 2007); Oliver Bernier, *Lafayette: Hero of Two Worlds* (New York: E. P. Dutton, 1983); Robert A. Selig, *Rochambeau in Connecticut, Tracing His Journey: Historic and Architectural Survey* (Hartford: Connecticut Historical Commission, 1999); Louis de Royamont, *La Fayette et Rochambeau au Pays de Washington: La Guerre de l'Indépendance Américaine, 1776–1783* (Grenoble, France: J. Rey, 1919); *The American Campaigns of* Rochambeau's *Army, 1780, 1781, 1782, 1783*, edited and translated by Howard C. Rice Jr. and Anne S. K. Brown (Princeton, N.J.: Princeton University Press, 1972).

30. See "Notes of the Week," *Suffragist*, September 14, 1918, 3; "Notes of the Week," *Suffragist*, December 21, 1918, 3.

31. The NWP had appealed to the legacies of French revolutionaries before. The March 14, 1914, cover of the *Suffragist* featured a cartoon of Lafayette and Friedrich Wilhelm Ludolf Gerhard Augustin von Steuben, a Prussian officer in the American Revolution, sitting upon a cloud looking down on the United States. In response to a sign posted on the United States that said "No Admission to Revolution," Lafayette said to Von Steuben, "That would have kept us out, old boy."

32. "Lafayette and Rochambeau," *Suffragist*, August 8, 1918, 4.

33. Ibid.

34. Ibid.

35. Ibid.

36. "Last Plans for the Protest Demonstration, August 6: Women from Many States Condemn President Wilson for Failing to Give Effective Help to Suffrage in the Senate," *Suffragist*, August 10, 1918, 5.

37. "Lafayette and Rochambeau," 4.

38. Cover of the *Suffragist*, August 10, 1918.

39. Mrs. Richard Wainwright, "An Appeal by the National Woman's Party to the Statue of Lafayette to Plead for Them," *Suffragist*, September 21, 1918, 4.

40. Wainwright, "An Appeal," 4. Quotation marks were added for clarity.

41. France's president at the time was socialist, Alexandre Varenne. For a discussion of woman suffrage in France in 1918, see Steven C. Hause with Anne R. Kenney, *Women's Suffrage and Social Politics in the French Third Republic* (Princeton, N.J.: Princeton University Press, 1984), 206–10. Other histories of French woman suffrage include Paul Smith, *Feminism and the Third Republic: Women's Political and Civil*

Rights in France, 1918–1945 (Oxford: Oxford University Press, 1996); William D. Irvine, "Women's Rights and the 'Rights of Man,'" in *Crisis and Renewal in France, 1918–1962,* eds. Kenneth Moure and Martin S. Alexander (New York: Berghahn, 2002), 46–65.

42. "The Idealism of the West," *Suffragist,* January 8, 1916, 4.

43. "Suffrage Movement in Great Britain," *Suffragist,* January 31, 1917, 3; "England First," *Suffragist,* February 16, 1918, 4; "English Victory Close," *Suffragist,* January 19, 1918, 4; "Woman's Movement in Italy," *Suffragist,* January 31, 1917, 3; "Suffrage Coming in Italy," *Suffragist,* February 23, 1918, 4; Winifred Mallon, "The First Duty of the Sixty-Fourth Congress," *Suffragist,* December 18, 1915, 3; "Paris Council Endorses Suffrage," *Suffragist,* November 23, 1918, 3; "Women in Hungarian Parliament," *Suffragist,* January 5, 1918, 3; "Suffrage in Hungary," *Suffragist,* February 16, 1918, 4; "First Use of Equal Suffrage in Switzerland," *Suffragist,* January 12, 1918, 4; "War and Women," *Suffragist,* February 9, 1918, 4; "Indian Women Working for Their Sex," *Suffragist,* May 9, 1918, 4; "The New Swedish Demand," *Suffragist,* February 16, 1918, 4; "Feminism in Norway," *Suffragist,* February 16, 1918, 4; "Women in Canadian Legislatures," *Suffragist,* February 16, 1918, 4; "A Woman Minister in Russia," *Suffragist,* February 23, 1918, 4; "Austrian Suffrage Agitation," *Suffragist,* February 23, 1918, 4; "Suffrage in Uruguay," *Suffragist,* March 9, 1918, 4; "A Congress of Slavic Women," *Suffragist,* July 20, 1918, 3; "Suffrage Landslide Predicted in Jamaica," *Suffragist,* September 28, 1918, 3; "Irish Women Make Demands," *Suffragist,* October 19, 1918, 3.

44. "Germany Outdistances the United States Senate," *Suffragist,* November 16, 1918, 6.

45. "Cheers Only for French Women," *Suffragist,* February 16, 1918, 4.

46. Hause and Kenney, *Women's Suffrage and Social Politics,* 210–11; "French Women Beginning to Demand," *Suffragist,* May 18, 1918, 5.

47. "French Women Beginning to Demand," *Suffragist,* May 18, 1918, 5.

48. See DuBois, "Woman Suffrage Around the World," 252–76.

49. The Ligue nationale pour le vote des femmes (LNVF) was formed in response to the more moderate methods of the Union francais pour le suffrage des femmes (UFSF). Hause and Kenney, *Women's Suffrage and Social Politics,* 172, 210.

50. "To Carrie Clinton Lane Chapman Catt," June 7[13], 1918, *PWW,* 48: 303–4.

51. Irvine, "Women's Rights," 46–47.

52. "Suffrage Moves Forward in France," July 13, 1918, 3.

53. "French Women Thank President Wilson," *Suffragist,* September 21, 1918, 3.

54. "An Address to the Senate," September 30, 1918, *PWW,* 51: 158.

55. Ibid., 159.

56. Ibid., 160.

57. "Suffrage Amendment Postponed: President Wilson Fails to Take Action Ensuring Its Passage," *Suffragist,* July 6, 1918, 6.

58. "Germany Outdistances the United States Senate," 6; "Miss Paul Speaks at National Headquarters," *Suffragist,* November 16, 1918, 4.

59. "Women Will Protest against the Thirty-Four Wilful Men," *Suffragist,* October 12, 1918, 13.

60. "Women's Protest against Disenfranchisement Broken Up by Federal Police," *Suffragist,* August 17, 1918, 5

61. Mary Columbus Akers, Bertha Williams, Hazel Le Brun, Alice De Ment, Ruth Creighton, Theresa Rehak, Lottie Rohr, Louise Batman, "The Appeal of a Munition Worker," *Congressional Record,* June 6, 1918. Reprinted in *Suffragist,* June 8, 1918, 7.

62. "Women's Protest against Disenfranchisement," 5; "Another Picket Line," *Suffragist,* May 25, 1918, 5.

63. Clara Wold, "Did You Ever Climb a Statue?" *Suffragist,* August 17, 1918, 6; "The Later Demonstrations," *Suffragist,* August 24, 1918, 5.

64. "Women's Protest against Disenfranchisement," 5.

65. "Picketing Thirty-four Wilful Senators," *Suffragist,* October 26, 1918, 8.

66. Miriam Cooke and Angela Woollacott, "Introduction," in *Gendering War Talk,* eds. Miriam Cooke and Angela Woollacott (Princeton, N.J.: Princeton University Press, 1993), xii.

67. See "The Election," *Suffragist,* November 2, 1918, 6.

68. In Oregon, Wyoming, Kansas, and Colorado, Republican senators replaced Democratic senators. "Women Voters Rebuke Democratic Party," *Suffragist,* November 16, 1918, 8.

69. "The End of the Session," *Suffragist,* November 23, 1918, 6.

70. "We Turn to the President," *Suffragist,* December 21, 1918, 4.

71. "Suffrage in the President's Message," *Suffragist,* December 7, 1918, 6.

72. "Conference of National Advisory Council," *Suffragist,* December 7, 1918, 8.

73. "National Advisory Council Demands Action," *Suffragist,* December 21, 1918, 5; "American Women Burn President Wilson's Meaningless Words on Democracy," *Suffragist,* December 21, 1918, 6–7. In late September 1918, the NWP burned Wilson's speeches, but the NWP did not do so in an organized fashion until late December. See "President's Words Burned as Suffragists Protest in Front of White House," *Suffragist,* September 28, 1918, 6–8.

74. "New Year's Day Protest," *Suffragist,* January 4, 1919, 7.

75. Elizabeth Kalb, "The Watch Fire Goes On," *Suffragist,* February 8, 1919, 8.

76. "President's Words Burned," 8.

77. Jason C. Flanagan, "Woodrow Wilson's 'Rhetorical Restructuring': The Transformation of the American Self and the Construction of the German Enemy," *Rhetoric & Public Affairs* 7 (2004): 115–48.

78. Woodrow Wilson, "An Address on Preparedness to the Manhattan Club," November 4, 1915, *PWW,* 35: 167.

79. "An Address in Pittsburgh on Preparedness," January 29, 1916, *PWW,* 36: 32.

80. Woodrow Wilson, "The Second Inaugural Address," March 5, 1917, *PWW,* 41: 335.

81. Mildred Morris, "The New Year Demonstration," *Suffragist,* January 11, 1919, 4.

82. Kalb, "The Watch Fire Goes On," 8.

83. "While Women Go to Jail," *Suffragist,* January 18, 1919, 4.

84. Ibid.

85. "Suffragists Protest at President's Meeting in New York: Burn President's Speeches," *Suffragist,* March 15, 1919, 4. Regarding the Boston demonstration, see "Reminding the President When He Landed in Boston," *Suffragist,* March 1, 1919, 6; "Women Jailed in Boston: Sixteen Women Sent to Prison for Protesting against Disenfranchisement," *Suffragist,* March 8, 1919, 4.

86. "The Demonstration of February 9," *Suffragist,* February 22, 1919, 10–11.

87. "Protected," *Suffragist,* May 17, 1919, 8.

88. See *Statutes of the United States of America Passed at the First Session of the Sixty-Sixth Congress, 1919, and Concurrent Resolutions of the Two Houses of Congress, Recent Treaties, and Executive Proclamations,* edited, printed and published by authority of Congress under the direction of the Secretary of State (Washington, D.C.: Government Printing Office, 1919), 362.

89. Reprinted in "President Asks Congress to Pass Amendment," *Suffragist,* May 24, 1919, 5.

90. "Senator Harris Gives the Sixty-Fourth Vote," *Suffragist,* May 17, 1919, 3; "Scrutinizing the Situation from Our Own Platform," *Suffragist,* May 17, 1919, 5.

91. "The Later Demonstrations," 5.

92. "In Prison," *Suffragist,* August 24, 1918, 7.

93. For reports on the NWP's experiences protesting the Senate, see "Preserving the Peace and Order of the Capitol," *Suffragist,* October 19, 1918, 8; "Woman's Party Protests against Wilful Senators," *Suffragist,* October 19, 1918, 6–7; "Picketing on the Eve of Election," *Suffragist,* November 9, 1918, 7; "Picketing Continued," *Suffragist,* November 2, 1918, 8.

94. "The Demonstration of February 9," 10–11.

95. "Suffragists Protest at President's Meeting in New York," 4.

96. "Women Jailed in Boston," 4.

97. "Picketing on the Eve of Election," 7; "Capitol Police Forced to Return Suffrage Banners," *Suffragist,* November 16, 1918, 5.

98. Quoted in "Women's Protest against Disenfranchisement Broken Up by Federal Police," *Suffragist,* August 17, 1918, 5.

99. "Suffragists Protest at President's Meeting in New York," 4.

100. "Protected," 8.

101. Matthew O'Brien, "Free Speech Issue Up to President Wilson," *Suffragist,* August 17, 2008, 7.

102. Annie G. Porritt, "The Suffrage Conference at Washington," *Suffragist,* December 28, 1918, 5. Later, in 1939, popular writer Agatha Christie published the story as a detective novel. The story was also published as "Ten Little Indians" in 1940.

AFTERWORD

1. By August 1920, the non-ratifying states were those led by governors who refused to call special sessions (e.g., Vermont and Connecticut), those that defeated the measure, or those whose constitutions specified that state assemblies could not vote on a constitutional amendment unless state legislators had been elected *after* the

amendment was submitted for ratification. On June 1, 1920, the US Supreme Court overruled an Ohio Supreme Court ruling that validated referenda on constitutional amendments. This ruling abrogated a clause in the Tennessee state constitution that prohibited its legislature from voting on a constitutional amendment submitted before the election of its legislators. For a summary of the ratification process, see Eleanor Flexner and Ellen Fitzpatrick, *Century of Struggle: The Woman's Rights Movement in the United States* (Cambridge: Belknap Press of Harvard University Press, 1996), 308–17. On the suffragists' and anti-suffragists' campaigns in Tennessee, see Anastasia Sims, "Armageddon in Tennessee: The Final Battle over the Nineteenth Amendment," in *One Woman, One Vote: Rediscovering the Woman Suffrage Movement,* ed. Marjorie Spruill Wheeler (Troutdale, Ore.: New Sage Press, 1995), 333–52.

2. Flexner and Fitzpatrick, *Century of Struggle,* 316. Burn's letter quoted from *Baltimore Sun,* September 5, 1920.

3. "Places League First," *Washington Post,* August 19, 1920, 1.

4. See, for example, Flexner and Fitzpatrick, *Century of Struggle,* 276; Linda J. Lumsden, *Rampant Women: Suffragists and the Right of Assembly* (Knoxville: University of Tennessee Press, 1997), 139.

5. "A National Campaign," *Suffragist,* July 5, 1919, 4.

6. Christine A. Lunardini, *From Equal Suffrage to Equal Rights: Alice Paul and the National Woman's Party, 1920–1928* (New York: New York University Press, 1986), 148.

7. "Tennessee Session to Begin Tomorrow," *New York Times,* August 8, 1920, 3.

8. NWP headquarters secretary to Miss Marion McG. Noyes, August 7, 1920, reel 4, National Woman's Party Papers, University of Maryland, College Park, McKeldin Library: hereafter, NWPP.

9. Alice Paul, "Why We Picketed," June 7, *New York Evening World,* reprinted in *Suffragist,* July 1920, 123.

10. Eleanor Taylor, "Picketing the Republican Party," *Suffragist,* July 1920, 126.

11. Miss Frega to Winfield Jones, August 3, 1920, NWPP, reel 4.

12. "Threaten Delay in Suffrage Vote," *New York Times,* August 15, 1920, 9.

13. Edgar B. Stewart to Alice Paul, July 16, 1920, NWPP, reel 4.

14. "National Woman's Party Is Active in Tennessee," *Washington Post,* August 3, 1920, 1.

15. "Cox Ready for Fight," *Washington Post,* August 5, 1920, 1. Also see "Cox Counts on Taft," *Washington Post,* August 6, 1920, 1; "Cox Changes Plans," *Washington Post,* August 12, 1920, 1, 7.

16. "National Woman's Party Is Active in Tennessee," 1.

17. "Harding Resumes to Help Suffrage," *New York Times,* August 6, 1920, 3.

18. "Cox Fights for Ohio," *Washington Post,* August 17, 1920, 1.

19. For a sample of press coverage that notes Baker's lobbying efforts, see "Urges Republicans to Ratify Suffrage," *New York Times,* August 2, 1920, 3; "Women Seeking Sixteen Votes in Tennessee; Open Week's Drive Before Special Session," *New York Times,* August 3, 1920, 11; "Tennessee Session to Begin Tomorrow," 3; "Tennessee Delays Vote on Suffrage; Beaten in Carolina," *New York Times,* August 18, 1920, 1, 3; "Colby to Proclaim Suffrage Promptly," *New York Times,* August 19,

1920, 1; "National Woman's Party Is Active in Tennessee; Cox Ready for Fight," *Washington Post*, August 5, 1920, 1; "Cox Counts on Taft; Cox Changes Plans; Sees Fight on Suffrage," *Washington Post*, August 16, 1920, 4; "Uncertainty Veils Fate of Suffrage," *Washington Post*, August 16, 1920, 4; "Cox Fights for Ohio," 1.

20. "Tennessee Delays Vote on Suffrage," 1, 3.

21. For instance, when Hal H. Clements, chairman of the Republican Committee of Tennessee, advised all Tennessee Republicans to support suffrage, the *New York Times* exclusively credited the NWP and quoted the *Suffragist*. "Urges Republicans to Ratify Suffrage," 3.

22. "Women Sixteen Votes in Tennessee," 11. Similarly, when the *New York Times* reported on the activities of the "National Suffragists," it exclusively featured reports from NWP headquarters. "Tennessee Session to Begin Tomorrow," 3.

23. "Colby to Proclaim Suffrage Promptly," 1. For other headlines featuring the NWP, see "Colby Proclaims Woman Suffrage," *New York Times*, August 27, 1920, 1, 3. The article later noted that Carrie Chapman Catt was similarly disappointed; "Laud Women Voters," *Washington Post*, August 27, 1920, 1. On coverage of the NWP after ratification, see "Colby Promises Early Proclamation of Amendment," *Washington Post*, August 19, 1920, 1; "Unfurling Suffrage Flag in Washington," *Washington Post*, August 19, 1920, 1; "Colby to Proclaim Suffrage Promptly;" "Colby Proclaims Suffrage Change," *New York Times*, August 27, 1920, 3; "Woman's Party Asks Data on Poll Laws in 9 States," *Washington Post*, August 21, 1920, 1.

24. See, for example, "Harding Resumes Help to Suffrage," 3; "Threaten Delay in Suffrage Vote," *New York Time*s, August 15, 1920, 9; "Expect Tennessee House Will Ratify," *Washington Post*, August 15, 1920, 6; "Long Fight to Win Votes for Women," *New York Times*, August 19, 1920, 2; "Colby Proclaims Woman Suffrage," 1, 3; "Laud Women Voters," 1.

25. "Women Spent $80,000 to Get 36th State," *New York Times*, August 22, 1920, 3.

26. "August 1, 1920: Data Requested by Post Office Regarding Present Circulation," NWPP, reel 4.

27. H. W. Brands, *Woodrow Wilson*, American Presidents series (New York: Times Books, 2003), 132–33; Arthur S. Link, *Woodrow Wilson: A Brief Biography* (Cleveland: World Publishing, 1963), 158–60.

28. Link, *Woodrow Wilson*, 161.

29. Ibid., 165.

30. Ibid., 166–68.

31. Ibid., 170–80.

32. *New Republic*, 16, August 10, 1918, 33–35.

33. Lunardini, *From Equal Suffrage*, 146.

34. Ibid., 148.

35. "Parties Planning to Get Women's Votes," *New York Times*, August 20, 1920, 3.

36. "Timely Topics Discussed by Capital Visitors," *Washington Post*, August 19, 1920, 6.

37. Mrs. Charles H. Sabin to Mrs. Clarence M. Smith, May 23, 1920, NWPP, reel 4, 1–2.

38. Link, *Woodrow Wilson,* 170.

39. "White and Hays Felicitate Women," *New York Times,* August 19, 1920, 1.

40. Ellen Carol DuBois, "Woman Suffrage around the World," in *Suffrage and Beyond: International Feminist Perspectives,* eds. Caroline Daley and Melanie Nolan (New York: New York University Press, 1994), 269–71.

41. Sheila Rowbotham, *Women in Movement: Feminism in Social Action* (New York: Routledge, 1992), 175–78.

42. On Alice Paul's activism between the 1920s and the 1960s, see Leila J. Rupp and Verta A. Taylor, *Survival in the Doldrums: The American Women's Rights Movement, 1945 to the 1960s* (New York: Oxford University Press, 1987).

43. DuBois, "Woman Suffrage around the World," 270–71.

44. See "International Conferences of Women," *Suffragist,* July 1920, 133, 146.

45. See Dorothy M. Brown, *Setting a Course: American Women in the 1920s* (Boston: Twayne Publishers, 1987); Marianne Hirsch and Evelyn Fox Keller, eds., *Conflicts in Feminism* (New York: Routledge, 1990); J. Stanley Lemons, *The Woman Citizen: Social Feminism in the 1920s* (Charlottesville: University Press of Virginia, 1990).

46. "The New South for Suffrage as a War Measure," *Suffragist,* September 14, 1918, 4; Sue S. White, "An Appeal from the South to the Western Voters," *Suffragist,* September 14, 1918, 4.

47. Marjorie Spruill Wheeler, *New Women of the New South: The Leaders of the Woman Suffrage Movement in the Southern States* (New York: Oxford University Press, 1993), 184.

48. *New York World,* February 18, 1919 (NAACP files, Suffrage, Library of Congress, Washington, D.C.).

49. *Branch Bulletin,* March 30, 1919 (NAACP files, Suffrage, Library of Congress, Washington, D.C.). The resolution and Paul's response both appear in this issue.

50. Walter White, cited in Rosalyn Terborg-Penn, "Afro-Americans in the Struggle for Woman Suffrage," PhD dissertation, Howard University, 1977 (University Microfilms International, Ann Arbor, Mich.), 298.

51. Paula Giddings, *When and Where I Enter: The Impact of Black Women on Race and Sex in America* (New York: William Morrow, 1984), 162–63.

52. Mary White Ovington to Alice Paul, July 9, 1920 (NAACP files, Suffrage, Library of Congress, Washington, D.C.).

53. Addie Hunton to Maggie Walker, February 23, 1921 (NAACP files, Suffrage, Library of Congress, Washington, D.C.). For more on African American women after the vote was secured, see Giddings, *When and Where,* 164–170.

54. Proceedings reprinted in *Suffragist:* "Victory for the Susan B. Anthony Amendment," *Suffragist,* June 14, 1919, 5–8. Also see "Suffrage Victory Today Predicted," *New York Times,* June 4, 1919, 17; Kenneth R. Johnson, "White Racial Attitudes as a Factor in the Arguments against the Nineteenth Amendment," *Phylon* 31 (1970): 31–37.

55. Nikki Brown, *Private Politics and Public Voices: Black Women's Activism from World War I to the New Deal* (Bloomington: Indiana University Press, 2006), xii; Giddings, *When and Where,* 171–81.

56. Nancy F. Cott also adds that only half of the overall electorate voted throughout the 1920s, and without a proper mechanism to measure how many women voted versus men, it is not clear just how little women voted. Nancy F. Cott, "Across the Great Divide: Women in Politics Before and After 1920," in *One Woman, One Vote,* 353–73; Paula Baker, "The Domestication of Politics: Women and American Political Society, 1780–1920," *American Historical Review* 89 (1984): 643–45.

57. "White and Hays Felicitate Women," 1.

58. Baker, "The Domestication of Politics," 644.

59. See "What of the Woman Vote?" *New York Times,* August 22, 1920, BRM2; "May Have Own Candidates," *Washington Post,* August 29, 1920, 26.

60. On the long history of the ERA debate, see Lunardini, *From Equal Suffrage;* Amy E. Butler, *Two Paths to Equality: Alice Paul and Ethel M. Smith in the ERA Debate, 1921–1926* (Albany: State University of New York Press, 2002); Susan D. Becker, *The Origins of the Equal Rights Amendment: American Feminism Between the Wars* (Westport, Conn.: Greenwood Press, 1981); Janet K. Boles, *The Politics of the Equal Rights Amendment: Conflict and the Decision Process* (New York: Longman, 1979); Mary A. Delsman, *Everything You Need to Know about *ERA (*the Equal Rights Amendment)* (Riverside, Calif.: Meranza Press, 1975); Chandra Silva, "Esto Perpetua: The Persistence and Transformation of Feminism in Idaho through the Struggle to Ratify the Equal Rights Amendment" (PhD diss., Washington State University, 2005); Caryn Ellen Neumann, "The National Woman's Party and the Equal Rights Amendment, 1945–1977" (PhD diss., Florida Atlantic University, 1994); Diane Elizabeth Hill, "International Law for Women's Rights: The Equality Treaties Campaign of the National Women's [*sic*] Party and Reactions of the United States State Department and the National League of Women Voters (1928–1938)" (PhD diss., University of California, Berkeley, 1999); Lynne M. O'Leary-Archer, "The Contentious Community: The Impact of Internecine Conflict of the National Woman's Party, 1920–1947" (PhD diss., University of Southern California, 1988).

61. Emma Wold to Mrs. Matilda Gage Carpenter, August 18, 1920, NWPP, reel 4, 1–2.

62. "Six Women Aspire to Capitol Hill," *Washington Post,* August 8, 1920, 36.

63. "Full Text of Governor Cox's Speech of Acceptance," *Washington Post,* August 8, 1920, 23.

64. Emma Wold to Mr. Frank Carroll, July 2, 1920, NWPP, reel 4, 2.

65. "From Helen Hamilton Gardener," August 16, 1918, in *The Papers of Woodrow Wilson,* hereafter *PWW,* ed. Arthur S. Link (Princeton, N.J.: Princeton University Press, 1978), 49: 268.

66. "From Helen Hamilton Gardener," June 17, 1918, *PWW,* 48: 340–41. For similar appeals, see "An Address to the President by Vira Boarman Whitehouse," October 25, 1917, *PWW,* 44: 440–41; "From Carrie Clinton Lane Chapman Catt," June 13, 1918, *PWW,* 48: 304.

67. "From Helen Hamilton Gardener," June 17, 1918.

68. Matthew Potolsky, *Mimesis* (New York: Routledge, 2006), 148.

69. Rene Girard, "Mimesis and Violence: Perspectives in Cultural Criticism," *Berkshire Review* 14 (1979): 9.

70. Potolsky, *Mimesis,* 149.

71. Marie-Jo Bonnet, "Gay Mimesis and Misogyny: Two Aspects of the Same Refusal of the Other?" *Journal of Homosexuality* 41 (2001): 275.

72. Enda McCaffrey, *The Gay Republic: Sexuality, Citizenship and Subversion in France* (Hampshire, UK: Ashgate Publishing, 2005), 201.

73. Annie G. Porrit, "Nationalizing of Suffrage Work," *Suffragist,* February 6, 1915, 5.

74. Mrs. C. L. Roberts to Alice Paul, August 20, 1920, NWPP, reel 4. Emphasis in original.

Bibliography

Alejandro, Robert. *Hermeneutics, Citizenship, and the Public Sphere.* Albany: State University of New York Press, 1993.

Allgor, Catherine. *Parlor Politics: In Which the Ladies of Washington Help Build a City and a Government.* Charlottesville: University Press of Virginia, 2000.

Anderson, Benedict. *Imagined Communities: Reflections on the Origin and Spread of Nationalism.* London: Verso, 1991.

Andrews, James. "Presidential Leadership and National Identity: Woodrow Wilson and the Meaning of America." In *The Presidency and Rhetorical Leadership,* edited by Leroy G. Dorsey, 129–44. College Station: Texas A&M University Press, 2002.

Ansolabehere, Stephen, Shigeo Hirano, and James M. Snyder Jr. "What Did the Primary Do to Party Loyalty in Congress?" In *Party, Process, and Political Change in Congress, Volume 2: Further Perspectives on the History of Congress,* edited by David W. Brady and Mathew D. McCubbins, 21–36. Stanford: Stanford University Press, 2007.

Anthias, Floya, and Nira Yuval-Davis. "Introduction." In *Woman-Nation-State,* edited by Nira Yuval-Davis and Floya Anthias, 1–15. New York: St. Martin's Press, 1989.

Aptheker, Bettina. *Woman's Legacy: Essays on Race, Sex, and Class in American History.* Amherst: University of Massachusetts Press, 1982.

Argersinger, Peter H. *Populism and Politics: William Alfred Peffer and the People's Party.* Lexington: University of Kentucky Press, 1974.

Asen, Robert. "A Discourse Theory of Citizenship." *Quarterly Journal of Speech* 90 (2004): 189–211.

Auchincloss, Louis. *Woodrow Wilson.* New York: Penguin Group, 2000.

Auerbach, Erich. *Mimesis: The Representation of Reality in Western Literature.* 50th anniversary ed. Translated by Willard R. Trask. Princeton, N.J.: Princeton University Press, 2003.

Ausland, Hayden W. "On Reading Plato Mimetically." *American Journal of Philology* 118 (1997): 371–416.

Avery, Dianne, and Alfred S. Konefsky. "The Daughters of Job: Property Rights and Women's Lives in Mid-Nineteenth-Century Massachusetts." *Law and History Review* 10 (1992): 323–56.

Baker, Jean H. *Affairs of Party: The Political Culture of Northern Democrats in the Mid-Nineteenth Century.* Ithaca, N.Y.: Cornell University Press, 1983.

———. *Sisters: The Lives of America's Suffragists.* New York: Hill and Wang, 2005.

———, ed. *Votes for Women: The Struggle for Suffrage Revisited.* Oxford: Oxford University Press, 2002.

Baker, John C. "Women, Language, and the Argument for Education Reform in Antebellum Ladies' Magazines." *Women and Language* 20 (1997): 49–52.

Baker, Paula. "The Domestication of Politics: Women and American Political Society, 1780–1920." *American Historical Review* 89 (1984): 620–47.

Bakhtin, Mikhail. *Rabelais and his World.* Trans. Helene Iswoldsky. Cambridge: MIT Press, 1968.

Balakrishnan, Gopal, ed. *Mapping the Nation.* London: Verso, 1996.

Balibar, Etienne. "The Nation Form: History and Ideology." In *Becoming National: A Reader,* edited by Geoff Eley and Ronald Grigor Suny, 132–50. New York: Oxford University Press, 1996.

Barber, Benjamin. *Strong Democracy: Participatory Politics for a New Age.* Berkeley: University of California Press, 1984.

Barnes, Donna A. *Farmers in Rebellion: The Rise and Fall of the Southern Farmers Alliance and People's Party in Texas.* Austin: University of Texas Press, 1984.

Basch, Norma. "Equity vs. Equality: Emerging Concepts of Women's Political Status in the Age of Jackson." *Journal of the Early Republic* 3 (1983): 297–318.

———. "Invisible Women: The Legal Fiction of Marital Unity in Nineteenth-Century America." *Feminist Studies* 5 (1979): 346–66.

———. "Relief in the Premises: Divorce as a Woman's Remedy in New York and Indiana, 1815–1870." *Law and History Review* 8 (1990): 1–24.

Bauer, Otto. "The Nation." In *Mapping the Nation,* edited by Gopal Balakrishnan, 39–77. London: Verso, 1996.

Beasley, Vanessa B. "Engendering Democratic Change: How Three U.S. Presidents Discussed Female Suffrage." *Rhetoric & Public Affairs* 5 (2002): 79–103.

———, ed. *Who Belongs in America? Presidents, Rhetoric, and Immigration.* College Station: Texas A&M University Press, 2006.

———. *You, the People: American National Identity in Presidential Rhetoric.* College Station: Texas A&M University Press, 2004.

Becker, Susan D. *The Origins of the Equal Rights Amendment: American Feminism between the Wars.* Westport, Conn.: Greenwood Press, 1981.

Bederman, Gail. *Manliness and Civilization: A Cultural History of Gender and Race in the United States, 1880–1917.* Chicago: University of Chicago Press, 1995.

Beer, Francis A., and Laura Brunell. "Women's Words: Gender and Rhetoric in the Gulf War Debate." In *Meanings of War & Peace,* edited by Francis A. Beer, 106–14. College Station: Texas A&M University Press, 2001.

Beeton, Beverly. "How the West Was Won for Woman Suffrage." In *One Woman, One Vote: Rediscovering the Woman Suffrage Movement,* edited by Marjorie Spruill Wheeler, 99–116. Troutdale, Ore.: New Sage Press, 1995.

———. *Women Vote in the West: The Woman Suffrage Movement, 1869–1896.* New York: Garland, 1986.

Belfiore, Elizabeth. "A Theory of Imitation in Plato's Republic." *Transactions of the American Philological Association* 114 (1984): 121–46.

Ben-Porat, Ziva. "Method in Madness: Notes on the Structure of Parody, Based on MAD TV Satires," *Poetics Today* 1 (1979): 245–72.

Benson, Lee. *The Concept of Jacksonian Democracy: New York as a Test Case.* Princeton, N.J.: Princeton University Press, 1961.

Benson, Mary S. *Women in Eighteenth Century America: A Study of Opinion and Social Usage.* New York: Columbia University Press, 1935.

Bernier, Oliver. *Lafayette: Hero of Two Worlds.* New York: E. P. Dutton, 1983.

Berthoff, Rowland. "Conventional Mentality: Free Blacks, Women, and Business Corporations as Unequal Persons, 1820–1870." *Journal of American History* 76 (1989): 753–84.

Bhabha, Homi K. *The Location of Culture.* London: Routledge, 2004.

Bibby, John F., and L. Sandy Maisel. *Two Parties—or More?* Boulder, Colo.: Westview Press, 2003.

Billington, Monroe Lee. *The Political South in the Twentieth Century.* New York: Scribner, 1975.

Binkley, Wilfred E. *American Political Parties: Their Natural History.* New York: Alfred A. Knopf, 1962.

———. *President and Congress.* New York: Alfred A. Knopf, 1947.

Black, Jason Edward. *"Words True to Both Hearts": Merging Native-U.S. Rhetoric in the Removal and Allotment of American Indians.* Tuscaloosa: University of Alabama Press, forthcoming.

Blackstone, William. *Commentaries on the Laws of England: A Facsimile of the First Edition, 1765–1769.* Chicago: University of Chicago Press, 1979.

Blair, Karen J. *The Clubwoman as Feminist: True Womanhood Redefined, 1868–1914.* New York: Holms and Meier, 1980.

Bland, Sidney Roderick. "Techniques of Persuasion: The National Woman's Party and Woman Suffrage, 1913–1919." PhD diss., George Washington University, 1972.

Blewett, Mary. *We Will Rise in Our Might: Workingwomen's Voices from Nineteenth-Century New England.* Ithaca, N.Y.: Cornell University Press, 1991.

Bloch, Ruth H. "American Feminine Ideals in Transition: The Rise of the Moral Mother, 1785–1815." *Feminist Studies* 4 (1978): 100–126.

———. "The Gendered Meanings of Virtue in Revolutionary America." *Signs* 13 (1987): 37–58.

Blom, Ida. "Gender and Nation in International Comparison." In *Gendered Nations: Nationalisms and Gender Order in the Long Nineteenth Century,* edited by Ida Blom, Karen Hagemann, and Catherine Hall, 3–26. Oxford: Berg, 2000.

Boles, Janet K. *The Politics of the Equal Rights Amendment: Conflict and the Decision Process.* New York: Longman, 1979.

Bonnet, Marie-Jo. "Gay Mimesis and Misogyny: Two Aspects of the Same Refusal of the Other?" *Journal of Homosexuality* 41 (2001): 265–80.

Borda, Jennifer L. "Woman Suffrage in the Progressive Era: A Coming of Age." In *Rhetoric and Reform in the Progressive Era,* edited by J. Michael Hogan, 339–86. East Lansing: Michigan State University Press, 2003.

———. "The Woman Suffrage Parades of 1910–1913: Possibilities and Limitations of an Early Feminist Rhetorical Strategy." *Western Journal of Communication* 66 (2002): 25–52.

Bordin, Ruth. *Women and Temperance: The Quest for Power and Liberty, 1873–1900.* Philadelphia: Temple University Press, 1981.

Boris, Eileen. "Reconstructing the 'Family': Women, Progressive Reform, and the Problem of Social Control." In *Gender, Class, Race, and Reform in the Progressive Era,* edited by Noralee Frankel and Nancy S. Dye, 73–86. Lexington: University Press of Kentucky, 1991.

Bosmajian, Haig A. "The Abrogation of the Suffragists' First Amendment Rights." *Western Journal of Speech Communication* 38 (1974): 218–32.

Boswell, Angela, and Judith N. McArthur, eds. *Women Shaping the South: Creating and Confronting Change.* Columbia: University of Missouri Press, 2006.

Bowen, Clarence Winthrop, ed. *The History of the Centennial Celebration of the Inauguration of George Washington as First President of the United States.* New York: D. Appleton, 1892.

Boxer, Marilyn J., and Jean H. Quataert. *Socialist Women: European Socialist Feminism in the Nineteenth and Early Twentieth Centuries.* New York: Elsevier, 1978.

Boyd, John D. *The Function of Mimesis and its Decline.* New York: Fordham University Press, 1980.

Boylan, Ann M. "Women and Politics in the Era before Seneca Falls." *Journal of the Early Republic* 10 (1990): 363–82.

Brands, H. W. *Woodrow Wilson.* New York: Times Books, 2003.

———. *T. R.: The Last Romantic.* New York: Basic Books, 1997.

Breen, William J. "Black Women and the Great War: Mobilization and Reform in the South." In *History of Women in the United States: Historical Articles on Women's Lives and Activities,* vol. 15, edited by Nancy F. Cott, 93–112. Munich: K. G. Saur, 1992.

Brown, Dorothy M. *Setting a Course: American Women in the 1920s.* Boston: Twayne Publishers, 1987.

Brown, Elsa Barkley. "'What Has Happened Here': The Politics of Difference in Women's History and Feminist Politics." *Feminist Studies* 18 (1992): 295–312.

Brown, Nikki. *Private Politics and Public Voices: Black Women's Activism from World War I to the New Deal.* Bloomington: Indiana University Press, 2006.

Brown, Roger H. *Redeeming the Republic: Federalists, Taxation, and the Origins of the Constitution.* Baltimore: Johns Hopkins University Press, 1993.

Browne, Stephen Howard. *Angelina Grimké, Rhetoric, Identity, and the Radical Imagination.* East Lansing: Michigan State University, 1999.

———. "Remembering Crispus Attucks: Race, and the Politics of Commemoration." *Quarterly Journal of Speech* 85 (1999): 169–87.

Brownmiller, Susan. *Against Our Will: Men, Women, and Rape.* New York: Fawcett Columbine, 1993.

Brummett, Barry. "Towards a Theory of Silence as a Political Strategy." *Quarterly Journal of Speech* 66 (1980): 289–303.

Bruner, M. Lane. *Strategies of Remembrance: The Rhetorical Dimensions of National Identity Construction.* Columbia: University of South Carolina Press, 2002.

Bryan, Dominic. *Orange Parades: The Politics of Ritual, Tradition and Control.* London: Pluto Press, 2000.

Bryden, Inga, and Janet Floyd, eds. *Domestic Space: Reading the Nineteenth-Century Interior.* Manchester, UK: Manchester University Press, 1999.

Buel, Richard, Jr. *Securing the Revolution: Ideology in American Politics, 1789–1815.* Ithaca, N.Y.: Cornell University Press, 1972.

Buhle, Mari Jo. *Women and American Socialism, 1870–1920.* Urbana: University of Illinois Press, 1981.

Burke, Kenneth. *A Grammar of Motives.* Berkeley: University of California Press, 1969.

Burton, David H. *The Learned Presidency: Theodore Roosevelt, William Howard Taft, Woodrow Wilson.* Cranbury, N.J.: Associated University Presses, 1988.

Butler, Amy E. *Two Paths to Equality: Alice Paul and Ethel M. Smith in the ERA Debate, 1921–1926.* Albany: State University of New York Press, 2002.

Butler, Melissa A. "Early Liberal Roots of Feminism: John Locke and the Attack on Patriarchy." *American Political Science Review* 72 (1978): 135–50.

Caesar, James W., Glen E. Thurow, Jeffrey Tulis, and Joseph M. Bessette. "The Rise of the Rhetorical Presidency." *Presidential Studies Quarterly* 11 (Spring 1981): 158–71.

Cameron, Ardis. *Radicals of the Worst Sort: Laboring Women in Lawrence, Massachusetts, 1860–1912.* Urbana: University of Illinois Press, 1993.

Campbell, Jacqueline Glass. "Seeking a Moral Economy of War: Confederate Women and Southern Nationalism in Civil War North Carolina." In *Women Shaping the South: Creating and Confronting Change,* edited by Angela Boswell and Judith N. McArthur, 74–96. Columbia: University of Missouri Press, 2006.

Campbell, Karlyn Kohrs. "Agency: Promiscuous and Protean." *Communication and Critical/Cultural Studies* 2 (2005): 1–19.

———. *Man Cannot Speak for Her,* vol. 1, *A Critical Study of Early Feminist Rhetoric.* Westport, Conn.: Praeger, 1989.

———. *Man Cannot Speak for Her,* vol. 2, *Key Texts of the Early Feminists.* Westport, Conn.: Praeger, 1989.

———. "The Rhetoric of Women's Liberation: An Oxymoron." *Quarterly Journal of Speech* 59 (1973): 74–86.

———. "Stanton's 'The Solitude of Self': A Rationale for Feminism." *Quarterly Journal of Speech* 66 (1980): 304–12.

Campbell, Karlyn Kohrs, and Kathleen Hall Jamieson. *Presidents Creating the Presidency: Deeds Done in Words.* Chicago: University of Chicago Press, 2008.

Casey, Michael W. "The First Female Public Speakers in America (1630–1840): Searching for Egalitarian Christian Primitivism." *Journal of Communication and Religion* 23 (2000): 1–28.

Cathcart, Robert S. "Movements: Confrontation as Rhetorical Form." *Southern Speech Communication Journal* 48 (1978): 233–47.

———. "New Approaches to the Study of Movements." *Western Speech* 36 (1972): 82–88.

Chafee, Zechariah, Jr. *Free Speech in the United States.* Cambridge: Harvard University Press, 1954.

Chan, Sucheng, ed. *Entry Denied: Exclusion and the Chinese Community in America, 1882–1943.* Philadelphia: Temple University Press, 1991.

———. "The Exclusion of Chinese Women, 1870–1943." In *A Heritage of Her Own: Toward a New Social History of American Women,* edited by Nancy F. Cott and Elizabeth H. Pleck, 75–125. New York: Simon and Schuster, 1979.

Charland, Maurice. "Constitutive Rhetoric: The Case of the Peuple Québécois." *Quarterly Journal of Speech* 73 (1987): 133–51.

Chester, Eric Thomas. *True Mission: Socialists and the Labor Party Question in the United States.* London: Pluto Press, 2004.

Chute, Marchette. *The First Liberty: A History of the Right to Vote in America, 1619–1850.* New York: Dutton, 1969.

Clanton, Gene. *Congressional Populism and the Crisis of the 1890s.* Lawrence: University of Kansas Press, 1998.

Clark, Thomas D. *The South since Reconstruction.* Indianapolis: Bobs-Merrill, 1973.

Cogan, Jacob Katz. "The Look Within: Property, Capacity, and Suffrage in Nineteenth-Century America." *Yale Law Journal* 107 (1997): 473–98.

Cogan, Jacob Katz, and Lori D. Ginzberg. "1846 Petition for Woman's Suffrage, New York State Constitutional Convention." *Signs* 22 (1997): 427–39.

Cohen, Jean L. "Strategy or Identity: New Theoretical Paradigms and Contemporary Social Movements." *Social Research* 52 (1985): 663–715.

Collier, Christopher. "The American People as Christian White Men of Property: Suffrage and Elections in Colonial and Early National America." In *Voting and the Spirit of American Democracy: Essays on the History of Voting and Voting Rights in America,* edited by Donald W. Rogers, 19–30. Urbana: University of Illinois Press, 1990.

Collins, Gail. *America's Women: Four Hundred Years of Dolls, Drudges, Helpmates, and Heroines.* NY: Harper Collins, 2004.

Conrad, Charles. "The Transformation of the 'Old Feminist' Movement." *Quarterly Journal of Speech* 67 (1981): 284–97.

Cooke, Miriam, and Angela Woollacott. "Introduction." In *Gendering War Talk,* edited by Miriam Cooke and Angela Woollacott, ix–xviii. Princeton, N.J.: Princeton University Press, 1993.

Corbett, Edward. "The Theory and Practice of Imitation in Classical Rhetoric." *College Composition and Communication* 22 (1971): 243–50.

Cott, Nancy F. "Across the Great Divide: Women in Politics Before and After 1920." In *One Woman, One Vote: Rediscovering the Woman Suffrage Movement,* edited by Marjorie Spruill Wheeler, 353–73. Troutdale, Ore.: New Sage Press, 1995.

———. "Divorce and the Changing Status of Women in Eighteenth Century Massachusetts." *William and Mary Quarterly,* 3rd series, 33 (1976): 586–614.

———. *The Grounding of Modern Feminism.* New Haven: Yale University Press, 1989.

———, ed. *History of Women in the United States: Historical Articles on Women's Lives and Activities,* vol. 19, part 1. Munich: K. G. Saur, 1992.

Croly, J. C. *The History of the Women's Club Movement in America.* New York: Henry B. Allen, 1898.

Cronin, Mary M. "Redefining Woman's Sphere: New England's Antebellum Female Textile Operatives' Magazines and the Response to the 'Cult of True Womanhood.'" *Journalism History* 25 (1999): 13–25.

Current, Richard N. *Northernizing the South.* Athens: University of Georgia Press, 1973.

Daley, Caroline, and Melanie Nolan, eds. *Suffrage and Beyond: International Feminist Perspectives.* New York: New York University Press, 1994.

Daniels, Roger. *Asian America: History of Chinese and Japanese in the United States since 1850.* Seattle: University of Washington Press, 1988.

———. "Chinese Exclusion: Causes and Consequences, 1882–1943." In *Who Belongs in America? Presidents, Rhetoric, and Immigration,* edited by Vanessa B. Beasley, 89–106. College Station: Texas A&M University Press, 2006.

Davis, Susan G. *Parades and Power: Street Theatre in Nineteenth-Century Philadelphia.* Philadelphia: Temple University Press, 1986.

DeGraaf, Lawrence B. "Race, Sex, and Region: Black Women in the America West, 1850–1920." *Pacific Historical Review* 49 (1980): 309–311.

Delsman, Mary A. *Everything You Need to Know about *ERA (*the Equal Rights Amendment).* Riverside, Calif.: Meranza Press, 1975.

De Pauw, Linda Grant. *Fortunes of War: New Jersey Women in the American Revolution.* Trenton: New Jersey Historical Commission, 1975.

De Royamont, Louis. *La Fayette et Rochambeau au Pays de Washington: La Guerre de l'Indépendance Américaine, 1776–1783.* Grenoble, France: J. Rey, 1919.

Deutsch, Sarah. "Landscape of Enclaves: Race Relations in the West, 1865–1990." In *Under Open Sky: Rethinking America's Western Past,* edited by William Cronon, George Miles, and Jay Gitlin, 110–31. New York: W. W. Norton, 1992.

Dexter, Elisabeth Anthony. *Colonial Women of Affairs: Women in Business and the Professions in America before 1776.* 2nd ed. New York: A. M. Kelley, 1972.

Dinkin, Robert J. *Voting in Provincial America: A Study of Elections in the Thirteen Colonies, 1689–1776.* Westport, Conn.: Greenwood Press, 1977.

Dippie, Brian. *The Vanishing American: White Attitudes and U.S. Indian Policy.* Lawrence: University of Kansas Press, 1991.

Ditz, Toby L. "Ownership and Obligation: Inheritance and Patriarchal Households in Connecticut, 1750–1820." *William and Mary Quarterly,* 3rd series, 47 (1990): 235–65.

Dorsey, Leroy G. "Preaching Morality in Modern America: Theodore Roosevelt's Rhetorical Progressivism." In *Rhetoric and Reform in the Progressive Era,* edited by J. Michael Hogan, 49–84. East Lansing: Michigan State University Press, 2003.

———, ed. *The Presidency and Rhetorical Leadership.* College Station: Texas A&M University Press, 2002.

Douglas, Ann. *The Feminization of American Culture.* New York: Anchor Press/Doubleday, 1977.

Dow, Bonnie J. "The 'Womanhood' Rationale in the Woman Suffrage Rhetoric of Frances E. Willard." *Southern Communication Journal* 56 (1991): 298–307.

Drinker, Sophie H. "Votes for Women in 18th-Century New Jersey." *Proceedings of the New Jersey Historical Society* 80 (1962): 34–42.

Druckman, Daniel. "Nationalism, Patriotism, and Group Loyalty: A Social Psychological Perspective." *Mershon International Studies Review* 38 (1994): 43–68.

Duberman, Martin. *Left Out: The Politics of Exclusion: Essays, 1964–1990.* New York: Basic Books, 1999.

Dubin, Michael J. *United States Congressional Elections, 1788–1997: The Official Results of the Elections of the 1st through 105th Congress.* Jefferson, N.C.: McFarland, 1998.

DuBois, Ellen Carol. *Feminism and Suffrage: The Emergence of an Independent Women's Movement in America, 1848–1869.* Ithaca, N.Y.: Cornell University Press, 1978.

———. *Harriot Stanton Blatch and the Winning of Woman Suffrage.* New Haven: Yale University Press, 1997.

———. "Introduction: The Invention of Women's Rights." In *Elizabeth Cady Stanton, Susan B. Anthony: Correspondence, Writings, Speeches,* edited by Gerda Lerner and Ellen Carol DuBois, 2–26. New York: Schocken Books, 1981.

———. "Outgrowing the Compact of the Fathers: Equal Rights, Woman Suffrage, and the United States Constitution, 1820–1878." *Journal of American History* 74 (1987): 836–62.

———. "Taking Law into Their Own Hands: Voting Women During Reconstruction." In *Voting and the Spirit of American Democracy: Essays on the History of Voting and Voting Rights in America,* edited by Donald W. Rogers, 67–81. Urbana: University of Illinois Press, 1990.

———. "Taking the Law into Our Own Hands: *Bradwell, Minor,* and Suffrage Militance in the 1870s." In *One Woman, One Vote: Rediscovering the Woman Suffrage Movement,* edited by Marjorie Spruill Wheeler, 82–98. Troutdale, Ore.: New Sage Press, 1995.

———. "Woman Suffrage around the World: Three Phases of Suffragist Internationalism." In *Suffrage and Beyond: International Feminist Perspectives,* edited by Caroline Daley and Melanie Nolan, 252–76. New York: New York University Press, 1994.

———. "Working Women, Class Relations, and Suffrage Militance: Harriot Stanton Blatch and the New York Woman Suffrage Movement, 1894–1909." *Journal of American History* 74 (1987): 34–58.

DuBois, Ellen Carol, Mari Jo Buhle, Temma Kaplan, Gerda Lerner, and Carroll Smith-Rosenberg. "Politics and Culture in Women's History: A Symposium." *Feminist Studies* 6 (1980): 26–64.

Duncan, Anne. *Performance and Identity in the Classical World.* Cambridge: Cambridge University Press, 2006.

Duncan, Christopher M. *The Anti-Federalists and Early American Political Thought.* DeKalb: Northern Illinois University Press, 1995.

Dura, Prasenjit. "Historicizing National Identity, or Who Imagines What and When." In *Becoming National: A Reader,* edited by Geoff Eley and Ronald Grigor Suny, 151–78. New York: Oxford University Press, 1996.

Durden, Robert F. *The Climax of Populism: The Election of 1896.* Lexington: University of Kentucky Press, 1965.

Dye, Nancy Schrom. *As Equals and as Sisters: Feminism, the Labor Movement, and the Women's Trade Union League of New York.* New York: Columbia University Press, 1980.

Early, Frances H. *A World without War: How U.S. Feminists and Pacifists Resisted World War I.* Syracuse: Syracuse University Press, 1997.

Ebert, Teresa L. "Gender and the Everyday: Toward a Postmodern Materialist Feminist Theory of Mimesis." In *"Turning the Century": Feminist Theory in the 1990s,* edited by Glynis Carr, 90–122. Cranbury, N.J.: Associated University Presses, 1992.

Edwards, Rebecca. *Angels in the Machinery: Gender in American Party Politics from the Civil War to the Progressive Era.* New York: Oxford University Press, 1997.

———. "Pioneers at the Polls: Woman Suffrage in the West." In *Votes for Women: The Struggle for Suffrage Revisited,* edited by Jean H. Baker, 151–74. Oxford: Oxford University Press, 2002.

Eley, Geoff, and Ronald Grigor Suny, eds. *Becoming National: A Reader.* New York: Oxford University Press, 1996.

———. "Introduction: From the Moment of Social History to the Work of Cultural Representation." In Eley and Suny, *Becoming National,* 3–38.

Else, G. "Imitation in the 5th Century." *Classical Philology* 53 (1958): 73–90.

Elshtain, Jean Bethke. "Antigone's Daughters." In *Feminism and Politics,* edited by Anne Phillips, 363–77. Oxford: Oxford University Press, 1998.

Enloe, Cynthia. *Maneuvers: The International Politics of Militarizing Women's Lives.* Los Angeles: University of California Press, 2000.

Evans, Richard J. *Comrades and Sisters: Feminism, Socialism and Pacifism in Europe, 1870–1945.* New York: St. Martin's Press, 1987.

———. *The Feminists: Women's Emancipation Movements in Europe, America, and Australasia, 1840–1920.* New York: Barnes & Noble, 1977.

Ferrell, Robert H. "Immigration and the Red Scare." In *Who Belongs in America? Presidents, Rhetoric, and Immigration,* edited by Vanessa B. Beasley, 134–48. College Station: Texas A&M University Press, 2006.

———. *Woodrow Wilson and World War I: 1917–1921.* New York: Harper & Row, 1985.

Fetherling, Dale. *Mother Jones, the Miners' Angel: A Portrait.* Carbondale: Southern Illinois University Press, 1974.

Flanagan, Jason C. "Woodrow Wilson's 'Rhetorical Restructuring': The Transformation of the American Self and the Construction of the German Enemy." *Rhetoric & Public Affairs* 7 (2004): 115–48.

Flexner, Eleanor, and Ellen Fitzpatrick. *Century of Struggle: The Woman's Rights*

Movement in the United States. Cambridge: Belknap Press of Harvard University Press, 1996.

Flexner, James Thomas. *George Washington and the New Nation (1783–1793).* Boston: Little, Brown, 1970.

Foner, Eric. "From Slavery to Citizenship: Blacks and the Right to Vote." In *Voting and the Spirit of American Democracy: Essays on the History of Voting and Voting Rights in America,* edited by Donald W. Rogers, 55–65. Urbana: University of Illinois Press, 1990.

Ford, Linda G. "Alice Paul and the Politics of Nonviolent Protest." In *Votes for Women: The Struggle for Suffrage Revisited,* edited by Jean H. Baker, 174–88. Oxford: Oxford University Press, 2002.

———. "Alice Paul and the Triumph of Militancy." In *One Woman, One Vote: Rediscovering the Woman Suffrage Movement,* edited by Marjorie Spruill Wheeler, 279–94. Troutdale, Ore.: New Sage Press, 1995.

———. *Iron-Jawed Angels: The Suffrage Militancy of the National Woman's Party, 1912–1920.* Lanham, Md.: University Press of America, 1991.

Formisano, Ronald P. *The Birth of Mass Political Parties: Michigan, 1827–1861.* Princeton, N.J.: Princeton University Press, 1970.

———. "Deferential-Participant Politics: The Early Republic's Political Culture." *American Political Science Review* 68 (1974): 473–87.

———. "Toward a Reorientation of Jacksonian Politics: A Review of the Literature, 1959–1975." *Journal of American History* 63 (1976–77): 42–65.

Frances, Hilary. "'Dare to be Free!': The Women's Freedom League and its Legacy." In *Votes for Women,* edited by June Purvis and Sandra Holton, 181–202. London: Routledge, 2000.

Frankel, Noralee, and Nancy S. Dye, eds. *Gender, Class, Race, and Reform in the Progressive Era.* Lexington: University Press of Kentucky, 1991.

Franklin, John Hope. *Reconstruction after the Civil War.* 2nd ed. Chicago: University of Chicago Press, 1994.

Freeman, Douglas Southall. *George Washington: A Biography,* vol. 6. New York: Charles Scribner's Sons, 1954.

Fuchs, Barbara. *Mimesis and Empire: The New World, Islam, and European Identities.* Cambridge: Cambridge University Press, 2001.

Gaines, James R. *For Liberty and Glory: Washington, Lafayette, and Their Revolutions.* New York: W. W. Norton, 2007.

Garroutte, Eva Marie. *Real Indians: Identity and the Survival of Native America.* Berkeley: University of California Press, 2003.

Gebauer, Gunter, and Christoph Wulf. *Mimesis: Culture, Art, & Society.* Translated by Don Reau. Berkeley: University of California Press, 1995.

Gerstle, Gary. *American Crucible: Race and Nation in the Twentieth Century.* Princeton, N.J.: Princeton University Press, 2001.

Gertzog, Irwin N. "Female Suffrage in New Jersey, 1790–1807." *Women & Politics* 11 (1990): 47–58.

Giddings, Paula. *When and Where I Enter: The Impact of Black Women on Race and Sex in America.* New York: W. Morrow, 1996.

Gifford, Carolyn De Swarte. "Home Protection: The WCTU's Conversion to Woman Suffrage." In *Gender, Ideology, and Action: Historical Perspectives on Women's Public Lives,* edited by Janet Sharistanian, 95–120. Westport, Conn.: Greenwood Press, 1986.

Gillespie, J. David. *Politics at the Periphery: Third Parties in Two-Party America.* Columbia: University of South Carolina Press, 1993.

Gilley, B. H. "Kate Gordon and Louisiana Woman Suffrage." In *History of Women in the United States: Historical Articles on Women's Lives and Activities,* vol. 19, edited by Nancy F. Cott, 254–71. Munich: K. G. Saur, 1992.

Ginzberg, Lori D. *Women and the Work of Benevolence: Morality, Politics, and Class in the 19th-Century United States.* New Haven: Yale University Press, 1990.

Girard, Rene. "Mimesis and Violence: Perspectives in Cultural Criticism." *Berkshire Review* 14 (1979): 9–19.

Gittell, Marilyn, and Teresa Shtob. "Changing Women's Roles in Political Volunteerism and Reform of the City." *Signs* 5 (1980 supplement): S67–S78.

Glenn, Evelyn Nakano. *Unequal Freedom: How Race and Gender Shaped American Citizenship and Labor.* Cambridge: Harvard University Press, 2002.

Goldberg, Michael Lewis. *An Army of Women: Gender and Politics in Gilded Age Kansas.* Baltimore: Johns Hopkins University Press, 1997.

———. "Non-Partisan and All-Partisan: Rethinking Woman Suffrage and Party Politics in Gilded Age Kansas." *Western Historical Quarterly* 25 (1994): 21–44.

Gordon, Ann D., ed. *African American Women and the Vote, 1837–1965.* Amherst: University of Massachusetts Press, 1997.

Gorn, Elliott J. *Mother Jones: The Most Dangerous Woman in America.* New York: Hill and Wang, 2001.

Gould, Lewis G. *The Modern American Presidency.* Lawrence: University Press of Kansas, 2003.

———. *The Presidency of Theodore Roosevelt.* Lawrence: University Press of Kansas, 1991.

Graham, Sara Hunter. "The Suffrage Renaissance: A New Image for a New Century, 1896–1910." In *One Woman, One Vote: Rediscovering the Woman Suffrage Movement,* edited by Marjorie Spruill Wheeler, 157–78. Troutdale, Ore.: New Sage Press, 1995.

———. "Woodrow Wilson, Alice Paul, and the Woman Suffrage Movement." *Political Science Quarterly* 98 (1983–1984): 665–79.

Green, Elna C. *Southern Strategies: Southern Women and the Woman Suffrage Question.* Chapel Hill: University of North Carolina Press, 1997.

Griffin, Leland M. "The Rhetoric of Historical Movements." *Quarterly Journal of Speech* 38 (1952): 184–88.

Griffith, Elisabeth. *In Her Own Right: The Life of Elizabeth Cady Stanton.* New York: Oxford University Press, 1984.

Griffiths, Gareth. *Women's Factory Work in World War I.* Wolfeboro Falls, N.H.: Alan Sutton, 1991.

Grimes, Alan. *The Puritan Ethic and Woman Suffrage.* New York: Oxford University Press, 1967.

Guide to U.S. Elections, vols. 1 and 2. 5th ed. Washington, D.C.: CQ Press, 2005.

Gulley, H. E. "Women and the Lost Cause: Preserving a Confederate Identity in the American Deep South." *Journal of Historical Geography* 19 (1993): 125–41.

Gundersen, Joan R. "Independence, Citizenship, and the American Revolution." *Signs* 13 (1987): 39–77.

Habermas, Jurgen. "The European Nation-State: Its Achievements and its Limits. On the Past and Future of Sovereignty and Citizenship." In *Mapping the Nation*, edited by Gopal Balakrishnan, 281–94. London: Verso, 1996.

Haney López, Ian F. *White by Law: The Legal Construction of Race*. New York: New York University Press, 1996.

Hargrove, Erwin C. *The President as Leader: Appealing to the Better Angels of Our Nature*. Lawrence: University Press of Kansas, 1998.

Harley, Sharon. "Northern Black Female Workers: Jacksonian Era." In *The Afro-American Woman: Struggles and Images*, edited by Sharon Harley and Rosalyn Terborg-Penn, 5–16. Port Washington, N.Y.: Kennikat Press, 1978.

———. "When Your Work Is Not Who You Are: The Development of a Working-Class Consciousness among Afro-American Women." In *Gender, Race, Class, and Reform in the Progressive Era*, edited by Noralee Frankel and Nancy S. Dye, 42–55. Lexington: University Press of Kentucky, 1991.

Harley, Sharon, and Rosalyn Terborg-Penn, eds. *The Afro-American Woman: Struggles and Images*. Port Washington, N.Y.: Kennikat Press, 1978.

Hartmann, Heidi. "Capitalism, Patriarchy, and Job Segregation by Sex." *Signs* 1 (1976): 137–69.

Hartz, Louis B. *The Liberal Tradition in America: An Interpretation of American Political Thought since the Revolution*. New York: Harcourt, Brace, & World, 1955.

Hatch, Alden. *Edith Bolling Wilson: First Lady Extraordinary*. New York: Dodd, Mead, 1961.

Hause, Steven C., with Anne R. Kenney. *Women's Suffrage and Social Politics in the French Third Republic*. Princeton, N.J.: Princeton University Press, 1984.

Hayden, Sara. "Negotiating Femininity and Power in the Early Twentieth Century West: Domestic Ideology and Feminine Style in Jeannette Rankin's Suffrage Rhetoric." *Communication Studies* 50 (1999): 83–102.

Hersh, Blanche Glassman. *The Slavery of Sex: Feminist Abolitionists in America*. Urbana: University of Illinois Press, 1978.

Hesseltine, William Best. *The Rise and Fall of Third Parties, from Anti-Masonry to Wallace*. Gloucester, Mass.: Public Affairs Press, 1957.

Hewitt, Nancy A. "Feminist Friends: Agrarian Quakers and the Emergence of Women's Rights in America." *Feminist Studies* 12 (1986): 27–49.

———. "Politicizing Domesticity: Anglo, Black, and Latin Women in Tampa's Progressive Movements." In *Gender, Race, Class, and Reform in the Progressive Era*, edited by Noralee Frankel and Nancy S. Dye, 25–41. Lexington: University Press of Kentucky, 1991.

Hicks, John D. *The Populist Revolt: A History of the Farmers' Alliance and the People's Party*. Lincoln: University of Nebraska Press, 1961.

Hill, Diane Elizabeth. "International Law for Women's Rights: The Equality Treaties Campaign of the National Women's [*sic*] Party and Reactions of the United States State Department and the National League of Women Voters (1928–1938)." PhD diss., University of California, Berkeley, 1999.

Hirsch, Marianne, and Evelyn Fox Keller, eds. *Conflicts in Feminism.* New York: Routledge, 1990.

Hobsbawm, E. J. *Nations and Nationalism since 1780: Programme, Myth, Reality.* 2nd ed. Cambridge: Cambridge University Press, 1992.

Hofstadter, Richard. *The Age of Reform: From Bryan to F.D.R.* New York: Alfred A. Knopf, 1968.

———. *The American Political Tradition and the Men Who Made It.* New York: Vintage Books, 1954.

———. *The Progressive Movement, 1900–1915.* Englewood Cliffs, N.J.: Prentice-Hall, 1963.

Hogan, J. Michael. "Introduction: Rhetoric and Reform in the Progressive Era." In *Rhetoric and Reform in the Progressive Era,* edited by J. Michael Hogan, vii–xvii. East Lansing: Michigan State University Press, 2003.

———. "Managing Dissent in the Catholic Church: A Reinterpretation of the Pastoral Letter on War and Peace." *Quarterly Journal of Speech* 75 (1989): 400–15.

———, ed. *Rhetoric and Reform in the Progressive Era.* Vol. 6 of *A Rhetorical History of the United States: Significant Moments in American Public Discourse,* edited by Martin J. Medhurst. East Lansing: Michigan State University Press, 2003.

Hoganson, Kristin L. *Fighting for American Manhood: How Gender Politics Provoked the Spanish-American and Philippine-American Wars.* New Haven: Yale University Press, 1998.

Holmes, Jonathan, and Adrian Streete, eds. *Refiguring Mimesis: Representation in Early Modern Literature.* Hertfordshire: University of Hertfordshire Press, 2005.

Holton, Sandra Stanley. "From Anti-Slavery to Suffrage Militancy: The Bright Circle, Elizabeth Cady Stanton and the British Women's Movement." In *Suffrage and Beyond: International Feminist Perspectives,* edited by Caroline Daley and Melanie Nolan, 213–33. New York: New York University Press, 1994.

———. "'To Educate Women into the Rebellion': Elizabeth Cady Stanton and the Creation of a Transatlantic Network of Radical Suffragists." *American Historical Review* 99 (1994): 1113–36.

Hoyt, Albert H. "The Name 'Columbia.'" *New England Historical and Genealogical Register* 40 (1886): 310–13.

Hutcheon, Linda. *A Theory of Parody: The Teachings of Twentieth-Century Art Forms.* New York: Methuen, 1985.

Huxman, Susan Schultz. "Perfecting the Rhetorical Vision of Woman's Rights: Elizabeth Cady Stanton, Anna Howard Shaw, and Carrie Chapman Catt." *Women's Studies in Communication* 23 (2000): 307–36.

Ijsseling, Samuel. *Mimesis: On Appearing and Being.* Kampen, Netherlands: Kok Pharos, 1997.

Iron-Jawed Angels. Home Box Office, 2004. DVD.

Irvine, William D. "Women's Right and the 'Rights of Man.'" In *Crisis and Renewal in France, 1918–1962,* edited by Kenneth Moure and Martin S. Alexander, 46–65. New York: Berghahn, 2002.

Irwin, Inez Haynes. *The Story of Alice Paul and the National Women's Party.* Fairfax, Va.: Denlinger's Publishers, 1977.

Isenberg, Nancy. *Sex and Citizenship in Antebellum America.* Chapel Hill: University of North Carolina Press, 1998.

Jacobs, Margaret D. "Resistance to the Rescue: The Indians of Bahapki and Mrs. Annie E. K. Bidwell." In *Writing the Range: Race, Class, and Culture in the Women's West,* edited by Elizabeth Jameson and Susan Armitage, 230–51. Norman: University of Oklahoma Press, 1997.

Jameson, Elizabeth, and Susan Armitage, eds. *Writing the Range: Race, Class, and Culture in the Women's West.* Norman: University of Oklahoma Press, 1997.

Jasinksi, James. "A Constitutive Framework for Rhetorical Historiography: Toward an Understanding of the Discursive (Re)Constitution of 'Constitution' in *The Federalist Papers.*" In *Doing Rhetorical History: Cases and Concepts,* edited by Kathleen J. Turner, 72–92. Tuscaloosa: University of Alabama Press, 1998.

Jayawardena, Kumari. *Feminism and Nationalism in the Third World.* 2nd ed. London: Zed Books, 1986.

Jeffrey, Julie Roy. "Women in the Southern Farmers' Alliance: A Reconsideration of the Role and Status of Women in the Late Nineteenth-Century South." *Feminist Studies* 3 (1975): 72–91.

Jensen, Kimberly. *Mobilizing Minerva: American Women in the First World War.* Urbana: University of Illinois Press, 2008.

Jenson, Deborah. *Trauma and its Representations: The Social Life of Mimesis in Post-Revolutionary France.* Baltimore: Johns Hopkins University Press, 2001.

Johnson, Kenneth R. "Kate Gordon and the Woman-Suffrage Movement in the South." In *History of Women in the United States: Historical Articles on Women's Lives and Activities,* vol. 19, edited by Nancy F. Cott, 226–52. Munich: K. G. Saur, 1992.

———. "White Racial Attitudes as a Factor in the Arguments against the Nineteenth Amendment." *Phylon* 31 (1970): 31–37.

Jones, Kathleen B. "Citizenship in a Woman-Friendly Polity." In *The Citizenship Debates: A Reade*r, edited by Gershon Shafir, 221–50. Minneapolis: University of Minnesota Press, 1998.

Jorgensen-Earp, Cheryl R. *"The Transfiguring Sword": The Just War of the Women's Social and Political Union.* Tuscaloosa: University of Alabama, 1997.

Kant, I. *Critique of Practical Reason and Other Works on the Theory of Ethics.* Translated by Thomas Kingsmill Abbott. London: Longmans, 1898.

Katz, Sherry J. "A Politics of Coalition: Socialist Women and the California Suffrage Movement, 1900–1911." In *One Woman, One Vote: Rediscovering the Woman Suffrage Movement,* edited by Marjorie Spruill Wheeler, 245–62. Troutdale, Ore.: New Sage Press, 1995.

Katzenstein, Caroline. *Lifting the Curtain: The State and National Woman Suffrage Campaigns in Pennsylvania as I Saw Them.* Philadelphia: Dorrance, 1955.

Kendall, Kathleen E. *Communication in the Presidential Primaries: Candidates and the Media: 1912–2000.* Westport, Conn.: Praeger Publishers, 2000.

Kent, Susan Kingsley. *Sex and Suffrage in Britain, 1860–1914*. Princeton, N.J.: Princeton University Press, 1987.

Kerber, Linda K. *Federalists in Dissent: Imagery and Ideology in Jeffersonian America*. Ithaca, N.Y.: Cornell University Press, 1970.

———. "'Ourselves and Our Daughters Forever': Women and the Constitution, 1787–1876." In *One Woman, One Vote: Rediscovering the Woman Suffrage Movement*, edited by Marjorie Spruill Wheeler, 21–36. Troutdale, Ore.: New Sage Press, 1995.

———. "The Paradox of Women's Citizenship in the Early Republic." *American Historical Review* 97 (1992): 349–78.

———. "The Republican Ideology of the Revolutionary Generation." *American Quarterly* 37 (1985): 474–95.

———. *Women of the Republic: Intellect and Ideology in Revolutionary America*. Chapel Hill: University of North Carolina Press, 1980.

Kerr, Andrea Moore. "White Women's Rights, Black Men's Wrongs, Free Love, Blackmail, and the Formation of the American Woman Suffrage Association." In *One Woman, One Vote: Rediscovering the Woman Suffrage Movement*, edited by Marjorie Spruill Wheeler, 61–80. Troutdale, Ore.: New Sage Press, 1995.

Kersh, Rogan. *Dreams of a More Perfect Union*. Ithaca, N.Y.: Cornell University Press, 2001.

Kessler-Harris, Alice. "Women, Work, and the Social Order." In *Liberating Women's History*, edited by Berenice A. Carroll, 330–43. Urbana: University of Illinois Press, 1976.

Kettner, James. "The Development of American Citizenship in the Revolutionary Era: The Idea of Volitional Allegiance." *American Journal of Legal History* 18 (1974): 208–12.

Key, V. O. *Politics, Parties, and Pressure Groups*. 5th ed. New York: Thomas Y. Crowell, 1964.

Keyssar, Alexander. *The Right to Vote: The Contested History of Democracy in United States*. New York: Basic Books, 2000.

Khan, B. Zorina. "Married Women's Property Laws and Female Commercial Activity: Evidence from United States Patent Records, 1790–1895." *Journal of Economic History* 56 (1996): 356–88.

Kleppner, Paul. *Who Voted? The Dynamics of Electoral Turnout, 1870–1980*. New York: Praeger, 1982.

Klinghoffer, Judith Apter, and Lois Elkis. "'The Petticoat Electors': Women's Suffrage in New Jersey, 1776–1807." *Journal of the Early Republic* 12 (1992): 159–93.

Kloppenberg, James T. "The Virtues of Liberalism: Christianity, Republicanism, and Ethics in Early American Political Discourse." *Journal of American History* 74 (1987): 9–33.

Knupfer, Anne Meis. *Toward a Tenderer Humanity and a Nobler Womanhood: African American Women's Clubs in Turn of the Century Chicago*. New York: New York University Press, 1996.

Kowal, Donna M. "One Cause, Two Paths: Militant v. Adjustive Strategies in the British and American Women's Suffrage Movements." *Communication Quarterly* 48 (2000): 240–55.

Kruman, Marc. *Between Authority and Liberty: State Constitution Making in Revolutionary America.* Chapel Hill: University of North Carolina Press, 1997.

Kuhlman, Erika A. *Petticoats and White Feathers: Gender Conformity, Race, and the Progressive Peace Movement, and the Debate Over War, 1895–1919.* Westport, Conn.: Greenwood Press, 1997.

Ladd-Taylor, Molly. "Hull House Goes to Washington: Women and the Children's Bureau." In *Gender, Class, Race, and Reform in the Progressive Era,* edited by Noralee Frankel and Nancy S. Dye, 110–26. Lexington: University Press of Kentucky, 1991.

Lake, Marilyn. "Between Old Worlds and New: Feminist Citizenship, Nation and Race, the Destabilisation of Identity." In *Suffrage and Beyond: International Feminist Perspectives,* edited by Caroline Daley and Melanie Nolan, 277–94. New York: New York University Press, 1994.

Lakey, George. "Technique and Ethos in Nonviolent Action: The Woman Suffrage Cause." *Sociological Inquiry* 38 (1968): 37–42.

Landes, Joan. *Women and the Public Sphere in the Age of the French Revolution.* Ithaca, N.Y.: Cornell University Press, 1988.

Landsman, Gail H. "The 'Other' as Political Symbol: Images of Indians in the Woman Suffrage Movement." *Ethnohistory* 39 (1992): 247–84.

Laracey, Mel. *Presidents and the People: The Partisan Story of Going Public.* College Station: Texas A&M University Press, 2002.

Larson, Thomas A. "Dolls, Vassals, and Drudges: Pioneer Women in the West." *Western Historical Quarterly* 3 (1972): 5–16.

———. "Woman Suffrage in Western America." *Utah Historical Quarterly* 38 (1970): 7–19.

Leff, Michael. "Hermeneutical Rhetoric." In *Rhetoric and Hermeneutics in Our Time: A Reader,* edited by Walter Jost and Michael J. Hyde, 196–214. New Haven: Yale University Press, 1997.

Lemons, J. Stanley. *The Woman Citizen: Social Feminism in the 1920s.* Charlottesville: University Press of Virginia, 1990.

Lerner, Elinor. "Immigrant and Working Class Involvement in the New York City Woman Suffrage Movement, 1905–1917: A Study in Progressive Era Politics." PhD diss., University of California, Berkeley, 1981.

Lerner, Gerda. "Black and White Women in Interaction and Confrontation." In *Prospects: An Annual of American Cultural Studies,* vol. 2, edited by Jack Salzman, 193–208. New York: Burt Franklin, 1976.

———. "The Lady and the Mill Girl: Changes in the Status of Women in the Age of Jackson." *American Studies* 10 (1969): 5–15.

Levin, Phyllis Lee. *Edith and Woodrow: The Wilson White House.* New York: Scribner, 2001.

Levine, Susan. *Labor's True Woman: Carpet Weavers, Industrialization, and Labor Reform in the Gilded Age.* Philadelphia: Temple University Press, 1984.

Lewis, Jan. "'Of Every Age Sex & Condition': The Representation of Women in the Constitution." *Journal of the Early Republic* 15 (1995): 359–88.

———. "The Republican Wife: Virtue and Seduction in the Early Republic." *William and Mary Quarterly* 44 (1987): 689–721.

Link, Arthur S. *Woodrow Wilson: A Brief Biography.* Cleveland: World Publishing, 1963.

Llobera, Josep R. *Foundations of National Identity: From Catalonia to Europe.* New York: Berghahn Books, 2004.

Locke, John. *An Essay Concerning Human Understanding.* Edited by Kenneth P. Winkler. Indianapolis: Hackett Publishing, 1996.

———. *The Second Treatise of Government.* New York: Barnes & Noble, 2004. Originally published 1690.

———. *Two Treatises of Government.* 2nd ed. Edited by Peter Laslett. London: Cambridge University Press, 1967.

Logan, Shirley Wilson. *"We Are Coming": The Persuasive Discourse of Nineteenth-Century Black Women.* Carbondale: Southern Illinois University Press, 1999.

———, ed. *With Pen and Voice: A Critical Anthology of Nineteenth-Century African-American Women.* Carbondale: Southern Illinois University Press, 1995.

Lucas, Stephen E. "The Rhetorical Ancestry of the Declaration of Independence." *Rhetoric & Public Affairs* 1 (1998): 143–84.

———. "Theodore Roosevelt's 'The Man with the Muck-Rake': A Reinterpretation." *Quarterly Journal of Speech* 59 (1973): 452–63.

Luibheid, Eithne. *Entry Denied: Policing Sexuality at the Border.* Minneapolis: University of Minnesota Press, 2002.

Luibheid, Eithne, and Lionel Cantu, eds. *Migrations: Sexuality, U.S. Citizenship, and Border Crossings.* Minneapolis: University of Minnesota Press, 2005.

Lumsden, Linda J. *Rampant Women: Suffragists and the Right of Assembly.* Knoxville: University of Tennessee Press, 1997.

———. "Suffragist: Making of a Militant." *Journalism and Mass Communication Quarterly* 72 (1995): 525–38.

Lunardini, Christine A. *From Equal Suffrage to Equal Rights: Alice Paul and the National Woman's Party, 1910–1928.* New York: New York University Press, 1986.

Lunardini, Christine A., and Thomas J. Knock. "Woodrow Wilson and Woman Suffrage: A New Look." *Political Science Quarterly* 95 (1980–1981): 655–71.

MacLeod, Arlene Elowe. "Hegemonic Relations and Gender Resistance: The New Veiling as Accommodating Protest in Cairo." *Signs* 17 (1992): 533–57.

Maddux, Kristy. "When Patriots Protest: The Anti-Suffrage Discursive Transformation of 1917." *Rhetoric & Public Affairs* 7 (2004): 283–310.

Magee, James. *Freedom of Expression.* Westport, Conn.: Greenwood Press, 2002.

Manzanas, Ana María, and Jesús Benito. *Intercultural Mediations: Hybridity and Mimesis in American Literatures.* Münster, Germany: Die Deutsche Bibliothek, 2003.

Marshall, T. H. *Citizenship and Social Class.* Cambridge, UK: Cambridge University Press, 1950.

Matthews, Glenna. *The Rise of the Public Woman.* New York: Oxford University Press, 1992.

Mayer, Tamar. "Gender Ironies of Nationalism: Setting the Stage." In *Gender Iro-*

nies of Nationalism: Sexing the Nation, edited by Tamar Mayer, 1–24. London: Routledge, 2000.

McCaffrey, Enda. *The Gay Republic: Sexuality, Citizenship and Subversion in France.* Hampshire, UK: Ashgate Publishing, 2005.

McCammon, Holly J. "'Out of the Parlors and into the Streets': The Changing Tactical Repertoire of the U.S. Women's Suffrage Movements." *Social Forces* 81 (2003): 787–818.

———. "Stirring Up Suffrage Sentiment: The Formation of State Woman Suffrage Organizations, 1866–1914." *Social Forces* 80 (2001): 449–80.

McCammon, Holly J., and Karen E. Campbell. "Winning the Vote in the West: The Political Successes of the Women's Suffrage Movements, 1866–1919." *Gender & Society* 15 (2001): 55–82.

McCammon, Holly J., Karen E. Campbell, Ellen M. Granberg, and Christine Mowery. "How Movements Win: Gendered Opportunity Structures and U.S. Women's Suffrage Movements, 1866–1919." *American Sociological Review* 66 (2001): 49–70.

McCormick, Richard P. "Ethno-Cultural Interpretations of Nineteenth-Century American Voting Behavior." *Political Science Quarterly* 89 (1974): 351–77.

———. *The History of Voting in New Jersey: A Study in the Development of Election Machinery, 1664–1911.* New Brunswick, N.J.: Rutgers University Press, 1953.

———. "New Perspectives on Jacksonian Politics." *American Historical Review* 65 (1956–60): 288–301.

McGee, Michael C. "In Search of 'The People': A Rhetorical Alternative." *Quarterly Journal of Speech* 61 (1975): 235–49.

McGerr, Michael. "Political Style and Women's Power, 1830–1930." *Journal of American History* 77 (1990): 864–85.

McKeon, Richard. "Literary Criticism and the Concept of Imitation in Antiquity." *Modern Philology* 34 (1936): 1–35.

McWilliams, Wilson Carey, and Michael T. Gibbons, eds. *The Federalists, the Antifederalists, and the American Political Tradition.* New York: Greenwood Press, 1992.

Mead, Rebecca J. *How the Vote Was Won: Woman Suffrage in the Western United States, 1868–1914.* New York: New York University Press, 2004.

Medhurst, Martin J., ed. *Beyond the Rhetorical Presidency.* College Station: Texas A&M University Press, 1996.

———. "A Tale of Two Constructs: The Rhetorical Presidency versus Presidential Rhetoric." In Medhurst, *Beyond the Rhetorical Presidency,* xi–xxvi.

Mehta, Uday S. "Liberal Strategies of Exclusion." *Politics and Society* 18 (1990): 427–54.

Melberg, Arne. *Theories of Mimesis.* Cambridge, UK: Cambridge University Press, 1995.

Melder, Keith. *The Beginnings of Sisterhood: The American Women's Rights Movement, 1800–1850.* New York: Schocken Books, 1977.

Merriam, Charles E., and Louise Overacker. *Primary Elections.* Chicago: University of Chicago Press, 1928.

Meyer, Herman. *The Poetics of Quotation in the European Novel.* Princeton, N.J.: Princeton University Press, 1968.

Mihesuah, Devon, ed. *Natives and Academics: Writing about American Indians.* Lincoln: University of Nebraska Press, 1998.

Milkis, Sidney M., and Michael Nelson. *The American Presidency: Origins and Developments: 1776–1998.* 3rd ed. Washington, D.C.: Congressional Quarterly Press, 1999.

Miller, Nathan. *Theodore Roosevelt: A Life.* New York: William Morrow, 1992.

Miller, Sally M., ed. *Race, Ethnicity, and Gender in Early Twentieth-Century American Socialism.* New York: Garland Publishing, 1996.

Miller, Worth Robert. *Oklahoma Populism: A History of the People's Party in the Oklahoma Territory.* Norman: University of Oklahoma Press, 1987.

Millis, Walter. *Road to War: America, 1914–1917.* Boston: Houghton Mifflin, 1935.

Mitchell, David. *Women on the Warpath: The Story of the Women of the First World War.* London: Lowe and Brydone, 1965.

Mohanty, Chandra Talpade. "Feminist Encounters: Locating the Politics of Experience." In *Feminism and Politics,* edited by Anne Phillips, 254–72. Oxford: Oxford University Press, 1998.

Moller, Herbert. "Sex Composition, and Correlated Culture Patterns of Colonial America." *William and Mary Quarterly* 2 (1945): 113–53.

Montesquieu. *The Spirit of the Laws.* Translated by Thomas Nugent. New York: Hafner Press, 1949.

Morgan, David. *Suffragists and Democrats: The Politics of Woman Suffrage in America.* East Lansing: Michigan State University Press, 1972.

Morgan, Edmund S. *Inventing the People: The Rise of Popular Sovereignty in England and America.* New York: Norton, 1988.

Morgan, Robin, ed. *Sisterhood Is Forever: The Women's Anthology for a New Millennium.* New York: Washington Square Press, 2003.

———, ed. *Sisterhood Is Global: The International Women's Movement Anthology.* New York: Feminist Press, 1996.

Morris, Richard B. *Studies in the History of American Law, with Special Reference to Seventeenth and Eighteenth Centuries.* 2nd ed. New York: Octagon Books, 1959.

Mowry, George E. *The Era of Theodore Roosevelt and the Birth of Modern America, 1900–1912.* New York: Harper and Row, 1958.

———. *Theodore Roosevelt and the Progressive Movement.* New York: Hill and Wang, 1946.

Murray, Judith Sargent. "On the Equality of the Sexes." *Massachusetts Magazine* 2 (March 1790): 132–35, (April 1790): 223–26.

Myres, Sandra L. "Suffering for Suffrage: Western Women and the Struggle for Political, Legal, and Economic Rights." In *Westering Women and the Frontier Experience, 1800–1915,* edited by Sandra L. Myres, 212–36. Albuquerque: University of New Mexico Press, 1982.

Nash, Howard P., Jr. *Third Parties in American Politics.* Washington, D.C.: Public Affairs Press, 1959.

National Association of Colored Women's Clubs (NACWC). *A History of the Club Movement among the Colored Women of the United States of America.* Washington, D.C.: NACWC, 1902.

Nelson, Michael, ed. *The Evolving Presidency: Addresses, Cases, Essays, Letters, Reports, Resolutions, Transcripts, and Other Landmark Documents, 1787–1998.* Washington, D.C.: Congressional Quarterly Press, 1999.

———. "Theodore Roosevelt's and William Howard Taft's Theories of Presidential Power." In Nelson, *The Evolving Presidency,* 93–94.

Ness, Immanuel, and James Ciment, eds. *The Encyclopedia of Third Parties in America,* vols. 1–3. Armonk, N.Y.: Sharpe Reference, 2000.

Neumann, Caryn Ellen. "The National Woman's Party and the Equal Rights Amendment, 1945–1977." PhD diss., Florida Atlantic University, 1994.

Newbold La Motte, Ellen. *The Backwash of War: The Human Wreckage of the Battlefield as Witnessed by an American Hospital Nurse.* New York: G. P. Putnam's Sons, 1934.

Newman, Louise Michele. *White Women's Rights: The Racial Origins of Feminism in the United States.* New York: Oxford University Press, 1999.

Norton, Mary Beth. "The Evolution of White Women's Experience in Early America." *American Historical Review* 89 (1984): 593–619.

———. *Founding Mothers and Fathers: Gendered Power and the Forming of American Society.* New York: Alfred A. Knopf, 1996.

———. *Liberty's Daughters: The Revolutionary Experience of American Women, 1750–1800.* Ithaca, N.Y.: Cornell University Press, 1996.

Nugent, Walter T. K. *The Tolerant Populists: Kansas Populism and Nativism.* Chicago: University of Chicago Press, 1963.

O'Leary-Archer, Lynne M. "The Contentious Community: The Impact of Internecine Conflict of the National Woman's Party, 1920–1947." PhD diss., University of Southern California, 1988.

Pardo, Thomas C. *The National Woman's Party Papers, 1913–1974: A Guide to the Microform Edition.* Sanford, N.C.: Microfilming Corporation of America, 1979.

Parker, Andrew, Mary Russo, Doris Sommer, and Patricia Yaeger. "Introduction." In *Nationalisms and Sexualities,* edited by Andrew Parker, Mary Russo, Doris Sommer, and Patricia Yaeger, 1–18. New York: Routledge, 1992.

Parsons, Stanley B. *The Populist Context: Rural versus Urban Power on a Great Plains Frontier.* Westport, Conn.: Greenwood Press, 1973.

Pateman, Carole. *The Disorder of Women: Democracy, Feminism, and Political Theory* Stanford: Stanford University Press, 1989.

———. *The Sexual Contract.* Stanford: Stanford University Press, 1988.

Patterson, David S. *The Search for Negotiated Peace: Women's Activism and Citizen Diplomacy in World War I.* New York: Routledge, 2008.

Pauley, Matthew A. *I Do Solemnly Swear: The President's Constitutional Oath.* Lanham, Md.: University Press of America, 1999.

Paulson, John. "Theodore Roosevelt and the Rhetoric of Citizenship: On Tour in New England, 1902." *Communication Quarterly* 50 (2002): 123–34.

Peffer, William A. *Populism, Its Rise and Fall.* Edited by Peter H. Argersinger. Lawrence: University of Kansas Press, 1992.

Peterson, Carla. "A 'Sign unto This Nation': Sojourner Truth, History, Orature, and Modernity." In *Black Women's Intellectual Traditions: Speaking Their Minds,* edited by Kristin Waters and Carol B. Conaway, 129–70. Burlington: University of Vermont Press, 2007.

Philbrook, Mary. "Woman's Suffrage in New Jersey Prior to 1807." *Proceedings of the New Jersey Historical Society* 57 (1939): 87–98.

Phillips, Anne, ed. *Feminism and Politics.* Oxford: Oxford University Press, 1998.

Pickering, Jean, and Suzanne Kehde, eds. *Narratives of Nostalgia, Gender, and Nationalism.* New York: New York University Press, 1997.

Plato. *Plato: The Collected Dialogues.* Edited by Edith Hamilton and Huntington Cairns. Translated by A. E. Taylor. Princeton, N.J.: Princeton University Press, 1989.

Pocock, J. G. A. *The Machiavellian Moment: Florentine Political Thought and the Atlantic Republican Tradition.* Princeton, N.J.: Princeton University Press, 1975.

———. *Virtue, Commerce, and History: Essays on Political Thought and History, Chiefly in the Eighteenth Century.* Cambridge: Harvard University Press, 1985.

Pole, J. R. "Suffrage Reform and the American Revolution in New Jersey." *Proceedings of the New Jersey Historical Society* 74 (1956): 173–93.

Porter, Kirk H., and Donald Bruce Johnson, comps. *National Party Platforms: 1840–1960.* Urbana: University of Illinois Press, 1961.

Portnoy, Alisse. *Their Right to Speak: Women's Activism in the Indian and Slave Debates.* Cambridge: Harvard University Press, 2005.

Potolsky, Matthew. *Mimesis.* New York: Routledge, 2006.

Potter, David M. *The South and the Sectional Conflict.* Baton Rouge: Louisiana State University Press, 1968.

Pringle, Henry F. *Theodore Roosevelt: A Biography.* New York: Harcourt, Brace, 1931.

Purvis, June, and Sandra Holton, eds. *Votes for Women.* London: Routledge, 2000.

Rabinowitz, Howard N. *The First New South.* Arlington Heights, Ill.: Harlan Davidson, 1992.

Rawls, John A. *A Theory of Justice.* Cambridge: Belknap Press of Harvard University Press, 1971.

Ray, Angela G. "The Permeable Public: Rituals of Citizenship in Antebellum Men's Debating Clubs." *Argumentation & Advocacy* 41 (2004): 1–16.

———. "The Rhetorical Ritual of Citizenship: Women's Voting as Public Performance, 1868–1875." *Quarterly Journal of Speech* 93 (2007): 1–26.

Ray, P. Orman. "The World-Wide Woman Suffrage Movement." *Journal of Comparative Legislation and International Law,* 3rd series, 1 (1919): 220–38.

Reardon, Betty A. *Sexism and the War System.* New York: Teachers College Press, 1985.

Rendall, Jane. "Citizenship, Culture, and Civilisation: The Languages of British Suffragists, 1866–1874." In *Suffrage and Beyond: International Feminist Perspectives,* edited by Caroline Daley and Melanie Nolan, 127–50. New York: New York University Press, 1994.

Reynolds, David. *Democracy Unbound: Progressive Challenges to the Two Party System.* Boston: South End Press, 1997.

Rice, Howard C., Jr., and Anne S. K. Brown, eds. *The American Campaigns of Rochambeau's Army, 1780, 1781, 1782, 1783.* Princeton, N.J.: Princeton University Press, 1972.

Rigolot, François. "The Renaissance Crisis of Exemplarity." *Journal of the History of Ideas* 59 (1998): 557–63.

Rodgers, Katharine M. "Republicanism: The Career of a Concept." *Journal of American History* 79 (1992): 11–38.

Rogers, Donald W. "Introduction: The Right to Vote in American History." In Rogers, *Voting and the Spirit of American Democracy,* 8–9.

———, ed. *Voting and the Spirit of American Democracy: Essays on the History of Voting and Voting Rights in America.* Urbana: University of Illinois Press, 1990.

Roosevelt, Theodore. "Debate on Proper Scope of Presidential Power and Leadership." In *The Evolving Presidency: Addresses, Cases, Essays, Letters, Reports, Resolutions, Transcripts, and Other Landmark Documents, 1787–1998,* 95. Washington, D.C.: Congressional Quarterly Press, 1999.

Rose, Margaret. *Parody/Metafiction.* London: Croom Helm, 1979.

Rosen, Andrew. *Rise Up, Women! The Militant Campaign of the Women's Social and Political Union, 1903–1914.* London: Routledge & Kegan Paul, 1974.

Rosenstone, Steven, Roy L. Behr, and Edward H. Lazarus. *Third Parties in America: Citizen Response to Major Party Failure.* Princeton, N.J.: Princeton University Press, 1984.

Rouse, Jacqueline A. "Atlanta's African-American Women's Attack on Segregation, 1900–1920." In *Gender, Class, Race, and Reform in the Progressive Era,* edited by Noralee Frankel and Nancy S. Dye, 10–23. Lexington: University Press of Kentucky, 1991.

Rousseau, Jean-Jacques. "Discourse on the Sciences and Arts." In *The First and Second Discourses,* edited by Roger D. Masters. New York: St. Martin's Press, 1964.

———. *The Social Contract.* Translated by Maurice Cranston. Middlesex, UK: Penguin Books, 1968.

Rowbotham, Sheila. *Women in Movement: Feminism in Social Action.* New York: Routledge, 1992.

Rupp, Leila J., and Verta A. Taylor. *Survival in the Doldrums: The American Women's Rights Movement, 1945 to the 1960s.* New York: Oxford University Press, 1987.

Ryan, Mary P. "The Power of Women's Networks: A Case Study of Female Moral Reform in Antebellum America." *Feminist Studies* 5 (1979): 66–85.

Sachs, Albie, and Joan Hoff Wilson. *Sexism and the Law: A Study of Male Beliefs and Legal Bias in Britain and the United States.* New York: Free Press, 1979.

Salmon, Marylynn. *Women and the Law of Property in Early America.* Chapel Hill: University of North Carolina Press, 1986.

Sandoval, Chela. "U.S. Third World Feminism: The Theory and Method of Oppositional Consciousness in the Postmodern World." *Genders* 10 (1991): 1–24.

Sapiro, Virginia. "Women, Citizenship, and Nationality: Immigration and Naturalization Policies in the United States." *Politics & Society* 13 (1984): 1–26.

Saunders, Frances Wright. *Ellen Axson Wilson: First Lady between Two Worlds.* Chapel Hill: University of North Carolina Press, 1985.

Saxton, Alexander. *The Indispensable Enemy: Labor and the Anti-Chinese Movement in California.* Berkeley: University of California Press, 1971.

Schechter, Patricia A. *Ida B. Wells-Barnett and American Reform, 1880–1930.* Chapel Hill: University of North Carolina Press, 2001.

Schneider, Dorothy, and Carl J. Schneider. *Into the Breach: American Women Overseas in World War I.* New York: Viking Press, 1991.

Schoen, Douglas E. *Declaring Independence: The Beginning of the End of the Two-Party System.* New York: Random House, 2008.

Schofield, Ann. "Rebel Girls and Union Maids: The Woman Question in the Journals of the AFL and IWW, 1905–1920." *Feminist Studies* 9 (1983): 335–58.

Schudson, Michael. *The Good Citizen: A History of American Civic Life.* New York: Free Press, 1998.

Seimers, David J. *Ratifying the Republic: Antifederalists and Federalists in Constitutional Time.* Stanford: Stanford University Press, 2002.

Selig, Robert A. *Rochambeau in Connecticut, Tracing His Journey: Historic and Architectural Survey.* Hartford: Connecticut Historical Commission, 1999.

Shachtman, Tom. *Edith and Woodrow: A Presidential Romance.* New York: G. P. Putnam's Sons, 1981.

Shafir, Gershon, ed. *The Citizenship Debates: A Reader.* Minneapolis: University of Minnesota Press, 1998.

———. "Introduction." In Shafir, *The Citizenship Debates,* 1–30.

Shalhope, Robert E. "Republicanism in Early American Historiography." *William and Mary Quarterly* 39 (1982): 334–56.

———. "Toward a Republican Synthesis: The Emergence of an Understanding of Republicanism in American Historiography." *William and Mary Quarterly* 29 (1972): 49–80.

Shammas, Carole. "Re-assessing the Married Woman's Property Acts." *Journal of Women's History* 6 (1994): 9–30.

Siegel, Reva B. "Home as Work: The First Woman's Rights Claims Concerning Wives' Household Labor, 1850–1880." *Yale Law Journal* 103 (1994): 1073–1217.

Sillars, Malcolm O. "Defining Movements Rhetorically: Casting the Widest Net." *Southern Speech Communication Journal* 46 (1980): 17–32.

Silva, Chandra. "Esto Perpetua: The Persistence and Transformation of Feminism in Idaho through the Struggle to Ratify the Equal Rights Amendment." PhD diss., Washington State University, 2005.

Simons, Herbert W. "Requirements, Problems, and Strategies: A Theory of Persuasion for Social Movements." *Quarterly Journal of Speech* 56 (1970): 1–11.

Sims, Anastasia. "Armageddon in Tennessee: The Final Battle over the Nineteenth Amendment." In *One Woman, One Vote: Rediscovering the Woman Suffrage Movement,* edited by Marjorie Spruill Wheeler, 333–52. Troutdale, Ore.: New Sage Press, 1995.

Sinclair, Barbara. "Party Leadership and Policy Change." In *Congress and Policy Change,* edited by Gerald C. Wright Jr., Leroy N. Rieselbach, and Lawrence C. Dodd. New York: Agathon Press, 2003.

Slagell, Amy R. "The Rhetorical Structure of Frances E. Willard's Campaign for Woman Suffrage, 1876–1896." *Rhetoric & Public Affairs* 4 (2001): 1–23.

Slaughter, Jane, and Robert Kern, eds. *European Women on the Left: Socialism, Feminism, and the Problems Faced by Political Women, 1880 to the Present.* Westport, Conn.: Greenwood Press, 1981.

Smallwood, Frank. *The Other Candidates: Third Parties in Presidential Elections.* Hanover, N.H.: University Press of New England, 1983.

Smith, Anthony D. "The Nation: Real or Imagined?" In *People, Nation and State: The Meaning of Ethnicity and Nationalism,* edited by Edward Mortimer, 36–42. London: I. B. Tauris, 1999.

Smith, Bonnie. *Changing Lives: Women in European History.* Lexington, Mass.: D. C. Heath, 1989.

———. *Ladies of the Leisure Class: The Bourgeoises of Northern France in the Nineteenth Century.* Princeton, N.J.: Princeton University Press, 1981.

Smith, Craig R. "The Aliens Are Coming: The Federalist Attack on the First Amendment." In *Who Belongs in America? Presidents, Rhetoric, and Immigration,* edited by Vanessa B. Beasley, 37–60. College Station: Texas A&M University Press, 2006.

Smith, Hilda L. *Reason's Disciples: Seventeenth Century English Feminists.* Urbana: University of Illinois Press, 1982.

Smith, Paul. *Feminism and the Third Republic: Women's Political and Civil Rights in France, 1918–1945.* Oxford: Oxford University Press, 1996.

Smith, Rogers M. *Civic Ideals: Conflicting Visions of Citizenship in U.S. History.* New Haven: Yale University Press, 1997.

Smith-Rosenberg, Carroll. "Beauty, the Beast, and the Militant Woman: A Case Study in Sex Roles and Social Stress in Jacksonian America." *American Quarterly* 23 (1971): 562–84.

———. "The Female World of Love and Ritual: Relations between Women in Nineteenth-Century America." *Signs* 1 (1975): 1–29.

Sörbom, Goran. *Mimesis and Art: Studies in the Origin and Early Development of an Aesthetic Vocabulary.* Stockholm: Svenska Bokforlaget, 1966.

Sowerwine, Charles. "Socialism, Feminism, and the Socialist Women's Movement from the French Revolution to World War II." In *Becoming Visible: Women in European History,* 3rd ed., edited by Renate Bridenthal, Merry E. Wiesner, and Susan Mosher Stuard, ch. 13. Boston: Houghton Mifflin, 2006.

Spitzer, Robert J. *The Right to Life Movement and Third Party Politics.* New York: Greenwood Press, 1987.

Sproule, J. Michael. *Propaganda and Democracy: The American Experience of Media and Mass Persuasion.* Cambridge, UK: Cambridge University Press, 1997.

Spruill, Julia Cherry. *Women's Life and Work in the Southern Colonies.* Chapel Hill: University of North Carolina Press, 1938.

Stanley, Amy Dru. "Conjugal Bonds and Wage Labor: Rights of Contract in the Age of Emancipation." *Journal of American History* 75 (1988): 471–500.

Stansell, Christine. *City of Women: Sex and Class in New York, 1789–1860.* Urbana: University of Illinois Press, 1982.

Steele, Thomas J. "The Figure of Columbia: Phillis Wheatley plus George Washington." *New England Quarterly* 54 (1981): 264–66.

Steinberg, Marc W. "The Roar of the Crowd: Repertoires of Discourse and Collective Action among the Spitafields Silk Weavers in Nineteenth-Century London." In *Repertoires & Cycles of Collective Action,* edited by Mark Traugott, 57–80. Durham, N.C.: Duke University Press, 1995.

Steinfeld, Robert J. "Property and Suffrage in the Early Republic." *Stanford Law Review* 41 (1998): 335–76.

Stepan, Nancy Leys. "Race, Gender, Science and Citizenship." *Gender and History* 10 (1998): 26–52.

Stevens, Doris. *Jailed for Freedom: American Women Win the Vote.* Edited by Carole O'Hare. Troutdale, Ore.: New Sage Press, 1995.

Stiglmayer, Alexandria, ed. *Mass Rape: The War against Women in Bosnia-Herzegovina.* Lincoln: University of Nebraska Press, 1994.

Stillion Southard, Belinda A. "Militancy, Power, and Identity: The Silent Sentinels as Women Fighting for Political Voice." *Rhetoric & Public Affairs* 10 (2007): 399–417.

Stone, Geoffrey R. *Perilous Times: Free Speech in Wartime: From the Sedition Act of the 1790s to the War on Terrorism.* New York: W. W. Norton, 2004.

Storing, Herbert J. *The Complete Anti-Federalist.* Chicago: University of Chicago Press, 1981.

Streitmatter, Roger. *Raising Her Voice: African-American Woman Journalists Who Changed History.* Lexington: University Press of Kentucky, 1994.

Strom, Sharon Hartman. "Leadership and Tactics in the American Woman Suffrage Movement: A New Perspective from Massachusetts." *Journal of American History* 62 (1975): 296–315.

Stuckey, Mary E. *Defining Americans: The Presidency and National Identity.* Lawrence: University Press of Kansas, 2004.

———. "'The Domain of Public Conscience': Woodrow Wilson and the Establishment of a Transcendent Political Order." *Rhetoric & Public Affairs* 6 (2003): 1–24.

Stuckey, Mary E., and Frederick J. Antczak. "The Rhetorical Presidency: Deepening Vision, Widening Exchange." *Communication Yearbook* 21 (1998): 405–41.

Sullivan, Dale. "Attitudes toward Imitation: Classical Culture and the Modern Temper." *Rhetoric Review* 8 (1989): 5–21.

———. "The Decline of Imitation in Eighteenth and Nineteenth Century Rhetoric." *Platte Valley Review* 20 (1992): 45–62.

Tax, Meredith. *The Rising of the Women: Feminist Solidarity and Class Conflict, 1880–1917.* Urbana: University of Illinois Press, 1991.

Terborg-Penn, Rosalyn. "African American Women and the Woman Suffrage Movement." In *One Woman, One Vote: Rediscovering the Woman Suffrage Movement,* edited by Marjorie Spruill Wheeler, 135–56. Troutdale, Ore.: New Sage Press, 1995.

———. "Afro-Americans in the Struggle for Woman Suffrage." PhD diss., Howard University, 1977.

———. "Discrimination against Afro-American Women in the Woman's Movement, 1830–1920." In *The Afro-American Woman: Struggles and Images,* edited by Sharon Harley and Rosalyn Terborg-Penn, 17–27. Port Washington, N.Y.: Kennikat Press, 1978.

Theodore, Alisse. "'A Right to Speak on the Subject': The U.S. Women's Antiremoval Petition Campaign, 1829–1831." *Rhetoric & Public Affairs* 5 (2002): 601–24.

Theriot, Nancy M. *Mothers and Daughters in Nineteenth-Century America: The Biosocial Construction of Femininity.* Lexington: University Press of Kentucky, 1996.

Thom, Deborah. *Nice Girls and Rude Girls: Women Workers in World War I.* London: I. B. Tauris, 1998.

Thompson, Roger. *Women in Stuart England and America: A Comparative Study.* London: Routledge, 1974.

Thornton, Russell, ed. *Studying Native America: Problems and Prospects.* Madison: University of Wisconsin Press, 1998.

Thurner, Manuela. "'Better Citizens Without the Ballot': American Anti-suffrage Women and Their Rationale during the Progressive Era." *Journal of Women's History* 5 (Spring 1993): 33–60.

Thurow, Glen E. "Dimensions of Presidential Character." In *Beyond the Rhetorical Presidency,* edited by Martin J. Medhurst, 15–29. College Station: Texas A&M University Press, 1996.

Tickner, J. Ann. *Gendering World Politics: Issues and Approaches in the Post–Cold War Era.* New York: Columbia University Press, 2001.

Tilly, Charles. "Citizenship, Identity and Social History." *International Review of Social History* 40 (1995): 1–17.

Tonn, Mari Boor. "Militant Motherhood: Labor's Mary Harris 'Mother' Jones." *Quarterly Journal of Speech* 82 (February 1996): 1–21.

Traugott, Mark, ed. *Repertoires and Cycles of Collective Action.* Durham, N.C.: Duke University Press, 1995.

Trivedi, Poonam. "'Bananas on a Mango Tree': Colonial Mimesis, Hybridity and Modern Indian Theatre." In *Refiguring Mimesis: Representation in Early Modern Literature,* edited by Jonathan Holmes and Adrian Streete, 99–116. Hertfordshire: University of Hertfordshire Press, 2005.

Tsitsiridis, Stavros. "Mimesis and Understanding: An Interpretation of Aristotle's *Poetics* 4.1448B–19." *Classical Quarterly* 55 (2005): 435–46.

Tulis, Jeffrey K. "Revising the Rhetorical Presidency." In *Beyond the Rhetorical Presidency,* edited by Martin J. Medhurst, 3–14. College Station: Texas A&M University Press, 1996.

———. *The Rhetorical Presidency.* Princeton, N.J.: Princeton University Press, 1987.

Turner, Edward Raymond. "Women's Suffrage in New Jersey: 1790–1807." *Smith College Studies in History* 1 (1916): 165–87.

Turner, Kathleen J., ed. *Doing Rhetorical History: Cases and Concepts.* Tuscaloosa: University of Alabama Press, 1998.

———. "Introduction: Rhetorical History as Social Construction." In Turner, *Doing Rhetorical History,* 1–15.

Verdenius, Willem Jacob. *Mimesis: Plato's Doctrine of Artistic Imitation and Its Meaning to Us.* Leiden, Holland: E. J. Brill, 1962.

Verdery, Katherine. "Whither 'Nation' and 'Nationalism'?" In *Mapping the Nation,* edited by Gopal Balakrishnan, 226–34. London: Verso, 1996.

Vicinus, Martha. *Suffer and Be Still: Women in the Victorian Age.* Bloomington: University of Indiana Press, 1977.

Wagner, Maryjo. "Farms, Families, and Reform: Women in the Farmers' Alliance and Populist Party." PhD diss., University of Oregon, 1986.

Walby, Sylvia. "Woman and Nation." In *Mapping the Nation,* edited by Gopal Balakrishnan, 235–54. London: Verso, 1996.

Wall, Wendy. "Gender and the 'Citizen Indian.'" In *Writing the Range: Race, Class, and Culture in the Women's West,* edited by Elizabeth Jameson and Susan Armitage, 202–29. Norman: University of Oklahoma Press, 1997.

Walzer, M. *Spheres of Justice.* New York: Basic Books, 1983.

Ware, Alan. *The American Direct Primary.* Cambridge, UK: Cambridge University Press, 2002.

Watkins, Marilyn P. *Rural Democracy: Family Farmers and Politics in Western Washington, 1890–1925.* Ithaca, N.Y.: Cornell University Press, 1995.

Watson, Harry L. *Jacksonian Politics and Community Conflict: The Emergence of the Second American Party System in Cumberland County, North Carolina.* Baton Rouge: Louisiana State University Press, 1981.

Wellman, Judith. *The Road to Seneca Falls: Elizabeth Cady Stanton and the First Woman's Rights Convention.* Urbana: University of Illinois Press, 2004.

Welter, Barbara. "The Cult of True Womanhood: 1820–1860." *American Quarterly* 18 (1966): 151–74.

Werbner, Pnina. "Political Motherhood and the Feminisation of Citizenship: Women's Activisms and the Transformation of the Public Sphere." In *Women, Citizenship and Difference,* edited by Nira Yuval-Davis and Pnina Werbner, 221–45. London: Zed Books, 1999.

Werbner, Pnina, and Nira Yuval-Davis. "Introduction." In *Women, Citizenship and Difference,* edited by Nira Yuval-Davis and Pnina Werbner, 221–45. London: Zed Books, 1999.

Wesley, Charles H. "Negro Suffrage in the Period of the Constitution." *Journal of Negro History* 32 (1947): 143–68.

Wheatley, Phillis. *Complete Writings.* Edited by Vincent Carretta. New York: Penguin Books, 2001.

Wheeler, Marjorie Spruill. "Editor's Introduction." In Wheeler, *One Woman, One Vote,* 277–79.

———. *New Women of the New South: The Leaders of the Woman Suffrage Movement in the Southern States.* New York: Oxford University Press, 1993.

———, ed. *One Woman, One Vote: Rediscovering the Woman Suffrage Movement.* Troutdale, Ore.: New Sage Press, 1995.

Wilentz, Sean. *A History of Suffrage in the United States.* 2nd ed. New York: AMS Press, 1971.

———. "On Class and Politics in Jacksonian America." *Reviews in American History* 10 (1982): 45–63.

———. "Property and Power: Suffrage Reform in the United States, 1787–1860." In *Voting and the Spirit of American Democracy: Essays on the History of Voting and Voting Rights in America,* edited by Donald W. Rogers, 31–41. Urbana: University of Illinois Press, 1990.

Wilkins, David E. *American Indian Sovereignty and the Supreme Court: The Masking of Justice.* Austin: University of Texas Press, 1997.

Williams, Rhys H. "Constructing the Public Good: Social Movements and Cultural Resources." *Social Problems* 42 (1995): 124–44.

Williamson, Chilton. *American Suffrage: From Property to Democracy, 1760–1860.* Princeton, N.J.: Princeton University Press, 1960.

Wills, Gary. *Lincoln at Gettysburg: The Words That Remade America.* New York: Touchstone, 1992.

Wilson, Edith Bolling. *My Memoir.* Indianapolis: Bobbs-Merrill, 1939.

Wilson, Joan Hoff. "The Illusion of Change: Women and the American Revolution." In *The American Revolution: Explorations in the History of American Radicalism,* edited by Alfred Young, 383–445. DeKalb: Northern Illinois University Press, 1976.

Wilson, Kirt. *The Reconstruction Desegregation Debate: The Politics of Equality and the Rhetoric of Place, 1870–1875.* East Lansing: Michigan State University Press, 2002.

Wolfensberger, Donald R. *Congress and the People: Deliberative Democracy on Trial.* Washington, D.C.: Woodrow Wilson Center Press, 2000.

Wolff, Francis. "The Three Pleasures of Mimesis According to Aristotle's *Poetics.*" In *The Artificial and the Natural: An Evolving Polarity,* edited by Bernadette Bensaude-Vincent and William R. Newman, 51–66. Cambridge: MIT Press, 2007.

Wood, Gordon S. *The Creation of the American Republic, 1776–1787.* Chapel Hill: University of North Carolina Press, 1969.

———. *The Radicalism of the American Revolution.* New York: Vintage Books, 1991.

Woodbury, Helen Laura Sumner. *Equal Suffrage: The Results of an Investigation in Colorado Made for the Collegiate Equal Suffrage League of New York State.* New York, 1909.

Woodham-Smith, Cecil Blanche Fitz Gerald. *Lonely Crusader: The Life of Florence Nightingale, 1890–1910.* New York: Whittlesey House, 1951.

Woolf, Virginia. *Three Guineas.* Edited by Michele Barrett. Harmondsworth: Penguin, 1993.

Wootton, David, ed. *The Essential Federalist and Anti-Federalist Papers.* Indianapolis: Hackett Publishing, 2003.

Wuthman, Leonard B. "The Militant-Moderate Agitator: Daniel O'Connell and Catholic Emancipation in Ireland." *Communication Quarterly* 30 (1982): 225–31.

Young, Iris Marion. "Polity and Group Difference: A Critique of the Ideal of Universal Citizenship." In *Feminism and Politics,* edited by Anne Phillips, 401–29. Oxford: Oxford University Press, 1998.

Young, Louise M. "Women's Place in American Politics: The Historical Perspective." *Journal of Politics* 38 (1976): 295–335.

Yuval-Davis, Nira. *Gender and Nation.* London: Sage Publications, 1997.

Yuval-Davis, Nira, and Pnina Werbner, eds. *Women, Citizenship and Difference.* London: Zed Books, 1999.

Zaeske, Susan. *Signatures of Citizenship: Petitioning, Antislavery, and Women's Political Identity.* Chapel Hill: University of North Carolina Press, 2003.

Zagarri, Rosemarie. "Morals, Manners, and the Republican Mother." *American Quarterly* 44 (1992): 192–216.

———. "The Rights of Man and Woman in Post-Revolutionary America." *William and Mary Quarterly* 55 (1998): 203–30.

Zangwill, Israel. "The Melting Pot." In *From the Ghetto to the Melting Pot: Israel Zangwill's Jewish Plays, Three Manuscripts.* Edited by Edna Nahshon. Detroit: Wayne State University Press, 2006.

Zarefsky, David. "The Presidency Has Always Been a Place for Rhetorical Leadership." In *The Presidency and Rhetorical Leadership,* edited by Leroy G. Dorsey, 20–41. College Station: Texas A&M University Press, 2002.

Index

Page numbers in italics refer to photos.